LIBRARY OF NEW TESTAMENT STUDIES

642

formerly the Journal for the Study of the New Testament Supplement series

Editor
Chris Keith

Editorial Board
Dale C. Allison, John M. G. Barclay, Lynn H. Cohick,
R. Alan Culpepper, Craig A. Evans, Robert Fowler, Simon
J. Gathercole, Juan Hernández Jr, John S. Kloppenborg,
Michael Labahn, Matthew V. Novenson, Love L. Sechrest,
Robert Wall, Catrin H. Williams, Brittany E. Wilson

The Politics of Salvation

*Lukan Soteriology, Atonement,
and the Victory of Christ*

by
Timothy W. Reardon

t&tclark
LONDON • NEW YORK • OXFORD • NEW DELHI • SYDNEY

T&T CLARK
Bloomsbury Publishing Plc
50 Bedford Square, London, WC1B 3DP, UK
1385 Broadway, New York, NY 10018, USA
29 Earlsfort Terrace, Dublin 2, Ireland

BLOOMSBURY, T&T CLARK and the T&T Clark logo
are trademarks of Bloomsbury Publishing Plc

First published in Great Britain 2021
This paperback edition published 2022

Copyright © Timothy W. Reardon, 2021

Timothy W. Reardon has asserted his right under the Copyright, Designs and Patents Act, 1988, to be identified as Author of this work.

For legal purposes the Acknowledgments on p. ix constitute an extension of this copyright page.

All rights reserved. No part of this publication may be reproduced or transmitted in any form or by any means, electronic or mechanical, including photocopying, recording, or any information storage or retrieval system, without prior permission in writing from the publishers.

Bloomsbury Publishing Plc does not have any control over, or responsibility for, any third-party websites referred to or in this book. All internet addresses given in this book were correct at the time of going to press. The author and publisher regret any inconvenience caused if addresses have changed or sites have ceased to exist, but can accept no responsibility for any such changes.

A catalogue record for this book is available from the British Library.

Library of Congress Cataloging-in-Publication Data
Names: Reardon, Timothy W., author.
Title: The politics of salvation : Lukan soteriology, atonement, and the victory of Christ / by Timothy W. Reardon.
Description: London ; New York : T&T Clark, 2021. | Series: The library of New Testament studies, 2513-8790 ; 642 | Includes bibliographical references and index. | Summary: "Timothy W. Reardon uncovers the Lukan salvation narrative developed within Acts, and its key themes that include its presentation of time and space, while also being attentive to overcoming a facile compartmentalization of religion and politics"– Provided by publisher.
Identifiers: LCCN 2020040411 (print) | LCCN 2020040412 (ebook) | ISBN 9780567696595 (hb) | ISBN 9780567696601 (epdf) | ISBN 9780567696625 (epub)
Subjects: LCSH: Bible. Luke–Criticism, interpretation, etc. | Bible. Acts–Criticism, interpretation, etc. | Salvation–Christianity–Biblical teaching.
Classification: LCC BS2589.6.S25 R43 2021 (print) | LCC BS2589.6.S25 (ebook) | DDC 226.4/06–dc23
LC record available at https://lccn.loc.gov/2020040411
LC ebook record available at https://lccn.loc.gov/2020040412

ISBN:	HB:	978-0-5676-9659-5
	PB:	978-0-5676-9857-5
	ePDF:	978-0-5676-9660-1
	ePUB:	978-0-5676-9662-5

Series: Library of New Testament Studies, ISSN 2513–8790, volume 642

Typeset by Integra Software Services Pvt. Ltd.

To find out more about our authors and books visit www.bloomsbury.com and sign up for our newsletters.

To Mariann, Junia Éinín, and Noa Dove

Contents

	Acknowledgments	ix
	Abbreviations	x
1	Defining Spaces: Religion, Politics, and Luke-Acts	1
	1.1 Defining Salvation	4
	1.2 Politics and Religion	5
	1.3 Lukan Salvation in Research	13
	1.4 Lukan Politics in Research	18
	1.5 Prospectus	27
2	An Inbreaking Salvation (Luke 1:68–79)	33
	2.1 Structure and Location	35
	2.2 God Has Redeemed God's People (Luke 1:68–75)	37
	2.3 Rome, Luke-Acts, and Cosmic Salvation	45
	2.4 John and the Dawn from on High (Luke 1:76–9)	51
	2.5 Conclusion	63
3	Jesus, Herald of God's Kingdom (Luke 4:18–19)	65
	3.1 From the Wilderness to Nazareth	66
	3.2 Jubilee	69
	3.3 He Has Anointed Me: Christology	76
	3.4 To Proclaim Good News to the Poor: Jesus and the Kingdom	78
	3.5 Release to the Captives: Jesus's Forgiveness	85
	3.6 Recovery of Sight to the Blind: Apprehending the Mystery	90
	3.7 The Lord's Acceptable Year: Jesus and Time	93
	3.8 Conclusion	96
4	Heaven Invading: The Holy Spirit, Church, and Salvific Space (Acts 2)	99
	4.1 Heaven and Cosmic-Comprehensive Space (Acts 2:1–4)	100
	4.2 Mapping the World (Acts 2:5–13)	116
	4.3 Peter's Speech (Acts 2:14–36)	121
	4.4 The Crowd Responds (Acts 2:37–47)	124
	4.5 Conclusion	131

5	The Mission of Salvation and Historical Recurrence (Acts 13:16–52)	133
	5.1 Setting the Scene	134
	5.2 Historical Recurrence (Acts 13:16–25)	136
	5.3 Those Dwelling in Jerusalem and Their Leaders (Acts 13:26–31)	144
	5.4 Good News of the Promise (Acts 13:32–7)	148
	5.5 The Epilogue (Acts 13:38–41)	151
	5.6 The Next Sabbath (Acts 13:42–52)	155
	5.7 Conclusion	160
6	Conclusion	163
	6.1 Summarizing the Story	164
	6.2 Luke-Acts and *Christus Victor*	166
	6.3 Contributions and Further Study	168

Bibliography	170
Index of Ancient Sources	200
Index of Modern Authors	231
Subject Index	238

Acknowledgments

Many have been a great support through the process of writing this monograph, but above all, I wish to thank my wife Mariann for her care and company—she is a more gracious companion than I have deserved—and our two daughters, Junia Éinín and Noa Dove, who have brought me joy and appropriate distractions from writing. I am also grateful for the years of support and sacrifice from my mother, Christine. In addition to these family members, I cannot forget my spiritual brothers, David Lilley and Bradley James Haas, whose examples in faith, life, and thought have made me a better thinker and person. My faith community, Pasadena Mennonite Church, has continued to be an immense support in prayer, meals, baby-sitting, and all sorts of other ways, and I am grateful as well for the financial support of Jeannette and David Scholer. Thanks go as well to Joel B. Green and Marianne Meye Thompson for their comments, direction, and insightful critique throughout the writing process. Others have read parts of this work and offered feedback, including John T. Carroll, David Hunsicker, Tommy Givens, and David Lilley. Thank you for your insights and your part in this process.

Abbreviations

AB	Anchor Bible
ABD	David Noel Freedman, ed., *The Anchor Bible Dictionary* (New York: Doubleday, 1992)
ABRL	Anchor Bible Reference Library
AcBib	Academia Biblica
ACNT	Augsburg Commentaries on the New Testament
AG	Archäologie und Geschichte
AGJU	Arbeiten zur Geschichte des antiken Judentums und des Urchristentums
AJEC	Ancient Judaism and Early Christianity
ANET	James B. Pritchard, ed., *Ancient Near Eastern Texts Relating to the Old Testament*, 3rd ed. (Princeton: Princeton University Press, 1969)
ANF	Ante-Nicene Fathers
ANQ	*Andover Newton Quarterly*
ANRW	Hildegard Temporini and Wolfgang Haase, eds., *Aufstieg und Niedergang der römischen Welt: Geschichte und Kultur Roms im Spiegel der neueren Forschung* (Berlin: de Gruyter, 1972–)
AnTh	*Anthropological Theory*
AOS	American Oriental Series
ASTI	*Annual of the Swedish Theological Institute*
AThR	*Australasian Theological Review*
ATR	*Anglican Theological Review*
BAFCS	*The Book of Acts in Its First Century Setting*
BBB	Bonner biblische Beiträge
BBR	*Bulletin for Biblical Research*
BDAG	W. Bauer, F. W. Danker, W. F. Arndt, and F. W. Gingrich, eds., *Greek-English Lexicon of the New Testament and Other Early Christian Literature*, 3rd ed. (Chicago: University of Chicago Press, 1999)

BECNT	Baker Exegetical Commentary on the New Testament
BETL	Bibliotheca ephemeridum theologicarum lovaniensium
Bib	*Biblica*
BiBh	*Bible Bhashyam*
BibInt	*Biblical Interpretation: A Journal of Contemporary Approaches*
BibInt	Biblical Interpretation Series
BJRL	*Bulletin of the John Rylands University Library of Manchester*
BSac	*Bibliotheca sacra*
BSem	The Biblical Seminar
BTB	*Biblical Theology Bulletin*
BZ	*Biblische Zeitschrift*
BZNW	Beihefte zur *ZNW*
CBQ	*Catholic Biblical Quarterly*
CBQMS	*Catholic Biblical Quarterly*, Monograph Series
CBR	*Currents in Biblical Research*
CCSS	Catholic Commentary on Sacred Scripture
ConBNT	Coniectanea biblica: New Testament
ConcJ	*Concordia Journal*
CTJ	*Calvin Theological Journal*
CurTM	*Currents in Theology and Mission*
DBSJ	*Detroit Baptist Seminary Journal*
DJG	Joel B. Green, Jeannine K. Brown, and Nicholas Perrin, eds., *Dictionary of Jesus and the Gospels*, 2nd ed. (Downers Grove, IL: InterVarsity Press, 2013)
DPL	G. F. Hawthorne and R. P. Martin, eds., *Dictionary of Paul and His Letters* (Downers Grove, IL: InterVarsity Press, 1993)
ECC	Eerdmans Critical Commentary
EDEJ	John J. Collins and Daniel C. Harlow, eds., *Eerdmans Dictionary of Early Judaism* (Grand Rapids: Eerdmans, 2010)
EH	Europäische Hochschulschriften
EKKNT	Evangelisch-Katholischer Kommentar zum Neuen Testament

Enc	*Encounter*
EpComm	Epworth Commentaries
ESS	Emerging Scholars Series
EvQ	*Evangelical Quarterly*
EvT	*Evangelische Theologie*
ExAud	*Ex auditu*
Exeg	*Exegetica*
Exp	*The Expositor*
ExpTim	*Expository Times*
FES	Finnish Exegetical Society
FN	*Filología neotestamentaria*
FRLANT	Forschungen zur Religion und Literatur des Alten und Neuen Testaments
FzB	Forschung zur Bibel
GNS	Good News Studies
HCS	Hellenistic Culture and Society
HerdBS	Herders biblische Studien
HNT	Handbuch zum Neuen Testament
HR	*History of Religions*
HTKNT	Herders theologischer Kommentar zum Neuen Testament
HTR	*Harvard Theological Review*
IBS	*Irish Biblical Studies*
ICC	International Critical Commentary
Int	*Interpretation*
JAAR	*Journal of the American Academy of Religion*
JAT	*Journal of Analytic Theology*
JBL	*Journal of Biblical Literature*
JEPTA	*Journal of the European Pentecostal Theological Association*
JPT	*Journal of Pentecostal Theology*
JPTSup	*Journal of Pentecostal Theology*, Supplement Series

JRS	*Journal of Roman Studies*
JSHJ	*Journal for the Study of the Historical Jesus*
JSJ	*Journal for the Study of Judaism in the Persian, Hellenistic and Roman Period*
JSJSup	*Journal for the Study of Judaism in the Persian, Hellenistic, and Roman Period*, Supplement Series
JSNT	*Journal for the Study of the New Testament*
JSNTSup	*Journal for the Study of the New Testament*, Supplement Series
JSOT	*Journal for the Study of the Old Testament*
JSOTSup	*Journal for the Study of the Old Testament*, Supplement Series
JTI	*Journal of Theological Interpretation*
JTISup	*Journal of Theological Interpretation*, Supplement Series
JTS	*Journal of Theological Studies*
JU	Judentum und Umwelt
KEK	Kritisch-exegetischer Kommentar über das Neue Testament (Meyer-Kommentar)
LCL	Loeb Classical Library
LD	Lectio divina
LLLA	The Little Library of Liberal Arts
LNTS	Library of New Testament Studies
MdB	Le Monde de la Bible
MQR	*Mennonite Quarterly Review*
NCB	New Century Bible
Neot	*Neotestamentica*
NIB	The New Interpreter's Bible
NIBCNT	New International Biblical Commentary on the New Testament
NICNT	New International Commentary on the New Testament
NICOT	New International Commentary on the Old Testament
NIDB	Katherine Doob Sakenfeld, ed., *New International Dictionary of the Bible*, 5 vols. (Nashville: Abingdon, 1987)
NIGTC	New International Greek Testament Commentary

NovT	*Novum Testamentum*
NovTSup	*Novum Testamentum*, Supplements
NTAbh	Neutestamentliche Abhandlungen
NTL	New Testament Library
NTOA	Novum Testamentum et Orbis Antiquus
NTS	*New Testament Studies*
NTT	New Testament Theology
OBO	Orbis biblicus et orientalis
ÖBS	Österreichische biblische Studien
OBT	Overtures to Biblical Theology
OGIS	W. Dittenberger, ed., *Orientis graeci inscriptiones selectae*, 2 vols. (Hirzel: Leipzig, 1903–5).
ÖTK	Ökumenischer Taschenbuch-Kommentar
OTL	Old Testament Library
PBC	People's Bible Commentary
PBM	Paternoster Biblical Monographs
PNTC	Pelican New Testament Commentaries
ProEccl	*Pro ecclesia*
PRSt	*Perspectives in Religious Studies*
PrTMS	Princeton Theological Monograph Series
PTMS	Pittsburgh Theological Monograph Series
QD	Quaestiones disputatae
R&T	*Religion and Theology*
RB	*Revue biblique*
REC	Reformed Expository Commentary
ResQ	*Restoration Quarterly*
RevExp	*Review and Expositor*
Rhet	*Rhetorica*
RTR	Reformed Theological Review
RV	Religionsgeschichtliche Volksbücher für die deutsche christliche Gegenwart

SANT	Studien zum Alten und Neuen Testaments
SacScr	*Sacra Scripta*
SBEC	Studies in the Bible and Early Christianity
SBFA	Studium Biblicum Franciscanum Analecta
SBL	Society of Biblical Literature
SBLDS	SBL Dissertation Series
SBLMS	SBL Monograph Series
SBLSBS	SBL Sources for Biblical Study
SBLSymS	SBL Symposium Series
SBS	Stuttgarter Bibelstudien
SBT	Studies in Biblical Theology
SClass	Studies in Classics
ScrH	Scripture and Hermeneutics
SJT	*Scottish Journal of Theology*
SNT	Studien zum Neuen Testament
SNTSMS	Society of New Testament Studies Monograph Series
SNTSU	Studien zum Neuen Testament und seiner Umwelt
SNTW	Studies of the New Testament and Its World
SP	Sacra pagina
SR	*Studies in Religion*
StBibLit	Studies in Biblical Literature (Lang)
ST	*Studia theologica*
STI	Studies in Theological Interpretation
SubBi	Subsidia Biblica
SVF	H. von Arnim, ed., *Stoicorum veterum fragmenta*, 4 vols. (Berlin: de Gruyter, 1964)
SVTQ	*St. Vladimir's Theological Quarterly*
TANZ	Texte und Arbeiten zum neutestamentlichen Zeitalter
TBü	Theologische Bücherei
TBT	*The Bible Today*

TDNT	Gerhard Kittel and Gerhard Friedrich, eds., *Theological Dictionary of the New Testament*, trans. Geoffrey W. Bromiley, 10 vols. (Grand Rapids: Eerdmans, 1964–)
TGST	Tesi Gregoriana, Serie Teologica
ThTo	*Theology Today*
TLZ	*Theologische Literaturzeitung*
TNTC	Tyndale New Testament Commentaries
TPINTC	TPI New Testament Commentaries
TS	*Theological Studies*
TynBul	*Tyndale Bulletin*
US	*Una Sancta*
VCSup	*Vigiliae christianae*, Supplements
VTSup	*Vetus Testamentum*, Supplements
WBC	Word Biblical Commentary
WC	Westminster Commentaries
WMANT	Wissenschaftliche Monographien zum Alten und Neuen Testament
WST	Walberberger Studien: Theologische Reihe
WUNT	Wissenschaftliche Untersuchungen zum Neuen Testament
WW	*Word and World*
ZBK	Zürcher Bibelkommentare
ZNW	*Zeitschrift für die neutestamentliche Wissenschaft*
ZTK	*Zeitschrift für Theologie und Kirche*

1

Defining Spaces: Religion, Politics, and Luke-Acts

Salvation has long been understood as a central theme of Luke-Acts, though the precise nature of this salvation remains contested.[1] Despite its recognized soteriological focus, Luke-Acts has been assessed as somewhat deficient, offering the *what* of salvation without fully delineating the *how*.[2] The *how* that Luke is said to be missing is a detailed means for achieving this salvation, generally understood in terms of atonement.[3] Nevertheless, there lie behind this assumption certain theological preconceptions that obscure Luke's answer for how salvation is achieved. This work will attempt to uncover some of these assumptions and demonstrate that this assessment is incorrect and that, conversely, Luke-Acts does demonstrate a holistic and complete "political" soteriology.[4]

---

[1] See Timothy W. Reardon, "Recent Trajectories and Themes in Lukan Soteriology," *CBR* 12 (2013): 77–95.

[2] On this "what" and "how" language, see Neal Flanagan, "The What and How of Salvation in Luke-Acts," in *Sin, Salvation, and the Spirit*, ed. Daniel Durken (Collegeville, MN: Liturgical Press, 1979), 203–13.

[3] My use of "Luke" throughout is not an assertion about the author's historical identity or psychology. I am concerned with the author as an "actantial role" embedded in the text. See Algirdas Julian Greimas and Joseph Courtés, *Semiotics and Language: An Analytical Dictionary* (Bloomington: Indiana University Press, 1982), 6.

[4] A general consensus affirmed the unity of Luke-Acts with Henry J. Cadbury, *The Making of Luke-Acts*, 3rd ed. (London: SPCK, 1968). However, after the publication of Mikeal C. Parsons and Richard I. Pervo's *Rethinking the Unity of Luke and Acts* (Minneapolis: Fortress, 1993), the question of Luke-Acts' unity remains contested (see Andrew F. Gregory, *The Reception of Luke and Acts in the Period before Irenaeus: Looking for Luke in the Second Century*, WUNT 2/169 (Tübingen: Mohr Siebeck, 2003); Andrew F. Gregory and C. Kavin Rowe, eds., *Rethinking the Unity and Reception of Luke and Acts* (Columbia: University of South Carolina Press, 2010); C. Kavin Rowe, "History, Hermeneutics and the Unity of Luke-Acts," *JSNT* 28 (2005): 131–57; idem, "Literary Unity and Reception History: Reading Luke-Acts as Luke and Acts," *JSNT* 29 (2007): 449–57; Robert W. Wall, "The Acts of the Apostles in Canonical Context," in *The New Testament as Canon: A Reader in Canonical Criticism*, eds. Robert W. Wall and Eugene M. Lemcio, JSNTSup 76 (Sheffield: JSOT Press, 1992), 110–28; Patricia Walters, *The Assumed Authorial Unity of Luke and Acts: A Reassessment of the Evidence*, SNTSMS 145 (Cambridge: Cambridge University Press, 2009)). For summaries of the debate, see Patrick E. Spencer, "The Unity of Luke-Acts: A Four-Bolted Hermeneutical Hinge," *CBR* 5 (2007): 341–66; Michael F. Bird, "The Unity of Luke-Acts in Recent Discussion," *JSNT* 29 (2007): 425–48. Criticism relates to Luke-Acts' theological, generic, canonical, historical, narrative, and authorial unity. My concern is with narrative unity. Joel B. Green ("Luke-Acts, or Luke and Acts? A Reaffirmation of Narrative Unity," in *Reading Acts Today: Essays in Honour of Loveday C. A. Alexander*, eds. Steve Walton, Thomas E. Philips, Lloyd K. Pietersen, and F. Scott Spencer, LNTS 427 (London: T&T Clark, 2011), 101–19) has argued that the texts themselves demonstrate a common narrative unity, and this is distinct from the benefits of reading the text canonically or with historical interest in composition, circulation, and authorship.

It is not a new observation that foreign theological categories have been unfairly imposed on Luke-Acts. Werner Georg Kümmel, nearly half a century ago, lamented prevalent theological accusations against Luke, including the unfair imposition of Pauline categories in assessing Luke's theology.[5] Nevertheless, this Pauline imposition continued.[6] Still, the issue runs somewhat deeper, encompassing at least the tendency to isolate religion (and salvation and atonement as narrowly religious realities) to a distinct, almost hermetically sealed sphere. With Lukan soteriology, this can be seen in the way salvation is often either spiritualized or eschatologized.[7] For some, Lukan salvation is an eschatological reality, presently unrealized. For others, salvation requires future consummation but is available now as "spiritual" or subjective forgiveness.[8] Still, for others, Lukan salvation unfolds in tangible and often public manifestations of physical, economic, and social salvation; nevertheless, the bedrock assumption remains the necessity of a "religious" mode of forgiveness to attend this public salvation. Certainly, Luke's Gospel opens with political prophecies of God's salvation and deliverance from enemies (1:71, 74) by the hands of a Davidic savior who brings peace in accordance with promises made to Israel's ancestors (cf. 1:30–3, 46–55, 67–79; 2:10–12). However, for various reasons, when salvation is presented with such politically construed language in Luke-Acts, critics frequently explain this away as marginal, emphasizing, instead, the spiritualization of these motifs and more subjectivized notions of forgiveness, peace, mercy, and so on.

This division of spheres derives, at least partially, from presupposed compartmentalization characteristic of modern, Western space.[9] Though such divisions as religion and politics, or even religion and the public sphere, seem natural, these delineations of space are discursive products of power consolidation. The modern imagination in many respects is rent by this categorical fault line, so that the divide between the political and religious defines the present and is assumed of the past. It is a discursive act from which NT interpretation and the study of Lukan soteriology are not immune.

Nevertheless, scholarship has increasingly found this distinction to be dubious, noting that the bifurcation of religious and political spheres does not faithfully represent the fluid interaction, indeed, the indissoluble unity, of political and religious phenomena in the first century. Simon Price, for one, in his work on the imperial cult, blames "Christianizing" tendencies for imposing foreign conceptions of the relationship between religion and politics onto antiquity: "The influence of prejudice and the imposition of arbitrary culture-bound categories, especially ones derived from

---

[5] Werner Georg Kümmel, "Current Theological Accusations against Luke," *ANQ* 16 (1975): 131–45.
[6] See, e.g., Ulrike Mittmann-Richert, *Der Sühnetod des Gottesknechts: Jesaja 53 im Lukasevangelium*, WUNT 220 (Tübingen: Mohr Siebeck, 2008).
[7] "Spiritual" is an inchoate term. For many, it has come to characterize "religion" as a personal, compartmentalized, and subjective experience distinct from the body. See, e.g., Karen Armstrong, *Islam: A Short History* (New York: Modern Library, 2002), ix.
[8] See below.
[9] On secular and liberal space, see Talal Asad, *Formations of the Secular: Christianity, Islam, Modernity* (Stanford: Stanford University Press, 2003); Timothy Fitzgerald, "Encompassing Religion: Privatized Religions and the Invention of Modern Politics," in *Religion and the Secular: Historical and Colonial Formations*, ed. Timothy Fitzgerald (London: Routledge, 2007), 211–40; idem, *The Ideology of Religious Studies* (Oxford: Oxford University Press, 2000), 3–32; Charles Taylor, *A Secular Age* (Cambridge, MA: Belknap, 2007).

Christianity, are a perennial problem in the study of the imperial cult ... The most pervasive [Christianization] is our assumption that politics and religion are separate areas."[10] It should, however, be debated whether this division of religion and politics is endemic to Christianity, or if this apparent element of modern Christianity is rather influenced by other cultural and paradigm-shaping forces. Nevertheless, echoing Price's sentiment, we should examine the soteriological assumptions we bring to Luke-Acts.

In this way, the title of this work is both provocative and problematic. It should be clear that I do not intend, by claiming that Lukan soteriology is political, that it should be understood as non-religious or relegated to some reductive political sphere, nor am I attending to religio-political reality as if religion is merely a veil for the political. My concern is to integrate something (politics) that has long been excised from Lukan soteriology. The term "religio-political" in itself has its own problems, reflecting implicitly the somewhat fashionable notion of a mutual embedding of these spheres in antiquity, yet this "embedding" tacitly asserts that these spheres remain distinguishable, even if muddled.[11] It is difficult to remove ourselves and our terminology from its own situatedness. Can we reimagine these categories that have become so distinct in our time?

At one level, this project investigates the association of Lukan politics and soteriology. My concern is not primarily whether Luke-Acts is pro-Roman, anti-Roman, or ambivalent vis-à-vis Rome. Though there are certainly ways in which Luke appropriates imperial ideological production and delegitimates political authorities, my contention is rather that salvation, grounded in God's initiatory covenant fidelity and Israel's restoration, is a theopolitical reality that takes up space in the world, made present in Jesus and manifest in the political body of the church participating in God's kingdom.[12] My thesis is that *Luke-Acts offers a complete, holistic, embodied, and political soteriology, cosmic in scope, that takes up space in the world and includes both the* what *and* how *of salvation, taking* Christus Victor *form*. In addition to a holistic *what* and the inclusion of the aforementioned *how* of salvation, I assess this soteriology as a *complete* soteriological scheme understood narratively: what is the beginning, middle, and end of salvation, and how is salvation achieved along this trajectory? This salvation is communal, present, and universal without denying the role of Israel or the particularity of any people. The contours of this will become clearer as we continue.

---

[10] Simon R. F. Price, *Rituals and Power: The Roman Imperial Cult in Asia Minor* (Cambridge: Cambridge University Press, 1984), 12. See also Brent Nongbri, *Before Religion: A History of a Modern Concept* (New Haven: Yale University Press, 2013), 11–12; idem, "Dislodging 'Embedded' Religion: A Brief Note on a Scholarly Trope," *Numen* 55 (2008): 442, 444; Mary Beard, John North, and Simon Price, *Religions of Rome*, 2 vols. (Cambridge: Cambridge University Press, 1998), 1:247; Jason P. Davies, *Rome's Religious History: Livy, Tacitus, and Ammianus on Their Gods* (Cambridge: Cambridge University Press, 2004), 7.

[11] On "embedding," see Beard, North, and Price, *Religions*, 1:43, 2:x; Mary Beard and Michael Crawford, *Rome in the Late Republic* (Ithaca, NY: Cornell University Press, 1985), 30. On the problem with this language, see Nongbri, *Religion*, 151–2; idem, "Dislodging."

[12] I continue to translate βασιλεία τοῦ θεοῦ spatially as "kingdom of God" rather than the de-spatialized "reign of God." On the importance of the spatial designation, see Karen J. Wenell, "Kingdom, Not Kingly Rule: Assessing the Kingdom of God as Sacred Space," *BibInt* 25 (2017): 206–33. Nevertheless, on the problems with this language, see Ada María Isasi-Díaz, "Kin-dom of God: A Mujerista Proposal," in *In Our Own Voices: Latino/a Renditions of Theology*, ed. Benjamín Valentín (Maryknoll, NY: Orbis, 2010), 171–89.

1.1 Defining Salvation

Soteriology is a considerably large topic that utilizes various other theological loci, such as Christology, ecclesiology, anthropology, and eschatology. Depending on how one understands such coordinate elements, salvation may refer to any number of realities, national deliverance, bodily healing, reconciliation with God, and so on. Here, I wish simply to establish an approach to soteriology.[13]

For our purposes, it is profitable to understand salvation narratively, with a beginning, middle, and end (cf. Aristotle, *Poet.* 1450b27).[14] This includes the state from which salvation is necessary (the beginning), the resultant state of salvation (the end), and the means by which salvation is achieved (the middle). No one element is coherent or complete on its own; the nature of the beginning is defined by the middle and end, the middle is defined by where it comes from and where it is going, and the end is a product of what led there. Defining one element recasts the whole scheme.

This is seen, for instance, in Christoph Stenschke's effort to clarify Lukan soteriology through anthropology.[15] Stenschke's formulation (focusing on gentiles) presumptively limits the investigatory scope in narrow moral-religious terms. Stenschke is responding primarily to the work of Jens Taeger, who maintains that Luke regards humanity as needing not salvation but simply correction, denying universal sinfulness.[16] For Stenschke, the Lukan person is defined by (1) universal ("spiritual") ignorance that can only be healed by God, (2) devotion to idols, (3) demonic cosmological oppression, and (4) debt and guilt incurred through sins. Lukan salvation is primarily deliverance from God's judgment and wrath. Though, certainly aspects of these observations are present, Stenschke's investigation narrowly circumscribes salvation's scope, providing a reductively religious anthropology demonstrating little concern for the social, economic, or political situation of human beings within their world.

I hope to move beyond restrictive anthropology. Luke's narrative is not the narrative of the universal (and de-particularized) human person but of God's people, Israel, their restoration, and their mission to be light to the nations (Isa. 49:6; Lk. 2:32; Acts 1:8; 13:47; 26:17–18). At Luke's outset, we find the *beginning* of our soteriological scheme firmly rooted in Israel's history, while the *middle* of God's unfolding salvation is told

---

[13] Though some make a distinction between salvation and a larger concept "soteriology" inclusive of salvation, in what follows salvation and soteriology are used interchangeably.

[14] Aristotle uses this definition of plot with tragedy. Paul Ricoeur applies the Aristotelian notion of plot to narrative (*Time and Narrative*, 3 vols. (Chicago: University of Chicago Press, 1984), 1:38–42).

[15] Christoph W. Stenschke, *Luke's Portrait of Gentiles Prior to Their Coming to Faith*, WUNT 2/108 (Tübingen: Mohr Siebeck, 1999); idem, "The Need for Salvation," in *Witness to the Gospel: The Theology of Acts*, eds. I. Howard Marshall and David Peterson (Grand Rapids: Eerdmans, 1998), 125–44. See also Fernando Méndez-Moratalla, *The Paradigm of Conversion in Luke*, JSNTSup 252 (London: T&T Clark, 2004), 218–19.

[16] Jens-W. Taeger (*Der Mensch und sein Heil: Studien zum Bild des Menschen und zur Sicht der Bekehrung bei Lukas*, SNT 14 (Gütersloh: Gütersloher Verlagshaus Mohn, 1982); idem, "Paulus und Lukas über den Menschen," *ZNW* 71 (1990): 96–108) reflects the traditional position, focusing on the Areopagus speech (Acts 17:16–34). See, e.g., Martin Dibelius, *Studies in the Acts of the Apostles* (New York: Scribner's Sons, 1956), 57; Rudolf Bultmann, *Theology of the New Testament*, 2 vols. (New York: Scribner's Sons, 1955), 2:117; Phillip Vielhauer, "On the 'Paulinism' of Acts," in *Studies in Luke-Acts: Essays Presented in Honor of Paul Schubert*, eds. Leander E. Keck and J. Louis Martyn (Nashville: Abingdon, 1966), 37.

through the end of Acts. The *end* (state) of salvation is not the same as the end of Acts;[17] rather, Acts' non-ending leaves us within the unfolding middle, the unfolding of history. Though there is an eschatological hope of full restoration, the state of salvation is experienced now. Within the particularity of this narrative, concepts like atonement and forgiveness of sins, traditional elements of soteriology, take on flesh.

1.2 Politics and Religion

Of primary importance is defining politics and religion. This task is both negative and positive. Negatively, I am critiquing the imposition of foreign delineations of space, such as those characterizing key soteriological elements as personal or private and thus religious rather than political.[18] Salvation's scope, when associated with religious categories, is a function of the realm in which *religion* operates. Demarcation of distinct political and religious spheres predetermines soteriological possibilities. Positively, we must develop a working definition for politics. This is not a description of an ancient category, but a redescriptive category through which we understand the text.[19] It is important to be transparent in this regard. Luke-Acts includes *political* elements, but does not itself define politics. I am not so much concerned about how Luke might understand politics, but how Luke-Acts is political.

1.2.1 Politics and Space

Politics at its base is concerned with the regulation of social activity and resources.[20] This may include what is colloquially understood as politics, namely, the art of governance, though I am not interested in such a restricted definition. A helpful starting place is Aristotle, whose focus is the organization of public affairs in the *polis*. Politics, for Aristotle, is a branch of ethics concerned with establishing a just society (cf. *Eth. nic.* 1181b15), a matter of life pertaining not to institutions primarily but to social interaction, as human being are "by nature" (φύσει) "political animals" (*Pol.* 1253a3). The focus is on the bottom-up development of natural (φύσις) sociopolitical relationships. For our purposes, politics is the ordering of resources, bodies, and relationships in social space. By space, I do not mean empty "place"; rather, space is a dynamic field of power inhabited by bodies, organizing in relationships in place.[21] To invoke politics is to invoke space and to invoke space is to invoke politics.

---

[17] This should not be confused with Hans Conzelmann's rigid periodization of history (see *The Theology of St. Luke* (New York: Harper & Row, 1961)).
[18] For a survey, see James B. Rive, "Graeco-Roman Religion in the Roman Empire: Old Assumptions and New Approaches," *CBR* 8 (2010): 240–99.
[19] A descriptive account is the observer's best attempt to reproduce an original classification system, while a redescriptive account uses a foreign classification system (Nongbri, *Religion*, 21–2).
[20] See Andrew Heywood, *Politics* (New York: Palgrave Macmillan, 2007), 2–11.
[21] From this perspective, Michel Foucault's emphasis on the organization of power in asymmetrical and often hierarchical structures that pervade social interactions at all levels, public and private, "outside, below and alongside" the state is helpful (*Power/Knowledge: Selected Interviews and Other Writings 1972–1977* (New York: Pantheon, 1980), 60).

This study uses language of space, referencing the discursive creation of discrete spaces such as religion and politics and the social production of spaces. Though at times this language might seem imprecise, appearing to drift between conceptual and physical space, we should resist the idea that these realms are so distinct. Conceptual distinctions are not merely subjective realities but tied to the construction of social space and how physical space is lived. The nature of space has been a consistent philosophical topic for millennia. Modern Kantian and Newtonian notions of space see space as a container or a Euclidean plane of pure extension, either an objective reality or a subjective *a priori* concept. Within the last half-century, however, theorists such as Henri Lefebvre, Michel Foucault, Michel de Certeau, Edward Soja, and Robert Sack, to name a few, have spoken of space in new ways, particularly as social, enacted, and lived space.[22]

A few particular critical approaches to space are helpful for this study. First, I appeal to "complex space," noting the work of Certeau and John Milbank. Milbank, utilizing Mikhail Bakhtin's "chronotope," which pertains to temporal and spatial representations of reality,[23] argues that the fundamental features of the Enlightenment chronotope are "the temporal figure of human growth from infancy to maturity" and "the spatial figure of organic coherence."[24] This modern chronotope emphasizes the liberative power of reason and overcoming mythical and hierarchical ways of envisioning space, resulting in "simple space" that is "suspended between the mass of atomic individuals on the one hand, and an absolute sovereign center on the other" (the modern nation-state). Mythical hierarchy is replaced by new metaphysical assumptions that guide rational inquiry and moral direction, and necessitate strict spatial compartmentalization (liberal space).[25] Pre-Enlightenment chronotopes (and, consequently, the Lukan chronotope), in comparison, are not characterized by strict spatial compartmentalization, flattening of "mythical hierarchies," or the progressive understanding of time; rather, pre-Enlightenment space is, Milbank argues, "complex space." In simple space, a centralized authority situates all competing interests under a single sovereign head; all political spaces are forced to subordinate themselves to the unified political center. In complex space, overlapping associations and jurisdictions coexist, though asymmetrically, in the same place.

Certeau, asserting the distinction between *space* and *place*, argues that alternate configurations of space exist at the margins. For Certeau, *place* exhibits "order," functioning according to what is "proper"—a singular and stable configuration of position aimed at uniformity generally defined by dominant cultural production. *Space*, however, is place in actualization, in temporal movement—"*space is practiced*

---

[22] Michel de Certeau, *The Practice of Everyday Life* (Berkeley: University of California Press, 1984), 91–130; Michel Foucault, *The Order of Things* (New York: Vintage Books, 1971); Henri Lefebvre, *The Production of Space* (Oxford: Blackwell, 1991); Robert Sack, *Human Territoriality: Its Theory and History* (Cambridge: Cambridge University Press, 1986); Edward Soja, *Thirdspace: Journeys to Los Angeles and Other Real-and-Imagined Places* (Malden, MA: Blackwell, 1996).

[23] Mikhail M. Bakhtin, "Forms of Time and the Chronotope in the Novel," in *The Dialogic Imagination: Four Essays by M. M. Bakhtin*, ed. Michael Holquist (Austin: University of Texas Press, 2002), 84–258.

[24] John Milbank, *The Word Made Strange: Theology, Language, Culture* (Oxford: Blackwell, 1997), 275.

[25] See Talal Asad, "Reading a Modern Classic: W. C. Smith's *The Meaning and End of Religion*," HR 40 (2001): 221.

place."²⁶ Luke-Acts enacts a specific spatial configuration characterized by God's kingdom in which salvation unfolds. Readings of Luke-Acts encumbered by flattened space imagine that the church's only recourse to being political is something like revolution, sectarianism, Constantinianism, or subordination characteristic of liberalism.²⁷ However, the church in Luke-Acts functions within *complex space*. It creates space within place, calling into question dominant conceptions of space and time, while simultaneously being not *against*, but *for* and rooted within the world. Rome and the church are not rigidly disciplined and restricted spheres, one "political" (state) and one "religious" (church);²⁸ they are two *poleis*, socially consisting spaces in complex space, claiming different authority.

Second, I appeal to the work of Lefebvre and Soja. Lefebvre's primary concern was breaking theoretical strangleholds on space that he saw as a product of "binary" thinking categorized as perceived space (material and physical space and the practices it engenders) and conceived space (ideational, mental, and conceptual systems developed to organize, arrange, divide, and subdue space). In order to overcome the closure of spatiality in perceived and conceived space, Lefebvre proposed a trilectics of spatiality,²⁹ which included a third space, a representational space, where space is actually lived and cannot be reduced, grasped, and closed by objective delineations or subjective conceptualizations of space. Lefebvre emphasized the socially constructed nature of space.

Soja, who systematized Lefebvre's work, perhaps more than Lefebvre would have permitted, coined the term "thirdspace" to describe Lefebvre's "lived space," presenting it as a tool for "othering" dominated space. Somewhat enigmatically, Soja defines thirdspace as "a secret and conjectured object, filled with illusions and allusions, a space that is common to all of us yet never able to be completely seen and understood, an 'unimaginable universe.'"³⁰ Soja adds, "Thirdspaces are always pushing against closure, they are productive of space in such a way as they fight against all 'permanent constructions.'"³¹ This has interesting implications for kingdom space as well as the role of heaven.³²

---

[26] Certeau, *Practice*, 117.

[27] These categories derive from William T. Cavanaugh, *Migrations of the Holy: God, State, and the Political Meaning of the Church* (Grand Rapids: Eerdmans, 2011), 56. For an example of liberal construal of church and space, see Martin Marty, *Politics, Religion, and the Common Good: Advancing a Distinctly American Conversation about Religion's Role in Our Shared Life* (San Francisco: Jossey-Bass, 2000), esp. 163.

[28] A common trope imposed on Luke-Acts is that of "church and state," where church and state represent the institutional equivalent of the ordered pair religion/politics. For Luke-Acts, this scheme is problematic. First, such portrayals risk uncritically associating Rome with the modern nation-state. Second, the categorization of the Christian community as "church" in this sense presumptuously limits the sphere of its authority. Third, this risks naturalizing "the state." Rome (et al.) and the church do not represent two distinct political and religious spheres in simple space, but two socio-religio-political authorities in complex space.

[29] Lefebvre, *Space*, 38–9. The phrase "trilectics of space" was coined by Edward Soja (*Thirdspace*, 8).

[30] Soja, *Thirdspace*, 56.

[31] Soja, *Thirdspace*, 61.

[32] See, e.g., Halvor Moxnes, "Kingdom Takes Place: Transformations of Place and Power in the Kingdom of God in the Gospel of Luke," in *Social Scientific Models for Interpreting the Bible: Essays by the Context Group in Honor of Bruce J. Malina*, ed. John J. Pilch, BibInt 53 (Leiden: Brill, 2001), 176–209; Matthew Sleeman, *Geography and the Ascension Narrative in Acts*, SNTSMS 146 (Cambridge: Cambridge University Press, 2009).

Third, I utilize Welsey Kort's analytical categories of narrative space. Kort delineates a threefold schema of narrative place-relations: cosmic-comprehensive, social-political, and personal-intimate space. It is the first two that will prove most applicable. First, narratives might reimagine *cosmic-comprehensive space*, which gives the reader "a sense of placement within a space that precedes, outstrips, and includes humans and their constructions."[33] Thus, the reader imagines a structure of the world extending beyond their social reality. Heaven, as a thirdspace, the location of Jesus's enthronement, or the realm of cosmic machinations, for example, invokes this dynamic. Second, *social-political space* is space "created by the relations of people to one another, the structure of those relations, and the laws and mores that regulate them." This social-political space is embedded in cosmic-comprehensive space. It is both a particular way of being in the world and the reality of the complex world to which one is subject.

The Jesus movement takes up, participates in, and produces space. Luke-Acts is a narrative of political and salvific space. This political space is not abstract; it is made up of bodies in a field of power defined by social organization. Indeed, the community in Acts is neither a reductively religious community nor a modern "church"; it is a people made of peoples, a theopolitical body ordered by and ordering space. This space runs deeper than objective perception or conceptual planning. The organization of this space, configuration of power relationships, distribution of goods, unified teleology, and community discipline are all elements of such political space. The Lukan Jesus does not simply set up a system of religious belief and practice or a way to interact with a discrete cosmological realm. Salvation incorporates a people as a political (and theological) reality, a theopolitical body.

1.2.2 Space and Religion

As the Enlightenment flattened space and banished mythical hierarchies, religion became defined in such a way that it did not infringe on the political. Enlightenment and post-Enlightenment political thought uniquely compartmentalized discrete spaces of existence—political, religious, economic, and so on—with politics being an essentially public practice and religion private. Relegation of religion to the private sphere, while politically expedient, fundamentally changed its nature, leaving the modern concept *religion* radically different than that of religion in antiquity, if such terminology is even applicable.[34]

---

[33] Wesley A. Kort, *Place and Space in Modern Fiction* (Gainesville: University Press of Florida, 2004), 19.

[34] Some view *religion* as a concept more applicable to delineations of Enlightenment and post-Enlightenment space. See Talal Asad, "The Construction of Religion as an Anthropological Category," in *Genealogies of Religion: Discipline and Reasons of Power in Christianity and Islam*, ed. Talal Asad (Baltimore: Johns Hopkins University Press, 1993), 27–54; William T. Cavanaugh, *The Myth of Religious Violence: Secular Ideology and the Roots of a Modern Conflict* (Oxford: Oxford University Press, 2009), 57–122; Jonathan Z. Smith, *Imagining Religion: From Babylon to Jonestown* (Chicago: University of Chicago Press, 1982); Nongbri, *Religion*. Daniel Boyarin challenges Asad's argument specifically (*Border Lines: The Partition of Judaeo-Christianity* (Philadelphia: University of Pennsylvania Press, 2004), 202–5), though Nongbri ably rebuts Boyarin (*Religion*, 54–5).

Theoretically, the political expedience involved in religious compartmentalization enables individuals to deliberate common issues through universal rational principles within the "public sphere" free from parochial or domineering external interests in order to determine the common good.[35] However, such public space is "*necessarily* articulated by power" so that in order to be heard in such space one must participate according to its rules and speak in its terms.[36] For religion to enter and participate, it must be "defined primarily by belief" and translate that belief to universal rational principles.[37]

Religion is, thus, reduced to a limited, privatized, and interior reality, rendering it, in relation to political space, relatively innocuous. Indeed, the boundaries of such a sphere are often movable depending on how political and public spaces organize power. John Locke maintained, for example, that not only was religion relegated to "soul maintenance," but also that the church as institution must be subsumed under state authority.[38] This power configuration enables not only a distinction between loyalty to God and to the state (where situations of conflict arise, the state assumes priority), but it also inscribes a division within the human person—the body belongs to the state and the soul to God. Indeed, Locke (and liberal society in his stead) inscribed this dualism onto the social body, reinforcing disciplinary, binary oppositions such as body/soul, public/private, reason/emotion, culture/nature, white/black, and so on.[39] Modern conceptions that proceed within this flattened religious space enable religion to be circumscribed and contained. As Talal Asad writes,

> It may be a happy accident that this effort of defining religion converges with the liberal demand in our time that it be kept quite separate from politics, law, and science—spaces in which varieties of power and reason articulate our distinctively modern life ... Yet this separation of religion from power is a modern Western norm, the product of a unique post-Reformation history.[40]

Modern attempts at defining religion emphasize variously personal belief, ultimate concern, and encounter with some numinous reality—that is, inner and heavenly realities, where an assumed two-level cosmos supposes a radical distinction between

---

[35] On the Enlightenment construction of public space, see Cavanaugh, *Migrations*, 46–55; idem, *Myth*, 77–85; Charles Taylor, *Modern Social Imaginaries* (Durham, NC: Duke University Press, 2007), 83–108. Alasdair MacIntyre has offered a sustained critique of the concept of universal common good ("The Political and Social Structures of the Common Good," in *Dependent Rational Animals: Why Human Beings Need the Virtues* (Chicago: Open Court, 1999), 129–46).

[36] Asad, *Formations*, 184.

[37] Asad, *Formations*, 186.

[38] For John Locke, "True and Saving Religion Consists in the Inward Persuasion of the Mind," in *A Letter Concerning Toleration*, ed. Patrick Romanell, LLLA 22 (New York: Liberal Arts, 1950), 18. Belief is no longer located in the body, allowing for a division of the person aligned well with the Cartesian self. On Locke, see also David Laird Dungan, *A History of the Synoptic Problem: The Canon, the Text, the Composition, and the Interpretation of the Gospels* (New York: Doubleday, 1999), 261–86; T. Fitzgerald, "Religion," 214–20.

[39] J. Kameron Carter demonstrates the deep racial logic to such bifurcations, showing that such racial thinking and the centering of whiteness is a foundational Enlightenment axiom (*Race: A Theological Account* (Oxford: Oxford University Press, 2008), 79–121).

[40] Asad, "Construction," 28.

the transcendent and immanent and the inner and outer. Such definitions search for a transhistorical and transcultural common religious kernel,[41] though even a cursory perusal of world religions textbooks demonstrates the difficulty of this task.[42] One textbook diagnoses the problem in this way:

> Because each [element] makes reference to an invisible (i.e. non-empirical) world that somehow lies outside of, or beyond, human history, the things we name as "religious" are commonly thought to be opposed to those institutions that we label as "political." We therefore operate under the assumption that, whereas religion is a matter of personal belief that can never be settled by rational debate, such things as politics are observable, public and thus open to rational debate.[43]

It continues, "[Religion] assumes an inner experience, which underlies religious behaviour."[44] The common framing of religion described here envisions a religious kernel defined apophatically by what politics is not. Religion pertains to the invisible, non-empirical, inward, non-rationally accessible aspects of existence distinct from that which is public (the visible, empirical, external, and rationally accessible—i.e., "real"). Religion, at least theoretically, has been successfully exiled. Though religious adherents might influence the public sphere, their religious concerns are separable from the political space they influence.

This understanding of religion is often retrojected onto ancient space, grounding religion in antiquity in a universal inward experience of the divine. External manifestations of religion represent an inner reality and are distinguishable from other aspects of society. Thus, André Jean Festugière writes in his treatise on ancient religion: "There is no true religion except that which is personal. True religion is, first of all, closeness to God. Every religious ceremony is but empty make-believe if the faithful who participate in it do not feel that thirst for the absolute, that anxious desire to enter into personal contact with the mysterious Being who is hidden behind appearances."[45] This existential criterion permeates analyses of topics such as the Augustan temple reforms, viewed as the response to a loss of general belief in the face of Roman globalization, utilized as political propaganda,[46] or the phenomenon of the mystery

---

[41] On the problem of definition, see Jonathan Z. Smith, "Religion, Religions, Religious," in *Critical Terms for Religious Studies*, ed. Mark C. Taylor (Chicago: University of Chicago Press, 1998), 269–84.

[42] Cf., e.g., Thomas A. Robinson and Hillary Rodrigues, eds., *World Religions: A Guide to the Essentials* (Peabody, MA: Hendrickson, 2006), 1–3; Ninian Smart, *The World's Religions: Old Traditions and Modern Transformations* (Cambridge: Cambridge University Press, 1989).

[43] Russell T. McCutcheon, "What Is Religion?" in *Introduction to World Religions*, ed. Christopher Partridge (Minneapolis: Fortress, 2005), 11.

[44] McCutcheon, "Religion," 12.

[45] André Jean Festugière, *Personal Religion among the Greeks* (Berkeley: University of California Press, 1954), 1.

[46] See Antonía Tripolitis, *Religions of the Hellenistic-Roman Age* (Grand Rapids: Eerdmans, 2002), 2; Luther H. Martin, *Hellenistic Religions: An Introduction* (New York: Oxford University Press, 1987), 3–15.

cults, which supposedly respond to the aforementioned existential anomie.[47] Critics, however, have doubted that such religious anomie was ever a reality,[48] not because such belief was actually rampant, but because cultic realities were simply part of unabridged social existence, not definitively a subjective experience.[49]

Thus, scholarship has called into question the traditional understanding of religion in antiquity,[50] emphasizing that religion was not a private, existential affair, but a vibrant communal, social, and civic enterprise that pervaded all levels of society.[51] There was not a distinct sphere of religion, but ethnic and communally located practices, and these rites cannot be easily (or at all) disentangled from the religio-political and ethnic milieu within which they are located. Such fictional disentangling makes antiquity easier to classify, but fundamentally ignores the nature of what is investigated. The criterion for these practices was not "belief"—not that Greeks, for instance, did not *believe* in the gods—nor was religion dependent primarily on a dislocated inner sphere; rather, such practices simply participated in and pervaded complex, hierarchical space, which was always political.

Of note is the development of "Judaism." A generation ago, Wilfred Cantwell Smith argued that the rise of Judaism as a distinct religion (the first such documented development) is witnessed in 2 Maccabees.[52] Specifically, observing the occurrence of Ἰουδαϊσμός in 2 Macc. 2:21; 8:1; 14:38—which originally referred to *Jewishness* or "a Jewish way of life"—Smith asserts that Ἰουδαϊσμός "eventually came to refer to the formal pattern or outward system of observances in which that quality found expression. Thus the concept 'Judaism' was born."[53] Brent Nongbri, for one, however, argues that 2 Maccabees does not demonstrate this shift from "Jewishness" to "Judaism." There did exist a struggle between intra-Jewish factions over Ἑλληνισμός

---

[47] Franz Cumont, *Oriental Religions in Roman Paganism* (Chicago: Open Court, 1911), 70–1; Richard Reitzenstein, *Hellenistic Mystery-Religions*, PTMS 15 (Pittsburgh: Pickwick, 1978), esp. 533–42; Wilhelm Heitmüller, *Taufe und Abendmahl im Urchristentum*, RV 1/22–3 (Tübingen: Mohr, 1911); Martin Brückner, *Der sterbende und auferstehende Gottheiland in den orientalischen Religionen und ihr Verhältnis zum Christentum*, RV 1/16 (Tübingen: Mohr, 1908).

[48] Rive notes, "The notion that traditional public cults and traditional Graeco-Roman deities were in any sort of decline during the Hellenistic and imperial periods depended on a set of highly dubious assumptions, and could be confirmed only by a very selective and even arbitrary use of evidence" ("Religion," 1).

[49] Even mystery cults were part of the larger social, polytheistic devotion. See Walter Burkert, *Ancient Mystery Cults* (Cambridge, MA: Harvard University Press, 1987), 10. Modern religious assumptions and historical endeavors designed to find the genetic link between Christianity and mystery cults have overemphasized these cults' personal elements, which are not stressed (Burkert, *Cults*, 28); cf. Ramsay MacMullen, *Paganism in the Roman Empire* (New Haven: Yale University Press, 1981), 55.

[50] See Price, *Rituals*, 15–16; Beard, North, and Price, *Religions*, 1:559; Rive, "Religion," 240–99.

[51] Beard, North, and Price, *Religions*, 1:114–40, esp. 134; Christiane Sourvinou-Inwood, "What Is *Polis* Religion?" in *Oxford Readings in Religion*, ed. Richard Buxton (Oxford: Oxford University Press, 2000), 13–37; ead., "Further Aspects of *Polis* Religion," in *Oxford Readings in Religion*, ed. Richard Buxton (Oxford: Oxford University Press, 2000), 38–55.

[52] Wilfred Cantwell Smith, *The Meaning and End of Religion: A New Approach to the Religious Traditions of Mankind* (New York: Macmillan, 1962).

[53] Smith, *Religion*, 72. Biblical translations similarly offer such anachronism. The NRSV, e.g., repeatedly translates Ἰουδαϊσμός as "Judaism" (2 Macc. 2:21; 14:38; *4 Macc*. 4.26; Gal. 1:13, 14) and once as "the Jewish faith" (2 Macc. 8:1). Ἑλληνισμός, however, which occurs only in 2 Macc. 4:13, is translated "Hellenization."

(Hellenism; 2 Macc. 4:13) and Ἰουδαϊσμός; however, such *-ismos* terminology refers to conflicting ethnic customs—communal ways of being—rather than "Paganism" versus "Judaism."[54] The juxtaposition of Ἑλληνισμός and Ἰουδαϊσμός in this literature makes it unlikely that one refers to a cultural phenomenon (Hellenism) and another a religious phenomenon (Judaism). The Maccabean revolt fought against "the destruction of the ancestral commonwealth" (τὴν τῆς προγονικῆς πολιτείας κατάλυσιν; 2 Macc. 8:17; cf. also 4:11; 13:14; *4 Macc.* 3.20; 8.7; 17.9), not for religious freedom in the modern sense.

There is more at stake here, however, than mere anachronism. Smith's presentation of Judaism as the foundational religion, which is to be distinguished from the positive inner experience of God ("faith"), is, as J. Kameron Carter has demonstrated, a variation on an Enlightenment theme whereby "Judaism" (and the Jews), in its supposed focus on material reality and parochialism, is juxtaposed to the universal and spiritual reality of Christianity.[55] Carter argues that such theological and racialized othering is foundational for the Enlightenment and the post-Enlightenment, modern West. For this work, it is not enough simply to note a tendency to impose a compartmentalized religious perspective on Scripture, but additionally it is important to be critically aware of presentations of Jews, "Judaism," and Jewishness, especially as juxtaposed to Christianity, and the church's relationship to Israel, in addition to the racialized logic of certain universalisms.[56]

All of this prefaces the uncontroversial observation that readers are formed by their contexts and this influences the way they interpret texts. Conceptions of religion, politics, and the space we inhabit influence the lenses through which we view Scripture. In what follows, I use the term *political* broadly, pertaining to the ordering of power, resources, and relationships within space, where space is a field of power inhabited by bodies organized in relationships. This does not exclude "the state," but it does exceed it. The invocation of politics involves a broadening of our soteriological scope, emphasizing the communal and embodied nature of salvation. Importantly, however, to invoke politics is not to exclude theology or religion. In this sense, the church is a theopolitical body.

The term *religion* is also problematic for the reasons outlined above. In what follows, I use the terms "religion" and "religious" in two ways. First, though understanding the difficulties in doing so, I use religion as a redescriptive term for an ancient phenomenon, not defined primarily by belief or privatized experience, but by a focus on the cosmological hierarchy within which the mundane world is embedded.[57] The

---

[54] See Nongbri, *Religion*, 46–50. On Ἑλληνισμός and Ἰουδαϊσμός, see Steve Mason, "Jews, Judeans, Judaizing, Judaism: Problems of Categorization in Ancient History," *JSJ* 38 (2007): 457–512. Shaye J. D. Cohen suggests the translation "Judeanness," regarding "Judaism" to be too restricted (*The Beginnings of Jewishness: Boundaries, Varieties, Uncertainties*, HCS 31 (Berkeley: University of California Press, 1999), 105–6). However, Cohen does recognize in 2 Maccabees the conversion of the term *Ioudaios* from an ethnic to a religious term. Mason aptly critiques Cohen's argument ("Jews," 494–5).

[55] Carter, *Race*, 4, 111–21. By "spiritual," Carter means a lack of focus on bodily reality.

[56] On Western Christianity's supersessionist appropriation of Israel's election, see Willie James Jennings, *The Christian Imagination: Theology and the Origins of Race* (New Haven: Yale University Press, 2010), 32–4.

[57] Though this description of the phenomenon religion/religious is itself problematic for a variety of reasons, it works at least functionally for this context where we speak of human relation to God or the gods. It is not meant to be a general definition for religion.

religious is not a discrete phenomenon. To say that salvation is religious, in this work, is not to isolate it from the political, to refer to privatized notions of faith and experience, or to restrict it to a series of practices that serve merely as a veil for the political, but, rather, to speak of an aspect of a whole.[58] Second, I often refer to reductively religious interpretations that impose modern restricted definitions of religion or the religious. When referring to religion/religious in this way, I include a descriptor in context such as "reductively" or "narrowly." This applies as well to the use of the term *spiritual*. This term is notoriously difficult to define, but it can commonly be utilized to denote concerns not primarily linked to the body. The history of research exhibits the modern tendency to create distinct spheres and retroject them on the text. We may not be able to escape this completely, but we should be aware where possible.

1.3 Lukan Salvation in Research

The bifurcated nature of our subject matter is exemplified by the necessity to trace two histories of interpretation, soteriology and politics. I begin with Lukan soteriology.[59]

1.3.1 Hans Conzelmann

Contemporary discussion begins with and emanates from Hans Conzelmann's seminal *Die Mitte der Zeit* (1954), which posits a three-stage development of *Heilsgeschichte* motivated by the apparent delay of the Parousia.[60] For Conzelmann, Luke is instrumental in institutionalizing the church, and Luke-Acts functions like the antitype of the Bultmannian "original kerygma," an anti-kerygma abandoning the *urchristliche* existential kerygma and appearing to mirror the failure of the modern church. Historicization of the kerygma shifts eschatological expectation to the distant future, leaving the church concerned primarily with its place in contemporary society. Luke acclimates the church to de-eschatologized simple space governed by Rome. Seeking only to be upstanding members of civil society, the church represents religion par excellence, relegated to its own sphere. Here, I note how "religion," even when conceptualized in compartmentalized terms, is defined by its relation and deference to dominant political space; thus, even with Conzelmann, we should not consider this soteriology apolitical.

---

[58] Even language of "integration" is problematic, insinuating component parts. Nevertheless, understanding that we exist on this side of the Enlightenment, unable to naively reintegrate what has been dis-integrated, language of integration perhaps speaks more properly of the lens through which moderns must necessarily view this holistic phenomenon.

[59] See further Reardon, "Trajectories."

[60] Conzelmann's three epochs include: (1) Israel and the Law, (2) Jesus, and (3) the church. For a critique, see Werner Georg Kümmel, "'Das Gesetz und die Propheten gehen bis Johannes': Lukas 16,16 im Zusammenhang der heilsgeschichtlichen Theologie der Lukasschriften," in *Verborum Veritas*, eds. Otto Böcher and Klaus Haacker (Wuppertal: Theologischer Verlag Rolf Brockhaus, 1970), 89–102; idem, "Accusations," 138. Joseph Fitzmyer accepts a modified tripartite scheme (*The Gospel According to Luke*, 2 vols., AB 28 (Garden City, NY: Doubleday, 1981–5), 2:1115). John T. Carroll highlights the continuity rather than division between epochs (*Response to the End of History: Eschatology and Situation in Luke-Acts*, SBLDS 92 (Atlanta: Scholars Press, 1988), 1–9).

Salvation, which he identifies as eschatological life and freedom from cosmological evil, is relegated to the past experience of Jesus and the future hope of his return. This salvation is primarily appropriated through a forgiveness of sins that is predicated on a neutral anthropology and ethical understanding of sin, in which some have no need for forgiveness (cf. 7:34; 15:3–7). Thus, the cross also loses import, or what Conzelmann calls "passion mysticism."[61] Forgiveness is associated not with Jesus's death but with his power.[62]

1.3.2 Howard Marshall

I. Howard Marshall's *Luke: Historian and Theologian* (1970) presents salvation as Luke-Acts' organizing principle, disputing significant points of Conzelmann's work.[63] Nevertheless, both Marshall and Conzelmann fundamentally assess Luke-Acts based on its faithfulness to a reconstructed early kerygma, though Marshall judges Luke closer to this kerygma than Conzelmann does. Marshall situates Lukan salvation within reductively religious space and distinguishes it from political or socioeconomic conceptions of salvation, concluding that Luke's increased soteriological lexicon is characterized by the narrowly "spiritual" sense with which he invests it.[64] Although situating Luke's soteriological language in relation to historical antecedents whose root concept is deliverance, Marshall argues for a development from "physical" to "moral and spiritual" deliverance, so that Luke-Acts emphasizes an existential soteriology where sins, not physical powers, hold people in bondage.[65] Marshall eschatologizes soteriological benefit that might accrue outside the religious sphere so that tangible political and socioeconomic reversal occur only in the future.[66] In this way, Marshall counters Conzelmann's claim that there is no salvation in the present era, yet by pushing most of the tangible soteriological elements to the eschaton, Marshall has left little more for the present than Conzelmann. Although Marshall mentions collateral elements of salvation, such as incorporation into community and healing, the different social, economic, and political effects associated with these collateral elements are not considered "salvation."

---

[61] Conzelmann, *Theology*, 201.
[62] Even Kümmel, who denies that Luke is "fundamentally impoverished" by its lack of an atonement theology, concedes that Luke has downplayed the significance of Jesus's death, and assumes that Jesus's atoning death is necessary for Luke to have a valid theology ("Accusations," 138). Many of Conzelmann's ideas have been critiqued. See, e.g., John Nolland, "Salvation-History and Eschatology," in *Witness to the Gospel: The Theology of Acts*, eds. I. Howard Marshall and David Peterson (Grand Rapids: Eerdmans, 1998), 63–81; Beverly Roberts Gaventa, "The Eschatology of Luke-Acts Revisited," *Enc* 43 (1982): 27–41; Anders E. Nielsen, "The Purpose of the Lucan Writings with Particular Reference to Eschatology," in *Luke-Acts: Scandinavian Perspectives*, ed. Petri Luomanen, FES 54 (Göttingen: Vandenhoeck & Ruprecht, 1991), 76–93.
[63] See also I. Howard Marshall, "The Development of the Concept of Redemption in the New Testament," in *Reconciliation and Hope: New Testament Essays on Atonement and Eschatology*, ed. Robert Banks (Exeter: Paternoster, 1974), 153–69.
[64] I. Howard Marshall, *Luke: Historian and Theologian*, 3rd ed. (Downers Grove, IL: IVP Academic, 1998), 92. Marshall consistently juxtaposes "spiritual" and "physical" salvation, leading to a subjective or existential soteriology.
[65] Marshall, *Historian*, 94.
[66] Marshall, *Historian*, 144.

1.3.3 The Cross and Expiation

A quintessential piece of this early kerygma for many scholars is Jesus's death as the means of salvation; however, many have determined Luke devoid of any such concept— or at least any developed one.[67] This determination is made for multiple reasons. First, with the exception of two mentions of Jesus's blood (Lk. 22:19–20; Acts 20:28), Luke-Acts lacks references connecting Jesus's death with forgiveness of sins or any positive benefit, though Jesus's death is repeatedly addressed.[68] Thus, many conclude that the Lukan Jesus's death is simply martyrdom.[69] Given that Luke occupies more space in the NT canon than any other author, the sheer scarcity of references to what many see as a cornerstone of Christian faith appears startling. Second, "forgiveness of sins" (ἄφεσις ἁμαρτιῶν) in Acts is tied to Jesus's exaltation (5:31), though never to his crucifixion (cf. 2:38; 3:19; 10:43; 13:38). Third, Luke has been accused of redacting his sources so as to remove connection between Jesus's suffering and salvation. Most glaringly, Luke contains no equivalent to the substitutionary formula ("a ransom for many") in Mk 10:45//Mt. 20:28 (cf. Lk. 22:24–30).[70] Fourth, though many note Luke-Acts' references to the Isaianic servant (Isa. 52:13–53:12; Lk. 22:37 = Isa. 53:12; Acts 8:32–33 = 53:7-8), there are no explicit allusions to this servant's vicarious death (cf. Isa. 53:11–12).[71] Some, such as Peter Doble and Robert J. Karris, have associated the Lukan Jesus's death with this Isaianic figure or the Righteous One of the Wisdom of Solomon without emphasizing vicarious expiation.[72] Others, however, have continued to argue for Jesus's expiatory death in Luke-Acts.[73]

---

[67] See, e.g., Conzelmann, *Theology*, 199–201; Ulrich Wilckens, *Die Missionsreden der Apostelgeschichte: Form- und traditionsgeschichtliche Untersuchungen* (Neukirchen-Vluyn: Neukirchen Verlag, 1961), 194; Marshall, *Historian*, 170–71; Cadbury, *Making*, 280–2; Walter E. Pilgrim, "The Death of Christ in Lukan Soteriology" (ThD diss., Princeton Theological Seminary, 1971).

[68] Michael Wolter attempts to bridge the gap between Luke and Paul by urging that Luke did not mention a connection between forgiveness of sins and Christ's death because of the *Missionssituation* of the speeches in Acts; i.e., it is only possible for those who already believe in the resurrection to accept Jesus's atoning death ("Jesu Tod und Sündenvergebung bei Lukas und Paulus," in *Reception of Paulinism in Acts; Réception du Paulinisme dans les Actes des Apôtres*, ed. Daniel Marguerat (Leuven: Uitgeverij Peeters, 2009), 34).

[69] Martin Dibelius, *From Tradition to Gospel* (Cambridge: James Clarke, 1971), 201; Brian E. Beck, "'Imitatio Christi' and the Lucan Passion Narrative," in *Suffering and Martyrdom in the New Testament: Studies Presented to G. M. Styler by the Cambridge New Testament Seminar*, eds. William Horbury and Brian McNeil (Cambridge: Cambridge University Press, 1981), 28–47; Greg Sterling, "*Mors philosophi*: The Death of Jesus in Luke," *HTR* 94 (2001): 398–9. For critiques of this view, see Dennis D. Sylva, ed., *Reimaging the Death of the Lukan Jesus*, BBB 73 (Frankfurt am Main: Anton Hain, 1990).

[70] Marshall has argued that Luke shifts his source material concerning substitutionary atonement (Mk 10:45) to Acts 20:28; however, Marshall fails to integrate a substitutionary understanding of Acts 20:28 into Luke-Acts as a whole ("The Place of Acts 20.28 in Luke's Theology of the Cross," in *Reading Acts Today: Essays in Honour of Loveday C. A. Alexander*, eds. Steve Walton, Thomas E. Philips, Lloyd K. Pietersen, and F. Scott Spencer, LNTS 427 (London: T&T Clark, 2011), 154–70).

[71] See, e.g., Cadbury, *Making*, 280. Specifically, Luke omits any mention of bearing the sins of many (Isa. 53:11–12).

[72] For Doble, Luke only alludes to the Wisdom of Solomon. Peter Doble, *The Paradox of Salvation: Luke's Theology of the Cross*, SNTSMS 87 (Cambridge: Cambridge University Press, 1996); Robert J. Karris, "Luke 23:47 and the Lukan View of Jesus's Death," in *Reimaging the Death of the Lukan Jesus*, ed. Dennis D. Sylva, BBB 73 (Frankfurt am Main: Anton Hain, 1990), 68–78.

[73] See recently, e.g., John Kimbell, *The Atonement in Lukan Theology* (Newcastle upon Tyne: Cambridge Scholars, 2014); Benjamin R. Wilson, *The Saving Cross of the Suffering Christ*, BZNW 223 (Berlin: de Gruyter, 2016).

Ulrike Mittmann-Richert, for one, has attempted to show that Luke's Gospel utilizes allusions to the Isaianic servant in order to portray Jesus's death as vicarious expiation.[74] However, as Joel Green has noted, though right to identify the importance of the Isaianic servant theme,[75] reliance on allusion to the servant's vicarious death is tenuous for a few reasons: (1) it is hard to imagine that Luke would rely on Isa. 53:12 so much without using the substitutionary phraseology somewhere; (2) given the several references to the necessity of Jesus's death, it is surprising that he does not associate these with the expiatory death of the Isaianic servant; and (3) Luke does not avoid drawing attention to an event associated with "the forgiveness of sins," but it happens to be Jesus's exaltation (cf. Acts 2:38; 3:19; 5:31; 10:43; 13:38).[76]

More problematically, however, Mittmann-Richert proceeds on a methodologically shaky ground. The thrust of her argument is not an inquiry concerning Luke-Acts on its own terms; rather, she begins by asking how Luke conforms to her own conception of legitimate atonement theology. She characterizes Luke as a ship captain whom others have accused of being "the saboteur of the gospel of the justification of the sinner by grace, diverting the ship from its course."[77] If this is so, she maintains, we should place him "in the lower deck of the ship, where his voice will not be so loud."[78] Decades after Kümmel questioned how appropriate it was "to view the Lucan theology 'through the spectacles of Pauline terminology,' "[79] Mittmann-Richert presumes that Luke is the Pauline Gospel.[80]

1.3.4 Resurrection and Exaltation

Luke, however, does explicitly associate forgiveness of sins with Jesus's resurrection and ascension/exaltation (Acts 5:31).[81] Cadbury declared, "The resurrection is therefore the significant thing about Jesus. His death is only the prelude."[82] However, some commentators have found more nuance in Luke's emphasis on the resurrection.

---

[74] Mittmann-Richert, *Sühnetod*. See also David Peterson, "Atonement Theology in Luke-Acts: Some Methodological Reflections," in *The New Testament in Its First-Century Setting: Essays on Context and Background in Honour of B. W. Winter on His 65th Birthday*, eds. P. J. Williams, Andrew D. Clarke, Peter M. Head, and David Instone-Brewer (Grand Rapids: Eerdmans, 2004), 56–71.

[75] See Marshall, *Historian*, 171–3; Joel B. Green, "The Death of Jesus, God's Servant," in *Reimaging the Death of the Lukan Jesus*, ed. Dennis D. Sylva, BBB 73 (Frankfurt am Main: Anton Hain, 1990), 1–28; Robert F. O'Toole, "How Does Luke Portray Jesus as Servant of YHWH," *Bib* 81 (2000): 328–46.

[76] Joel B. Green, "'Was It Not Necessary for the Messiah to Suffer These Things and Enter into His Glory?': The Significance of Jesus's Death for Luke's Soteriology," in *The Spirit and Christ in the New Testament and Christian Theology: Essays in Honor of Max Turner*, eds. I. Howard Marshall, Volker Rabens, and Cornelius Bennema (Grand Rapids: Eerdmans, 2012), 71–85. See also Hans Jörg Sellner, *Das Heil Gottes: Studien zur Soteriologie des lukanischen Doppelwerks*, BZNW 152 (Berlin: de Gruyter, 2007), 406–8.

[77] "der das Schiff vom Kurs ablenkenden Saboteur des Evangeliums von der Rechtfertigung des Sünders aus Gnaden" (Mittmann-Richert, *Sühnetod*, 16).

[78] Mittmann-Richert, *Sühnetod*, 43.

[79] Kümmel, "Accusations," 136.

[80] Mittmann-Richert, *Sühnetod*, 313.

[81] On the relation between resurrection, ascension, and exaltation, see Kevin L. Anderson, "*But God Raised Him from the Dead*": *The Theology of Jesus's Resurrection in Luke-Acts*, PBM (Waynesboro, GA: Paternoster, 2006).

[82] Cadbury, *Making*, 280.

Kevin Anderson maintains, "the resurrection of Jesus occupies, not the centre, but the *focus* of Lukan soteriology."[83]

Recently, Torsten Jantsch has argued a particularly resurrection-centric soteriology.[84] Forgiveness, he argues, is asserted through God's compassion, and the time of salvation remains only a promise until Jesus ascends to the Father where he fully realizes his "Christ-Sein." Jantsch's soteriology is characterized by a strict distinction between "physical" and "religious" salvation. Religious salvation pertains to forgiveness, release from eschatological judgment, and eternal life. It is individual and universal.[85] Jantsch repeatedly refers to this spiritual, eschatological salvation as "comprehensive" (*umfassenderes*) or full-fledged (*vollumfänglich*),[86] yet this can be done only by ignoring present aspects of salvation. Jantsch critiques those who emphasize embodied elements of salvation as myopic, though his own soteriology is disembodied and restricted to an inner, subjective reality. Thus, it is somewhat surprising that Jantsch faults those who argue for cross-centered atonement as influenced by theological assumptions, when much the same appears to be at work in his strict bifurcation between religious/physical and present/future salvation. This extends to his treatment of Luke's concern for Israel and David, which he sees as a "problem" needing to be solved. Yet, this is a problem only if one supposes that salvation must be de-historicized and unshackled from an apparent embarrassing connection to Israel.[87]

1.3.5 Embodied Salvation

For some, the cross and resurrection, viewed within the totality of Jesus's life, is as an example of vindication and reversal.[88] Thus, Richard Glöckner, for one, eschews the notion of a particular salvific moment altogether.[89] Jesus's crucifixion is the consummation of Jesus's identification with the lowly, and God's exaltation of Jesus is a reversal solidifying salvation. This reversal is often tied to a more embodied, holistic, and social salvation. Joel Green and Mark Allan Powell, for instance, have advocated a more holistic soteriology,[90] specifically, noting the communal, religious, economic, and social aspects of present salvation. Further, it is increasingly recognized that this

---

[83] K. L. Anderson, *God Raised*, 31.

[84] Torsten Jantsch, *Jesus, der Retter: Die Soteriologie des lukanischen Doppelwerks*, WUNT 381 (Tübingen: Mohr Siebeck, 2017).

[85] On this, Jantsch cites Flanagan's word-study on salvation in Luke-Acts, which imposes *a priori* discrete categories of physical and "transcendental" salvation (*Jesus*, 41; Flanagan, "Salvation," 203–13).

[86] E.g., Jantsch, *Jesus*, 44, 344.

[87] See Anthony Buzzard, "Acts 1:6 and the Eclipse of the Biblical Kingdom," *EvQ* 66, no. 3 (1994): 197–215; Jason Maston, "How Wrong Were the Disciples about the Kingdom? Thoughts on Acts 1:6," *ExpTim* 126 (2015): 169–78. On the anti-Jewish universalization of modern, Enlightenment-era theology, see Jennings, *Imagination*, 119–68.

[88] See, esp., Richard Glöckner, *Die Verkündigung des Heils beim Evangelisten Lukas*, WST 9 (Mainz: Matthias Grunewald, 1975), 107–8.

[89] Glöckner, *Verkündigung*, 113.

[90] Mark Allan Powell, "Salvation in Luke-Acts," *WW* 12 (1992): 5–10; Joel B. Green, "'The Message of Salvation' in Luke-Acts," *ExAud* 5 (1989): 21–34; idem, "Death of Jesus"; idem, "'Salvation to the End of the Earth': God as the Saviour in the Acts of the Apostles," in *Witness to the Gospel: The Theology of Acts*, eds. I. Howard Marshall and David Peterson (Grand Rapids: Eerdmans, 1998), 83–106.

embodied salvation is not formulated for a departicularized, universal humanity, but is grounded in the historical, political community of Israel. Several commentators note that Lukan salvation must be understood within the frame of Israel's restoration, emphasizing communal salvation and the "New Exodus."[91]

1.3.6 Summary

Since Conzelmann, Lukan soteriology remains an unsettled topic. For some salvation supposes a dichotomous, individualistic, and subjective salvation. Political or more embodied and social elements have been explained away to uncover a more significant, eternal (reductively religious) salvation. For others, increasingly, embodied salvation is important but either eschatologized or distanced from what Luke-Acts still lacks, a distinctly religious means of reconciliation with God, a "how" for attaining forgiveness of sins. Even where political, social, and economic elements are invoked, this is distinguished from the sphere of religious "atonement." I contend that such a distinction is not proper to Luke-Acts. However, such an understanding of salvation requires attention to Lukan politics.

1.4 Lukan Politics in Research

Most discussions of Lukan politics understandably begin with Luke-Acts' relationship with Rome. If the political rhetoric of Luke 1–2 develops within the larger narrative, one might expect a polemic developed with Rome.[92] However, almost universally, scholars see no such thing. Consensus for nearly three centuries has viewed Luke-Acts as one way or another amenable to Roman power. For many, Luke offers a defense of the church to Rome (*apologia pro ecclesia*). For others, Luke makes a case for the Roman Empire to the church (*apologia pro imperio*). For still others, more benignly, Luke is unconcerned with politics at all.[93] Generally, these positions are based on

---

[91] Max Turner, *Power from on High: The Spirit in Israel's Restoration and Witness in Luke-Acts*, JPTSup 9 (Sheffield: Sheffield Academic Press, 1996); idem, "The Spirit and Salvation in Luke-Acts," in *The Holy Spirit and Christian Origins*, eds. Graham N. Stanton, Bruce W. Longenecker, and Stephen C. Barton (Grand Rapids: Eerdmans, 2004), 103–16; David W. Pao, *Acts and the Isaianic New Exodus* (Grand Rapids: Baker Academic, 2002); Michael Fuller, *The Restoration of Israel: Israel's Re-gathering and the Fate of the Nations in Early Jewish Literature and Luke-Acts*, BZNW 132 (Berlin: de Gruyter, 2006); W. Gil Shin, "The 'Exodus' in Jerusalem (Luke 9:31): A Lukan Form of Israel's Restoration Hope" (PhD diss., Fuller Theological Seminary, 2016).

[92] Conzelmann considered Luke 1–2 as non-Lukan and thus ignored them (*Theology*, 16, 118, 172). See Paul Minear's critique, "Luke's Use of the Birth Stories," in *Studies in Luke-Acts: Essays Presented in Honor of Paul Schubert*, eds. Leander E. Keck and J. Louis Martyn (Nashville: Abingdon, 1966), 111–30.

[93] On Acts as apologetic, see Loveday C. A. Alexander, "The Acts of the Apostles as an Apologetic Text," in *Apologetics in the Roman Empire: Pagans, Jews, and Christians*, eds. Mark Edwards, Martin Goodman, and Simon Price (Oxford: Oxford University Press, 1999), 15–44. For an extensive *Forschungsberichte* of Lukan politics and apology, see Steve Walton, "The State They Were In: Luke's View of the Roman Empire," in *Rome in the Bible and the Early Church*, ed. Peter Oakes (Carlisle: Paternoster, 2002), 1–41; more recently, Matthew L. Skinner, "Who Speaks for (or against)

several factors, including certain positive portrayals of Romans within Luke, a positive appraisal of Roman jurisprudence, Luke's redaction of politically sensitive material in his sources, an assumed bifurcation between religious and political spheres, the Parousia's delay, and an allegorization or redaction-critical rejection of the remaining politically sensitive material. Some have questioned this old consensus, but such positions remain in the minority.

1.4.1 Luke-Acts as Political Apologetic

Beginning with the C. A. Heumann's contention that Luke's purpose is an *apologia pro ecclesia* to a Roman official, Theophilus (1720),[94] Luke-Acts has commonly been seen as a defensive document addressing a crisis moment in the church rather than written for ecclesial edification. Generally, this crisis concerns the relationship between church and state, showing Christianity as nonthreatening to the political status quo. This political apologetic's ability to present a plausible purpose for Luke-Acts derived from significant elements of the text and related to pressing contemporary political questions has not only given it durability but also legitimates a characterization of the church and state as occupying distinct but complementary societal roles in modern space. Acts is prime territory for such political legitimation because it alone represents a sustained canonical narrative of the early church. Even where the political apologetic is not seen as the main purpose of the book, the assumption of Luke's view of Roman political power as positive and complementary to the church's distinct religious role passes through the DNA of Lukan scholarship from Heumann to the present.

1.4.1.1 Apologia pro Paulus

The predominant stream of interpretation in the nineteenth century, influenced by the Tübingen school and first articulated by Matthias Schneckenburger, identified the crisis as Pauline Christianity's reception by the Jewish Christian church, an *apologia*

Rome?" in *Reading Acts in the Discourses of Masculinity and Politics*, eds. Eric D. Barreto, Matthew L. Skinner, and Steve Walton, LNTS 559 (London: Bloomsbury T&T Clark, 2017), 107–25. See also Paul Walasaky, "*And So We Came to Rome*": *The Political Perspective of St. Luke*, SNTSMS 49 (Cambridge: Cambridge University Press, 1983), 1–14; Philip Esler, *Community and Gospel in Luke-Acts: The Social and Political Motivations of Lucan Theology*, SNTSMS 57 (Cambridge: Cambridge University Press, 1987), 205–14; Robert Maddox, *The Purpose of Luke-Acts*, SNTW (London: T&T Clark, 1982), 19–23; Stephen Pattison, "A Study of the Apologetic Function of the Summaries of Acts" (PhD diss., Emory University, 1990), 10–35; Alexandru Neagoe, *The Trial of the Gospel: An Apologetic Reading of Luke's Trial Narratives*, SNTSMS 116 (Cambridge: Cambridge University Press, 2002), 3–22; Friedrich W. Horn, "Die Haltung des Lukas zum römischen Staat im Evangelium und in der Apostelgeschichte," in *The Unity of Luke-Acts*, ed. Joseph Verheyden, BETL 142 (Leuven: Leuven University Press, 1999), 203–24.

[94] Christoph August Heumann, "Dissertatio de Theophilo, cui Lucas Historiam Sacram Inscripsit," in *Bibliotheca Historico-Philologico-Theologica*, ed. Johann Andreas Grimm, Classis IV (Bremen: Hermanni Brauer, 1720), 483–505. Cf. Henry J. Cadbury, "The Purpose Expressed in Luke's Preface," *Exp* 21 (1921): 437.

pro Paulus.⁹⁵ Though Schneckenburger alludes to a related political apologetic, Eduard Zeller, building on Schneckenburger's work, more explicitly develops this secondary political apologetic as a subset of the *apologia pro ecclesia*. For Zeller, Luke is concerned to demonstrate to a Jewish Christian church in Rome that Pauline Christianity is neither politically subversive nor threatens the stability of the church by advocating a *religio illicita* among the gentiles.⁹⁶ Though directed to the church, the concern is ultimately Rome's view of the church.

Zeller's Acts portrays a deferential church, devoid of political concern other than a desire to be good citizens. This submissive church's subordination to the political legitimacy of the Roman state presupposes a division of political and religious spheres reminiscent of Zeller's own political activism and mirrors Zeller's treatise on church and state interaction from the 1870s, *Staat und Kirche*.⁹⁷ In *Staat und Kirche*, concerned with German political debates over the *Kirchenfrage*—the role of the church in the modern state—Zeller argues for the institutional superiority of the state over the church.⁹⁸ For the purpose of national unity, he advocated for state control over social programs and the state's right to oversee and regulate the church. The church must restrict itself to all things private and narrowly religious. Zeller's elevation of the political apologetic in Acts and the church's subordination to Roman power mirror the configuration of church–state relations that he advocated in Germany. His presentation of biblical history participates in and justifies the configuration of contemporary space, and subsequent scholarship has been impacted by this stance often unaware of its ideological foundation. That is, contemporary scholarship on Luke-Acts often begins unawares with the liberal delineation of space advocated by Zeller and the *Kirchenfrage*.

1.4.1.2 Apologia pro Ecclesia

By the end of the nineteenth century, enthusiasm for the *apologia pro Paulus* was waning, and, in 1897, Johannes Weiss abandoned it, arguing instead that Acts was written to a gentile audience for the purpose of overcoming Jewish accusations, a

---

[95] Matthias Schneckenburger, *Über den Zweck der Apostelgeschichte: Zugleich eine Ergänzung der neueren Commentare* (Bern: Christian Fischer, 1841), 244–51. More recently, A. J. Mattill, Jr., "The Purpose of Acts: Schneckenburger Reconsidered," in *Apostolic History and the Gospel: Biblical and Historical Essays Presented to F. F. Bruce*, eds. W. Ward Gasque and Ralph P. Martin (Exeter: Paternoster, 1970), 108–22; Robert W. Wall, "Acts of the Apostles: Introduction, Commentary, and Reflections," in *Acts, Introduction to Epistolary Literature, Romans, 1 Corinthians*, ed. Leander E. Keck, NIB 10 (Nashville: Abingdon, 1994), 8–9. Others advocate an apology to the church on Paul's behalf but believe that this apology concerns Gnosticism: Charles H. Talbert, *Luke and the Gnostics: An Examination of Lucan Purpose* (Nashville: Abingdon, 1966), 111–15; C. K. Barrett, *Luke the Historian in Recent Study* (Philadelphia: Fortress, 1961), 63. The categories in this section largely follow Walton's classification, though Walton does not include the *apologia pro Paulus* ("State," 2–12). Neagoe classifies this view as "an apologia for Paul" (*Trial*, 6–8).
[96] Eduard Zeller, *Die Apostelgeschichte: Nach ihrem Inhalt und Ursprung kritisch untersucht* (Stuttgart: Carl Mäcken, 1854), 364–75; W. Ward Gasque, *A History of the Interpretation of the Acts of the Apostles*, 2nd ed. (Peabody, MA: Hendrickson, 1975), 49.
[97] Eduard Zeller, *Staat und Kirche: Vorlesungen an der Universität zu Berlin gehalten* (Leipzig: Fues's, 1873).
[98] Michael B. Gross, *The War against Catholicism: Liberalism and the Anti-Catholic Imagination in Nineteenth-Century Germany* (Ann Arbor: University of Michigan Press, 2004), 216.

resurgence of the *apologia pro ecclesia*.[99] For Weiss, the Christian community faced two accusations: (1) the church was apostate from Judaism, and (2) the new religion was dangerous to the state. Note that the concern for a politically deferential church has not abated.

Weiss argued that Luke aims to show that the church is practicing a *religio licita* through its connection to Judaism. Though an official *religio licita* status has been advocated to differing degrees by several commentators,[100] others have noted the lack of evidence for such an official status.[101] A single text from Tertullian is often cited, in which he defends the link between Jewish and Christian religion (*Apol.* 21); however, he does not refer to an official *religio licita* status. Jewish religious practice was generally tolerated because of its antiquity, and, although there is evidence of local decrees made for Jewish toleration, these related only to specific instances.[102] If Luke-Acts was written to gain toleration from a gentile audience, there is little evidence that this pertained to an official legal standing—since no such standing appears to have existed.

Though the *apologia pro ecclesia* remained the dominant view through the midtwentieth century, most scholars abandoned the idea that Luke makes this defense by linking Christianity with Judaism. Instead, it was argued that Luke appeals to a general Roman sense of justice.[103] Conzelmann later contributed to the *apologia pro ecclesia* by attributing Luke's political deference to the Parousia's delay, where the church's perseverance within the world necessitated negotiating a world dominated by Rome. Conzelmann's work has been profoundly influential, and the groundwork he laid remains foundational for contemporary scholarship.[104]

---

[99] Johannes Weiss, *Über die Absicht und den literarischen Charakter der Apostelgeschichte* (Göttingen: Vandenhoeck & Ruprecht, 1897), 56–60.

[100] F. J. Foakes-Jackson and Kirsopp Lake, *The Beginnings of Christianity: Part I: The Acts of the Apostles*, 5 vols. (London: Macmillan, 1920), 2:180; Burton Scott Easton, *Early Christianity: The Purpose of Acts and Other Papers* (Greenwich, CT: Seabury, 1954), 33–57; Cadbury, *Making*, 299–316.

[101] Henry J. Cadbury, "Some Foibles of New Testament Scholarship," *JAAR* 26 (1958): 213–16; Conzelmann, *Theology*, 144–8; idem, *Acts of the Apostles*, Hermeneia (Philadelphia: Fortress, 1987), lxvii–lxviii; Esler, *Community*, 211–14; Maddox, *Purpose*, 91–3; Paula Fredriksen, "Mandatory Retirement: Ideas in the Study of Christian Origins Whose Time Has Come to Go," *SR* 35 (2006): 231–46.

[102] Tessa Rajack, "Was There a Roman Charter for the Jews?" *JRS* 74 (1984): 107–23; Philip A. Harland, *Associations, Synagogues, and Congregations: Claiming a Place in Ancient Mediterranean Society* (Minneapolis: Fortress, 2003), 221–2.

[103] Conzelmann, *Theology*, 137–49; Ernst Haenchen, *The Acts of the Apostles: A Commentary* (Philadelphia: Westminster, 1971), 100.

[104] Cf., e.g., F. F. Bruce, *The Book of Acts*, 2nd ed., NICNT (Grand Rapids: Eerdmans, 1988), 8–13, 22; Harry W. Tajra, *The Trial of St. Paul: A Juridical Exegesis of the Second Half of the Acts of the Apostles*, WUNT 2/35 (Tübingen: Mohr Siebeck, 1989), 199; Erika Heusler, *Kapitalprozess im lukanischen Doppelwerk: Die Verfahren gegen Jesus und Paulus in exegetischer und rechtshistorischer Analyse*, NTAbh 38 (Münster: Aschendorff, 2000), 259–60; Brent Kinman, *Jesus' Entry into Jerusalem: In the Context of Lukan Theology and the Politics of His Day*, AGJU 28 (Leiden: Brill, 1995), 91–103; Hans Klein, "Jesus und der römische Staat in der Sicht des Lukasevangeliums zugleich ein Beitrag zum Verhältnis von Kirche und Staat," *SacScr* 13 (2015): 139–52; Joachim Molthagen, "Rom als Garant des Rechts und als apokalyptisches Ungeheuer: Christliche Antworten auf Anfeindungen durch Staat und Gesellschaft im späten 1. Jahrhundert n. Chr.," in *Gemeinschaft am Evangelium*, eds. Edwin Brandt, Paul S. Fiddes, and Joachim Molthagen (Leipzig: Evangelische, 1996), 127–42; Drew W. Billings, *Acts of the Apostles and the Rhetoric of Roman Imperialism* (Cambridge: Cambridge University Press, 2017).

1.4.1.3 Apologia pro Imperio

Paul Walaskay, in his monograph "*And So We Came to Rome*," reverses the traditional apology, seeing Luke-Acts as an apology written to the church to extol the Roman Empire's benefits. Walaskay proceeds to fill every possible gap of interpretive indeterminacy in the text with a pro-Roman reading, and his position is unabashedly thorough in its compartmentalization of religious and political space. For example, Walaskay writes of Jesus's positive acceptance of the centurion's authority in Lk. 7:6–9: "For Luke's reader this means that the representatives of the empire have rightful authority over the earthly realm, while the church, through the word of Jesus which continues in the church, has authority over the unseen, but powerful, world of spirits."[105] This conclusion does not follow from the evidence. Walaskay's arguments assume too much about Luke's enthusiastically pro-Roman stance, and the *apologia pro imperio* has few supporters.[106]

1.4.2 Luke-Acts as Legitimation

Philip Esler follows an altogether different path, maintaining that the appearance of Rome in Luke-Acts is altogether positive, yet no longer ascribing an apologetic motive to Luke.[107] Esler concludes that Luke's purpose is to legitimate the decisions and worldviews of those new Christians whose livelihoods might conflict with their Christian faith, including Roman soldiers and administrative officials within Luke's community.[108] Esler maintains that Luke's narrative provides legitimation through the creation of a symbolic universe in which Rome and Christianity need not be at odds. There is a good deal to commend about his understanding of Luke-Acts' presentation of a symbolic worldview. However, Esler's thesis is highly speculative. It is doubtful that we can reconstruct the community for which the work was written with the degree of specificity Esler employs.[109] Several others, such as Seyoon Kim and Christopher

---

[105] Walaskay, *Rome*, 34.
[106] On this, see Maddox, *Purpose*, 96–7; Vernon K. Robbins, "Luke-Acts: A Mixed Population Seeks a Home in the Roman Empire," in *Images of Empire*, ed. Loveday C. A. Alexander, JSOTSup 122 (Sheffield: JSOT Press, 1991), 202–21; Daniel Marguerat, *The First Christian Historian: Writing the "Acts of the Apostles,"* SNTSMS 121 (Cambridge: Cambridge University Press, 2002), 76–7; Martin Meiser, "Lukas und die römische Staatsmacht," in *Zwischen den Reichen: Neues Testament und Römische Herrschaft*, eds. Michael Labahn and Jürgen Zangenberg, TANZ 36 (Tübingen: Francke, 2002), 190. Klaus Wengst argues that Conzelmann's and Walaskay's respective positions can be mutually inclusive (*Pax Romana and the Peace of Jesus Christ* (Philadelphia: Fortress, 1987), 105).
[107] Esler, *Community*.
[108] Esler, *Community*, 210. Here, Walton rightly critiques Esler's high level of mirror reading ("State," 8). If we accept Hans von Campenhausen's claim that there were no Christian soldiers until 175 CE (*Der Kriegsdienst der Christen in der Kirche des Altertums* (Stuttgart: Wissenschaftliche, 1957), 206), then Esler's speculative reconstruction becomes all the more dubious.
[109] See Dale C. Allison, Jr., "Was There a 'Lukan Community'?" *IBS* 10 (1988): 62–70; Stephen C. Barton, "Can We Identify Gospel Audiences?" in *The Gospels for All Christians: Rethinking the Gospel Audiences*, ed. Richard Bauckham (Grand Rapids: Eerdmans, 1998), 173–94. See also Isak J. du Plessis, "The Lukan Audience—Rediscovered? Some Reactions to Bauckham's Theory," *Neot* 34 (2000): 243–61; Craig Blomberg, "The Gospel for Specific Communities and All Christians," in *The Audience of the Gospels: The Origin and Function of the Gospels in Early Christianity*, ed. Edward W. Klink III, LNTS 353 (London: T&T Clark, 2010), 111–33.

Bryan, have affirmed Esler's concern for legitimation, while both advocating a view of Luke-Acts with an undeniably positive perception of Rome.[110] More recently, Drew Billings has argued that Acts forges a persona for Paul that conforms to "standards of representation amplified during the reign of Trajan, in order to forge a place for 'the Way' within the Roman Empire and to depict the mission of God in the language of Roman power."[111] More speculatively, Stefan Nordgaard has argued that Luke attempts to legitimate life in the church specifically to Theophilus, a Roman aristocrat, going as far as to soften ethical demands when moving from Luke to Acts to make Christianity more palatable.[112]

1.4.3 Luke-Acts as Non-Political

Rather than a political apologetic to or for Rome, Eric Franklin argues that the main purpose of Luke-Acts is theological. For Franklin, Luke presents Roman power as sometimes capricious and occasionally corrupt, but, mainly, "Luke's purpose seems to be to present additional material regarding Jewish perversity rather than to make a defense of Roman practices."[113] Jacob Jervell similarly argues that Acts primarily evinces a theological purpose.[114] He does assert, "The Roman Empire represents the gentiles in hostility against the Messiah of God";[115] however, Jervell understands politics as the art of statecraft and judges the church to be passive and politically harmless (until the eschaton).[116] Loveday C. A. Alexander has argued a position essentially parallel to Jervell's, although she does not say that Luke-Acts is not political.[117] For Alexander, Luke-Acts primarily contains an internal Jewish polemic, and she questions the idea that Luke is an apology in the strict sense.[118]

1.4.4 Luke-Acts as Politically Subversive

Some critics have begun to recognize that Luke-Acts' picture of the political world is not as deferential to Rome as once thought. Though offering different understandings of politics and the extent of the Lukan political critique, these voices have been gaining momentum, offering an alternative to the standard pro-Roman reading of Luke-Acts.

---

[110] Seyoon Kim, *Christ and Caesar: The Gospel and the Roman Empire in the Writings of Paul and Luke* (Grand Rapids: Eerdmans, 2008), 75–199; Christopher Bryan, *Render to Caesar: Jesus, the Early Church and the Roman Superpower* (Oxford: Oxford University Press, 2005), 95–107.
[111] Billings, *Acts*, 122.
[112] Stefan Nordgaard, *Possessions and Family in the Writings of Luke* (Copenhagen: Museum Tusculanum Press, 2017). On legitimation, see also Joshua Yoder, *Representatives of Roman Rule: Roman Provincial Governors in Luke-Acts*, BZNW 209 (Berlin: de Gruyter, 2014).
[113] Eric Franklin, *Christ the Lord: A Study in the Purpose and Theology of Luke-Acts* (Philadelphia: Westminster, 1975), 137.
[114] Jacob Jervell, *Die Apostelgeschichte: Übersetzt und erklärt*, KEK 3 (Göttingen: Vandenhoeck & Ruprecht, 1998), 86–90; idem, *The Theology of the Acts of the Apostles*, NTT (Cambridge: Cambridge University Press, 1996), 15–16, 100–6, 134.
[115] Jervell, *Theology*, 106.
[116] Jervell, *Theology*, 101.
[117] Alexander, "Apologetic," 15–44.
[118] Alexander, "Apologetic," 43.

1.4.4.1 Richard J. Cassidy

A major shift occurred with the work of Richard Cassidy.[119] For Cassidy, Jesus was not set on instantiating his own political kingdom, nor did he present himself as a kingly messiah: "Rather than seeking to establish a kingdom of his own, Luke's Jesus espouses social patterns and practices based on service and humility and does not take a definite position with regard to any of the existing forms of government."[120] Was Jesus political? Yes. Did he envision a new state? No. In Cassidy's assessment, Luke's politics is exemplified in patterns of living that subvert the ordered existence undergirding the Roman way of life and political structure. Cassidy's Lukan Jesus functions generally within the public sphere, attempting to reshape civil society. Cassidy also critiques the long-held division between religion and politics, writing, "no passage in the Gospel of Luke portrays Jesus teaching ... as though there were *two* realms to be respected, God's and Caesar's."[121] Here, he only means that Jesus may legitimately critique governing powers. This, however, has led to criticism that Cassidy has overzealously applied political and social categories to nearly everything in Luke-Acts.[122]

1.4.4.2 C. Kavin Rowe

The most significant work published on Lukan politics since Cassidy is C. Kavin Rowe's *World Upside Down*. Rowe argues for an expanded notion of politics, calling into question earlier understandings of Luke-Acts' relation to politics as "politics *simpliciter*," or statecraft.[123] The community of Christ acts politically by instantiating a new vision for social interaction that can only be called "apocalyptic." Rowe generalizes this Lukan politics pithily: "New culture, yes—coup, no."[124] On the one hand, the church stands in dialectical tension with "culture." On the other hand, Luke makes a direct appeal to Roman law, claiming that Christians conform to it better than even Roman jurists understand. The church is a model of justice, while its apocalyptic existence turns the world on its head. Rowe's use of "apocalyptic" for Acts may seem strange to some; its closest derivation appears to be from Barthian theology and contemporary debates

---

[119] Richard J. Cassidy, *Jesus, Politics, and Society: A Study of Luke's Gospel* (Maryknoll, NY: Orbis Books, 1978); idem, *Society and Politics in the Acts of the Apostles* (Maryknoll, NY: Orbis Books, 1987); idem, *Christians and Roman Rule in the New Testament: New Perspectives* (New York: Crossroad, 2001); idem, "Paul's Proclamation of *Lord* Jesus as a Chained Prisoner in Rome: Luke's Ending Is in His Beginning," in *Luke-Acts and Empire: Essays in Honor of Robert L. Brawley*, eds. David Rhoads, David Esterline, and Jae Won Lee, PrTMS 151 (Eugene, OR: Pickwick, 2011), 142–53; Richard J. Cassidy and Philip Scharper, eds., *Political Issues in Luke-Acts* (Maryknoll, NY: Orbis Books, 1983).

[120] Cassidy, *Jesus*, 66.

[121] Cassidy, *Christians*, 28.

[122] Walton, "State," 33; cf. Robert F. O'Toole, "Review of *Society and Politics in the Acts of the Apostles*, by Richard J. Cassidy, *Bib* 70 (1989): 427. See, similarly, Karl Allen Kuhn, *The Kingdom according to Luke and Acts: A Social, Literary, and Theological Introduction* (Grand Rapids: Baker Academic, 2015).

[123] C. Kavin Rowe, *World Upside Down: Reading Acts in the Greco-Roman Age* (Oxford: Oxford University Press, 2009), 4.

[124] Rowe, *World*, 5.

about the apocalyptic Paul.¹²⁵ This emphasis presents the Acts church itself as God's apocalyptic revelation, not simply as a social change movement.¹²⁶ Thus, Luke need not oppose specific Roman officials or the political apparatus; the church's mere existence is a socially and cosmically transforming apocalyptic reality.

1.4.4.3 Lukan Critique of Roman Political Language

Other scholars have drawn attention to the symbolic language employed by Luke-Acts. The works of both Gary Gilbert and Stefan Schreiber offer a nuanced picture of Luke-Acts' appropriation of political language and concepts characterizing Jesus in contrast to governing authorities. Gilbert argues forcefully that Luke offers an "alternative vision of world history" that rivals Rome's claim to be ruler of the world through a demonstration of Luke's creative appropriation of Roman imperial themes.¹²⁷ He writes, "By contesting Rome's claims, transposing Roman expressions of authority to Jesus and the early church, and offering alternative models of world rule, Luke-Acts creates a counter-discourse that responds to and resists Roman imperial authority and, in so doing, seeks to constitute an understanding of being a Christian in the Roman world."¹²⁸ Schreiber's work focuses specifically on Luke 1–2 and its similarity to conceptions of a golden age in Roman ideology, emphasizing the conflict between two world orders.¹²⁹ These presentations do not imagine a political critique that encompasses only institutions; instead, this critique is leveled at one's entire conception of the world.

1.4.4.4 Kazuhiko Yamazaki-Ransom

Kazuhiko Yamazaki-Ransom has more directly sought to upend traditional interpretation of Lukan politics, arguing that Luke situates Roman rule within a cosmic context that pits God's kingdom against Satan's, which is directly associated with Rome.¹³⁰ From this position, Luke-Acts is decidedly anti-Roman. Yamazaki-Ransom compares different models of political relationships between God, Israel, and gentiles, supposing that Luke is arguing for a particular, ideal, interim political relationship. Thus, the models are static, without appreciation for temporal development, assuming Jesus's Parousia to be a distant addendum, seeming to perpetuate Conzelmann's error.

---

[125] E.g., Rowe, *World*, 140. On the apocalyptic Paul, see Ernst Käsemann, "The Beginnings of Christian Theology," in *New Testament Questions of Today* (Philadelphia: Fortress, 1969), 82–107; J. Louis Martyn, *Theological Issues in the Letters of Paul* (Nashville: Abingdon, 1997), 85–156; Beverly Roberts Gaventa, *Our Mother Saint Paul* (Louisville: Westminster John Knox, 2007), 125–49.
[126] Rowe, *World*, 4.
[127] Gary Gilbert, "Roman Propaganda and Christian Identity in the Worldview of Luke-Acts," in *Contextualizing Acts: Lukan Narrative and Greco-Roman Discourse*, eds. Todd C. Penner and Caroline Vander Stichele, SBLSymS 20 (Leiden: Brill, 2004), 233–56.
[128] Gary Gilbert, "Luke-Acts and the Negotiation of Authority and Identity in the Roman World," in *Multivalence of Biblical Texts and Theological Meanings*, ed. Christine Helmer, SBLSymS 37 (Atlanta: Society of Biblical Literature, 2006), 87.
[129] Stefan Schreiber, *Weihnachtspolitik: Lukas 1–2 und das Goldene Zeitalter*, NTOA 82 (Göttingen: Vandenhoeck & Ruprecht, 2009), 90.
[130] Kazuhiko Yamazaki-Ransom, *The Roman Empire in Luke's Narrative*, LNTS 404 (New York: T&T Clark, 2010).

There is reason to doubt Luke's concern for an interim political ideal. In Luke-Acts, rather than practical political dialogue, we find idealistic portraits of Jesus, the Davidic Messiah (e.g., Acts 2:22–36; 13:22–3, 34–7), and a promise that the disciples will witness before rulers and kings, testifying to God's rule and the resurrection. Nothing about Jesus's prediction or the disciples' discussion of their witness indicates that this discourse will be conciliatory (cf., e.g., Lk. 21:12–19; Acts 1:6–8; 3:11–16; 5:29–32; 26:15–18). Acts does not provide a practical guide on church–state relations. On the contrary, Acts presents a narrative where idealistic confrontation with near-universal "ignorance" (3:17; 13:27; 17:23, 30) simply declares the reality of God's kingdom (1:3; 8:12; 14:22; 19:8; 20:25; 28:23, 31) and the movement of God's Word (6:7; 12:24; 17:13). The church does not wait in perseverance but participates in God's work, turning the world from "Satan's authority" (Acts 26:18).

Nevertheless, the great strength of Yamazaki-Ransom's work is the clear assessment of Luke's negative presentation of political powers in relation to the church and God's kingdom, particularly those powers' allegiance with the demonic.[131]

1.4.5 Postcolonial Interpretation

Finally, I note the insights of postcolonial interpretations, which have emphasized both empire critical readings and Luke-Acts' ambivalence to Rome. Yong-Sung Ahn, for instance, highlights this ambivalence,[132] and Gilberto J. Medina argues that Luke is an "expression of colonial resistance literature" that adopts a rhetoric of congeniality as a means of survival.[133] However, Rubén Muñoz-Larrondo, focusing on Herod in Acts 12, argues that Acts is more openly anti-imperial than Medina supposes.[134] In a similar vein, Amanda Miller, noting stories of reversal, sees Lukan reversal as "a celebration of and call to *de*stabilize and even overturn the political and economic status quo."[135] My attention to Lukan politics leaves room for ambivalence or a strategy of negotiation; nevertheless, my argument echoes Miller's "celebration" of the destabilizing elements of Lukan soteriology.

1.4.6 Summary

Our focus has been on avoiding readings that reinscribe modern fault lines while asserting objectivity. We have seen that some of the standard political interpretations of Acts have roots in liberal political spatial organization, though this has generally been obscured. This is not to say that those who hold to the traditional view of Lukan

---

[131] See, similarly, Pyung Soo Seo, *Luke's Jesus in the Roman Empire and the Emperor in the Gospel of Luke* (Eugene, OR: Pickwick, 2015).

[132] Yong-Sung Ahn, *The Reign of God and Rome in Luke's Passion Narrative: An East Asian Global Perspective*, BibInt 80 (Leiden: Brill, 2006).

[133] Gilberto J. Medina, "The Lukan Writings as Colonial Counter-Discourse: A Postcolonial Reading of Luke's Ideological Stance of Duplicity, Resistance, and Survival," (PhD diss., Vanderbilt University, 2005).

[134] Rubén Muñoz-Larrondo, *A Postcolonial Reading of the Acts of the Apostles*, StBibLit 147 (New York: Peter Lang, 2012).

[135] Amanda C. Miller, *Rumors of Resistance: Status Reversals and Hidden Transcripts in the Gospel of Luke*, ESS (Minneapolis: Fortress, 2014), 29.

politics wish to reassert this ideological framing, only that this genealogy should be recognized and critiqued in our interpretations. Inevitably, of course, we will never be free from such realities. Nevertheless, we saw that many of the standard assumptions about Luke's political practicality have been critiqued and several dissenting voices have offered nuanced arguments calling traditional views into question. There is increasing recognition that Luke's portrayal of authorities is not altogether rosy, nor is his picture of the church's response to leadership necessarily deferential. In particular, Rowe's emphasis on the formational, ecclesial social imaginary, Gilbert's and Schreiber's respective emphases on the creative consumption of dominant imagery, and Yamazaki-Ransom's reformulated portrayal of Roman leadership within Luke-Acts offer helpful ways forward as we investigate Luke-Acts' political soteriology.

1.5 Prospectus

My thesis is that *Luke-Acts offers a complete, holistic, embodied, and political soteriology, cosmic in scope, that takes up space in the world and includes both the* what *and* how *of salvation, taking* Christus Victor *form*. Approaching this soteriology narratively, Luke-Acts offers a "complete" scheme in which the content and means of salvation can be articulated with a clear and coherent beginning, middle, and end. My primary contention is with those who argue that Luke-Acts lacks an objective means by which to secure atonement or forgiveness of sins. Luke does not speak, at least in any developed way, of "ransom" (e.g., Mt. 20:28; Mk 10:45) or vicarious expiation. Nevertheless, my assertion is not that Luke does in fact significantly incorporate such means of atonement, as others have claimed, but that this approach has been problematic from the start, assuming theological foundations that obscure Luke's message.

The precise nature of Lukan soteriology must be developed in the following chapters. However, preliminarily, I note that, as conceived by Luke, atonement does not culminate but begins with God's forgiveness. Jesus does not satisfy a legal demand or offer God supererogatory restitution for humanity's past sins through death, thereby making forgiveness available. Rather, the narrative *opens* with God's turning and offering forgiveness. Yet, importantly, this forgiveness is not a simple declaration that one accepts personally, receiving absolution; it demands an often costly response where one enters into a social reality. Forgiveness—a productive act, expecting repentance, formation, and the reordering of space—initiates a process of release, organizing bodies justly in space, whereby the world is reconciled with God, and thus does not forgo but "satisfies" and manifests God's justice.[136] This atonement is not simply personal but social and cosmic. It is a spatial salvation where God's gracious offer of forgiveness is an offer to put

---

[136] Gustav Aulén argues that in the *Christus Victor* scheme "there is no satisfaction of God's justice" (*Christus Victor: An Historical Study of the Three Main Types of the Idea of Atonement* (London: SPCK, 1931), 145-6). This only maintains within a certain notion of justice presupposed by satisfaction theories (whether the Anselmian or penal satisfaction), whereby a just balance must be restored concerning past wrongs, an action of which humans are themselves incapable. I argue that this conception of justice is not at home in Luke-Acts.

things right, to reconcile the world—including the (social) space of the mundane world that people inhabit in their bodies and to which they are subject—to heaven.

In narrative terms, the *beginning* assumes not simply a people that need to have their sins forgiven in a narrowly religious sense. Luke focuses on those needing redemption and release, including the oppressed, captive, blind, poor, and the sinner in the reordering of social-political space. The world needs release from its captivity to world powers, social structures, and blindness, indelibly tied to demonic idolatry. More specifically, this beginning is located in *Israel's* restoration for the good of the whole world. Luke's salvific narrative begins not with a universalized, departicularized human situation, but with Israel and the formation of a political body made of peoples joining to Israel within the Davidic tent (Acts 15:13–18). With this beginning, the *end* state of salvation involves overcoming unjust relationships, a just ordering of the world that eschews violence, exploitation, and exclusion, a release from demonic idolatry and reconciliation to God, joined to Israel, and participating in the Davidic blessings (cf. Acts 13:34; Isa. 55:1–5). For Luke, this end is a cosmic reordering reconciling the world to heaven, not simply God to individuals. The question remains then, how does Luke propose that this situation needing salvation is remedied (the *middle*)? What brings this world from this state of un-salvation to salvation?

I argue that an integral aspect of "how" this Lukan salvation narrative is structured and unfolds, though not sufficient in itself, is best expressed in *Christus Victor* terms, or what John Driver calls the Conflict-Victory-Liberation model.[137] Presentations of *Christus Victor* take many shapes; however, with respect to his understanding of atonement, the author of Luke-Acts has certain similarities with Irenaeus's work (see esp. *Haer.* 5.21). My interest in Irenaeus derives not from an assumption that Irenaeus is interpreting Luke-Acts, nor do I wish to read Irenaeus back into Luke. My interest is rather more modest. Irenaeus simply provides a *Christus Victor* presentation that helps to illumine and draw our attention to elements already present in Luke-Acts' own soteriology. My discussion of Irenaeus does not exhaust the richness of, nor do complete justice to, Irenaean soteriology, focusing on only a segment of his presentation. Though returning to him at points, Irenaeus is not a central focus of the following chapters; rather, Irenaeus's work provides some framing for what follows.

As is common among *Christus Victor* presentations, with Irenaeus, the *beginning*, the state from which one is saved, is captivity (*Haer.* 5.21). Compare the narrative of conflict with which Luke opens, namely, the need for deliverance (1:69) from the "hands of our enemies" (1:71, 74)—a captivity understood in national, theological, and sociopolitical terms. We learn quickly, however, that this conflict in social-political space is intimately connected to cosmic actors, specifically the devil (4:1–13). Both Irenaeus and Luke emphasize the need for release from powers, specifically Satan (*Haer.* 3.18.6; *Epid.* 17, 83).[138]

---

[137] Aulén, *Christus*; John Driver, *Understanding Atonement for the Mission of the Church* (Scottsdale, PA: Herald Press, 1986), 71–86.

[138] Irenaeus highlights sin as a force under which humanity is imprisoned in a way that Luke does not (*Epid.* 37). Additionally, Satan plays a noticeably more salient role in *Adversus haereses*, where Irenaeus emphasizes Satan as the fallen power as opposed to the creator god of the Gnostics, than in *Epideixis tou apostolikou kerygmatos*.

Further, salvation (release) in *Christus Victor* models comes by God's initiative and God's decisive redemptive action. Gustav Aulén distinguished the *Christus Victor* model by its focus on God's "continuous" action of redemption for humanity,[139] rather than, for example, a human act directed at affecting God or satisfying a legal demand.[140] Arguably, we discover this emphasis on God's continuous initiative in Luke-Acts establishing justness. The early church portrayed redemption from Satan in various ways. Origen references payment to Satan and Satan's own self-deception (*Comm. Matt.* 16.8; *Comm. Rom.* 2.13.29). Gregory of Nyssa's famous "fishhook" analogy speaks of God tricking Satan with Jesus's death as a payment (*Great Catechism* 5.21–6; cf. Augustine, *Serm.* 263.1; see also Ambrose, *Ep.* 41.7; Basil, *Ep.* 261.2). However, the idea of paying ransom to Satan is rejected by others, such as Gregory of Nazianzus (*Or.* 45.22; cf. 39.13; see later Anselm, *Cur Deus Homo?* 1.3–7). Indeed, such a ransom payment is not found in Luke-Acts, which might lead one to assume that Luke-Acts lacks this *Christus Victor* perspective. Nevertheless, even on this point, Irenaeus proves instructive. For Irenaeus, sacrificial metaphors are less prevalent. Neither does God trick Satan, pay ransom, or require payment.[141] Though Irenaeus references redeeming humanity from captivity to "the apostasy," contrary to Gregory of Nyssa, he holds that the devil tyrannized humanity *unjustly* and does not have just claim over humanity (*Haer.* 5.1.1); hence, God does not redeem humanity through payment to Satan.[142] Rather, Satan is conquered through Jesus's obedience (*Haer.* 3.18.6; 5.16.3, 21.2–3; *Epid.* 34) and "persuasion" (*Haer.* 4.20.10, 37.1–4; 5.1.1).[143]

Irenaeus's distinct emphasis on persuasion is particularly helpful. Whereas, for some, Satan is defeated through a just ransom payment or trickery, Irenaeus argues that Satan is defeated instead by persuasion (*Haer.* 5.1.1), where the object of persuasion is humanity. Irenaeus maintains that human beings, who are immature and need teaching, are held prisoner by Satan and his deception. Rather than defeating Satan through violence, Jesus encounters Satan with means that eschew Satan's own violence. To be clear, persuasion is not some idealistic confidence in dialogue, but a posture that rejects the domination and imposed violence of worldly realities, generally and as a means of achieving and a component part of God's restored and reconciled Creation.

---

[139] Aulén argues that this view exhibits continuity of divine operation. Salvation is accomplished by God's self in Christ, enabling God to be reconciled to the world.

[140] Aulén's characterizations of atonement types are not without problems. Aulén (*Christus*, 145–6), for instance, argues that "there is no satisfaction of God's justice" in the "classic" model, what he calls a discontinuity of justice and merit. The distinction between justice/merit and action directed toward God by humans on the one hand and release and God's unmerited action for humanity on the other is analytically helpful, but this discussion of justice requires more nuance, and does not reflect the concern for justice in both Irenaeus and Luke-Acts.

[141] Whether Irenaeus portrays God as paying ransom is contested. The primary text of concern is *Haer.* 5.1.1. See the discussion in Chapter 4.

[142] See William P. Loewe, "Irenaeus' Soteriology: *Christus Victor* Revisited," *ATR* 67 (1985): 5. *Contra* Neil Forsyth, *The Old Enemy: Satan and the Combat Myth* (Princeton: Princeton University Press, 1987), 335–8; Stanley J. Grenz, *Theology for the Community of God* (Grand Rapids: Eerdmans, 1994), 341.

[143] On Jesus's obedience, see John I. Hochban, "St. Irenaeus on the Atonement," *TS* 7 (1946): 543; Daniel Wanke, *Das Kreuz Christi bei Irenäus von Lyon*, BZNW 99 (Berlin: de Gruyter, 2000), 205–73.

Violent imposition and domination is of Satan (*Haer.* 4.20.10; 5.1.1).[144] Jesus defeats Satan through obedience to God, persuading humanity of Satan's lies, freeing humanity from its captivity. For Irenaeus, not only is this demonstrated in Jesus's crucifixion, which functions as a revelation of injustice, it is also witnessed at Jesus's temptation where Jesus exposes the lies that have bound humanity (*Haer.* 5.21.2–3). Indeed, Jesus's whole life of faithfulness demonstrates (gives "knowledge" of) God's true justice and covenant faithfulness (*Haer.* 2.20.3; 3.5.2; 5.16.3, 21.2–3; *Epid.* 34).[145]

Though this *Christus Victor* motif is important, release itself is not salvation, and Irenaeus's presentation exhibits multiple atonement motifs.[146] Salvation, for Irenaeus, necessitates participation in Christ's life, and thus Christ's body, a theopolitical reality.[147] This is common to both Irenaeus and Luke-Acts. Through persuasion, humanity is invited to fidelity/obedience, overcoming ignorance, immaturity, and captivity, freeing them for participation in obedience and new life with God (*Haer.* 3.18.5; 5.1.1, 16.3), a new life characterized by imitation, taking on Christ's life in fidelity and obedience to God.[148] Thus, while appropriation of Jesus's teaching and obedience ("knowledge," *moral exemplar*) is crucial, the embodied nature of this "knowledge" is emphasized so that God reconciles humanity not simply through cognitive knowledge, but through embodied obedience (*Haer.* 5.16.3), and imitation and embodied obedience, effected by "knowledge" and persuasion, are directly linked to overcoming Satanic captivity. Incorporation into Christ's body, the political body functioning according to this obedience and justness, is the *end* in much the same way that, for Luke-Acts, as demonstrated below, incorporation into the community of Jesus that participates in God's kingdom space functions as an end anticipating fulfillment.

---

[144] *Contra* Hans Boersma, who asserts Irenaeus and atonement more generally requires a necessary violence (*Violence, Hospitality, and the Cross: Reappropriating the Atonement Tradition* (Grand Rapids: Baker Academic, 2004)). Adam Kotsko ably critiques Boersma on this point (*The Politics of Redemption: The Social Logic of Salvation* (London: Bloomsbury T&T Clark, 2010), 55–62).

[145] Loewe argues that Irenaeus's soteriology is primarily noetic ("*Christus*"). To say that Lukan soteriology is concerned with "knowledge," however, is not to reduce it to subjective appropriation.

[146] Rightly, then, Kathryn Tanner (*Christ the Key* (Cambridge: Cambridge University Press, 2010), 253–4) and Oliver D. Crisp ("Is Ransom Enough?" *JAT* 3 (2015), doi:10.12978/jat.2015–3.141117021715a) critique Aulén's "ransom" theory for failure to see the importance of incarnation as the mechanism of atonement. See also Boersma, *Violence*, 126. On Irenaeus's use of multiple atonement models, see Hans Boersma, "Redemptive Hospitality in Irenaeus: A Model for Ecumenicity in a Violent World," *ProEccl* 11 (2002): 207–26; idem, *Violence*, 121–32.

[147] On the necessity of human participation and imitation, see Trevor A. Hart, "Irenaeus, Recapitulation, and Physical Redemption," in *Christ in Our Place: The Humanity of God in Christ for the Reconciliation of the World*, eds. Trevor A. Hart and Daniel P. Thimell (Exeter: Paternoster, 1989), 152–81; Thomas Finger, "Christus Victor and the Creeds: Some Historical Considerations," *MQR* 72 (1998): 46, 49; Boersma, *Violence*, 129–32.

[148] Irenaeus studies have understood the human situation in primarily two ways (Boersma, "Hospitality"). First, the evolutionary approach sees humans as immature needing growth. Adam and Eve were not perfect but immature. The incarnation represents God's presence among humanity perfecting God's image. See Demetrios J. Constantelos, "Irenaeos of Lyons and His Central Views on Human Nature," *SVTQ* 33 (1989): 351–63; Denis Minns, *Irenaeus: An Introduction*, 2nd ed. (London: T&T Clark, 2010), 56–82. Second, the restoration approach imagines that humans are held captive, but Christ's coming removed that which held humans in bondage. See John Lawson, *The Biblical Theology of Saint Irenaeus* (London: Epworth, 1948), 192–7. Boersma rightly argues that they are both present and not mutually exclusive. See also Douglas Farrow, "St. Irenaeus of Lyons: The Church and the World," *ProEccl* 4 (1995): 333–55.

In what follows, one should not expect that I will spend significant time arguing for the *absence* of other atonement motifs. An author may avail herself of multiple metaphors. Indeed, as we just noted, a *moral exemplar* component is integral for Irenaeus and will be for Luke. Victory over Satan through fidelity/obedience and embodied justness, the revelatory nature of Jesus's crucifixion, and Jesus as teacher imparting such knowledge in embodied practice are all elements of Luke's salvific narrative.

Reading Luke's salvation through the lens of Irenaeus emphasizes overcoming imposed bifurcations such as body/spirit and religion/politics. Irenaeus's own anti-gnostic impulse led him to emphasize the importance of Christ's incarnation and embodiment. J. Kameron Carter writes, "Irenaeus understood his struggle against the ancient Gnostic movement, particularly in its Valentinian variant, as a struggle over the meaning of the body both individually and as a sociopolitical arrangement—that is, as tied to or indicative of the body politic."[149] Carter adds that Christ's birth and life (not simply his death) "imprint a new modality of existence on [humankind], a modality of the cross, the ascetical model of life that refuses to tyrannically possess the world (*Haer.* 5.18.3; *Epid.* 34)."[150] Here again, we return to the importance of persuasion and obedience as not only strategies but modes of being that, through Christ's life and death, structure a political body. Moreover, this is not simply the departicularized, universal political body of Christ, but the political body of Christ, the Jewish Messiah, who recapitulates the life of the covenant people. With this, I do not appeal to Irenaeus in order to read Luke in an Irenaean mode, but to appeal to Irenaeus as a conversation partner who enlightens elements already present to Luke.

What follows does not unfold topically, but rather surveys the narrative of God's inbreaking salvation by attending to four important waypoints along the journey: The Benedictus (Lk. 1:68–79), Jesus's Nazareth sermon (4:18–19), Peter's Pentecost address (Acts 2), and Paul's address in Pisidian Antioch (13:13–52). These passages are recognized, each in their way, as important or programmatic passages that offer beginnings of sorts: to the Lukan narrative, to Jesus's ministry, to the apostles' mission, and to Paul's synagogue preaching.[151] However, in each chapter, attention is not restricted to these verses; rather, I attempt to see how these passages fit within the surrounding narrative.

Chapter 2 investigates the Benedictus (Lk. 1:68–79). The Benedictus is particularly interesting not only because of its preponderance of salvation-related terminology, but also because it presents what appears to be a markedly political salvation, including the promised Davidic deliverer. Commentary on this passage exhibits well the modern

---

[149] Carter, *Race*, 11.
[150] Carter, *Race*, 28.
[151] See, e.g., Holly Beers, *The Followers of Jesus as the Servant: Luke's Model from Isaiah for the Disciples in Luke-Acts*, LNTS 535 (New York: Bloomsbury T&T Clark, 2015), 160; Darrell L. Bock, *Luke*, 2 vols., BECNT (Grand Rapids: Baker Academic, 1994), 1:394; François Bovon, *Luke*, 3 vols., Hermeneia (Minneapolis: Fortress, 2002–13), 1:157; Joel B. Green, *The Gospel of Luke*, NICNT (Grand Rapids: Eerdmans, 1997), 207; Richard I. Pervo, *Acts: A Commentary*, Hermeneia (Minneapolis: Fortress, 2009), 74. The Benedictus is the only passage of the four that has significant debate concerning its programmatic nature. However, as Bock notes, this passage helps set "the theological tone of Luke Acts" (*Luke*, 1:172).

tendency to bifurcate space between political and religious spheres. Nevertheless, the Benedictus helps set the trajectory of the ensuing narrative.

Chapter 3 focuses on Jesus's Nazareth sermon and its Jubilee vision (4:18–19). Here we find the inaugural explication of Jesus's gospel, and the promised Davidic deliverer beginning his mission. Having just left the wilderness victorious over the devil, this passage gives us an explicit entry way into the cosmic drama with Satan and an introduction to the Jubilee era. This Jubilee speaks of real tangible release and reordering of social-political space. What is particularly interesting about the Jubilee, however, is its traditional association with the Day of Atonement, as a social-spatial extension of atonement cosmic ordering.

In Chapter 4, I address Peter's Pentecost sermon, though primarily the events surrounding it (Acts 1–2), including Jesus's ascension and the presentation of cosmic-comprehensive space. Focus is on heaven's place within the narrative, the unfolding cosmic drama related to Jesus's ascension, the way Luke characterizes space so as to reorder one's vision of social-political space, the eschatological event of the Spirit's outpouring, and the incorporation of the early community. Here, the elements of salvation, baptism, and so on lead to a community of those "being saved," participating in what looks like a Jubilee economy.

Finally, Chapter 5 focuses on Paul's sermon in Pisidian Antioch. There, Paul proclaims, as Peter before him, the Davidide who fulfills the promise to Israel's ancestors. However, Paul's message comes also as a warning to join faithfully to what God is now doing. This message of hope for Israel is concurrently a message of hope for the nations. However, this passage, as others, has language that has traditionally been understood as distinctly religious, including, in true Pauline form, a reference to "justification." How this is to be understood in terms of Israel's restoration is important. With this last chapter, we are reminded once again that this cosmic salvation and reconciliation is not an abstract event; it is directly tied and anchored in Israel, its election, and its mission to the nations.

Luke-Acts offers a comprehensive vision of holistic reconciliation of the world to God that is in many ways political. By invoking politics, my concern is not primarily whether Luke-Acts is pro-Roman, anti-Roman, or ambivalent vis-à-vis Rome, though I do think that his characterization of space calls certain aspects of Roman self-presentation, soteriology, and cosmic legitimation into question. More positively, Luke-Acts presents a picture of God's cosmic restoration in terms of a kingdom that simply is, under Jesus's lordship, who simply is Lord. The strategy of this kingdom and Lord is not violence or domination. Rather, Luke's gospel attests to the enduring nature of what really is, apocalyptically revealing the true structure of the universe. The church exists within *this* world, participating in and producing space of *this* kingdom, impacting the world which it occupies. The church's life is not an exercise in waiting but participation in the true authoritative structure of the cosmos in complex space. What follows focuses on the presentation of this soteriological vision. Having attended to these texts and this narrative, we will be in a better position to assess both the *what* and *how* of Lukan soteriology.

2

An Inbreaking Salvation (Luke 1:68–79)

Our discussion of the Lukan salvation narrative begins with the Benedictus (Lk. 1:68–79), a passage that helps introduce and set expectations for God's subsequently unfolding salvation. These twelve verses represent the densest concentration of soteriological language within Luke-Acts,[1] and much of this terminology is overtly political.[2] Even the language that many identify as more properly religious, such as "forgiveness of sins," has political connotations. This passage is crucial not only because of its content and position in the narrative, but because it is a site of contestation between political and religious notions of salvation. My contention is that the Benedictus sets a framework for Luke-Acts' salvation narrative and that the language that is traditionally deemed discretely religious is, rather, indissolubly *both* political *and* religious, contributing to Luke-Acts' overall theopolitical soteriology.

Lukan scholars have tended to isolate the different political and religious aspects of Zechariah's prophecy, ultimately emphasizing one while downplaying the other, with preference usually given to a personal, subjective, and spiritual sense.[3] Zechariah's political language is generally understood in two ways, as metaphorical and/or as pertaining distinctly to the future.[4] Both such interpretations essentially exclude present political and social manifestations of the prophecy.[5] The Benedictus is, thus,

---

[1] By soteriological language, I mean language typically associated with salvation, however defined, including redemption (λύτρωσις), salvation (σωτηρία), deliverance (ῥύομαι), and forgiveness of sins (ἄφεσις ἁμαρτιῶν).

[2] On politics, see Chapter 1.

[3] See, e.g., William F. Arndt, *The Gospel According to St. Luke* (St. Louis: Concordia, 1956), 66–9; Darrell L. Bock, *Proclamation from Prophecy and Pattern: Lucan Old Testament Christology*, JSNTSup 12 (Sheffield: Sheffield Academic Press, 1987), 73; G. B. Caird, *The Gospel of St. Luke*, PNTC (New York: Seabury, 1963), 58; L. Daniel Chrupcała, *Everyone Will See the Salvation of God: Studies in Lukan Theology*, SBFA 83 (Milan: Edizioni Terra Santa, 2015), 59; Hans Klein, *Das Lukasevangelium*, KEK 1/3 (Göttingen: Vandenhoeck & Ruprecht, 2006), 121–3; Friedrich Gustav Lang, "Abraham geschworen—uns geben Syntax und Sinn im Benediktus (1.68–79)," *NTS* 56 (2010): 506; Marshall, *Historian*, 99; Stenschke, *Portrait*, 253.

[4] Often, interpretations are nuanced, emphasizing a future political consummation. Others, however, contend that the language is solely religious—e.g., Arndt, *Luke*, 66–9; Luke Timothy Johnson, *The Gospel of Luke*, SP (Collegeville, MN: Liturgical Press, 1991), 48.

[5] Eschatologizing interpretations are not summarily wrong. Clearly, the *end* of salvation is not reached by Acts' end. Yet, most eschatologizing interpretations inscribe a body/soul and politics/religion dichotomy on time, envisioning the present manifestation of salvation as relegated to the religious or spiritual, as opposed to the political hopes of the eschaton.

often cast in a reductively religious idiom, and reference to "forgiveness of sins" (v. 77), in particular, is taken by many to signal a shift away from the political and toward a more narrowly religious focus.[6]

For some, this categorical division between politics and religion is exhibited in the prophecy's very structure.[7] While the first section is viewed as predominantly political (vv. 68–75), the second section gives way to a more narrowly religious or spiritual reading (vv. 76–9). This transition from political to religious idiom is thought to mirror a general conceptual transition in Luke-Acts (and early Christianity more broadly) away from political, material, perhaps militaristic, and Jewish salvific expectation to a more "Christian" and "spiritual" hope. Luke's supposed move toward universalization, depoliticization, and a reductively spiritual religion aligns, in respects, to the Enlightenment compartmentalization of religion and often depends on the binary Jewish/Christian, where "Judaism" becomes a primordial darkness from which the Jesus movement emerges and distinguishes itself.[8]

Nevertheless, the determination to deemphasize the political does not result simply from a desire for narrowly religious readings; rather, the move to spiritualize or shift the political aspects of the Benedictus to the future stems, at least in part, from a real interpretive conundrum: If we are to accept that God visits through the Davidic horn to bring about Israel's political liberation, where is it? For some, Luke-Acts, outside of Luke 1–2, shows no tangible manifestation of this political deliverance;[9] thus, it is argued, Luke has either deemphasized political deliverance or marginalized Luke 1–2.[10]

---

[6] E.g., Caird, *Luke*, 58; Fitzmyer, *Luke*, 1:386; Stenschke, *Portrait*, 253; Lang, "Abraham," 509.

[7] E.g., Marshall, who emphasizes a transition from an OT, physical notion of salvation to what he identifies as the "spiritual" salvation located in Luke and the NT (*Historian*, 94; idem, "Redemption," 154–6). See also Mark Coleridge, *The Birth of the Lukan Narrative: Narrative as Christology in Luke 1–2*, JSNTSup 88 (Sheffield: JSOT Press, 1993), 123.

[8] Bock, for instance, contrasts the "Christian hope" of the Benedictus to "contemporary Judaism, which tended to emphasize the earthly physical elements of salvation" (*Luke*, 1:190). Raymond E. Brown similarly contrasts "Jewish expectation" and "early Christianity" in the early chapters of Luke (*The Birth of the Messiah: A Commentary on the Infancy Narratives in Matthew and Luke* (Garden City, NY: Doubleday, 1979), 312). J. Massyngberde Ford, in an attempt to argue for a universal, justice-oriented Jesus, discards the parochial Jewishness of the Benedictus, arguing that Luke includes it only to reject it (*My Enemy Is My Guest: Jesus and Violence in Luke* (Maryknoll, NY: Orbis Books, 1984), 25–8). This betrays a tendency to see "Judaism" or Jewish conceptions of salvation as a foil for what is properly "Christian." J. Kameron Carter locates in this juxtaposition the foundational racial logic of modern Western thought: "The Jews were the mirror in which the European and eventually the Euro-American Occident could religiously and thus racially conceive itself through the difference of Orientalism … Having racialized Jews as a people of the Orient and thus Judaism as a 'religion' of the East, Jews were then deemed inferior to Christians of the Occident or the West" (*Race*, 4). Judaism was a material religion that "enslave[d] them to the material, empirical world" (*Race*, 105).

[9] E.g., Ford, *Enemy*, 25–8; Daniel Gerber, "*Il vous est né un Sauveur*": *La construction du sens sotériologique de la venue de Jésus en Luc-Actes*, MdB 58 (Geneva: Labor et Fides, 2008), 56.

[10] For some, this incongruity results from Luke's inclusion, either uncritically or intentionally, of source material at odds with his later presentation. On major theories concerning the Benedictus's composition, see Bock, *Luke*, 1:173–4; Fitzmyer, *Luke*, 1:377–8; Richard J. Dillon, *The Hymns of Saint Luke: Lyricism and Narrative Strategy in Luke 1–2*, CBQMS 50 (Washington, DC: Catholic Biblical Association of America, 2013), 1–5. Others have rightly focused on the text's final form and its placement in the narrative, e.g., Michael Wolter, *Das Lukasevangelium*, HNT 5 (Tübingen: Mohr Siebeck, 2008), 110–11; Coleridge, *Birth*, 17–28; David L. Tiede, *Luke*, ACNT (Minneapolis: Augsburg, 1988), 61. Dillon has argued that such a synchronic approach fails to appreciate Luke's

Many critics maintain that Luke-Acts, following its opening chapters, is actually rather deferential to political authorities, leading to the conclusion that the political themes of Luke 1–2 must be metaphorical or non-Lukan. Additionally, at Acts' conclusion, the people (the Jews) remain divided over Jesus as Messiah (Acts 28:23–8) and Rome persists in power. Is *this* the salvation of which Zechariah spoke?

Yet, the Benedictus functions like a scaffolding, leaving multiple gaps to be filled. It remains to be determined what the Benedictus's political deliverance looks like more fully, how it is implemented, and the timeline of its implementation, questions with which the disciples similarly struggle (e.g., Lk. 19:11; Acts 1:6–8). Zechariah's prophecy provides us with an entry into this discussion; it does not complete it. Within this framework, we need not assume politics as usual. The Benedictus, for instance, amid its discussion of a Davidic king and deliverance from enemies, makes no mention of military might or violent imposition.[11] Rather, the deliverance of which God is the subject climaxes with the way of peace.

Focusing on the Benedictus, we begin to fill out the *beginning*, *middle*, and *end* of salvation with elements that prove enduring through Luke-Acts. This prophecy's privileged place at the beginning of the narrative and its provenance, within the narrative, from the Holy Spirit, speaks to its importance. In what follows, I will work through the major sections of the Benedictus, showing an emerging picture of Luke-Acts' holistic soteriological narrative that includes cosmic, political, and religious elements, grounded in Israel's redemption, which is already taking a *Christus Victor* form.

2.1 Structure and Location

The Benedictus is situated at a key moment. Luke 1, though dealing with both Jesus's and John's births, builds climatically to Jesus's birth (2:1–7). Zechariah's prophecy sits in the penultimate place of this climax, declaring God's salvific work to be realized in the coming Davidic king (v. 69; cf. 1:27, 32; 2:4, 11). In this position, Jesus's birth

---

intentional dialogue with his original source, which, he argues, is transparent to the reader (*Hymns*, 5–6). However, it is unlikely that a general reader would be so attuned. This analysis relies heavily on a recognition of alterations to a specific pre-Christian Baptist hymn. Even if this Baptist source existed, however, there is no evidence that such a hypothetical text was widely available.

[11] Though some assert that Luke has used stylized martial language in the Benedictus (C. F. Evans, *Saint Luke*, TPINTC (London: SCM, 1990), 182; Herman Hendrickx, *The Third Gospel for the Third World*, 4 vols. (Collegeville, MN: Liturgical Press, 1996), 1:154; Paul Winter, "Magnificat and Benedictus—Maccabaean Psalms?" *BJRL* 37 (1954-5): 328–47; J. Massyngbaerde Ford, "Zealotism and the Lukan Infancy Narratives," *NovT* 18 (1976): 285), the text has no explicit reference to violence as a salvific means. Douglas Jones links the Benedictus's opening to the "Hymn of the Return" in the War Scroll (1QM XIV, 4) ("The Background and Character of the Lukan Psalms," *JTS* 19 (1968): 19–56). Though the Benedictus shares themes with certain Qumranic hymns, these themes are found in OT literature more broadly. More significant are the persistent elements of the Qumranic war hymns that are not present in the Benedictus or Luke 1–2. Though the Qumranic hymns describe God's deliverance through "the blood of guilty corpses" (1QM XIV, 3), for example, the Benedictus does not invoke bloodshed. The antecedents for the Benedictus's language are too broad and any allusion to violence too obscure to identify this hymn, in its Lukan form, as a Zealot revolutionary hymn.

becomes the narrative fulfillment of the Benedictus's messianic pronouncement. Rather than the Benedictus serving as mere ornamentation, Jesus must be understood through the lens of the Benedictus as it foreshadows his appearance.[12] Additionally, the prophecy's proximity to Augustus's census (2:1–2) invites the reader to compare its claims with the demonstration of imperial authority expressed in the census. This comparison is bolstered by the announcement of Jesus's birth by a heavenly army (v. 13), with Jesus declared Savior (σωτήρ), Christ (χριστός), and Lord (κύριος), born in David's city (v. 11). The Benedictus and the angelic announcement flank Augustus's imperial action, inviting a critical juxtaposition between Augustus and this hoped-for Messiah.[13]

The occasion for the Benedictus is a question concerning John's identity (v. 66), yet the prophecy delays discussion of John until v. 76, beginning, instead, by praising God and discussing the hoped for horn of salvation (vv. 68–9). Some have argued that this beginning would fit more appropriately after v. 64.[14] There, Zechariah's mouth is opened, ushering forth praises to God. However, the Benedictus addresses both Zechariah's praise and the question concerning the child's future (v. 66). John's significance can be understood only in relation to the Messiah.[15]

The prophecy, though exhibiting a "ramshackle" construction,[16] contains two recognizable sections, each a distinct sentence (vv. 68–75, 76–9).[17] The first major unit (vv. 68–75) is recognized by most commentators to emphasize a national and political restoration.[18] The second major unit (vv. 76–9) relates the current event, John's birth, to the soteriological project just declared (vv. 68–75). The unity of the two sections is demonstrated in thematic and terminological overlap, tying together Jesus and John within God's overall salvific work.

---

[12] *Contra* Brown's claim that the Lukan hymns are "appendages and can easily be excised so that the reader would never miss them" (*Birth*, 244).

[13] The political tension is palpable through the opening scenes in other ways: Davidic kingship allusions (1:27, 32–3, 69; 2:4, 11, 26), liberative soteriological language (1:46–55, 68–79; 2:11, 25, 29–31), and general political themes (1:46–55, 67–79; 2:1–4, 10–14, 25).

[14] E.g., C. F. Evans, *Luke*, 181.

[15] On the parallelism between John and Jesus in Luke 1–2, see Green, *Luke*, 50.

[16] Stephen Farris, *The Hymns of Luke's Infancy Narratives: Their Origin, Meaning and Significance*, JSNTSup 9 (Sheffield: JSOT Press, 1985), 133; C. F. Evans, *Luke*, 181. Several commentators note that the hymn appears to be a cento of OT citations, often viewed as having little theological intention. See Fitzmyer, *Luke*, 1:377; Winter, "Magnificat," 333.

[17] Several commentators note that these two sections represent distinct genres, a *berakah*, a blessing to God (vv. 68–75), and a *genethliakon*, a prophecy in honor of a child's birth (vv. 76–9) (e.g., I. Howard Marshall, *The Gospel of Luke: A Commentary on the Greek Text*, NIGTC (Grand Rapids: Eerdmans, 1978), 86; Dillon, *Hymns*, 57–8; Bovon, *Luke*, 1:67). Examples of such combined blessing and prophecy are found elsewhere. Dillon notes mixed forms in the Psalms: Pss. 81:6; 85:9; 89:3, 20; 108:8 (*Hymns*, 58, 70). Note also a similar shift to personal address of a fated child in Vergil, *Eclogue* 4.19. See Gottfried Erdmann, *Die Vorgeschichten des Lukas- und Matthäus-Evangeliums und Vergils vierte Ekloge* (Göttingen: Vandenhoeck & Ruprecht, 1932), 10.

[18] See, e.g., Caird, *Luke*, 58; E. Earle Ellis, *The Gospel of Luke*, 2nd ed., NCB (London: Oliphants, 1974), 77–8; Marshall, *Historian*, 94–102; Richard Bauckham, "The Restoration of Israel in Luke-Acts," in *Restoration: Old Testament, Jewish, and Christian Perspectives*, ed. James M. Scott, JSJSup 72 (Leiden: Brill, 2001), 435–88.

2.2 God Has Redeemed God's People (Luke 1:68-75)

This first major section weaves together a pastiche of Jewish imagery such as exodus-like liberation, Abrahamic covenant, and hope for a Davidic messianic figure. The prophecy signals that Israel's hoped-for national restoration has begun and attention is given to God's salvific action and messianic agent.[19] In this section, I attend first to the initial statement of God's intervention (vv. 68-70) and its characterization as national restoration, then to salvation and covenant in vv. 71-5 and, finally, to the context of Roman imperialism and soteriology. Here, we find the basis for a communal and holistic salvation taking place in social-political space.

2.2.1 God's Intervention (Luke 1:68-70)

This first subsection invites the reader into a national and political frame from its opening blessing: "Blessed be the Lord God of Israel" (εὐλογητὸς κύριος ὁ θεὸς τοῦ Ἰσραήλ).[20] Though the phrase "the God of Israel" (ὁ θεὸς τοῦ Ἰσραήλ) is rare in the NT (Mt. 15:31; Acts 13:17),[21] in the LXX, this blessing formula occurs often with remembrance of God's past actions for Israel and specifically in Davidic contexts (cf. 1 Sam. 25:32; 1 Kgs 1:48; 8:15; 1 Chron. 16:36; 2 Chron. 2:12[11]; 6:4; Pss. 41[40]:13[14]; 72[71]:18).[22] Such a beginning coheres with Luke's opening chapters more broadly, which emphasize national restoration, deliverance, and a restricted geographical scope centered on Judea.[23]

Gabriel's inclusion (1:19, 26) further grounds us in a narrative highlighting national and communal restoration, harkening back to Daniel 9,[24] where Daniel prays

---

[19] On the importance of Israel's restoration in Luke-Acts, see Jacob Jervell, *Luke and the People of God: A New Look at Luke-Acts* (Minneapolis: Augsburg, 1972), 41-74; Arthur W. Wainwright, "Luke and the Restoration of the Kingdom to Israel," *ExpTim* 89 (1977): 76-9; David Ravens, *Luke and the Restoration of Israel*, JSNTSup 119 (Sheffield: Sheffield Academic Press, 1995); Vittorio Fusco, "Luke-Acts and the Future of Israel," *NovT* 38 (1996): 1-17; Turner, *Power*; Bauckham, "Restoration," 435-88; Fuller, *Restoration*.

[20] In the LXX, the form generally appears without the genitive article (Gen. 9:26; 1 Sam. 25:32; 1 Kgs 1:48; 8:15; 1 Chron. 16:36; 2 Chron. 2:12[11]; 6:4; Pss. 41[40]:13[14]; 72[71]:18; 106[105]:48 LXX). See also Gen. 9:26; 1 Chron. 29:10; Tob. 3:11; 13:18 ℵ; *Ps. Sol.* 2.37; 1QM XIII, 2; XIV, 4; 4Q503; *Shemoneh 'Esreh*.

[21] In Luke-Acts, mention of Israel's God occurs in other forms: the God of Abraham, Isaac, and Jacob (Lk. 20:37; Acts 3:13; 7:32), the God of our Fathers (Acts 3:13; 5:30; 7:32; 22:14; 24:14), and the God of Jacob (7:46).

[22] We also find other themes from the Benedictus echoed in these passages, such as covenant (1 Kgs 8:21; 1 Chron. 16:15-18), salvation from enemies (1 Chron. 16:23; Ps. 41:11-12; 72:12-14; 106:4, 8-11, 43, 47), and allusions to God's exodus liberation (1 Kgs 8:16, 21; 1 Chron. 16:19-22; 2 Chron. 6:5; Ps. 106:7-12, 21).

[23] Luke opens in Judea (1:5) at the temple (vv. 8-9); John's purpose is eschatologically tinged as national renewal in the spirit and power of Elijah (1:16-17; Mal. 3:1; 4:5-6; Sir. 48:10); Jesus is a Davidide (v. 27) who will assume David's throne over Jacob (vv. 32-3; cf. Isa. 9:6-7); and the Magnificat's language anticipates political and economic liberation (vv. 46-55) in keeping with God's covenant faithfulness and mercy (vv. 54-5).

[24] Gabriel appears only twice within the OT, Dan. 8:16; 9:21.

concerning Israel's collective sins that led to national destruction and exile (vv. 4–16, 20), citing the exodus as a paradigm for restoration from exile (vv. 15, 17–19). Here, Daniel prays not for his own sins but for Israel's. These collective sins affect the people, a political body, as a whole, and forgiveness of Israel's sins results in restoration, giving support for understanding forgiveness later in the Benedictus (v. 77) as communal and referring to restoration.

Gabriel's appearance to Zechariah in the temple (Lk. 1:8–20) is reminiscent of Gabriel approaching Daniel during the evening sacrifice (Dan. 9:20–7). Gabriel, hearing Daniel's prayer for restoration, declares a time of atoning for the people and Jerusalem, so that their exile is in itself a cleansing (ἀπαλείφω) of sin before communal restoration (v. 24 LXX; cf. Isa. 40:2). I address further how Luke incorporates themes from Dan. 9:24–7, including Jubilee, in later chapters, yet, here, the prominence of an anointed one (Dan. 9:26 LXX; χριστός) who will bring judgment to the city (vv. 26–7) is notable.[25] The inclusion of Gabriel in Luke 1 and the anticipation raised by God's intervention and the coming Davidide in the beginning of the Benedictus suggest that now this hope of communal restoration is being realized.

In the Benedictus, Zechariah initially describes God's salvific movement in three interrelated actions: God has visited (ἐπεσκέψατο), freed (ἐποίησεν λύτρωσιν) God's people, and raised up (ἤγειρεν) a horn of salvation.[26] God visits to deliver through this Davidic horn.[27] God's visiting or looking down has ample precedent in the LXX where ἐπισκέπτομαι (I visit, look on) and ἐπισκοπή (visitation) are used of both God's salvation/providence[28] and God's judgment on both Israel and the nations.[29] In God's archetypal "visitation," the exodus, God *looked down* (ἐπισκέπτομαι) and brought redemption for God's people (Exod. 4:31).[30] The paradigmatic nature of this exodus-like deliverance is seen, for example, in Ps. 106(105), whose language is echoed in the Benedictus. There, the psalmist refers to God's past deliverance from the hand of enemies (v. 10; cf. Lk. 1:71, 74) as a pattern for God's current "visitation" (v. 5). Similarly, Psalm 80(79) pleads for God's salvation (σῴζω, vv. 3, 4, 8, 20), asking God to save as in the exodus (vv. 8–19), and anticipating what appears to be a Davidic king (v. 18; cf. Ps. 110:1). Though often referring to foreign oppressors, this visitation could also apply to deliverance from the powerful within Israel (see Isa. 10:1–3; 23:17; 24:22; 29:6).

---

[25] Additional elements of this prophecy can be attuned to Luke: Jesus's table-turning in the temple (Lk. 19:45–6; Dan. 9:26), a new διαθήκη (Lk. 22:20; Dan. 9:27), the desolating abomination (Dan. 9:27; 11:31; 12:11; Lk. 21:20; cf. Mt. 24:14–15; Mk 13:14; 1 Macc. 1:54; 6:7), and coming war and destruction (Lk. 21:20–4; Dan. 9:27).

[26] The verbs here are prophetic aorists, describing what God has purposed and set in motion (cf. Exod. 4:31; Isa. 43:1; 44:23). On the prophetic aorist, see Marshall, *Theologian*, 99; Dillon, *Hymns*, 58; idem, "The Benedictus in Micro- and Macrocontext," *CBQ* 68 (2006): 468–69.

[27] Each aorist verb in this sequence is, thus, linked by an epexegetical καί.

[28] Exod. 3:16; 4:31; 13:19; Pss. 80(79):15; 106(105):4; Jer. 15:15; 29(36):10; 30(37):20; 32(39):41; Zeph. 2:7; Sir. 35:18; cf. CD I, 7; *T. Jud.* 23.5.

[29] Exod. 32:34; Pss. 59(58):5(6); 89(88):32(33); Sir. 2:14; Jer. 5:9, 29; 9:9(8); 11:22; 15:15; 27(34):8; 29(36):32; 36(43):31; 44(51):13, 29; Lam. 4:22; Hos. 4:14; Sir. 35:18; cf. 1QS III, 13–15, 18; IV, 9; CD VII, 9; VIII, 2–3; XIX, 15; *T. Levi* 4.3. Some texts show God's salvation and judgment as a singular reality (Isa. 24:21–3; Jer. 15:15; 30[37]:20; Sir. 35:18; cf. Isa. 35:4).

[30] Cf. Exod. 3:16; 4:31; 13:19; 32:34; Pss. 80(79):15; 106(105):4.

Such visitation is obviously deliverance. The term λύτρωσις (deliverance/redemption, v. 68) is a multivalent term that conjures both sociopolitical and cultic connotations.³¹ Though, in the LXX, λύτρωσις κτλ. often refer to ransoming people or property (e.g., Exod. 21:30; 30:12; Lev. 25:26; Num. 3:49; Prov. 6:35; 13:8),³² the verb λυτρόω and the verbal noun λύτρωσις in particular focus on release or deliverance, with a ransom payment (λύτρον) either secondary or absent.³³ Thus, λύτρωσις need not imply a ransom payment, but simply deliverance as in the exodus. This comports with the Benedictus's emphasis on deliverance from enemies and national restoration without implying economic exchange.³⁴ There is no need to see a mixing of metaphors.³⁵ This sense of λύτρωσις as deliverance for the people corresponds to the larger context of national restoration in Luke's early chapters.

However, as Green rightly asserts, the degree to which the political language can be taken "literally" depends on how Jews in first-century Palestine understood their "life-circumstances."³⁶ There is, of course, no monolithic Jewish understanding of life-circumstances in the first century; nevertheless, several scholars note that many Jews believed that they remained in exile due to the diaspora and foreign domination.³⁷

---

[31] The precise wording of v. 68 is unique, but similar language appears in Ps. 111(110):9. The term λύτρον derives etymologically from λύω, as the instrument or means (-τρον) of release (Herbert Weir Smyth, *A Greek Grammar for Colleges* (New York: American, 1920), 232). λυτρόω is the activity of releasing, with λύτρωσις as its verbal noun and λυτρωτής as the agent of λύτρωσις.

[32] It is notable that several occurrences of λύτρον occur in relation to the Jubilee year (Lev. 25:24, 26, 51–2; 27:31; cf. Isa. 63:4).

[33] Exod. 6:6; 15:13; Deut. 7:8; 9:26; 13:5(6); 15:15; 21:8; 24:18; 2 Sam. 7:23; 1 Chron. 17:21; Neh. 1:10; Pss. 74(73):2; 77(76):16; 106(105):10; Isa. 43:1; 44:22–3; 63:9; Jer. 31:11; Mic. 4:10; 6:4; Zech. 10:8. Isaiah 52:3 uses λυτρόω without reference to a price. Outside of the LXX, λύτρωσις is used to describe the payment of a ransom price or pledge (Plutarch, *Arat.* 11.2; POxy 1130.12); however, the term also generally means release in situations where there is explicitly no ransom price paid (Diogenes Laertius 1.45).

[34] Most scholars admit that λύτρωσις here has a political sense. E.g., Frederick W. Danker, *Jesus and the New Age According to St. Luke: A Commentary on the Third Gospel* (St. Louis: Clayton, 1972), 19; Fitzmyer, *Luke*, 1:386; Leon Morris, *Luke: An Introduction and Commentary*, TNTC 3 (Grand Rapids: Eerdmans, 1974), 87–8; Alfred Plummer, *A Critical and Exegetical Commentary on the Gospel According to St. Luke*, ICC (New York: Scribner's Sons, 1902), 40; Heinz Schürmann, *Das Lukasevangelium*, 2 vols., HTKNT 3 (Freiberg: Herder, 1969), 1:91; Eduard Schweizer, *The Good News According to Luke* (Atlanta: John Knox, 1984), 42. Some dampen the political elements by emphasizing λύτρωσις as a cultic term (e.g., L. T. Johnson, *Luke*, 46; Klein, *Lukasevangelium*, 123).

[35] Or perhaps, more aptly, the metaphor of "ransom" from slavery serves the trope of liberation with specific attention to release. This is not to deny associations with debt slavery, but only to emphasize that as that metaphor is employed, it need not put an emphasis on payment. Luke utilizes the theme of debt especially as he appropriates salvation from second Isaiah. On this see, John Sietze Bergsma, *The Jubilee from Leviticus to Qumran: A History of Interpretation*, VTSup 115 (Leiden: Brill, 2007), 192. The themes of debt-slavery release and liberation more broadly are not at odds. Anthony Giambrone notes the importance of the debt metaphor in Luke and unmerited forgiveness (*Sacramental Charity, Creditor Christology, and the Economy of Salvation in Luke's Gospel*, WUNT 2/439 (Tübingen: Mohr Siebeck, 2017)); See also Klaus Baltzer, "Liberation from Debt Slavery after the Exile in Second Isaiah and Nehemiah," in *Ancient Israelite Religion: Essays in Honor of Frank Moore Cross*, eds. Patrick D. Miller Jr., Paul D. Hanson, and S. Dean McBride (Philadelphia: Fortress, 1987), 477–84).

[36] Green, *Luke*, 115.

[37] Tob. 13; 14:5; 2 Macc. 2:7; 1QM I, 3; 4Q504 4, 7–14; 6, 7–17; cf. Isa. 43:14; 1 Macc. 4:11; cf. Dan. 9; *T. Levi* 16–17; *Ass. Mos.* 3; *Jub.* 1.7–18. See Peter R. Ackroyd, *Exile and Restoration: A Study of Hebrew Thought of the Sixth Century B.C.*, OTL (Philadelphia: Westminster, 1968), 232–56; Craig A. Evans, "Jesus and the Continuing Exile of Israel," in *Jesus and the Restoration of Israel: A*

Richard Bauckham maintains that we should not only speak about continuing exile "but of continuing exile *and subjugation*."[38] This understanding can already be seen in Ezra and Nehemiah. In Ezra 9:8, though God has brought the people back to the land, their state is still conceived as slavery:

> But now for a brief moment favor has been shown by the lord our God, who has left us a remnant, and given us a stake in his holy place, in order that he may brighten our eyes and grant us a little sustenance in our slavery.

Nehemiah 9:36-7 echoes Ezra's assessment, noting particularly that their state of slavery is the result of their collective sins:

> Here we are, slaves to this day—slaves in the land that you gave to our ancestors to enjoy its fruit and its good gifts. Its rich yield goes to the kings whom you have set over us because of our sins; they have power also over our bodies and over our livestock at their pleasure, and we are in great distress.

Of the three NT uses of the term λύτρωσις, two are found in Luke as transparent references to Israel's restoration (1:68; 2:38; cf. Heb. 9:12). Elsewhere, Luke speaks of *awaited deliverance* (ἀπολύτρωσις, 21:28), concern for Israel's *embodied/political deliverance* (λυτρόω) (24:21), and describes Moses as a *deliverer* (λυτρωτής, Acts 7:35; cf. 3:22). The theme of deliverance (λύτρωσις) cannot be isolated as a phenomenon unique to the Benedictus and unrepresentative of Luke-Acts as a whole.

The agent of this deliverance and visitation is the Davidic "horn of salvation" (v. 69). The horn was a symbol of strength that had developed a close connection with the Davidic line,[39] and the advent of a Davidic king represents a particularly potent form of God's covenant remembrance (cf. 2 Sam. 7:8-16; 23:5; 1 Kgs 8:23-4; 2 Chron. 13:5; 21:7; Ps. 89:3-4; Isa. 11:10-16; 55:3; Ezek. 34:22; 37:24; cf. 4Q174; Sir. 45:25).[40] This Davidic theme connects the Benedictus to Luke-Acts more broadly as Jesus is

---

Critical Assessment of N. T. Wright's Jesus and the Victory of God, ed. Carey C. Newman (Downers Grove, IL: InterVarsity Press, 1999), 77-100; idem, "Aspects of Exile and Restoration in the Proclamation of Jesus and the Gospels," in *Exile: Old Testament, Jewish, and Christian Conceptions*, ed. James M. Scott, JSJSup 56 (Leiden: Brill, 1997), 299-328; James M. Scott, "Exile and the Self-Understanding of Diaspora Jews in the Greco-Roman Period," in *Exile: Old Testament, Jewish, and Christian Conceptions*, ed. James M. Scott, JSJSup 56 (Leiden: Brill, 1997), 173-218; Bauckham, "Restoration," 435-88; N. T. Wright, *The New Testament and the People of God, Vol. 1 of Christian Origins and the Question of God* (Minneapolis: Fortress, 1992), 268-9. For a contrary view, see Steven M. Bryan, "The End of Exile: The Reception of Jeremiah's Prediction of a Seventy-Year Exile," *JBL* 137 (2018): 107-26.

[38] Bauckham, "Restoration," 436-7.

[39] 1 Sam. 2:1, 10; 2 Sam. 22:3; Pss. 18:2; 75:4-5, 10; 89:17, 24; 112:9; 132:17; 148:14; Ezek. 29:21; Jer. 48:25. Note reference to "the Davidic shoot" in the *Shemoneh 'Esrah* 15 (Emil Schürer, *The History of the Jewish People in the Age of Jesus Christ [175 B.C.-A.D. 135]*, eds. Geza Vermes and Fergus Millar, 2nd ed. (Edinburgh: T&T Clark, 1973), 2:458).

[40] Mark L. Strauss, *The Davidic Messiah in Luke-Acts: The Promise and Its Fulfillment in Lukan Christology*, JSNTSup 110 (Sheffield: Sheffield Academic Press, 1995), 292-7.

repeatedly described in Davidic terms.[41] Indeed, Jesus's Davidic identity is an aspect of each focal passage we investigate, and David's invocation raises expectation of national restoration and a particular political dynasty, presented later as the restored Davidic "booth" (Acts 15:16-17; cf. Amos 9:11-12).[42] Throughout Luke-Acts, characteristically Davidic hopes are placed on Jesus: appeal to a perpetual Davidic line;[43] peace,[44] righteousness, justice, and concern for the poor;[45] mercy and covenant faithfulness;[46] the Messiah's Spirit anointing;[47] concern for the gentiles;[48] abundance;[49] and salvation.[50]

Visitation language continues into the following narrative, where Jesus, the Davidide, embodies God's visitation (Lk. 7:16; 19:44; Acts 15:14; cf. Lk. 9:38; Acts 4:29). So, when Jesus raises a widow's son (7:11-17), the bystanders respond that God has visited (ἐπισκέπτομαι) God's people (v. 16). Both here and in the Benedictus the beneficiary is the people (ὁ λαός), and the agent is Jesus, motivated by compassion (σπλαγχνίζομαι, 7:13; cf. 1:77).[51] Later, after arriving in Jerusalem, Jesus laments Jerusalem's ignorance concerning the things of peace (19:42; cf. 1:79), having not recognized their visitation (ἐπισκοπή, 19:44), Jesus's coming. As a result, desolation will come (19:43-4; 21:20; cf. Dan. 9:26). By Acts 15, God's visitation includes gentiles incorporated into the restored Davidic tent (vv. 14-17).

---

[41] Lk. 1:27, 32, 69; 2:11; 3:31; 18:38-9; 20:42; 22:69; Acts 2:25-36; 5:31; 7:55-6; 13:22-3, 34-7; 15:16. See Robert F. O'Toole, *Luke's Presentation of Jesus: A Christology*, SubBi 25 (Rome: Pontifical Biblical Institute, 2004), 139; Strauss, *Messiah*; Scott W. Hahn, "Kingdom and Church in Luke-Acts: From Davidic Christology to Kingdom Eschatology," in *Reading Luke: Interpretation, Reflection, and Formation*, eds. Craig G. Bartholomew, Joel B. Green, and Anthony C. Thistleton, ScrH 6 (Gloucestershire: University of Gloucestershire Press, 2005), 294-326; Yuzuru Miura, *David in Luke-Acts: His Portrayal in the Light of Early Judaism*, WUNT 2/232 (Tübingen: Mohr Siebeck, 2007); Sarah Harris, *The Davidic Shepherd King in the Lukan Narrative*, LNTS 558 (London: Bloomsbury T&T Clark, 2016).

[42] See the association between David and national restoration found in *Psalms of Solomon* 17-18 and its resonances with the Benedictus: the Davidide, the Lord Christ (χριστὸς κύριος, 17.32; cf. Lk. 2:11), acts as the agent of God's salvation (17.3; cf. Lk. 3:6; 8:33), in keeping with God's promises (17.4). The Davidide will gather a people (17.26) who are under foreign subjugation due to their sin (17.5-10), removing unrighteousness, condemning sinners, and directing people in righteous acts (18.8). The enemies from whom the Davidic Messiah liberates the people are multiple, including both Jewish and gentile opponents (17.21-5). See Kenneth Atkinson, *I Cried to the Lord: A Study of the Psalms of Solomon's Historical Background and Social Setting*, JSJSup 84 (Leiden: Brill, 2004), 129-79; Miura, *David*, 203-5.

[43] Gen. 49:10; 2 Sam. 7:12-17; Jer. 33:17, 20-1; Ezek. 37:24-5; Lk. 1:33; cf. Acts 2:34; 3:15; 5:30; 10:40; 13:30, 33-7.

[44] Isa. 9:6-7; 11:6-9; Ezek. 34:23-5; Mic. 5:4-5; Lk. 1:79; 2:14, 29; 7:50; 8:48; 10:5-6; 14:32; 19:38, 42; 24:36; Acts 9:31; 10:36; cf. Lk. 12:51.

[45] Isa. 9:7; 11:4; 16:5; Jer. 22:3-4; 23:5-6; 33:14-15; Lk. 1:17, 52-3, 75; 4:18; 6:20; 7:22; 14:13, 21; 16:19-31; 18:22; 19:18; 21:1-4; Acts 10:35; 17:31; 24:25.

[46] Isa. 16:5; 55:3; Lk. 1:50, 54, 58, 72, 78.

[47] Isa. 11:2; Acts 2:33; Lk. 3:22; 4:1, 14, 18.

[48] Isa. 11:10; 55:3-5; Lk. 2:32; 24:47; Acts 9:15; 10:35; 11:18; 13:46-8; 15:3, 7, 14-17; 21:19; 26:20, 23.

[49] Isa. 25:6-10; 55:1-5.

[50] Jer. 23:6; 30:8-9; 33:15-16; Ezek. 34:22-4; cf. Hos. 3:5; Amos 9:11-12; Lk. 1:68, 71, 77; 19:9; Acts 4:12; 7:25; 13:26; 16:17.

[51] This idea is not unprecedented. Sirach notes, e.g., Samuel as such an agent of God's visitation (ἐπισκέπτομαι) (46:13-15).

Here, at the outset of the Benedictus, Luke continues the theme of national deliverance already developing within his opening chapter. This deliverance, spoken of by the prophets, is God's visitation through a Davidic heir, and the audience is invited to understand the present moment as a time of fulfillment of this salvation.

2.2.2 Salvation and Covenant Fidelity (Luke 1:71–75)

Zechariah proceeds to delineate what was spoken through prophets and is now being realized in God's visitation: salvation from enemies (v. 71) and fulfillment of the oath sworn to Abraham (v. 73).[52] Salvation (σωτηρία) has already been linked with the promised Davidide, and will later be linked to the forgiveness of sins (v. 77). Here, salvation continues to occupy the domain of national deliverance, characterized as salvation "from our enemies" (ἐξ ἐχθρῶν ἡμῶν, v. 71) and "from the hand of all who hate us" (ἐκ χειρὸς πάντων τῶν μισούντων ἡμᾶς, v. 74). Again, this language is reminiscent of Ps. 106(105):10 and its invocation of the exodus paradigm.[53]

The Benedictus's use of ῥύομαι (deliver) further enforces this notion of embodied deliverance. The LXX uses ῥύομαι when referring to God's deliverance in the exodus,[54] while Israel is in the land,[55] on their return to the land,[56] generally,[57] and in God's future restoration of Israel.[58] The NT similarly utilizes the term for such embodied liberation.[59] Notably, the term is often used in conjunction with David, who both delivers the people and is delivered by God.[60] In such contexts, ῥύομαι is often connected with σωτηρία (2 Sam. 22:18, 41; Pss. 37:20; 54:13; 68:5; 88:24). The Benedictus exploits this notion by linking national restoration and the raising up of a Davidic savior (cf. Lk. 2:11; Acts 13:22–3).

The identity of the "enemies" to which the passage refers remains, at this point, somewhat vague, though the context implies tangible, social-political enemies. Although narrative proximity to Augustus's census gives reason to include Rome among this group (cf. 19:43), blanket equivalence between these enemies and Rome would be unwarranted. Israel's enemies could also include their own leadership and Israel's aristocracy (e.g., Isa. 1:24; 3:13–15; 5:7–10, 14; 10:2; *Pss. Sol.* 17.21–5). As the

---

[52] While the clause beginning with ὅρκον particularizes the covenant (διαθήκη), it is not necessary to explain the use of the accusative ὅρκον as a case of attraction to διαθήκη (e.g., Fitzmyer, *Luke*, 384). Rather, another possible explanation is that the accusatives (σωτηρίαν, v. 71; ὅρκον, v. 73) are objects of λαλέω (v. 70).

[53] Cf. Lev. 26:17; Deut. 30:17; 32:41, 43; Pss. 21(20):8(9); 44(43):10(11); 68(67):1(2); 83(82):2(3); 106(105):42.

[54] Exod. 5:23; 6:6; 12:27; 14:30; Judg. 8:34; Pss. 22(21):4(5); 81(80):7(8); 106(105):43.

[55] Josh. 21:22, 31; 2 Kgs 18:32.

[56] Ezra 8:31; Neh. 9:28; 1 Macc. 12:15; 1 Esd. 8:60; 3 *Macc.* 6.10, 39.

[57] Job 5:20; Pss. 22(21):8(9); 34(33):17(18), 19(20); 37(36):40; 41(40):1(2); 72(71):12; 91(90):14; 97(96):10; Isa. 1:17; Wis. 2:18.

[58] Isa. 44:6; 47:4; 48:17, 20; 49:7, 25, 26; 52:9; 54:5, 8; 59:20; 63:16; Ezek. 13:21, 23; 37:23; Mic. 4:10; 5:6(5).

[59] Cf. Mt. 27:43; Rom. 15:31; 2 Cor. 1:10; 2 Thess. 3:21; 2 Tim. 3:11; 4:17, 18; 2 Pet. 2:7, 9.

[60] E.g., 2 Sam. 12:7; 14:16; 19:10; 22:18, 44, 49; Pss. 6:5; 7:2; 17:18, 20, 44, 49; 30:16; 33:5; 53:9; 55:14.

narrative develops, the Herodian line,[61] Pilate,[62] and the high priests[63] provide distinct opposition to the developing movement, and Satan plays an important role as well (Lk. 4:1–13; 10:17–19; 13:16; 22:3, 53; Acts 5:3; 10:38; 26:18). Nevertheless, these enemies are also not restricted to spiritual or symbolic enemies.[64] The text gives no indication that this is the case. As with God's visitation and deliverance, the antecedent for the Benedictus's language in the LXX is the historical (and embodied) plight of God's people (Israel) and God's intervention (cf., e.g., Deut. 30:7; 32:41; 2 Sam. 22:18, 41; Pss. 21[20]:8[9]; 68[67]:1[2]; Bar. 4:18, 21).

The basis of this salvation is God's historic covenant fidelity to Israel (v. 72). God brings this deliverance in order to enact mercy (ποιῆσαι ἔλεος) and "to remember his holy covenant" made with "our ancestors" (μετὰ τῶν πατέρων ἡμῶν, cf. Mic. 7:20; 1 Macc. 4:10). Specifically, Zechariah references the Abrahamic covenant (v. 73; cf. Acts 3:25; 7:8), the covenant that God remembers when Israel is in Egypt (cf. Exod. 2:24; 6:5; 4Q378 11, 2–3; 4Q504 1–2 V, 9; *LAB* 30.7). The movement of the Benedictus, however, suggests that God's continual covenant fidelity through Mosaic and Davidic covenants, representing God's faithfulness through time, is similarly in view.[65] Most often, ἔλεος (mercy) is used in the LXX to render חסד, which frequently denotes God's covenant fidelity and loyalty.[66] This mercy can serve as the basis of God's unmerited forgiveness of iniquity (e.g., Num. 14:19; Ps. 25:7; Isa. 54:8), a theme found in v. 77. Of the six times that Luke-Acts employs ἔλεος, five occur in the Magnificat and the Benedictus (1:50, 54, 58, 72, 78; 10:37), highlighting the parallels between the two. In both, God's covenant faithfulness leads to saving action for Israel as a political body.

Deliverance then leads to the aforementioned political body serving (λατρεύω) God in holiness (ὁσιότης) and justness/righteousness (δικαιοσύνη) (vv. 74–5).[67] There

---

[61] Lk. 3:19; 9:7–9; 13:31; 23:6–12; Acts 4:27; 12:1–4, 21–3; 23:35.
[62] Lk. 13:1; 23:1–5, 13–25; Acts 4:27.
[63] Lk. 9:22; 19:47–8; 20:1, 19–26; 22:1–6, 52–3, 54, 66–71; 23:1–5, 10, 13; 24:20; Acts 4:5–6, 23; 5:17–18, 21–4, 27; 7:1; 9:1–2, 14, 21; 22:5, 30; 23:2–5, 14; 24:1; 25:2, 15; 26:10, 12.
[64] Gerber asserts, "The symbolic force of the words certainly wins out over their literal sense" (La force symbolique des mots l'emporte très certainement sur leur sens littéral) (*Sauveur*, 56). See also Lang, "Abraham," 506.
[65] R. E. Brown, *Birth*, 372, 389; Farris, *Hymns*, 73; Strauss, *Messiah*, 102; C. F. Evans, *Luke*, 185; Walter Kaiser, "The Blessing of David: The Charter for Humanity," in *The Law and the Prophets: Old Testament Studies Prepared in Honor of Oswald Thompson Allis*, eds. John H. Skilton, Milton C. Fisher, and Leslie W. Sloat (Nutley, NJ: Presbyterian and Reformed, 1974), 309.
[66] E.g., Exod. 20:6; 34:7; Deut. 5:10; 7:9, 12; 2 Chron. 6:14; Ezra 3:11; Neh. 1:5; 9:32; Ps. 98:3; Isa. 54:10; Dan. 9:4.
[67] This pair of virtues, holiness (ὁσιότης) and justness/righteousness (δικαιοσύνη), occurs in multiple contexts. In Wis. 9:3, this pair designates the virtues by which humanity should govern the world. In Hellenistic literature, this pair represents a set of cardinal virtues (Marcus Aurelius 12.1; Plutarch, *Mor.* 857A; Plato, *Prot.* 333B; Dionysius Halicarnassus, *Ant. rom.* 4.9.2; Philo, *Sacr.* 57; *Spec. Leg.* 1.304; *Virt.* 47). Philo notes that Abraham specifically demonstrated ὁσιότης to God and δικαιοσύνη toward human beings (*Abr.* 208; see also *Spec. Leg.* 2.63). Notably, in Deut. 9:5, the people are told that it is not because they might have ὁσιότης and δικαιοσύνη that they are inheriting the land, but because of the inhabiting nations' wickedness. Thus, it is remarkable that the people will now, indeed, embody holiness and justness/righteousness. See also Klaus Berger, *Die Gesetzesauslegung Jesu: Ihr historischer Hintergrund im Judentum und im Alten Testament*, WMANT 40 (Neukirchen-Vluyn: Neukirchener Verlag, 1972), 142–76.

is no reason to extricate this service from the overall political and liberative themes.[68] The people's service, λατρεύω, should be distinguished from λειτουργέω, the service of the priests (cf. Lk. 1:23).[69] The former (λατρεύω) is not restricted to the cultic sphere,[70] or to personal morality. This service (λατρεύω) implicates the totality of one's life (cf. Deut. 10:12; Josh. 24:14). Further, national concern is not distinguishable from a discrete moral-ethical sphere; it makes no sense in this context to talk of national restoration apart from Israel's repentance and service to God. The latter does not supersede and subordinate the former.[71] Rather, the phrase, "to serve God in holiness and justness/righteousness," describes in ideal terms the covenant people's entire mode of life in deliverance.[72]

This theme of national restoration continues into the subsequent narrative. For example, Simeon, who is waiting for Israel's consolation (παράκλησις, 2:25), promised by the Spirit to see the Lord Christ (χριστὸς κύριος, v. 26) before he dies, claims to have seen, in Jesus, God's instrument of salvation (σωτήριον). Simeon directly alludes to Israel's restoration and return from exile in Isa. 40:5, where Isaiah speaks of the day when all will see God's salvation. This is substantiated by the earlier mention of Israel's consolation (παράκλησιν τοῦ Ἰσραήλ, Lk. 2:25), an allusion to the hope for restoration from that same passage (Isa. 40:1–2). A few verses later, this instrument of salvation (σωτήριον) is referenced again in relation to John's ministry preparing the Lord's way, citing Isa. 40:3–5 (Lk. 3:4–6; cf. Acts 28:26–8; Isa. 6:9–10). This Isaianic citation invokes the broader LXX usage of σωτήριον as a term for deliverance.[73] The importance of this theme is underlined by its reappearance at the end of Acts (28:28), where, when in Rome, Isaiah is again alluded to (Isa. 6:9–10; Acts 28:26–7), and Paul declares that salvation (σωτήριον) has been sent to the gentiles (cf. 11:18; 15:6–21).

2.2.3 Summary

As noted above, most scholars recognize that this segment of the Benedictus (vv. 68–75) presents salvation as a political and national deliverance. However, my contention is that this political and national focus does not fade in favor of a more reductively spiritual salvation as the prophecy (and Luke-Acts) continues. Here, we have the foundation for a salvation taking up space in the world—a communal, national, and religio-political salvation, promising restoration for Israel as a political body. The *beginning* of this salvation narrative identifies the salvific need as deliverance from enemies and those who hate God's people. Yet, it is not simply a salvation *from*, but also a salvation *to* reordered social-political space characterized by a people living in holiness and righteousness. This is groundwork for a theopolitical soteriology, and as

---

[68] *Contra*, e.g., Farris, *Hymns*, 138; Schürmann, *Lukas*, 1:88; R. E. Brown, *Birth*, 372; Danker, *Luke*, 19.
[69] Hermann Strathmann, "λατρεύω, λατρεία," *TDNT* 4:61.
[70] Fitzmyer, *Luke*, 1:385.
[71] The exodus's continually stated purpose was that Israel may go worship (λατρεύω) God in the desert (Exod. 3:12; 4:23; 7:16; 8:1, 20; 9:1, 13; 10:3, 7–8, 11, 24, 26; 12:31).
[72] Fitzmyer, *Luke*, 1:385.
[73] Pss. 28(27):8; 62(61):7(8); 98(97):2–3; 106(105):4; Jon. 2:9; Isa. 26:1; 33:20; 51:5–6, 8; 56:1; 60:18; 63:1.

we move into the second major section (vv. 76–9), we have noted already how national deliverance is tied to communal forgiveness and grounded in covenant mercy.

Before turning to the second section (vv. 76–9), however, it is important to note that this salvation unfolds within a particular conception of cosmic-comprehensive space, inhabited by Israel's God, who is Most High. Nevertheless, within Luke's world, this vision competes with other visions of cosmic-comprehensive space that justify and animate those imposing order on space, such as Rome, whose political ideology is also firmly located within a religio-political discourse.

2.3 Rome, Luke-Acts, and Cosmic Salvation

To this point, we have noted how Luke's presentation of salvation depends on its embeddedness in Israel's history and the story of God's deliverance, but Luke-Acts is a work created within multiple worlds. Luke-Acts also engages with a Greco-Roman world having its own salvation narratives, including those pertaining to Roman imperial conquest. Indeed, the Benedictus and its cotext creatively consume dominant cultural production in order to present Jesus as savior, while delegitimizing Roman imperial ideology concerning salvation. This Roman ideology is not simply about the emperor's efficaciousness, but about an entire vision of cosmic-comprehensive space, and what might often be understood as a political and secular salvation is actually profoundly religious and theopolitical.

Greco-Roman salvation rarely ever refers to an afterlife;[74] rather, salvation has more to do with present wellbeing. Thus, a doctor (Lucian, *Ocyp.* 78), statesperson (Plutarch, *Cor.* 11.2), or philosopher (Dio Chrysostom, *Alex.*18) could be called savior (*soter/* σωτήρ).[75] For Luke-Acts, certain such salvific benefits as social reformation, healing, exorcism, raising the lowly, and peace are tied to Jesus. For the Roman world, it is Caesar who provides salvation (*salus/*σωτηρία), bringing peace and restoring order (cf. Philo, *Leg. Gai.* 149–51; *OGIS* 458). The age of Roman salvation was a golden age (Vergil, *Georg.* 1.24–43; *Ecl.* 4; *Aen.* 6.788–94; Lucan, *Bell. civ.* 1.45–66; Horace, *Carm.* 15.4–7; Augustus, *Res ges.* 12; Seneca, *Clem.* 2.1.4),[76] and Caesar, as ultimate benefactor, brought salvation through his *auctoritas* at the behest of the gods to keep the peace and prosperity of Roman dominion.[77] This salvation would be part of the cultural encyclopedia of Luke-Acts' model reader. The Benedictus, which is, in its narrative syntax, juxtaposed to the ubiquity of Roman authority (cf. 2:1–2), mirrors elements of this Roman soteriology (see below). Yet, it does not work within the discourse of Roman authority, but isolates key mythic elements and reconfigures them within a unique discourse.

---

[74] Jason Moralee, *"For Salvation's Sake": Provincial Loyalty, Personal Religion, and Epigraphic Production in the Roman and Late Antique Near East*, SClass (New York: Routledge, 2004), 17. On scholarly overemphasis of the afterlife as a major element of salvation in "mystery cults," see Burkert, *Cults*, 28.

[75] See Werner Foerster, "σωτήρ," *TDNT* 7:1003–12.

[76] See Schreiber, *Weihnachtspolitik*, 105–62.

[77] Frederick W. Danker, *Benefactor: Epigraphic Study of a Greco-Roman and New Testament Semantic Field* (St Louis: Clayton, 1982), 324.

Augustus's appearance—the quintessential imperial personality,[78] exercising his imperial authority in the census (2:1–2)—is wedged between two distinct divine revelatory moments (1:67–79; 2:8–14), the second of which proclaims the birth of a savior (σωτήρ) who is the Lord Christ (χριστὸς κύριος), in David's city (2:11). The Benedictus does not simply utilize certain words elsewhere employed for Roman soteriology, but the structure of this presentation itself encourages such a reading.

Several critics, however, maintain that Luke's inclusion of Augustus appeals rather to the benefit of the *Pax Romana* as the worldly political force enabling Jesus's more narrowly religious salvation to thrive.[79] Christopher Bryan writes, for example: "One thing is perfectly clear: Luke here shows Mary and Joseph loyally obeying Caesar Augustus' decree, and in so doing, *identifying* themselves with the Roman Empire."[80] This assertion cannot be maintained. First, if the text were emphasizing the boon of the Roman Empire, it is unlikely that it would have used the occasion of a census to make this point, especially in such proximity to the preceding and subsequent political language. Census-taking and the imposed tax system were notoriously burdensome. Clifford Ando, for example, notes: "The tax rebellion in Egypt during the prefecture of Cornelius Gallus was probably associated with the initial imposition of the Roman tax system and, therefore, with the census. So, too, the Cappadocian Cieti revolted against their king Archelaus … when he attempted to impose a Roman-style census" (cf. Strabo, *Geogr.* 17.1.53; Tacitus, *Ann.* 6.41.1; cf. idem, *Hist.* 4.74).[81] Similar census-based upheaval is referenced in Acts 5:37 with Judas the Galilean. Richard Horsley argues that this census would have been especially troublesome for Jews, citing census and taxation as an affront to the first commandment, testing their loyalty to God alone (cf. 2 Sam. 24; Josephus, *War* 2.118; cf. 2.433; *Ant.* 18.23–6).[82] Indeed, the Synoptic Gospels, with the sole exception of Lk. 3:1, consistently relate Caesar to taxation (Mt. 22:17, 21; Mk 12:14, 16–17; Lk. 2:1; 20:22, 24–5; 23:2).[83] And with respect to Jesus's birth, Norman Beck notes, "What would be more oppressive than to force a poor pregnant woman to have to travel a great distance on foot or riding a donkey during the final days of her pregnancy and then to have to experience labor and childbirth far from home among the unsanitary conditions of animal feeding and manure?"[84] From this perspective, it seems more appropriate to say that Joseph and Mary do not *identify* with Rome; they are *subject* to Rome.

---

[78] Cf. Clifford Ando, *Imperial Ideology and Provincial Loyalty in the Roman Empire* (Berkeley: University of California Press, 2000), 294.

[79] Horst R. Moehring, "Census in Luke as an Apologetic Device," in *Studies in New Testament and Early Christian Literature: Essays in Honor of Allen P. Wikgren*, ed. David Edward Aune, NovTSup 33 (Leiden: Brill, 1972), 144–60; C. Bryan, *Render*, 98–9; R. E. Brown, *Birth*, 416–17; Robbins, "Luke-Acts," 202.

[80] C. Bryan, *Render*, 98. See also R. E. Brown, *Birth*, 416–17.

[81] Ando, *Ideology*, 352. See also Stephen L. Dyson, "Native Revolt Patterns in the Roman Empire," ANRW 2.3 (1975): 138–75.

[82] Richard A. Horsley, *The Liberation of Christmas: The Infancy Narratives in Social Context* (New York: Crossroad, 1989), 37.

[83] Horsley (*Christmas*, 38) does not note the exception of Lk. 3:1.

[84] Norman Beck, *Anti-Roman Cryptograms in the New Testament: Hidden Transcripts of Hope and Liberation*, StBibLit 127 (New York: Peter Lang, 2010), 104.

Second, positive appraisal of Rome and its authority assumes that Luke affirms Roman authority over the civilized world (οἰκουμένη, 2:1). However, this is not directly apparent. Though noting here a census of the ostensibly civilized world, Lukan geography extends the transmission of God's word beyond the boundaries of Rome's version of the civilized world (Acts 2:9–11; 8:26–40). A case could be made that Luke's use of the term οἰκουμένη parodies Augustan self-presentation in Lk. 2:1, delegitimating this piece of Roman ideology.

Authority over the *orbis terrarum*/οἰκουμένη—and the peace brought to it by the Romans—is a central element of Roman self-presentation (see, e.g., Diodorus Siculus 40.4; Polybius 1.1.5; 1.2.7; 3.1.4–5; 3.4.2–3; 6.2.3; Dionysius of Halicarnassus, *Ant. rom.* 1.3.3–5).[85] In Greco-Roman writings, coins, and images, Rome is portrayed as victorious, having conquered the entire globe, which is fated and sustained by the gods. Coins from Augustus's reign picture on the reverse Victoria mounted on a globe. Others portray Victoria on the obverse with the reverse showing Caesar mounting his foot on the *orbis terrarum*.[86] The theme of domination of the civilized world continues throughout the first and into the second century with various representations of emperors receiving the globe from Jupiter (Hadrian), the globe held by Roma or Italia (Trajan), and proclaiming *Paci orb[is] terr[arum]* (Vespasian), but in each case making clear that Rome exercised authority over the *orbis terrarum*.[87]

Greco-Roman authors clearly saw Rome as "conqueror of land and ruler of the entire civilized world" (Pliny the Elder, *Nat.* 36.118; see also Cicero, *Balb.* 16; *Leg. man.* 56; *Sest.* 67), a status bestowed by fate and divine favor (Vergil, *Aen.* 1.278–9; Cicero, *Phil.* 6.19; Livy 1.16.6–8; Pliny the Elder, *Nat.* 3.38–9). However, the limit of the *orbis terrarum* was not the physical extent of the globe. There were in fact places that Rome was unable or unwilling to conquer. Strabo defines the civilized world (οἰκουμένη) in terms of habitability (οἰκήσιμα) (*Geogr.* 2.5.8; cf. Dionysius of Halicarnassus, *Ant. rom.* 1.3.3), dismissing the need to conquer savage peoples and miserable climates that extend beyond the boundary of the οἰκουμένη. The Romans, rather, so it goes, rule the most desirous parts of the civilized world (*Geogr.* 17.3.25). Plutarch even claims that Rome rules beyond the limits of the civilized world by extending its rule further than Gaul (*Caesar* 23.3).

However, there remains some incongruity between Rome's self-presentation as ruler of the civilized world and the reality of several "civilized" peoples left unconquered.

---

[85] Stefan Weinstock, *Divus Julius* (Oxford: Clarendon, 1971), 40–53; Ando, *Ideology*, 63, 277–335. See also Andreas Lindemann, "*Orbis romanus* und οἰκουμένη: Römischer und urchristlicher Universalismus," in *Christ and the Emperor: The Gospel Evidence*, eds. Gilbert Van Belle and Joseph Verheyden (Leuven: Peeters, 2014), 51–100; Barbara Rossing, "(Re)Claiming *Oikoumene*? Empire, Ecumenism and the Discipleship of Equals," in *Walk in the Ways of Wisdom: Essays in Honor of Elisabeth Schüssler Fiorenza*, eds. Shelly Matthews, Cynthia Briggs Kittredge, and Melanie Johnson-DeBaufre (Harrisburg: Trinity, 2003), 74–87; ead., "Turning the Empire (οἰκουμένη) Upside Down," in *Reading Acts in the Discourses of Masculinity and Politics*, eds. Eric D. Barreto, Matthew L. Skinner, and Steve Walton, LNTS 559 (London: Bloomsbury T&T Clark, 2017), 148–55.

[86] See Weinstock, *Julius*, plate 5.

[87] See Paul Zanker, *The Power of Images in the Age of Augustus* (Ann Arbor: University of Michigan Press, 1988), 81, 83.

For instance, Rome had notorious difficulty with the Parthians, an empire within the civilized world that did not bow to Roman authority (*auctoritas*). Early imperial writers speak of Rome's destiny to conquer the Parthians, Indians, Chinese, and Garamantes (Vergil, *Aen.* 6.791–5; Horace, *Carm.* 3.5.1–4). However, when this did not occur with respect to the Parthians, some settled for Roman recovery of battle standards lost in conflict to the Parthians as a sign of Roman authority (cf. Lucan, *Bell. civ.* 1.18–32; Florus 2.24.63). Further, Rome was known to have trade relations with India and China, though never extending *imperium* over them (Strabo, *Geogr.* 2.5.12; Pliny the Elder, *Nat.* 11.26; 37.78).

Luke-Acts—which includes a preponderance of the term οἰκουμένη among the NT (Lk. 2:1; 4:5; 21:26; Acts 11:28; 17:6, 31; 19:27; 24:5; cf. Mt. 24:14; Rom. 10:18; Heb. 1:6; 2:5; Rev. 3:10; 12:9; 16:14)—clearly portrays the οἰκουμένη as extending beyond Rome (Acts 2:9–11). At Lk. 2:1–2, however, οἰκουμένη is presented in Roman terms as part of a Roman decree. Luke portrays Augustus enacting the Roman script of worldly *imperium*. "Civilized world" is language of domination, a dominance subverted by the infant king, the shepherd's welcome, and the cosmic (apocalyptic) announcement from an angelic army concerning the Savior and Lord.

Reference to the civilized world (οἰκουμένη) recurs during Jesus's temptation, where the devil offers Jesus authority over the civilized world in exchange for idolatrous worship (Lk. 4:5–7).[88] The mimicry of Roman ideology is apparent, casting such authority over the civilized world (οἰκουμένη) as idolatrous and subject to diabolic patronage rather than to Rome's preferred benefactor, Jupiter (cf. Ovid, *Metam.* 15.858–61, 868–70). Luke, here, implies that Rome's rule is delegated by Satan, leaving Rome to function as an instrument of Satan.[89] Satan's authority, however, is itself delegated ("because [this authority over the kingdoms of the earth] has been given to me" [4:6], presumably by God [cf. Job 1:11–12; 2:5–6; Zech. 3:1; Jn 12:31; *Asc. Isa.* 2.3–4]). Conversely, Jesus's rule is repeatedly tied to God directly (e.g., 1:32, 69; 2:11; 3:22; 4:18; 9:26–7, 35), and he need not submit to Satan's authority, allowing him to reject the temptation of the politics of domination.

Luke's inclusion of Augustus specifically is important. The specter of Augustus loomed large over subsequent emperors. As Karl Galinsky notes, "[Augustus] was not only *pater patriae* [father of the fatherland], but the father of the world, *pater orbis*" (Ovid, *Fasti* 2.130).[90] The peace and prosperity of the civilized world (οἰκουμένη) were linked to Augustus's salvation. Succeeding emperors relied on perpetuating Augustus's persona and charisma in their own rule.[91] The Julio-Claudian emperors derived their authority from Augustus's charisma, and the

---

[88] Though the multiple kingdoms might lead some to disqualify Rome from consideration, Roman *imperium* often functioned by exerting *auctoritas* over kingdoms, not abolishing them.
[89] See Yamazaki-Ransom, *Empire*, 87–97.
[90] Karl Galinsky, *Augustan Culture: An Interpretive Introduction* (Princeton: Princeton University Press, 1996), 29.
[91] Ando, *Ideology*, 411; Price, *Rituals*, 58; Marianne Palmer Bonz, *The Past as Legacy: Luke-Acts and Ancient Epic* (Minneapolis: Fortress, 2000), 69.

Flavian dynasty relied on their own reestablishing of rituals and forms of Augustan rule.⁹² In fact, an integrated system of images tied to Augustus's charisma was established during his rule, bolstering a mythology of the empire that remained largely in place despite minor changes for two centuries.⁹³ Virtues of the empire such as *Pax* (peace), *Victoria* (victory), and *Salus* (salvation) were declared to be *Augusti* (of Augustus).⁹⁴

Luke's narrative presentation juxtaposes two cosmological orders distinguished in part by their respective saviors. As Luke sets the world stage, the birth of the Savior (σωτήρ) is situated within the reign of the paradigmatic savior, Augustus (Pliny the Younger, *Ep.* 52; Florus, 2.24.64; Suetonius, *Nero* 13.2; *Vesp.* 9.1; Lucan, *Bell. civ.* 1.60; Josephus, *War* 7.158; Vergil, *Ecl.* 1.6-8, 17-20; Horace, *Carm.* 15.4-16).⁹⁵ Gary Gilbert writes, "By the end of the first century the title of savior and benefaction of peace were almost inextricably bound together with Rome and the emperor."⁹⁶ The oft-quoted Priene calendar inscription explicates this of Augustus:

> Since the divine Providence that has ordered our lives ... has set the world in good order by introducing Augustus, whom she filled with virtue for the benefit (εὐεργεσία) of all humankind, by granting him as savior (σωτήρ) to us and those who will come after us, ending war and ordering peace (εἰρήνη), and Caesar, by appearing (ἐπιφαίνω), surpassed the hopes of all those anticipating good news (εὐαγγέλια), going beyond not only those who had been benefactors (εὐεργέτης) before him, but also leaving no hope for those who will come in the future of surpassing him, the god's [Augustus's] birthday began this good news (εὐαγγελίζω) to the world thanks to him.
>
> (*OGIS* 458, my translation)

Augustus brings good news of peace and salvation. He is a benefactor beyond all imagined hopes, and his status is divinely arranged, cosmically linked, and undeniably religious (see also Suetonius, *Aug.* 94; Vergil, *Aen.* 6.788-807). It is this Augustus who appears in Lk. 2:1-2 between the proclamation of the Davidic savior's appearance—freeing from oppression and enemies and teaching his people to walk in the ways of peace—and Jesus's birth as the "Savior, the Lord Messiah in the city of David" announced by an angelic army.⁹⁷

Augustus's salvation was not restricted to politics *simpliciter*. He was embedded in a saving cosmic order (cf. Lucan, *Bell. civ.* 1.33-66). From the beginning of the fourth

---

⁹² Ando, *Ideology*, 33, 294.
⁹³ Zanker, *Images*, 237, 338.
⁹⁴ Ando, *Ideology*, 292.
⁹⁵ Gilbert, "Identity," 238.
⁹⁶ Gilbert, *Multivalence*, 100. See also J. Rufus Fears, "The Cult of Virtues and Roman Imperial Ideology," *ANRW* 2.17.2 (1981): 807.
⁹⁷ See the comparison between Luke's presentation of Jesus as σωτήρ in Lk. 2:11 and the Priene calendar in Franz Jung, ΣΩΤΗΡ: *Studien zur Rezeption eines hellenistischen Ehrentitels im Neuen Testament*, NTAbh 39 (Münster: Aschendorff, 2002), 274-9.

century BCE, Romans venerated the goddess *Salus Publica* who guaranteed "salvation" (*salus*) (Livy 9.43.25, 10.1.9), and while Roman tradition had typically rejected giving kings divine honors, by Augustus's death, "a specifically Roman imperial ideology was established around symbols and slogans that advertised the emperor's role in 'saving' the state from its enemies."[98] In fact, after Augustus's death, the god *Salus Publica* (public salvation) gradually became first *Salus Augusta*, taking on the feminine name associated with Augustus, then by the reign of Vespasian she became *Salus Augusti* (Augustan salvation).[99] Lorenz Winkler argues that this shift to the masculine genitive *Augusti* indicates that *Salus* had ceased to be distinct from the emperor.[100] Further, Augustan salvation assured the *pax deorum* (gods' peace);[101] Augustus was able to restore peace between the gods and humanity that had been disturbed during the civil war.[102]

The name *Augustus* itself embraced a broad range of meanings, including "stately," "dignified," and "holy,"[103] derived from *auger*, a role he held as Jupiter's representative on earth.[104] For many, the name Augustus was an indication of his divine status. Dio Cassius writes that the name indicates that he is "more than human, for all the most honored and sacred things are called *augusta*" (53.16.18). Florus writes: "the name of Augustus was deemed more holy and venerable [than Romulus], in order that, while he dwelt on earth, he might be given a name and title that raised him to the rank of a deity" (2.34.66); and Ovid adds, "Augustus alone bears a name that ranks with Jove supreme" (*Fasti*, 1.608; cf. Phil. 2:9–11). Ando notes: "Modern translators and dictionaries rob texts from this era of much of their power when they render the words 'sacred' and 'divine' as 'imperial,' as though Augustus had been merely a man."[105] Augustus established an all-encompassing religio-political salvation and ordering of social-space embedded in a conception of cosmic-comprehensive space and authority.

Salvation here was no matter of mere deliverance, an isolated political reality. *Salus Augusti* was political and religious; it was a cosmological vision.[106] For Luke-Acts, similarly, we do not find Rome occupying the role of political savior and Jesus, the religious savior; rather, we have two saviors and two kingdoms, neither relegated to discrete spheres. Luke's opening invites a conflict of interpretations over this cosmological order and authority, a conflict starkly presented in Jesus's temptation as the difference between Satan's authority and God's by way of Jesus (Lk. 4:1–13; cf. Acts 26:18). This cosmological conflict, in subsequent chapters of this study, becomes more explicit, noting the underlying struggle between Satan and Jesus. Yet, here, we note that

---

[98] Moralee, *Salvation's Sake*, 17.
[99] Moralee, *Salvation's Sake*, 20.
[100] Lorenz Winkler, *Salus: Vom Staatskult zur politischen Idee: Eine archäologische Untersuchung*, AG 4 (Heidelberg: Archäologie und Geschichte, 1995), 95; Fears, "Virtues," 887.
[101] Allen Brent, "Luke-Acts and the Imperial Cult in Asia Minor," *JTS* 48 (1997): 421.
[102] Fears, "Virtues," 885–6.
[103] Zanker, *Images*, 98.
[104] Ovid, *Metam.* 15.858–61, 868–70.
[105] Ando, *Images*, 393.
[106] The term "cosmological" in this study has and continues to speak of an all-encompassing reality that exceeds human, mundane space but does not exclude it.

this cosmological struggle does not unfold over their heads, so to speak, but is manifest simultaneously in social-political space.

Luke-Acts engages with the dominant cultural production of its historical milieu. As Gilbert writes, "Luke-Acts invokes the language used to legitimize imperial authority, but by identifying Jesus as savior and stressing that peace has been established through him (and therefore not Rome), the narrative negates Rome's hegemonic claim."[107] Not only does the narrative negate Rome's hegemonic claim, it negates an entire view of cosmological order. Though Luke-Acts has been accused of simply repackaging the same oppressive structures in Christian garb,[108] the appropriation involves rather a distancing from and reconfiguration of those structures, a reality made particularly clear in Jesus's ministry.

2.4 John and the Dawn from on High (Luke 1:76-9)

As we move to the second major segment of Zechariah's prophecy, one might detect a shift at this juncture to a more "religious" and "spiritual" salvation at odds with the political salvation of vv. 68-75, especially in the language of forgiveness of sins (v. 77). Nevertheless, the passage continues to emphasize holistic salvation, building on the social, political, and religious salvation of the first section (vv. 68-75). In what follows, I first consider forgiveness of sins and John's role in this scheme, followed by a discussion of the remaining elements of this unfolding salvation showing how they reinforce the national and theopolitical hope of vv. 68-75.

2.4.1 John and Forgiveness of Sins

This section is set apart by its transition to the future tense (κληθήσῃ) and its focus on John. The δέ (but/now) at v. 76 functions as a mild contrastive conjunction indicating movement into something new, yet the pre-positioned καί indicates a continuity with what has come before.[109] Seemingly, the previous material (vv. 68-75) prepares for John, who will bring the knowledge of salvation, yet what this means remains contested.

2.4.1.1 *John, Prophet of Reformation and Restoration*

Zechariah declares that John will be called the prophet of the Most High (v. 76), confirming Gabriel's announcement to Zechariah in vv. 13-17. There, Gabriel claims that John will cause rejoicing and be filled with the spirit and power of Elijah (vv. 14, 17; cf. 2 Kgs 2:9-15). Invoking Elijah, John is expected not only to bring reform

---

[107] Gilbert, *Multivalence*, 101.
[108] E.g., Warren Carter, "Singing in the Reign: Performing Luke's Songs and Negotiating the Roman Empire (Luke 1-2)," in *Luke-Acts and Empire: Essays in Honor of Robert L. Brawley*, eds. David Rhoads, David Esterline, and Jae Won Lee, PrTMS (Eugene, OR: Pickwick, 2011), 42-3.
[109] See Wolter, *Lukasevangelium*, 115.

(v. 16) but also to prepare the people for the Lord's coming,[110] a role expressed in two key scriptural allusions, Isa. 40:3 and Mal. 3:1 (vv. 17, 76; 3:4–6).

The allusion to Isa. 40:3 (Lk. 1:76) draws our attention to that passage, which addresses the end of exile. There, God directs the prophet (or priests [LXX]), after declaring comfort to Jerusalem, to tell Jerusalem that her service is complete and her penalty paid (MT). The LXX, however, reframes this debt language, referring to Jerusalem's humility (ταπείνωσις), rather than service, reaching fulfillment and her (collective) sin loosed/released (λύω) rather than paid (cf. Lam. 4:22).[111] The announcement of "forgiveness of sins" in Lk. 1:77 correlates with such an announcement of national restoration. Nevertheless, the anticipation of restoration also comes with an expectation for social reorganization. John's preaching is portrayed through the lens of Isaianic ecological metaphor, leveled mountains and filled valleys (40:4; Lk. 3:5), bringing to mind the moral and social renewal more straightforwardly delineated in the Magnificat (1:52–3). John comes as a preacher of renewal (3:7–18) to prepare *a people* for the Lord's coming and restoration.

The allusion to Mal. 3:1, "I am sending my messenger and he will prepare the way before my coming," similarly invokes God's visitation and reform. Though Mal. 3:1 centers on temple reformation—a role Jesus will later take up (cf. 19:44; 19:45–8)—Malachi's concern is much broader, the people's collective ethical existence. The messenger of Malachi declares God's judgment against those who do not fear God: sorcerers; adulterers; and those who lie in God's name, defraud hired laborers, oppress the widow, strike the orphan, and withhold justice from the resident alien (3:5). This restoration vision is one of completely reformed social-political space. Thus, when Gabriel announces that John has come to turn fathers' hearts to children and the wicked to the thoughts of the just (1:17; cf. Sir. 48:10), this goes hand in hand with preparing God's way(s) (Isa. 40:3–5; Lk. 1:77; 3:4–6).[112]

2.4.1.2 Knowledge of Salvation and the Forgiveness of Sins

John, as prophet of the Most High, prepares the way by giving knowledge (τοῦ δοῦναι γνῶσιν) of salvation (σωτηρία) to God's people, in the forgiveness of their sins (ἐν ἀφέσει ἁμαρτιῶν αὐτῶν). An interpretive crux of this subsection is the reference to "forgiveness of sins." Forgiveness of sins is a distinctly Lukan phrase, appearing at key moments throughout Luke-Acts (Lk. 1:77; 3:3; 24:47; Acts 2:38; 5:31; 10:43; 13:38; 26:18; cf. Lk. 4:18) and relatively few times outside of Luke-Acts (cf. Rom. 4:7;

---

[110] Cf. Mal. 4:5–6; 1 Kgs 17–18; Sir. 48:1–15; Mk 1:1–4; Mt. 3:1–6; 11:10; Jn 3:28. See Christian Blumenthal, "Elija bei Lukas," *BZ* 61 (2017): 86–103. Nowhere in Luke-Acts is John identified *as* Elijah. Rather, he comes in the spirit and power of Elijah (Lk. 1:17). Unlike the other Synoptic Gospels, which make more of a connection between John and Elijah (Mt. 11:14; 17:2; Mk 9:13; cf. Jn 1:21, 25), in Luke, John appears to function as an Elijianic type, though not Elijah *redivivus*.

[111] Luke appears to be working with the LXX given, e.g., his relatively faithful rendering of Isa. 40:3–5 in Lk. 3:4–6.

[112] Notably, John's preparatory work appears successful. Characters addressed by John in Luke 3 appear prepared prior to Jesus's arrival—e.g., centurions (Lk. 3:14; 7:11; Acts 10:1–48) and tax collectors (Lk. 3:12; 5:27–8; 19:1–10).

Col. 1:14; Eph. 1:7; Heb. 9:22; 10:18; Jas 5:15; 1 Jn 1:9; 2:12). For many, forgiveness of sins, here, represents a Lukan interjection into a political milieu that reshapes the prophecy in a more narrowly spiritual direction.[113] However, forgiveness refers to more than personal relational repair with God and includes Israel's restoration.

The prepositional phrase, "in/by the forgiveness of sins," modifies the infinitival clause, "to give knowledge of forgiveness to his people" (τοῦ δοῦναι γνῶσιν σωτηρίας τῷ λαῷ αὐτοῦ), one of two purposive infinitive clauses explicating John's "coming before the Lord": John comes (1) to prepare the Lord's way and (2) to *give* the knowledge of salvation. Implicitly, the latter helps achieve the former. The Lord's way is prepared by John's giving this knowledge. How does John give this knowledge; and what exactly is it?

Generally, there have been two approaches to defining γνῶσις (knowledge) in this text. First, some see this knowledge as factual knowledge about a *future* coming salvation. With this understanding, John gives information concerning a salvation yet to be realized. Understanding γνῶσις in this way leaves the prepositional phrase, "in the forgiveness of sins," to function adjectivally, modifying salvation (σωτηρία), but risks confining salvation to a reductive forgiveness.[114] Verse 77 is then understood to mean that John comes to give factual knowledge *about* a *future* salvation consisting in forgiveness of sins.

Understanding John's mission as giving awareness of a future salvation is attractive to some commentators for a couple of reasons.[115] First, outside of Lk. 1:77 and 3:3, Luke-Acts connects neither John nor his baptism to the forgiveness of sins (Lk. 24:47; Acts 2:38; 3:19; 5:31; 10:43; 13:38; 26:18); rather, John offers only a baptism of repentance (Acts 13:24; 19:4). John's baptism is portrayed as incomplete (Acts 18:25; 19:1–5), lacking, in particular, the Spirit, an element some tie directly to salvation (Acts 2:38; 9:17; 10:33–4; 11:15–17).[116] Thus, disassociating John from forgiveness preserves the apparent coherence of the narrative. Second, this interpretation preserves Jesus's unique relation to forgiveness.

Nevertheless, a second approach argues that knowledge (γνῶσις), here, should be understood in the Semitic sense of acknowledgement, practical knowledge, or confirmation.[117] Hans Sellner notes that this conception of γνῶσις, found within the LXX, relates less to apprehension of logical facts and more to the understanding and experience of a reality that may still remain somewhat concealed in its totality.[118] The phrase "knowledge of salvation" (γνῶσις σωτηρίας) is not found elsewhere in the NT

---

[113] E.g., Fitzmyer, *Luke*, 1:386; Coleridge, *Birth*, 123; Caird, *Luke*, 58; Norval Geldenhuys, *Commentary on the Gospel of Luke*, NICNT (Grand Rapids: Eerdmans, 1956), 93; Klein, *Lukasevangelium*, 121, 124; Bovon, *Luke*, 1:75; Marshall, *Gospel*, 99; Stenschke, *Portrait*, 253.

[114] Sellner finds this reduction to be the major problem with this interpretation (*Heil*, 56). Conversely, O'Toole remarks that "forgiveness of sins is an alternative Lucan expression for salvation" (*Christology*, 127).

[115] E.g., Joachim Gnilka, "Der Hymnus des Zacharias," *BZ* 6 (1962): 233; Farris, *Hymns*, 139–40; Klein, *Lukasevangelium*, 125.

[116] E.g., Turner, *Power*, 137, 418–27; Green, "Saviour," 94–5; idem, "Servant," 10. Cf. Lk. 2:38; 9:17; 10:43–4; 11:15–17.

[117] Bovon, *Luke*, 1:75; R. E. Brown, *Birth*, 373; Rudolf Bultmann, "γινώσκω, γνῶσις, ἐπιγινώσκω, ἐπίγνωσις," *TDNT* 1 (1964): 689–714; Thomas Kaut, *Befreier und befreites Volk*, BBB 77 (Frankfurt am Main: Anton Hain, 1990), 187–8; Sellner, *Heil*, 58; Philipp Vielhauer, "Das Benedictus des Zacharias (Lk 1,68–79)," in *Aufsätze zum Neuen Testament*, TBü 31 (Munich: Kaiser, 1965), 41.

[118] See Sellner, *Heil*, 58.

or the LXX, but a similar idea appears in Ps. 97:2 LXX where God "makes known" salvation. There, knowledge does not concern the *fact* of salvation; rather, salvation is made known through its *enactment*, publicly manifest before the nations. Similarly, in the NT, γνῶσις often refers to an experience, acquaintance, or understanding rather than mere factual knowledge (2 Cor 2:14; 4:6; Phil. 3:8; 2 Pet. 3:18; cf. Lk. 11:52). If we adopt this sense of γνῶσις, the prepositional phrase, "in forgiveness" in v. 77, functions adverbially and instrumentally to modify the infinitive "to give" (δοῦναι), so that John gives an experience of or acquaintance with salvation through his role as the herald of God's forgiveness (or his baptism, 3:3).[119] The key is that this salvation remains partially concealed in its totality, even if John proclaims and demonstrates its inbreaking. In this way, salvation is not reduced to forgiveness of sins, but made manifest and demonstrated in forgiveness, which need not simply be the absolution of past wrongs, but a productive reality with social implications for release (vv. 68, 71, 74, 78–79) and a renewed community living in holiness and righteousness (v. 75) and walking the way of peace (v. 79). This conforms to the picture of salvation already presented in the Benedictus.

By this reading, making salvation known through the declaration of God's turning in forgiveness uncovers the impending reality of God's redemption. Forgiveness, as we saw with Dan. 9:24–7, is presupposed by and initiates God's redemption; it is the inauguration of salvation, not its totality. Thus, John's baptism, declaring God's turning in forgiveness, makes known that God's salvation is at hand. Coupled with the Benedictus's declaration of forgiveness are Scriptural allusions to Israel's communal restoration (Isa. 40:2; 44:21–2; 55:7).[120] In the OT, Israel's exile is the result of collective and generational sins[121] that have driven the people from the land.[122] God's forgiving sins means that God turns once again to act for the people in their need and to restore them (Isa. 43:25; 44:22; Dan. 9:18).

This national concern continues throughout Luke-Acts, where references to forgiveness of sins occur citing Israelite ties (Acts 2:14, 22, 29, 39; 3:12, 25; 10:42; 13:16–17, 26, 32; 22:14), the Davidic Messiah (2:25–36; 13:22–3, 33–7), the prophet like Moses and the exodus (3:22–4; 13:17–23), and Israel's repentance (5:31). Jesus's proclamations of forgiveness are signs of this new movement of God (Lk. 5:20–5; 7:48–9; 23:34; cf. 4:18–19), inaugurated with John's announcement of God's forgiveness, where the people confront God's turning to act for salvation. This is the reality that

---

[119] E.g., Walter Radl, *Der Ursprung Jesu: Traditionsgeschichtliche Untersuchungen zu Lukas 1–2*, HerdBS 7 (Freiberg: Herder, 1996), 116; Bovon, *Luke*, 1:75; Tiede, *Luke*, 63; Dillon, *Hymns*, 477 n. 55; Pierre Benoit, "L'enfance de Jean-Baptiste selon Luc I," *NTS* 3 (1957): 189–90; Vielhauer, "Benedictus," 41; R. E. Brown, *Birth*, 373; Kaut, *Befreier*, 187–8.

[120] On the connection between forgiveness of sins and restoration, see Ben F. Meyer, *The Aims of Jesus* (London: SCM, 1979), 161, 221; N. T. Wright, *Jesus and the Victory of God*, vol. 2 of *Christian Origins and the Question of God* (Minneapolis: Fortress, 1996), 268–74; Brant Pitre, *Jesus, the Tribulation, and the End of the Exile: Restoration Eschatology and the Origin of the Atonement* (Grand Rapids: Baker Academic, 2005), 288.

[121] 1 Kgs 14:15–16; 2 Kgs 17:21–3; 21:11–15; 23:26–7; 24:2–4; Pss. 79:8–10; 106:6; 109:13–15; Jer. 2:9; 14:20; 15:4; 16:10–13; Lam. 5:7.

[122] Ezra 9:6–7, 13; Neh. 9:16–31; Isa. 1:14; 2:6; Lam. 4:22; Dan. 9:16.

is *made known* in John's proclamation, while remaining concealed in its totality and incomplete in its implementation.

For some, however, who accept this notion of γνῶσις (knowledge) as proper to the Benedictus, another tension remains. Associating forgiveness with John appears incongruous with the rest of Luke-Acts.[123] Outside of the two primary associations of forgiveness with John, forgiveness is linked exclusively to Jesus and his name (5:20–5; 7:48–9; 24:47; Acts 2:38; 5:31; 10:43; 13:38; 22:16; cf. Lk. 4:18; 23:34), and explicitly to his ascension (Acts 5:31).

Similarly, Luke's portrait of John's baptism (3:3) as "for (εἰς) the forgiveness of sins" (Mk 1:4; cf. Mt. 3:11) appears at odds with the apostles' baptismal formula in Acts 2:38. This later baptismal formula modifies John's by proclaiming a baptism *in the name of Jesus* for the forgiveness of sins and *the reception of the Holy Spirit*. Nevertheless, the apparent differences are relatively minor. John (Lk. 3:3) does not demand that people be baptized into his own name, nor does he himself offer the gift of the Spirit, whom he explicitly claims the Messiah will bring (3:16).[124] Neither does John forgive; rather, he announces God's forgiveness. Yet, it is this prerogative to even declare God's forgiveness and administer a baptism for forgiveness, apart from Jesus, that is apparently problematic.

For some, assigning a different meaning to each εἰς (into/for) in these parallel formulas mitigates this problem by relegating John's baptism to a baptism of promise and elevating the apostles' baptism to one of realized forgiveness. Thus, εἰς in Lk. 3:3, in this interpretation, describes a baptism *that leads toward a future but yet unrealized* (εἰς) forgiveness, and εἰς in Acts 2:38 describes a baptism *for* (εἰς) forgiveness *now*.[125] However, given the parallel formulas in Lk. 3:3 and Acts 2:38, it seems unlikely that the sense should be so drastically different.[126]

The general reason for deciding in favor of different senses of εἰς (Lk. 3:3; Acts 2:38) is not grammatical but based on assumptions of context. For instance, Darrell Bock argues that John cannot offer forgiveness simply because that is not his role as preparer. Yet, this assumption misplaces the role of forgiveness in the overall soteriological scheme. Forgiveness is not the total substance of salvation but its inauguration, especially given its association with the inauguration ritual, baptism (Lk. 3:3; Acts 2:38; 10:43). Forgiveness is the moment of God's turning, by God's own initiative, to restore relationship and bring an unfolding salvation (Acts 5:31). In Isaianic terms, John Goldingay notes: "The idea is not that Israel returns to Yahweh and therefore Yahweh forgives it and restores it; it is rather that Yahweh forgives it and restores it,

---

[123] E.g., Klein, *Lukasevangelium*, 122–3; Sellner, *Heil*, 55–8; Ford, *Enemy*, 27.

[124] On the continuity between John's and the apostles' respective baptisms, see Joel B. Green, "From 'John's Baptism' to 'Baptism in the Name of the Lord Jesus': The Significance of Baptism in Luke-Acts," in *Baptism, the New Testament and the Church: Historical and Contemporary Studies in Honor of R. E. O. White*, eds. Stanley E. Porter and Anthony R. Cross, JSNTSup 171 (Sheffield: Sheffield Academic Press, 1999), 157–72.

[125] Bock, *Luke*, 1:289; Walter Schmithals, *Das Evangelium nach Lukas*, ZBK 3.1 (Zürich: TVZ, 1980), 50. Against such a view see Sellner, *Heil*, 60; C. F. Evans, *Luke*, 236.

[126] On the further interpretive issues concerning εἰς in Acts 2:38, see Chapter 4.

and this action must draw Israel to return to Yahweh (Isa. 44:21–2)."[127] According to John's message, God demands nothing for forgiveness, no just equivalence for sins committed, only repentance (3:3), but repentance is not a word or an apology; it is a turning, reordered and reconciled life. It is to be a tree that bears fruit worthy of repentance (vv. 8–9).[128]

John brings a baptism of repentance for participation in God's forgiveness in order to prepare and inaugurate God's initiatory salvific movement. John's baptism and announcement of forgiveness is not distinct from Jesus's mission, but always points forward to Jesus (vv. 15–17).[129] This forgiveness, which is productive of a social space defined by an economy of forgiveness, is not an end in itself, but representative of God's initiative and covenant faithfulness, resulting in the national restoration and communal salvation envisioned in the first segment of the Benedictus (vv. 68–75). Knowledge of this forgiveness is socially productive precisely because it is embodied and social and not simply personal and cognitive. It comes through baptism, an embodied inaugural act that orders bodies in space.[130] This theme of knowledge is important moving forward.

2.4.1.3 John Our Priest

John's association with forgiveness coheres with his priestly characterization. As Jesus's Davidic pedigree is utilized to situate him as the expected Davidide (1:32–3, 69; 2:4, 11), Luke-Acts similarly foregrounds John's priestly lineage. Both of John's parents are explicitly described as descendants of Aaron (1:5), and we first meet Zechariah performing priestly duties (1:8–23). Additionally, Gabriel's declaration that John must not drink wine or strong drink (1:15) echoes both the Nazarite vow (Num. 6:3) and specific instructions given to Aaron and his sons (Lev. 10:9).

Being a priest and a prophet are not mutually exclusive. Functioning in a priestly role does not exclude one from a prophetic role (see Jn 11:51; Josephus, *War* 1.68–9; *Ant.* 13.299–300). According to Josephus, Aaron demonstrated the ability to prophesy (*Ant.* 3.192), an ability that Josephus, himself a priest, claimed to have (*War* 3.352, 399–408). Similarly, both Jeremiah and Ezekiel were priests before being

---

[127] John Goldingay, *The Theology of the Book of Isaiah* (Downers Grove, IL: IVP Academic, 2014), 66.

[128] For more on repentance, see Joel B. Green, *Body, Soul, and Human Life: The Nature of Humanity*, STI (Grand Rapids: Baker Academic, 2008), 106–39; idem, *Conversion in Luke-Acts: Divine Action, Human Cognition, and the People of God* (Grand Rapids: Baker Academic, 2015); Guy D. Nave Jr., *The Role and Function of Repentance in Luke-Acts*, AcBib 4 (Leiden: Brill, 2002); Méndez-Moratalla, *Conversion*. Bauckham links repentance and turning language (ἐπιστρέφω, Lk. 1:16–17), which is used continuously in Luke-Acts (Lk. 17:4; 22:32; Acts 3:19, 26; 9:35; 11:21; 14:15; 15:19; 26:18, 20; 28:27), to the prophetic hope for return from exile (Isa. 59:6; Jer. 16:15; 23:3; 24:6; 29:10; 32:37; 50:19; Ezek. 39:27; Hos. 6:1; 11:11) ("Restoration," 440).

[129] Despite this, John A. Darr rightly notes that Luke's characterization of John is as reformer and preparer but not as herald of Jesus (*On Character Building: The Reader and the Rhetoric of Characterization in Luke-Acts*, LCBI (Louisville: Westminster John Knox, 1992), 60–84). Though announcing the coming one (Lk. 3:15–17; Acts 13:25), John nowhere identifies or confesses Jesus as the Christ in Luke.

[130] See the discussion on this in Chapter 4.

called as prophets (Jer. 1:1; Ezek. 1:3). Conversely, Elijah, a prophet in whose spirit and power John comes, performed certain priestly functions (e.g., 1 Kgs 18:20-40); even in Malachi, the messenger preparing the Lord's way (3:1) comes as the prophet Elijah (4:5-6), with specific concern for the temple (3:1, 4) and the covenant with Levi (2:8; 3:3-4).[131]

Particularly interesting, however, are the parallels between John and Samuel, another prophet enacting priestly functions (e.g., 1 Sam. 2:18, 25; 7:17; 10:8; 11:14-15; 13:8-9).[132] John's birth echoes Samuel's. Elizabeth's barrenness (Lk. 1:7), often noted as reminiscent of Sarah's barrenness (Gen. 18:11), similarly brings to mind Hannah before Samuel's birth (1 Sam. 1:5; 2:5). Hannah's petition to God for a son includes a pledge to offer him as a Nazarite (1:11, 15, 22, 28; cf. Lk. 1:15). Consider also how John's role as forerunner and anointer of Jesus, the Davidic king, parallels Samuel's relation to David (1 Sam. 9:16; 16:1-13).[133] Indeed, just as Samuel was an intermediate figure who ushered in a new era for Israel under the Davidic monarchy, John helps prepare the way for the coming Davidide (cf. Acts 13:20-5).

Finally, consider John's and Samuel's relationships with prevailing Jewish leadership. Samuel is contrasted to the priestly leaders of his youth (1 Sam. 2:27-36), and John similarly appears, coming from the wilderness, juxtaposed to the Jerusalem and priestly aristocracy (Lk. 3:2; cf. 7:30; 11:52; 20:1-19). John's baptism, in his priestly role, provides a means of atonement (i.e., forgiveness of sins) away from the temple in Jerusalem, implicitly subverting its authority.[134] This comes as part of a movement of salvation and restoration that does not explicitly exclude the leadership, but certainly does not proceed from, depend on, or leave intact the authority structures assumed by the Jerusalem leadership. Indeed, it is worth noting that Jesus's Parable of the Vineyard, in which he critiques the prevailing leadership, is prefaced by a conflict over authority in which Jesus asks the Jerusalem leadership if it accepts John's baptism as divinely authorized (20:1-19). This invocation of John not only attests to Jesus's authority, but also participates in a critique of the prevailing authorities.

John's emergence in Luke 3 bears out this tension. In vv. 1-2, John's appearance, coming in the wilderness, is juxtaposed to Roman, Herodian, and Jewish leadership.

---

[131] See also Jaroslav Rindoš, *He of Whom It Is Written: John the Baptist and Elijah in Luke*, ÖBS 38 (Frankfurt am Main: Peter Lang, 2010), 229; David George Clark, "Elijah as Eschatological High Priest: An Examination of the Elijah Tradition in Mal 3: 24-5"(PhD diss., University of Notre Dame, 1975), 89-90; Andrew E. Hill, *Malachi: A New Translation with Introduction and Commentary*, AB 25D (New York: Doubleday, 1998), 379.

[132] On these parallels, see Rindoš, *John*, 44-55. Luke-Acts shows Samuel elsewhere as an important transition figure (Acts 3:24; 13:20).

[133] Other similarities include the focus on the temple (1 Sam. 1:7, 9, 24; Lk. 1:8-23; 2:22-38, 41-51; 4:9-12; 18:10; 19:45-21:6; 23:45; 24:53; Acts 2:46; 3:1-10; 4:1; 5:20-6, 42; 21:26-30; 22:17; 24:6, 12, 18; 25:8; 26:21) and the similar responses of Hannah and Elizabeth to news of promised conception (1 Sam. 1:19-20; Lk. 1:24-5).

[134] See Jonathan Klawans, *Impurity and Sin in Ancient Judaism* (Oxford: Oxford University Press, 2000), 138-43 (cf. Mt. 3:2, 6, 8, 11; Mk 1:5). Klawans argues that the historical John offered baptism as an atonement ritual. Robert L. Webb similarly notes the atoning function of John's baptism and its function as an alternative to the temple (*John the Baptizer: A Socio-Historical Study*, JSNTSup 62 (Sheffield: JSOT Press, 1991), 190-4, 203-5).

The distinction between these spaces of authority and the wilderness is taken up below (Chapter 3); however, it is worth preliminarily noting that John comes in the wilderness and receives God's word (cf. 1 Sam. 3:1), followed by the Isaianic ecological metaphor of reform and reorganization of power (Lk. 3:4–6; Isa. 40:3–5). John's baptism in this context comes as more than an unauthorized cultic ritual (at least if understood as narrowly religious). John's activity speaks of God's movement outside the bounds of normal power structures, and should cause those who are reliant on status quo organization to be concerned.[135] This is characteristic of this salvation (cf. 1:77; 3:5) that reorders social-political space.

2.4.2 Salvation Dawning: Mercy, Visitation, and Redemption

Forgiveness of sins anticipates the national restoration already announced in vv. 68–75. In this section, I focus on several key elements that reappear in the remaining material of vv. 76–9 and link salvation in the two main units of Zechariah's prophecy: (1) mercy and covenant faithfulness, (2) visitation, and (3) redemption, which is presented negatively as release and positively as walking the way of peace. Rather than taking a reductively religious turn, the salvation explicated in these latter verses in terms of mercy, light, and the way of peace continues to emphasize the national redemption and theopolitical salvation of the whole prophecy.

2.4.2.1 Through Our God's Tender Mercy

The salvation made known through the forgiveness of sins is made available through (διά) the mercy of "our God." This mercy (ἔλεος) draws the audience back to v. 72, where mercy refers explicitly to God's covenant remembrance. Here, however, ἐλέους (mercy) modifies σπλάγχνον (affection).[136] At the time of Luke's composition, σπλάγχνον κτλ. were used to translate the Hebrew term רחמים (compassion), with emphasis on God's compassion, where the LXX had previously used the term οἰκτιρμός (compassion) (cf. *T. Zeb.* 3; 8.2, 6; Phil. 2:1; Col. 3:12).[137] The combination of God's mercy (ἔλεος) and compassion (οἰκτιρμός) occurs several times in the LXX to translate חסד (covenant fidelity) and רחמים (compassion).[138] In Isa. 63:15 LXX, Isaiah appeals to God's mercy (ἔλεος) and compassion (οἰκτιρμός) so that God might remember Israel and redeem

---

[135] Consider John's arrest (Lk. 3:19–20; cf. Mt. 14:3–5; Mk 6:17–19). Luke notes that Herod is upset that John has critiqued his choice of wife. Nevertheless, this critique is not apolitical. Herod is most likely concerned about John's opinion because of the popular sway John held with the populace. This motivation is stated explicitly by Josephus (*Ant.* 18.116–19). Further, Luke adds more generally "and concerning all the evil which he did."

[136] On this tender mercy, see Maarten J. J. Menken, "The Position of σπλαγχνίζεσθαι and σπλάγχνα in the Gospel of Luke," *NovT* 30 (1988): 112.

[137] Helmut Koester, "σπλάγχνον, σπλαγχνίζομαι, εὔσπλαγχνος, πολύσπλαγχνος, ἄσπλαγχνος," *TDNT* 7: 552–5.

[138] Pss. 25(24):6; 40(39):11(12); 51(50):1(3); 69(68):16(17); 103(102):4; Isa. 63:15; Hos. 2:21; Zech. 7:9; Sir. 5:6; cf. 1QS II, 1.

the people from their adversaries (63:15–19; cf. Sir. 5:6). God's merciful compassion/affection is shown in God's tangible action of restoration and salvation.

2.4.2.2 Visitation from on High

The language of visitation also reappears with the ἀνατολή (dawn/branch) visiting (ἐπισκέπτομαι)[139] from on high (v. 78). Understood by most recent commentators to be messianic,[140] the term ἀνατολή could mean "dawn" (cf. Jer. 23:5; Ezek. 16:7; 17:10; Zech. 3:8, 6:12) or "branch/shoot" (Isa. 9:11; 11:11, 14; cf. Mt. 2:2, 9; Rev. 7:2), specifically a Davidic branch. The fact that the ἀνατολή shines on those in darkness and its spatial location (ἐξ ὕψους) suggest that the plain reading refers to some sort of luminary. Others, however, have posited an intentional ambiguity (v. 69).[141] The corresponding verb ἀνατέλλω (rise) is used in the LXX to translate both "sprout/branch" (צמח) or "rise" (זרח), which have both been connected to traditional messianic texts (e.g., Num. 24:17; Jer. 23:5; Zech. 3:8; 6:12; cf. CD VII, 18–21; 1QM XI, 6–7; 4Q175 9–13; T. Levi 4.2–4; 18.2–4; T. Jud. 24.1). Connecting ἀνατολή to a Davidic branch is not improbable (cf. Isa. 11:1; Jer. 23:5–6; Zech. 3:8; 6:12; *Shemoneh Esrah* 15; cf. Rev. 22:16).[142] Nevertheless, in the immediate context, that allusion is more difficult to substantiate. In any case, the dawn's visitation parallels the earlier visitation (v. 68), and undoubtedly refers to Jesus's coming advent and earthly mission.[143]

2.4.2.3 To Shine on Those in Darkness

God's visitation brings redemption (cf. λύτρωσις, v. 68) from enemies. Here, release comes through this dawn (ἀνατολή) from on high shining on those sitting in darkness and the shadow of death and, positively, guiding "our feet in the way of peace" (v. 79). Importantly, this enlightenment is not subjective or reductively religious.

The juxtaposition of darkness and light is a common theme in Jewish and early Christian writing (Lk. 2:32; Col. 1:12–14; Jas 1:17; 1 Pet. 2:9; *1 Clem.* 59.2; *Jos. Asen.* 8.9; *T. Levi* 19.1). Whereas darkness represents the work of cosmological evil (Isa. 5:20), light is a metaphor for God's presence (Exod. 12:21; Deut. 33:2; Pss. 27:1; 36:9; 118:27; Isa. 2:5). This language, however, is not relegated to cosmological or spiritual functionaries. Salvation—deliverance and restoration—itself is often described in Isaiah, for instance,

---

[139] Some texts present ἐπισκέπτομαι in the future (א* B L W Θ) and others in the aorist (א² A C D Ξ *f*¹·¹³ 33). Most scholars prefer the future, judging the aorist to be an assimilation from ἐπεσκέψατο in v. 68 (Bruce M. Metzger, *A Textual Commentary on the Greek New Testament*, 2nd ed. (Stuttgart: Deutsche Bibelgesellschaft, 1994), 110).

[140] E.g., Farris, *Hymns*, 141; Ulrike Mittmann-Richert, *Magnifikat und Benediktus: Die ältesten Zeugnisse der judenchristlichen Tradition von der Geburt des Messias*, WUNT 2/90 (Tübingen: Mohr Siebeck, 1996), 121–6; Strauss, *Messiah*, 103–8; Simon Gathercole, "The Heavenly ἀνατολή (Luke 1:78–9)," *JTS* 56 (2005): 471–88; Bock, *Luke*, 1:191. *Pace* Vielhauer, "Benediktus," 38.

[141] Gnilka, "Hymnus," 228–9; Marshall, *Gospel*, 95; Bock, *Luke*, 192.

[142] Cf. also Ps. 132(131):17; Jer. 23:5–6. John J. Collins also notes that the branch metaphor was also found elsewhere in the ANE (John J. Collins, *The Scepter and the Star: The Messiahs of the Dead Sea Scrolls and Other Ancient Literature*, ABRL (New York: Doubleday, 1995), 29).

[143] *Contra* Jantsch, who argues that visitation refers to Jesus's Parousia (*Jesus*, 147–9).

as illumination (Isa. 60:1-3; cf. 42:7; 49:6). God's light is characterized by justice (51:4-5) and is juxtaposed to the injustice perpetrated by the people, experienced by the people at the hands of their leaders (2:5-11), and implemented by foreign nations (9:2; 42:7; 49:9-10; 51:5; 59:8-9).

The texts most explicitly alluded to by the Benedictus use this light metaphor not as inner illumination or existential enlightenment but as release from oppression and captivity (cf. Isa. 9:2[1]; 42:7; Ps. 107[106]:10, 14; Mic. 7:8). Isaiah 9:2(1), for example, concerns deliverance coming to those in darkness and the shadow of death, clearly addressing Israel as a people with hopes of collective redemption. When light shines on them, the oppressor's rod is broken (v. 3), war ceases (v. 4), and a Davidide brings peace and a kingdom characterized by justness/righteousness (δικαιοσύνη) (vv. 5-6).[144] These themes are echoed by the Benedictus's concern for the Davidide (Lk. 1:69), peace (v. 79), a political space ruled by justness/righteousness (v. 75), but most saliently by concern for those in darkness (σκότος) and the shadow of death (σκιὰ θανάτου) (v. 79). Sitting in the shadow of death is used in the OT to speak of deep suffering (Job 3:5; Pss. 23[22]:4; 88[87]:6[7]),[145] but it is also used to describe captivity and Israel's oppression (Pss. 44[43]:19[20]; 107[106]:10, 14; Jer. 13:16). In Isaiah 9, it is clearly the latter.[146] Similarly, Isa. 42:7 refers to those "sitting in darkness" with clear sociopolitical connotations.[147] Those sitting in darkness are in prison, and the reference is tied to God's servant who brings forth justice for the nations (vv. 1, 4). Darkness is tangible injustice and God's light is its rectification through the servant. In Isa. 58:10, light going forth and shining on all refers to acts of justice.

These manifestations of light language in Isaiah find particular resonance with Luke-Acts and its notion of salvation. Although it would be convenient to identify such light language as *physical* release, it is precisely the dichotomy assumed by such an assertion that both Isaiah and Luke-Acts deny. It is more proper to call the reality of light *embodied*, in such a way that it includes the personal, social, and communal, while not being reduced to the reductively spiritual, physical, or material. In Isaiah 59, for instance, the people await justice and salvation, expecting light but receiving only darkness, and because of this they are blinded themselves (vv. 9-15). Whereas the Benedictus pairs forgiveness of sins with the appearance of a shining light, the removal of darkness, and peace, Isaiah ties the people's sins (rebellions, injustice, oppression, etc.) to absence of light (59:9). The source of this light is God, and the sense is that when the people's light shines forth, this is a participation in God's light and just way of being, a coming out from darkness supposing a just ordering of social space that is embedded in and reconciled to cosmic-comprehensive space and specifically to the God of Israel.

---

[144] Conversely, condemnation is declared by God against Babylon who is ordered to go into darkness (Isa. 47:1 LXX).

[145] Sellner, *Heil*, 68.

[146] Similar light language is attributed to Augustus by Horace, who writes: "Bring back the light, dear leader, to your country; for when your face shines like spring upon the citizens, the day passes more happily and the sun's radiance is brighter" (*Carm.* 4.5.5-8).

[147] Pao, *Exodus*, 184; Yamazaki-Ransom, *Empire*, 153-4.

For Luke-Acts, light is a means of divine revelation that proceeds from God/heaven (Lk. 2:32; Acts 9:3; 12:7; 16:29; 22:9, 11; 26:13). At points, this light inhabits, fills, and characterizes persons (Lk. 11:33–6; 16:8), though not simply in terms of personal enlightenment, but with expectation to be ordered by God's justness/righteousness as children of light (Lk. 11:42; 16:8–9). Of particular interest are Luke-Acts' programmatic allusions to Isa. 49:6 (Lk. 2:32; Acts 1:8; 13:47; 26:17–18, 23; cf. Rom. 2:17–19) to describe the unfolding salvific mission.[148] In Isa. 49, the servant is given as a light to the nations so that salvation might reach the end of the earth (v. 6). This salvation is not simply a personally repaired relationship with God, but the instantiation of justice, release, and restoration. Those in darkness are prisoners who, in conjunction with their release from darkness, eat, drink, and experience salvation (vv. 8–9). Paul, in Acts, summarizes his own mission, as conveyed to him by God, as opening the eyes of the nations, so that they might turn from darkness to light, from Satan's authority to God's authority (Acts 26:16–18). The movement *into* light is, simultaneously, *away from* the sphere of the demonic authority, which is directly related to the organization of power within social-political space (cf. Lk. 4:5–7). Paul's mission that the nations might see—and Jesus's proclamation to bring sight to the blind (Lk. 4:18)—may be personal, but it is not individualistic. It involves participation in another authoritative space governed by God's light, justness/righteousness, and authority. This light involves true reconciliation with God and forgiveness of sins, yet this cannot be conceived separately from embodied salvation, the organization of power in social-political space, and communal existence serving God in justness and holiness (cf. Lk. 1:74–5). Indeed, Sellner is correct to say, "With a [narrowly] spiritualizing interpretation, the power of the [light] image would be largely destroyed."[149]

2.4.2.4 *The Way of Peace*

The ultimate word of the Benedictus is peace (εἰρήνη, v. 79); the dawn visits, positively, to guide "our feet in the way of peace," a formational reality that resonates with the earlier assertion of release so that the people might serve God in holiness and justness/righteousness (vv. 74–5). Both ideas speak to an ethical way of being, though v. 79 places emphasis on guidance from the messianic dawn/branch. This peace, given the generally septuagintal characteristics of Luke's early chapters, invokes a Hebraic notion of peace as wellbeing and plenty.[150] Gerhard von Rad notes of OT conceptions of peace: "We are struck by the negative fact that there is no specific text in which [peace] denotes the specifically spiritual attitude of inward peace." Rather, "שָׁלוֹם [peace] is an emphatically social concept."[151]

---

[148] David L. Tiede argues that the allusion to Isa. 49:6 perhaps serves as the "thematic statement of Luke's entire narrative" (*Prophecy and History in Luke-Acts* (Philadelphia: Fortress, 1980), 31).

[149] "Wäre mit einer spiritualisierenden Deutung die Kraft des Bildes weitgehend zerstört" (Sellner, *Heil*, 69). More personal interpretations of such language can be found arguably in the NT and elsewhere (e.g., 2 Cor. 4:4–6; Col. 1:12–13; 1 Thess. 5:4–7; cf. 1 Pet. 2:9; *Jos. Asen.* 8.9; 15.12). However, the contextual clues that allow for such interpretation are missing in the Benedictus.

[150] Sellner, *Heil*, 69; Werner Foerster and Gerhard von Rad, "εἰρήνη," *TDNT* 2:402–17.

[151] Foerster and Rad, *TDNT* 2:406.

In Isaiah, peace is a salient element of national restoration. In Isa. 52:7–10, a messenger declares (εὐαγγελίζω) the news of peace, announcing salvation (σωτηρία) and God's reign (v. 7). Peace and salvation are parallel concepts tied to Jerusalem's restoration (v. 9). This hope envisions God's having returned to Zion, demonstrating strength before the nations, so that the ends of the earth will see God's salvation (v. 10). Elsewhere in Isaiah, peace is a benefit bestowed by the coming Davidide (9:7), when the wolf will lie down with the lamb (11:6–10). Nevertheless, this peace requires justness/righteousness. Isaiah's condemnation of the people's injustice (59:6), oppression of workers (58:3), distortion of the Sabbath (58:13–14), and so on is related to their ignorance of the "way of peace" (ὁδὸν εἰρήνης) (59:8; cf. 2:3–4), the exact phrase we find in the Benedictus.

When investigating peace (εἰρήνη) in Luke-Acts, one discovers not only that the Benedictus does not relegate peace to an inner disposition, but also that one is hard-pressed to find such a meaning throughout Luke-Acts.[152] In the whole of Luke-Acts, Willard M. Swartley argues, peace is not merely personal but "relational" and "structural."[153] Consider Peter's statement to Cornelius that God sent the word to Israel, proclaiming the good news (εὐαγγελίζω) of peace through Jesus the Christ, who is Lord (κύριος) of all (Acts 10:36). This language draws on political announcements of good news, and designating Jesus "Lord of all" appropriates a title for Caesar (cf. Dio Chrysostom, *Def.* 4; Epictetus, *Diatr.* 4.1.12; Josephus *Ant.* 16.118; Lucan, *Bell. civ.* 9.20; Martial, *Epig.* 8.2.5–6). Jesus, not Caesar, effects peace, which lends significance to the close juxtaposition of the dawn's (ἀνατολή) guidance in peace with Caesar's census (Lk. 2:1–2). The repentance, reform, and restoration encapsulated in guiding Israel's feet in the way of peace prefigures Peter's christological declaration in Acts 10:36.

The Roman ideology of peace was prevalent and based on a particularly violent subjugation.[154] Constantly, the god *Pax* is portrayed with *Victoria* and the *orbis terrarum* (οἰκουμένη, civilized world) under foot.[155] Zanker notes how the panel decorating the Ara Pacis in Rome depicting the *pax augusta* is set opposite a picture of *Roma* enthroned on a mound of armor: "The viewer was meant to read the two images together and understand the message, the blessings of peace had been won and made secure by the newly fortified *virtus* of Roman arms."[156] Roman peace was something imposed on and dictated to subjects, not something that represented the confluence of equals.[157] Gerardo Zampaglione writes, "Almost all Roman writers agreed that spreading peace among mankind meant subjecting other peoples to

---

[152] Luke 1:79; 2:14, 29; 7:50; 8:48; 10:5–6; 11:21; 12:51; 14:32; 19:38, 42; 24:36; Acts 7:26; 9:31; 10:36; 12:20; 15:33; 16:36; 24:2.

[153] Willard M. Swartley, "Politics and Peace (Eirēnē) in Luke's Gospel," in *Political Issues in Luke-Acts*, eds. Richard J. Cassidy and Philip J. Scharper (Maryknoll, NY: Orbis Books, 1983), 18–37.

[154] See J. Rufus Fears, "The Theology of Victory at Rome: Approaches and Problems," *ANRW* 2.17.2 (1981): 912–13.

[155] Wengst, *Pax*, 11–12; Zanker, *Images*, 85.

[156] Zanker, *Images*, 175.

[157] Gerardo Zampaglione, *The Idea of Peace in Antiquity* (Notre Dame: University of Notre Dame Press, 1973), 133.

Roman dominion" (see Tacitus *Agr.* 30; Polybius 1.3.1–6; Vergil, *Aen.* 6.850–3).[158] Importantly, for our purposes, peace is also here intimately tied to salvation (*Salus*) as it is in Luke-Acts (e.g., Lk. 2:29; 7:50; 8:48; 19:42). This peace was ensured by *pietas* and the favor of the gods. Augustus in particular was able to restore peace between the gods and people.[159]

Luke's use of peace invokes this language of imperial authority and associates Jesus with what is supposedly Augustus's blessing.[160] However, the imagery is more complex than a simple appropriation of a Roman theme. Luke does not simply overtake Roman conceptions of *pax* or portray Jesus as a substitute Caesar; rather Roman articulations of peace are placed in tension with those from the Jewish tradition and their particular contextualization in Luke's soteriology. The militaristic corollaries of Roman peace find no analog in Luke-Acts. How is this peace characterized? The means of achieving this peace remain opaque in the Benedictus, though the Davidic horn is central and the dawn from on high teaches the way of peace, highlighting themes of discipleship, knowledge, obedience, and imitation that develop in Luke-Acts.

However, consider our discussion already of Jesus's temptation (4:1–13). There, Jesus denies authority over the world through the devil's patronage and, implicitly, the politics of domination, foregoing the temptation to become another Caesar. Instead, Jesus asserts an alternate authority into which he will, in his ministry, live and by which he will gather others to participate in the social-political reality of God's kingdom. This is not a kingdom vying for space in conflict with or domination over other mundane kingdoms; rather, God's kingdom produces its own spaces of participation in complex space. Luke has thus begun to orient his readers to a way of peace that is not a strategy of domination but obedient involvement in God's just cosmic ordering that, though leading through the cross, is ultimately victorious and enduring. The way of peace is journeyed through imitating and embodying the teaching and life of Jesus (the dawn from on high) and producing and participating in alternate social-political space. The *end* state of salvation is characterized by peace, wholeness, and the reconciliation of all things, where God's restored and delivered people serve God together in justness/righteousness and holiness (1:74–5).

2.5 Conclusion

In this chapter, I investigated the Benedictus as a programmatic and foundational passage for Lukan soteriology. Rather than a disjointed mixture of political and religious concepts, discretely defined, Zechariah's prophecy speaks coherently of God's inbreaking salvation and Israel's restoration, a theopolitical salvation taking up space

---

[158] Zampaglione, *Peace*, 135.
[159] Fears, "Virtues," 885–6.
[160] Gilbert, "Identity," 242.

within the world and dependent on a particular narrative of God's covenant fidelity to Israel. Language such as forgiveness of sins, mercy, light, and peace does not show a spiritualizing turn but conforms to the idiom of national restoration. Further, the prophecy proves to be more than a foreign addition and relic of an antiquated notion of parochial and political redemption; rather, it prepares for a salvation taking place in social-political and cosmic-comprehensive space.

The salvation described in the Benedictus coheres with the Irenaean *Christus Victor* framework we noted in Chapter 1. The prophecy identifies the primary salvific need (the beginning) as *release*, specifically from tangible enemies. Though the precise nature of these enemies remains obscure, the release itself (the middle) is characterized by God's paradigmatic exodus deliverance and the context of Roman imperialism. Though no mention is made of Satan in Zechariah's prophecy, I noted how Luke ties cosmic powers with the organization of social-political space, and the significance of Satan and other powers will become clearer as this investigation continues. Release comes through the activity of a Davidic heir, a horn of salvation, who will guide the people in the way of peace. This "guidance," also, is an early indication of the moral formation component (*moral exemplar*) raised more saliently in the upcoming narrative.

Further, this salvation unfolds through the *continuity of God's action* for God's people. The Davidide does not come to "persuade" God or to achieve God's forgiveness, but God visits through the Davidic horn to effect release and—as will become clearer in subsequent chapters—to *persuade* Israel to respond to God's salvation—not to offer restitution to God in order to achieve forgiveness. John announces a forgiveness available through repentance, which he invites all to take on through the embodied ritual of baptism, giving *knowledge* of God's salvation, and pointing to the one who is to come. Forgiveness is introduced into this scheme not as a spiritualization of the earlier political salvation—that is, as redefining release in terms of release from sin, reductively—but as the inaugural element of God's turning to bring comprehensive restoration to which the people are called to join. Forgiveness is not the totality or outcome of salvation; it is not the end, but the beginning. It is not simply personal absolution, but a participatory and socially productive reality entered through embodied repentance.

The salvation of the Benedictus takes place in space. Its *end* is a reformed social-political reality, in which God's people serve God in holiness and justness/righteousness, having walked the road of peace. Moving to Chapter 3, my focus will be particularly on the emergence of this Davidic Messiah, the call to participate in the alternate social-political space of God's kingdom "today," and obedience and imitation in discipleship as elements of an embodied and inbreaking soteriological reality.

3

Jesus, Herald of God's Kingdom (Luke 4:18–19)

In his inaugural address in Nazareth, Jesus gives what most maintain is the programmatic exposition of his gospel and mission.[1] Though frequenting synagogues (4:15, 16–30, 33–7, 44; 6:6; 13:10), this is the only example of Jesus's synagogue teaching, giving insight into his central message. This chapter attends primarily to Jesus's mixed citation from Isaiah (vv. 18–19; Isa. 58:6; 61:1–2) as a lens through which to view Jesus, his ministry, and the developing salvation narrative. After assessing the context of Jesus's movement from the wilderness to Nazareth, the structure of the mixed Isaianic prophecy, and the diachronic development of a Jubilee tradition, I focus on the particular elements of vv. 18–19 and how they illumine Jesus's mission in Luke, helping us better understand Luke-Acts salvation narrative and *Christus Victor* form.

Zechariah's prophecy presented a salvation narrative in which a Davidic savior played a central role. In this chapter, I discuss how this Davidic savior, Jesus, begins his mission, proclaiming God's kingdom, and announcing Jubilee. The theme of Jubilee will prove important for a couple of reasons. First, it draws our attention to release in terms of good news for the poor and participation in God's kingdom. Second, it characterizes this release as cosmic reconciliation and a social-spatial extension of atonement. That is, Jubilee speaks of an order being reconciled to God's way of ordering (to God's kingdom). It is not simply individuals that must be reconciled to God, but social-political space. Space, as I am using the concept, is not simply extension or a container, but a socially produced and inhabited reality. Space is a dynamic field of power inhabited by bodies organized in relationships. Jubilee signals a cosmic atonement and reconciliation of inhabited space to God's order. All of this points to salvation as a spatial reality, as reconciling the mundane world to heaven (see further Chapter 4) and Jubilee order.

Additionally, this chapter more fully discusses the cosmic drama that was introduced in Chapter 2. Jesus's battle with Satan frames this Nazareth pericope and proves integral to the development of Luke's Gospel. The Jubilee release announced by Jesus narratively finds connection to this cosmic drama. In this way, we see further connection to atonement as release from Satan. Key to this release is understanding Satan's connection to worldly authorities and the persisting communal and political nature of Luke's soteriology.

---

[1] Green, *Luke*, 207; Klein, *Lukasevangelium*, 184; Marshall, *Gospel*, 177–8; John Nolland, *Luke*, 3 vols., WBC 35A–C (Dallas: Word, 1989–93), 1:195.

3.1 From the Wilderness to Nazareth

We begin with attention not simply to where Jesus is, Nazareth, but from where he came. Jesus comes to Galilee by way of the desert, and his arrival is like that of marginal space impinging on normalized place.

3.1.1 Wilderness Space

The wilderness is no ancillary theme in these early chapters; rather, it provides the major setting for John's growth (1:80) and preaching (3:2, 4) and the place of Jesus's anointing (3:21–2) and temptation (4:1–13).[2] James Resseguie, in his discussion of Luke's "spiritual landscape," has offered a somewhat negative assessment of the wilderness: "The desert represents the world at its edges, untamed, uninhabitable land that threatens the pleasant fertility of inhabited spaces and human existence."[3] Though the desert, for Resseguie, may be a place where transformation happens (precisely when faced with its difficulty), it is still a place that threatens "inhabited space." Nevertheless, it is precisely this latter element that constitutes its positive import.

The wilderness can represent many things—encounter, renewal, purification, preparation—and with John, it is a place of repentance and atonement, of coming to terms with God. Most saliently, however, the wilderness recapitulates Israel's exodus from Egypt, and in this mold, wilderness space, for those hoping for deliverance from Rome, was a locus for fomenting revolt (Josephus, *War* 2.261–3; *Ant.* 20.97–9, 167–72; cf. Acts 5:36; 21:28).[4] Wilderness, in this way, is characterized as a space opposed to inhabited place. Inhabited space can be totalized, dominant, and disciplined space. It is the space of "civilization," which so often codifies space to benefit the dominant and subjugate the marginalized.[5]

This sort of opposition is implicit in Luke's final chronological marker (3:1–2). Through John, the message of God's inbreaking salvation (i.e., God's word) comes forth in the wilderness, that space opposed to those paragons of dominant rule in Jerusalem, the inhabited place par excellence, including Herod, who later beheads John; Pilate, who oversees Jesus's execution; the Jewish leadership; and of course, ruling from Rome, Caesar. This same spatial juxtaposition is found on Jesus's lips in 7:24–7, where the rich in royal palaces are opposed to a desert prophet.

Wilderness factors importantly in the temptation scene (4:1–13). There, Jesus is tested as Israel was in the wilderness (v. 2; cf. Exod. 16:4; 17:2; Deut. 8:2), showing

---

[2] Jesus's baptism occurs in the Jordan river. Some commentators have noted that this is a different location than "the desert," so that the desert and the Jordan serve different functions (Bock, *Luke*, 1:286; Bovon, *Luke*, 1:121; Schürmann, *Lukas*, 1:155). Yet, this is overcritical, as wilderness is more than a place on a map. John is identified with desert space, as is his preaching (3:2, 4). The entire activity of Luke 3 is associated with desert space, including Jesus's baptism.

[3] James L. Resseguie, *Spiritual Landscape: Images of the Spiritual Life in the Gospel of Luke* (Peabody, MA: Hendrickson, 2004), 12.

[4] See C. A. Evans, "Israel," 81. Cf. Isa. 35:1–2; 40:3–5; Ezek. 20:33–44; Hos. 2:14–23.

[5] On space, see the discussion in Chapter 1. It is helpful to understand space as practiced place. Space is a socially produced reality within which people participate. Spaces such as the "city," the "wilderness," or "inhabited place" can bring with them connotations of power and social organization that may be in tension.

himself as the faithful Son of God (vv. 3, 9). Jesus does battle with the devil, rejecting his temptations, juxtaposing the authoritative space of the devil (see esp. vv. 5–8), the world's kingdoms, with the obedience of God's faithful servant, and by this obedience achieving at least temporary victory over the devil (cf. Irenaeus, *Haer.* 5.21.2). Jesus's rejection of authority on the devil's terms is a rejection of dominant inhabited space. Wilderness, however, is not simply the place where the devil resides for testing. Demonic actors show up throughout Luke's Gospel, and Jesus's final temptation takes place in Jerusalem through the Jerusalem authorities (22:53) and Jesus's own disciple (22:3). The devil represents the cosmic reality of such inhabited space threatening untamed space conceived at its margins.[6]

Wilderness represents space away from mapped place. Similarly, God's kingdom is an alternate, cosmically legitimated space impinging on and reorganizing dominant places. In a way, Jesus's coming and kingdom message is as wilderness invading. Thus, rather than a threat to human existence, the wilderness represents its possibility. And so, Jesus returns to the wilderness habitually in prayer and with his disciples for respite from the war being waged in inhabited spaces, a war with unjustness, un-wholeness, sin, and the demonic (e.g., 4:42; 5:16). Even the feeding of the five thousand (9:10–17) appears to be a staging ground in the wilderness, appropriately situated just before Jesus begins his march to Jerusalem (9:51). Thus, Jesus's coming to Nazareth is a movement from wilderness to inhabited place, anticipating the spatial tension to come.

3.1.2 Jesus Comes to Nazareth

Uniquely among the Synoptic Gospels, Luke's first full scene of Jesus's ministry occurs in Nazareth (cf. Mt. 13:54–8; Mk 6:1–6), though narratively this is not his first destination (4:14–15). In Jesus's previous preaching, the response appears overwhelmingly positive (v. 15); however, this cannot be said of Nazareth (vv. 28–30), even if those in the Nazareth synagogue initially respond favorably (v. 22). Here, Jesus presents himself as the herald of "good news" (v. 18; cf. vv. 43–4), and the content of this good news concerns God's kingdom (cf. 4:43; 8:1; 16:16; Acts 8:12).

The first segment of the Nazareth pericope (vv. 16–21) is structured chiastically, emphasizing the quotation from Isaiah at its center (vv. 18–19):

A. He stood to read (v. 16)
    B. The scroll of the prophet Isaiah was given to him (v. 17)
        C. And after opening the scroll, he found the place … (v. 17)
            D. *Isaiah 58:6; 61:1–2* (vv. 18–19)
        C'. And after closing the scroll (v. 20)
    B'. And giving it back to the attendant (v. 20)
A'. He sat down (v. 20)

---

[6] Delores S. Williams employs wilderness centrally as a place of resistance, survival, and transformational encounter with Jesus. In doing so, she critiques dominant cultural attempts to "civilize" wilderness (*Sisters in the Wilderness: The Challenge of Womanist God-Talk* (Maryknoll, NY: Orbis Books, 1993), 108–39).

The citation comes primarily from Isa. 61:1–2, amended with a phrase from Isa. 58:6. This redemption prophecy highlights an anointed figure who heralds good news of Jubilee release. What Luke includes of Isa. 61:1–2 is taken almost verbatim from the LXX, with the exception of v. 19 where κηρύξαι (to preach) is used instead of καλέσαι (to call), though the sense is essentially the same.

A few other items are of note. First, the phrase "to heal the broken hearted" (ἰάσασθαι τοὺς συντετριμμένους τῇ καρδίᾳ, Isa. 61:1) is omitted for no clear reason.[7] Second, and more notably, the place where Luke stops his citation is just before the phrase "the day of our God's vengeance" (Isa. 61:2). This phrase occurs in Isaiah as a couplet with "the Lord's acceptable year." Ending the citation where it does could intentionally exclude violence. Yet, it should be noted that God's judgment is not foreign to Luke-Acts (e.g., Lk. 3:9; 10:14–15; 11:32; 13:28). Richard B. Hays may likely be correct that the day of vengeance/recompense (ἀνταπόδοσις) of God hovers metapleptically over the text with a certain ambiguity, promising a day of God's action as either benefit or woe depending on one's relationship to God's justice.[8] Nevertheless, in its current form, greater emphasis is placed on the ultimate word, "acceptable" (δεκτός).[9] The Lord's acceptable year has been identified as an allusion to Jubilee.[10] Further, "acceptable" (δεκτός) links this citation with the crowd's reaction in Nazareth, where somewhat ironically the prophet of the Lord's acceptable year is not found acceptable (δεκτός) in his own hometown (v. 24).

Finally, the most significant emendation to the passage is the addition of a phrase from Isa. 58:6, "to send those having been oppressed in release" (ἄφεσις). Isaiah 58 links to Isa. 61 by way of *gezerah shawah*. That is, each passage's use of ἄφεσις (release), the only two uses of the noun in Isaiah LXX, creates a link that encourages mutual interpretation. This link is dependent on the LXX, since the MT uses two different Hebrew words (דרור, חפשי).[11] Isaiah 58:6 is part of a larger segment (56:1–58:14) bracketed by an inclusio concerning the Sabbath (56:1–8; 58:13–14),[12] and although Isa. 61 is associated with Jubilee, the close connection between the Sabbath and Jubilee

---

[7] Some manuscripts include the phrase (A Θ f¹), but the manuscript evidence is decidedly in favor of its omission (א B D f¹³ 33).

[8] Richard B. Hays, *Echoes of Scripture in the Gospels* (Waco, TX: Baylor University Press, 2016), 225–8.

[9] Danker, *Luke*, 59.

[10] Regarding Isaiah, the Jubilee link has widespread support: Walther Zimmerli, "Das 'Gnadenjahr des Herrn,'" in *Archäologie und Altes Testament*, eds. Arnulf Kuschke and Ernst Kutsch (Tübingen: Mohr Siebeck, 1970), 321–32; Robert B. Sloan, *The Favorable Year of the Lord: A Study of Jubilary Theology in the Gospel of Luke* (Austin: Schola, 1977), 39–41; Walter Brueggemann, *Isaiah*, 2 vols., WC (Louisville: Westminster John Knox, 1998), 2:214; Brevard S. Childs, *Isaiah*, OTL (Louisville: Westminster John Knox, 2001), 505; Bradley C. Gregory, "The Postexilic Exile in Third Isaiah: Isaiah 61:1–3 in Light of Second Temple Hermeneutics," *JBL* 126 (2007): 475–96; Shalom M. Paul, *Isaiah 40–66*, ECC (Grand Rapids: Eerdmans, 2011), 538; John Goldingay, *A Critical and Exegetical Commentary on Isaiah 56–66*, ICC 24.4 (London: Bloomsbury T&T Clark, 2014), 300. Pace John J. Collins, "A Herald of Good Tidings: Isaiah 61:1–3 and Its Actualization in the Dead Sea Scrolls," in *The Quest for Context and Meaning: Studies in Biblical Intertextuality in Honor of James A. Sanders*, eds. Craig A. Evans and Shemaryahu Talmon (Leiden: Brill, 1997), 228.

[11] Still, these passages could also be linked in the Hebrew. Both emphasize the poor (עני, Isa. 58:7; 61:1) and an acceptable (רצון) time (Isa. 58:5; 61:1).

[12] Claus Westermann, *Isaiah 40–66*, OTL (Philadelphia: Westminster, 1969), 340.

makes this link particularly apt. Indeed, it is this release (ἄφεσις, דרור in Lev. 25:8; Ezek. 46:17; Isa. 61:1) that encapsulates the Jubilee imagery and correlates with the socioeconomic focus of Isa. 58. The nature of this Jubilee imagery is important for our investigation.

3.2 Jubilee

Most scholars acknowledge the Jubilee imagery of Jesus's citation,[13] though a few question whether this imagery is intentional or should have any bearing on how Jesus's mission is understood.[14] These scholars contend that such political or economic concerns do not comport with what they see as either Jesus's more spiritual-moral concerns or as Luke's Gospel's lack of Jubilee imagery elsewhere. Concerning the former, our general argument has called and continues to call this reduction of Luke-Acts' message into question. Concerning the latter, both Robert B. Sloan and Sharon Ringe have made compelling cases that Jubilee is represented throughout Luke.[15] However, it should also be considered that mention of Jubilee here is part of a narrative framing device. It is not necessary for Luke to make repeated, overt references to the Jubilee theme. Rather, considering the programmatic nature of this opening section to Jesus's ministry, the reader is presented with a lens through which to view the narrative. More importantly, the Jubilee theme need not carry all the weight of our argument. It is part of a cluster of concepts that point toward a holistic and cosmic restoration.

One should not expect that Jesus simply announces the enactment of Jubilee legislation and that this enactment should be strewn about his ministry.[16] Recent work

---

[13] E.g., M. V. Abraham, "Good News to the Poor in Luke's Gospel," *BiBh* 14 (1988): 72–3; Samuele Bacchiocchi, *From Sabbath to Sunday: A Historical Investigation of the Rise of Sunday Observance* (Rome: Pontifical Gregorian University, 1977), 20–1; Walter J. Houston, "'Today in Your Very Hearing': Some Comments on the Christological Use of the Old Testament," in *The Glory of Christ in the New Testament: Studies in Christology in Memory of George Bradford Caird*, eds. L. D. Hurst and N. T. Wright (Oxford: Clarendon, 1987), 37–47; B. J. Koet, *Five Studies on Interpretation of Scripture in Luke-Acts* (Leuven: Leuven University Press, 1989), 25; Walter E. Pilgrim, *Good News to the Poor: Wealth and Poverty in Luke-Acts* (Minneapolis: Augsburg, 1981), 71; Sharon H. Ringe, *Jubilee, Liberation, and the Biblical Jubilee: Images for Ethics and Christology* (Eugene, OR: Wipf and Stock, 1985), 36–45; James A. Sanders, "From Isaiah 61 to Luke 4," in *Luke and Scripture: The Function of Sacred Tradition in Luke-Acts*, eds. Craig A. Evans and James A. Sanders (Minneapolis: Fortress, 1993), 62; August Strobel, "Die Ausrufung des Jobeljahrs in der Nazarethpredigt Jesu: Zur apokalyptischen Tradition Lc 4,16–30," in *Jesus in Nazareth*, ed. Walther Eltester, BZNW 40 (Berlin: de Gruyter, 1972), 38–50. See the survey in Christopher J. Schreck, "Luke 4,16–30: The Nazareth Pericope in Modern Exegesis: A History of Interpretation" (STD diss., Katholieke Universiteit Leuven, 1990), 414–18.

[14] Turner, *Power*, 244; Pao, *Exodus*, 77; L. T. Johnson, *Luke*, 81; Robert C. Tannehill, *The Narrative Unity of Luke-Acts: A Literary Interpretation*, 2 vols. (Philadelphia: Fortress, 1986–90), 1:68.

[15] Ringe, *Jesus*; Sloan, *Favorable*, 111–53. Sloan in particular notes how Jubilee themes appear in the Sermon on the Plain (6:20–38) and in the Lord's Prayer (11:2–4), the importance of forgiveness, and Luke's distinctive use of εὐαγγελίζω. See also Nicholas Perrin and Joel B. Green, "Jubilee," *DJG*, 2nd ed., 450–2.

[16] *Pace* John H. Yoder, *The Politics of Jesus: Vicit Agnus Noster*, 2nd ed. (Grand Rapids: Eerdmans, 1994), 28–33, 60–75; André Trocmé, *Jesus and the Nonviolent Revolution* (Scottdale, PA: Herald, 1998), 27–40.

on the development of the Jubilee concept has demonstrated that Jubilee imagery as adopted in the Second Temple period was not simply the bare application of legislation from Lev. 25; rather, the Jubilee conception went through a diachronic transformation that involved, among other things, its emergence as an eschatological hope.[17] Though Jubilee certainly retains its sociopolitical sense, it is not a social program, strictly speaking. Jubilee themes, when immersed in the Isaianic context, provide a lens for envisioning an era of eschatological deliverance and restoration. This diachronic transformation is important, though this investigation is limited to what is immediately important for understanding our text.

3.2.1 Leviticus 25

The Jubilee Year first appears in Lev. 25:8–55, where it is said to be celebrated every fifty years beginning on the tenth day of the seventh month, the Day of Atonement (vv. 8–9). The connection between Jubilee and the Day of Atonement links Jubilee to the cultic system. It is not simply a mundane social mandate. This year is characterized by the proclamation of release (דרור, v. 10) in which property is returned to its ancestral occupants, land lies fallow, debts are forgiven, and slaves are released. The Jubilee year has a connection with the Sabbath year (Lev. 25:1–7; Deut. 15:1–18; Jer. 34:8–22).

Leviticus 25 mentions on multiple occasions that the Israelites should obey this legislation because they are slaves brought out of Egypt (vv. 38, 42, 55). John Sietze Bergsma contends that the legislation conceives of "the entire territory controlled by Israel [as] analogous to a temple estate, and the Israelites themselves were sacred slaves, having been dedicated to YHWH through the exodus experience."[18] Behind this release is the reassertion of YHWH's kingship over Israel in a way that mirrors the release (דרור) proclaimed by Near Eastern kings at their enthronement.[19] The biggest difference between the Near Eastern expression of royal largess and Jubilee is that Jubilee was cyclical and ordained directly by God, not by a human (even if thought divine) king.[20] Indeed, Israel was originally a kingless society, and God's royal lordship is asserted in such a festival.[21] Helmer Ringgren also supposes that the Davidic king, as God's son and representative, would have had a prominent place in announcing this year of release.[22]

Behind both the royal proclamation and the priestly connection to atonement is the importance of establishing order and justice. When a Near Eastern king proclaimed release, there were definite socioeconomic motivations in overcoming destabilizing inequality. This inequality was understood as a mal-ordering of cosmic space, and

---

[17] See esp. Bergsma, *Jubilee*; J. A. Sanders, "From."
[18] Bergsma, *Jubilee*, 295.
[19] Bergsma, *Jubilee*, 92. See also Jacob Milgrom, *Leviticus: A New Translation with Introduction and Commentary*, 3 vols., AB 3–3B (New York: Doubleday, 2000–2007), 3:2166–69; *ANET* 378–9; Jer. 34:8–22.
[20] Milgrom, *Leviticus*, 3:2169.
[21] See Moshe Weinfeld, *Social Justice in Ancient Israel and in the Ancient Near East* (Minneapolis: Fortress, 1995), 7–15.
[22] Helmer Ringgren, *The Messiah in the Old Testament*, SBT 18 (London: SCM, 1956), 22.

rectifying action was needed to restore cosmic order.²³ Jubilee, similarly, demonstrates concern with ordering, and its connection to the Day of Atonement places it within a cosmic context. The linking of the two events enables what Adriana Destro and Mauro Pesce call "collective ritual expiation,"²⁴ a communally enacted canceling of debts as an extension of atonement. They write, "The conversion and the forgiveness of sins [that are requisite parts of the Day of Atonement] require the reconstitution of a relationship of equality between members of the people."²⁵ That is, the full realization of atonement as conversion and forgiveness is brought only through full social/cosmic reformation. Luke similarly calls such conversion "repentance." Repentance is a necessary correlate to the new offer of forgiveness (Lk. 3:3; 17:3–4; 24:42; Acts 2:38; 3:19; 8:22; 28:18–20), yet this requires fruits of repentance that are explicitly social (Lk. 3:7–14). Jubilee demonstrates a communal repentance and restoration that is the spatial extension of the Day of Atonement.²⁶ Indeed, if Jubilee does present a lens through which to view Jesus's ministry, Jesus's specific social-ethical vision, forgiveness, and repentance-preaching should be understood as a manifestation and extension of this Jubilee/atonement space.

Robert S. Kawashima has shown that both the Day of Atonement and Jubilee are concerned with cosmic purgation and order.²⁷ He writes that "the Jubilee Year symbolizes and completes an atonement of socioeconomic pollution."²⁸ Again, Jubilee is characterized not as a narrowly socioeconomic reality but as an extension of the purgation and cosmic ordering of atonement. Such socioeconomic pollution was seen in Israelites' and Israelite land's being out of proper place. The return of land, the manumission of slaves, and the forgiveness of debts restored cosmic order in a way analogous to the purgation of the temple on the Day of Atonement.²⁹ Jubilee extends the cleansing of the temple to all creation, and in this way the coupling of Jubilee and atonement images a spatially extended atonement that easily transitions to an eschatological (spatial-temporal) vision where all things are restored as God intends. There is liberation realized in the remaking of space.³⁰

---

[23] See, e.g., "Joy at the Accession of Mer-ne-Ptah," where it is celebrated that "normality has come down (again) into its place" (*ANET* 378).

[24] Adriana Destro and Mauro Pesce, "Forgiveness of Sins without a Victim: Jesus and the Levitical Jubilee," in *Sacrifice in Religious Experience*, ed. Albert I. Baumgarten, SHR 93 (Leiden: Brill, 2002), 163.

[25] Destro and Pesce, "Forgiveness," 164.

[26] Destro and Pesce add, "Just as Jubilee means the reintegration of debtors, so the forgiveness of sins means the pacification and re-equilibrium among men and their reciprocal relationships" ("Forgiveness," 164). See also the association of God's forgiveness of sins with the year of the release in 1Q22 III, 6–7.

[27] Robert S. Kawashima, "The Jubilee Year and the Return of Cosmic Purity," *CBQ* 65 (2003): 370–89. See also Gordon J. Wenham, *The Book of Leviticus*, NICOT (Grand Rapids: Eerdmans, 1979), 317; Perrin and Green, "Jubilee," 450.

[28] Kawashima, "Jubilee," 371.

[29] On the Day of Atonement's functioning primarily to cleanse the sanctuary and not the offerer, see Jacob Milgrom, "Israel's Sanctuary: The Priestly 'Picture of Dorian Gray,'" *RB* 83 (1976): 390–9; idem, *Leviticus*, 1:254. Milgrom's assertions have, however, been contested by his student Roy E. Gane (*Cult of Character: Purification Offerings, Day of Atonement, and Theodicy* (Winona Lake, IN: Eisenbrauns, 2005), esp. 106–43).

[30] Cf. Erhard Gerstenberger, *Leviticus: A Commentary*, OTL (Louisville: Westminster John Knox, 1996), 378.

3.2.2 Isaiah 58 and 61

These cosmic themes involving social reordering are developed in Isaiah. As noted above, Isa. 61 makes use of Jubilee in its proclamation of release. However, Isaiah does not advocate the implementation of Levitical legislation on a fifty (or forty-nine)-year cycle; rather, Jubilee becomes a qualitative framework for a coming era of righteousness, undergoing corporate reapplication to an eschatological restoration.[31] Concern for releasing captives and giving sight to the blind recalls the Benedictus's concern for salvation from enemies (1:71, 74) and light for those in darkness (v. 79), resulting in serving God in holiness and justness/righteousness (vv. 74–5). Isaiah 61 announces the coming of this just order.

One of the most prominent connections to Jubilee in Isa. 61 is the proclamation of release (דרור, ἄφεσις).[32] The use of דרור (release) is relatively rare in the MT, occurring only six times (Lev. 25:10; Isa. 61:1; Jer. 34:8, 15, 17; Ezek. 46:17). In Lev. 25:10, the year of Jubilee is a time "to proclaim release" (קראתם דרור), and in Isa. 61:1 an anointed herald proclaims release (לקרא לשבוים דרור) to captives. Further, the later reference to a year of release in Ezek. 46:17 shows that the Jubilee year, even if not implemented, remained in the prophetic imagination through the exile.[33] Indeed, if, as some commentators assert, Jubilee imagery is behind the release in Jer. 34:8, דרור (release) appears to be specialized terminology linked to Jubilee.[34]

The Jubilee allusion is further strengthened when we consider that Israel's enslavement and exile on account of her sins in Isa. 40–66 requires a redeemer (גאל).[35] This imagery helps to frame Israel's deliverance in Jubilee terms, where the term "redeemed" (גאל) is used repeatedly of those redeemed through Jubilee (Lev. 25:25–6, 30, 33, 48–9, 54). Though the imagery is that of debt-slavery,[36] the prominent concern is deliverance and release, not exactitude in balanced reciprocity.[37] It is this emphasis on deliverance/release that allows for the overlapping of exile and Jubilee metaphors. Second (and Third) Isaiah's well-attested portrayal of the Babylonian exile in terms of exodus (e.g., 43:1–2, 14–21; 48:20–2; 51:9–11; 52:3–6; 63:7–14) includes the dimension

---

[31] Bergsma, *Jubilee*, 299.
[32] See Childs, *Isaiah*, 505; Paul, *Isaiah*, 538; Goldingay, *Isaiah*, 300.
[33] See B. C. Gregory, *Postexilic*, 484.
[34] B. C. Gregory rejects John J. Collins' assertion that דרור refers simply to manumission with no Jubilee concern ("Herald," 228). On Jeremiah, see William L. Holladay, *Jeremiah*, 2 vols., Hermeneia (Minneapolis: Fortress, 1986–9), 2:238–40; Jack R. Lundbom, *Jeremiah: A New Translation with Introduction and Commentary*, 3 vols., AB 21–21C (New York: Doubleday, 1999–2004), 2:560–1.
[35] Isaiah 41:14; 43:1, 14; 44:6, 22–4; 47:4; 48:17, 20; 49:7, 26; 51:10; 52:3, 9; 54:5, 8; 59:20; 60:16; 62:12; 63:9, 16.
[36] On debt-slavery as a metaphor for captivity in Isa. 40–66, see Bergsma, *Jubilee*, 192.
[37] Gary A. Anderson's comment on debt imagery in Scripture is apt: The mistake of a generation of biblical scholars has been "to assume that Jewish thinking about forgiveness of sins was determined by rules of strict financial propriety" (*Sin: A History* (New Haven: Yale University Press, 2009), 110). Indeed, the economic reciprocity mentioned in Isa. 40:2, for example, does emphasize consequences of sin but is not dependent on precise economic equivalence. This passage appears to be dependent on Jer. 16:18, which emphasizes double repayment for idolatry. Isaiah 40:2 announces that this punishment is over. Isaiah 61:7 builds on 40:2 to indicate that now God will give a double portion and everlasting joy.

of release from slavery caused by sin (e.g., 40:2; 42:24; 44:22; 50:1). God, here, functions as redeemer (גאל, cf. Exod. 6:6; 15:13), and Jubilee release, where we find similar need of a redeemer (גאל), provides apt imagery for God's new exodus-like deliverance.

The other major allusion to Jubilee in Isa. 61, "the Lord's acceptable year," is also amenable to a new exodus/Jubilee interpretation. The Lord's acceptable *year* is representative of a Jubilee *era* of righteousness/justness. Indeed, this righteousness is what is hoped for in the socioeconomic vision of Isa. 58 (cf. esp. vv. 6–9). Here, the hope is not simply deliverance but a new social economy and political existence. "The acceptable year" appears to be a comment on the "acceptable time" of 49:8, which is characterized as a day of salvation to restore Israel.[38] Altering "time" to "year" alludes to both the Jubilee year in Lev. 25:13 (cf. v. 10) as well as the "year of release" in Jer. 34:8.[39] The use of "acceptable" (רצון; δεκτός) in both 49:8 and 61:2 indicates a time of God's turning. As John Goldingay writes: "This is the moment when Yhwh accepts the people again instead of rejecting them" (cf. 60:10).[40] If the new exodus is understood not simply as release, but as release into a specific sociopolitical existence characterized by justness/righteousness, the cosmic-social wholeness of the Jubilee year provides an ideal counterpart.[41]

Additionally, both Isa. 58 and 61, with whatever Jubilee allusions they contain, are associated with atonement in later tradition. 11QMelch II, 7–9 directly relates the eschatological year of Jubilee with forgiveness of sins, while Isa. 57:14–58:14 is identified in the Talmud (*b. Meg.* 31a) as a reading for the Day of Atonement.[42] A major reason for this latter link is concern with fasting in Isa. 58:3, 6, the Day of Atonement being the only required fast in the Torah (Lev. 23:26–32). The socioeconomic expansion of this fast by Isaiah, as noted above, is foreshadowed in the Jubilee's cosmic-social concern in Leviticus and its relation to the Day of Atonement. Indeed, Luke's combination of Isa. 58 and 61 points to this very reality, where the acceptable (δεκτός) fast (58:5) represents properly restored relationships characteristic of the acceptable (δεκτός) year (61:2), so that once again this link between atonement and Jubilee is implied. In fact, Bergsma writes that "the prophetic author of Isa. 58 saw in the Jubilee the authentic social expression of the meaning of the Day of Atonement, which was the fast *par excellence* in traditional Israelite law."[43]

Finally, Isa. 58 further connects to Jubilee with its emphasis on Sabbath, which is intimately related to the Jubilee Year (Lev. 25:1–7; 26:2, 34–5).[44] This Sabbath theology

---

[38] B. C. Gregory, "Postexilic," 486.
[39] Goldingay, *Isaiah*, 301.
[40] Goldingay, *Isaiah*, 301.
[41] The connection between national restoration and Jubilee wholeness can be found in Leviticus as well, where chs. 25–6 exhibit clear framing (25:1; 26:46). The Jubilee legislation, which is interwoven with general ethical demands, is thus linked to the threatened punishment of exile for disobedience (26:27–39) and promised restoration (26:40–5). See G. A. Anderson, *Sin*, 66–74.
[42] George Foot Moore, *Judaism in the First Centuries of the Christian Era: The Age of the Tannaim*, 3 vols. (Cambridge, MA: Harvard University Press, 1946–9), 2:69.
[43] Bergsma, *Jubilee*, 197.
[44] The connection between the Day of Atonement and the Year of Jubilee has been noted in particular by Thomas D. Hanks (*God So Loved the Third World: The Bible, the Reformation, and Liberation Theologies* (Maryknoll, NY: Orbis Books, 1983), 97–104). See also Bergsma, *Jubilee*, 195–8.

utilizes Jubilee practices of justice (56:1; 58:2, 13): freeing of debt-slaves (58:6, 9; Lev. 25:39–55), no longer abusing workers (Isa. 58:3; Lev. 25:36, 39, 43, 46, 53), sharing food and shelter with needy kin (Isa. 58:7, 10; Lev. 25:35–8)—even, some suggest, refusing to charge interest on loans (Isa. 58:4; Lev. 25:35–8).[45] Thus, it is apparent that Isa. 58 and 61 emphasize the extension of atonement in Jubilee "release" in proper cosmic-social ordering, a theme already evident in Leviticus.

3.2.3 Daniel 9

Daniel 9 has already proven important for Luke. In Chapter 2, I discussed the importance of Daniel 9 for the imagery of Luke's early chapters. It is also notable that Gabriel's declaration to Daniel concerning Israel's restoration refers to weeks of years (9:24–7). The nearest biblical precedent for this language comes from the calculation of the Jubilee (Lev. 25:8); thus, most scholars see here a reference to ten Jubilee cycles.[46] It is noteworthy then that this Jubilee imagery is linked intimately with atonement imagery. Daniel's intercessory prayers beg for communal forgiveness and release from bondage (9:3–20), and Gabriel responds by indicating that the tenth Jubilee will put an end to sin, atone for iniquity, and "bring an everlasting righteousness," undoubtedly an image of an eschatological era (v. 24).

3.2.4 11QMelchizedek

One final text, 11QMelchizedek, is particularly interesting for our study because it not only builds on Jubilee themes that develop through Leviticus, Isaiah, and Daniel, but it also represents a somewhat similar reflection to Luke on Isa. 61:1–2, with explicit relation to Jubilee, a Davidic figure, redemption of "captives" (particularly from the demonic force of Belial), and atonement.[47] The text opens with a reference to the Jubilee Year (11QMelch II, 2; Lev. 25:13) and deliverance (דרור) for captives (lines 4–5). These captives will be freed from their iniquities on the Day of Atonement that begins the tenth Jubilee (lines 6–8; cf. *1 En.* 91.12–17; 93), and freedom from the hand of Belial is announced at a trumpet blast (line 25; cf. Lev. 25:9). The association between communal deliverance, Jubilee-like release, and the Day of Atonement is even more direct here than in Isaiah.

Interestingly, the text states that this is Melchizedek's acceptable year rather than the Lord's (line 9). Bergsma writes, "Melchizedek is seen as personally enacting a Jubilee on behalf of the 'captives' who are somehow associated with him (his 'inheritance'), in much the same way that Isaiah 61:1–2 portrays a messianic figure personally enacting Jubilee

---

[45] Bergsma, *Jubilee*, 196.
[46] James A. Montgomery, *A Critical and Exegetical Commentary on the Book of Daniel*, ICC (Edinburgh: T&T Clark, 1927), 373; John J. Collins, *Daniel*, Hermeneia (Minneapolis: Fortress, 1993), 352; Bergsma, *Jubilee*, 225 n. 62.
[47] On 11QMelchizedek, see M. de Jonge and A. S. van der Woude, "11Q Melchizedek and the New Testament," *NTS* 12 (1966): 301–26; Joseph A. Fitzmyer, "Further Light on Melchizedek from Qumran Cave 11," *JBL* 86 (1967): 25–41; Merril P. Miller, "The Function of Isa 61:1–2 in 11Q Melchizedek," *JBL* 88 (1969): 467–9; J. A. Sanders, "From," 56–7; Bergsma, *Jubilee*, 277–91.

on behalf of the 'poor of Zion.'"[48] Though Daniel 9, for instance, portrayed this messianic figure to come at the tenth Jubilee in royal terms, the invocation of Melchizedek (who also comes during the tenth Jubilee, lines 6–9) seems to indicate a composite priestly royal figure (cf. Gen. 14:18–20; Ps. 110:4; Heb. 5:5–10; 6:20; 7:1–28).[49]

A messianic figure announces the era of salvation and peace (cf. Isa. 52:7) as anticipated in Isa. 61:1–2. It will be a time of God's favor and vengeance, in which captives will be freed and sins forgiven. The Davidic/royal description is apparent, though the priestly connection is dependent on this figure's association with the Day of Atonement. For some, concern for social renewal seems absent. Collins notes, for instance, that "in contrast to Isa. 61, the liberation is not economic but relief from the burden of sin, an idea that may be suggested by the reference to the Day of Atonement in Lev. 25:9,"[50] and Bergsma asserts that here there is a reabsorption of Jubilee into the Day of Atonement, which he claims also occurs in Lk. 4:16–21.[51] However, this is unlikely. Though deliverance involves freedom from iniquity (line 6), this is not at odds with the previous presentations of the era of Jubilee release. Association with the Day of Atonement has not and does not here mean that this release obscures the sociopolitical effects of Jubilee. Indeed, as I have argued, Jubilee is an extension of, not a couplet with, atonement, so that freeing from iniquity is an aspect of holistic release. Nor should we understand the battle with Belial (lines 12–14) to be reduced to spiritual actors. Such demonic realities are intimately tied to embodied forces (see, on Belial, 1QM I, 10–15; XIII, 1–15; cf. *Mart. Isa.* 2.4). Rather than a reabsorption of Jubilee into the atonement, emphasis on this Melchizedek figure highlights the importance of holistic atonement that is extended in Jubilee. The Jubilee announcement speaks prophetically of coming release. In the end, this passage resembles Lk. 4:16–21 in many ways, even if Luke conceives of the benefits of Jubilee in more universal terms.

3.2.5 Summary

This brief survey gives us some conceptual background for Jesus's announcement of Jubilee release. Jubilee has developed a sense of eschatological expectation, and its link to atonement envisions social-political ordering as an element of cosmic atonement. Jubilee is important for this investigation as it conceptualizes a social and theopolitical salvation that extends beyond personal forgiveness to incorporate a cosmic-comprehensive reordering comparable in scope to our Irenaean *Christus Victor* scheme, imagining an embodied release from oppressive structures and not just personal sin. Thus, Jubilee is not simply an era, but an eschatological configuration of space, a proper ordering of cosmic and social-political reality centered on Jesus. It is a "cosmic purgation" reconciling the world to God's way of ordering, a spatial atonement.

---

[48] Bergsma, *Jubilee*, 282.
[49] So Bergsma, *Jubilee*, 304; *pace* de Jonge and van der Woude, "Melchizedek," 305; J. J. Collins, "Herald," 230.
[50] J. J. Collins, "Herald," 230.
[51] Bergsma, *Jubilee*, 284–5.

3.3 He Has Anointed Me: Christology

Utilizing this Isaianic message (58:6; 61:1–2), Luke presents Jesus's ministry in Jubilee terms. Several elements of this are important. The "acceptable year of the Lord" is fulfilled "today" (Lk. 4:21) in what appears as a Jubilee era. The implications of this announcement are, on the surface, of sociopolitical import. As Daniel 9 and 11QMelchizedek imagine a Davidic figure, the Lukan Davidic Messiah is undoubtedly linked to the anointed one in Lk. 4:18. Much as 11QMelchizedek presented the scope of release in terms of cosmic actors (Belial), so we have already seen that Jesus battles Satan (4:1–13). Finally, and importantly, we saw the relationship between Jubilee and national restoration (Isa. 61:1–2; Dan. 9:24–7), a theme that has been important in Luke thus far. In the following sections, the different elements of Jesus's Nazareth declaration are investigated in order to develop a broader picture of this unfolding salvation.

From the start, Jesus makes this address about himself, repeating the first-person pronoun, "me" ([ἐ]με) three times. The initial structure of the citation emphasizes this "me" by placing the pronoun after distinct consecutive clauses: The Spirit of the Lord is on *me*; he has anointed *me*; to proclaim good news to the poor, he has sent *me*.[52]

Elsewhere in Luke-Acts, the term χρίω (anoint, v. 18) is used clearly linking Jesus to David (Acts 4:27),[53] and in Luke 4, the Davidic imagery is similarly palpable for the attentive reader (e.g., 1:32, 69; 2:11). Reference to "anointing" with the Holy Spirit (4:18) draws the reader back to Jesus's recent baptism (3:21–2), where God's words over Jesus, "You are my beloved Son, in you I am well pleased," allude to Ps. 2:7, which is also used by Paul to describe Jesus's resurrection as a Davidic enthronement (Acts 13:33).[54] Jesus's mention of anointing refers to the already-established Davidic theme.[55] Jesus is the Spirit-anointed king, declaring an era of release.

This Davidic theme permeates the citation from Isa. 61 as well. Walter Brueggemann writes, "The juxtaposition of 'spirit' and 'anoint' is bound to recall in Israel the old narrative of the authorization of David with the same two features" (1 Sam. 16:13; 2 Sam. 23:1–2).[56] Most often, such anointing was associated with kings (1 Sam. 9:16; 10:1; 2 Sam. 2:7; 5:17; 12:7; 19:10; 1 Kgs 1:34; 5:1; 19:15; 2 Kgs 9:3, 6, 12 et al.). Nevertheless, others have noted allusions to the Isaianic servant.[57] Some Lukan scholars see Jesus here

---

[52] So Nolland, *Luke*, 1:192; Bovon, *Luke*, 1:154; Green, *Luke*, 210; Fitzmyer, *Luke*, 1:532. Pace Wolter, *Lukasevangelium*, 192. It is not clear from the Greek whether the infinitival clause ("to proclaim good news to the poor") should go with the preceding or following material, yet the Hebrew original appears to place the clause with the latter, "he sent me."

[53] See Strauss, *Messiah*, 226–33.

[54] This is not to discount allusions to Gen. 22:2 or Isa. 42:1; 44:1, though these are less prominent. Codex Bezae mimics Ps. 2:7 at Lk. 3:22.

[55] So N. T. Wright, *People*, 378–80; Bock, *Proclamation*, 105–11; Robert F. O'Toole, "Jesus as the Christ in Luke 4,16–30," *Bib* 76 (1995): 498–522; Wolter, *Lukasevangelium*, 192; C. Kavin Rowe, *Early Narrative Christology: The Lord in the Gospel of Luke* (Grand Rapids: Baker Academic, 2006), 78–9; Miura, *David*, 214.

[56] Brueggemann, *Isaiah*, 213.

[57] See Goldingay, *Isaiah*, 293; Beers, *Followers*, 1; Pao, *Exodus*, 76–7.

embodying both Davidic and Isaianic servant elements.[58] Brevard Childs's assertion concerning the Christian utilization of Isaiah is appropriate here: "the final shape of the Isaianic corpus is such that the resonance between the eschatological Messiah and the suffering servant was soon heard by the Christian church as a legitimate reader response to its scriptures in linking servant and Messiah."[59] Luke 4:18–19 represents Jesus as such a composite Davidic and Isaianic servant figure.

Nevertheless, despite the apparent Davidic theme, critics are not wrong to highlight the prophetic theme as well.[60] Though there is little corroborating evidence in the OT for prophetic anointing, where the rite of anointing with oil was used of kings, priests, and physical objects but not prophets,[61] there is such prophetic anointing in the DSS (1QM XI, 7–8; CD II, 12; III, 9; VI, 1),[62] and the Holy Spirit is related to prophetic empowerment in Luke-Acts (Lk. 1:41–2, 67; 12:12; Acts 1:8; 2:4, 17–18; 4:31; 11:28; 28:25).[63] Further, Jesus is portrayed in prophetic terms throughout Luke-Acts (7:39; 9:8, 19; 13:34–5; 22:64; 24:19; Acts 3:22–3; 7:37). Indeed, Jesus's self-comparison to Elijah and Elisha (4:25–7) and the explicit affirmation of his prophetic status (v. 24) dominates the latter segment of this pericope.[64]

These prophetic themes, however, need not diminish the Davidic picture. The two themes coexist in Lukan Christology as is evident, for example, from Acts 3:12–26 where Peter, before designating Jesus as the prophet like Moses, twice calls Jesus *Christ* (χριστός, vv. 18, 20),[65] or elsewhere where Luke depicts David himself as a prophet (Acts 1:16; 4:25; cf. 2 Sam. 23:2; Josephus, *Ant.* 6.166). Further, there are sources in antiquity that see Mosaic and Davidic roles as overlapping.[66] For instance, the Midrash on the Psalms states: "Whatever Moses did, David did" (1.2). As Moses became a king, David became a king, as Moses built an altar, David built an altar (see also *Sipra Deut.* 26.1.C). In Luke-Acts, Jesus's journey is both Davidic (e.g., Acts 13:22–3) and Mosaic (e.g., Acts 7:35–8).

This is not a comprehensive investigation of Lukan Christology, but it helps situate the Isaianic quotation within this moment of Luke-Acts. Jesus is the Davidic representative governing social/cosmic space. When Jesus shows up, salvation has arrived (Lk. 19:5, 9), so that salvation emanates from Jesus, and soteriological space,

---

[58] On the Isaianic servant, see Beers, *Followers*; Pao, *Exodus*, 76–7; B. J. Koet, "Isaiah in Luke-Acts," in *Isaiah in the New Testament*, eds. Steve Moyise and Maarten J. J. Menken (London: T&T Clark, 2005), 79–100.
[59] Childs, *Isaiah*, 505.
[60] So Fitzmyer, *Luke*, 1:529–30, 532; L. T. Johnson, *Luke*, 81.
[61] Goldingay notes at least one apparent exception in the OT, 1 Kgs 19:16, yet this passage only proves the point, being essentially metaphorical (*Isaiah*, 296).
[62] See Paul, *Isaiah*, 539.
[63] See also Tg. Isa. 61:1.
[64] See John C. Poirer, "Jesus as an Elijianic Figure in Luke 4:16–30," *CBQ* 71 (2009): 349–63.
[65] So Turner, *Power*, 266; Michael Prior, *Jesus the Liberator: Nazareth Liberation Theology (Luke 4.16–30)*, BSem 26 (Sheffield: Sheffield Academic Press, 1995), 137–8; Green, *Luke*, 212; Nolland, *Luke*, 1:196. It is likely, given Luke's tendency to use Christological titles somewhat promiscuously (Conzelmann, *Theology*, 170–4), that Luke thinks in both prophetic and messianic terms (Tiede, *Prophecy*, 46).
[66] See Miura, *David*, 235.

the proper and atoning ordering of social-political space in conformity to God's (cosmic) ordering and Jesus's Jubilee proclamation, is produced in relation to him.

3.4 To Proclaim Good News to the Poor: Jesus and the Kingdom

The first prong of Jesus's proclamation is good news to the poor, a declaration that generalizes Jesus's overall message. "Good news," of course, carries some weight. It is a message of meaning, of political import. This is a message of hope and a new reality for the poor. Though the other Synoptic Gospels will use the noun εὐαγγέλιον (good news),[67] a term that never occurs in Luke and only twice in Acts (15:7; 20:24), only Luke, outside of a single occurrence in Mt. 11:5, uses the verb form εὐαγγελίζω (proclaim good news), and he does so twenty-five times.[68] The terminological choice could exhibit a desire to perpetuate the link between Jesus's ministry and the Isaianic era.[69] Thus, Matthew similarly uses the verb rather than his otherwise marked preference for the noun (εὐαγγέλιον) on the one occasion where he refers to Isa. 61:1 (Mt. 11:5; cf. Lk. 7:22).

It is well documented that "good news" in antiquity frequently occurred in political contexts.[70] Josephus, for instance, can speak of how the news of Vespasian's ascension to power spread eastward, provoking festivals and sacrifices in response to the "good news" (εὐαγγέλιον) (*War* 4.618), and the Priene inscription (see Chapter 2) speaks of the good news of the new era of peace brought about by Augustus's birth, the savior (*OGIS* 458).[71] The use of εὐαγγελίζω (proclaim good news) in the LXX is not drastically different. There, the typical understandings of victory in battle (1 Sam. 31:9; 2 Sam. 4:10; 1 Chron. 10:9; Ps. 68[67]:11[12]) and a king's ascension (1 Kgs 1:42) remain. Additionally, the term is used in relation to messengers sent by God (Nah. 1[2]:15[1]), God's victory (2 Sam. 18:19, 20, 31), and God's salvation and deliverance (Pss. 40[39]:9[10]; 96[95]:2; Isa. 40:9; 52:7; 60:6; Nah. 1[2]:15[1]). We must resist the urge to classify such uses as either "religious" or "secular," as if the ascension of a king is distinctly secular. This heralding of good news is a cosmic-comprehensive event, declaring the presence of God's kingdom (4:43; 8:1; 16:16).

3.4.1 Proclaiming God's Kingdom

If Jesus is here making a declaration concerning God's kingdom, we must understand how that kingdom functions, especially as a spatial reality. "Kingdom of God" is of

---

[67] Mt. 4:23; 9:35; 24:14; 26:13; Mk 1:1, 14, 15; 8:35; 10:29; 13:10; 14:9; 16:15.
[68] Lk. 1:19; 2:10; 3:18; 4:18, 43; 7:22; 8:1; 9:6; 16:16; 20:1; Acts 5:42; 8:4, 12, 25, 35, 40; 10:36; 11:20; 13:32; 14:7, 15, 21; 15:35; 16:10; 17:18.
[69] Isaiah uses εὐαγγελίζω (proclaim good news) six times (40:9 x2; 52:7 x2; 60:6; 61:1) but never uses the noun form.
[70] Gerhard Friedrich, "εὐαγγελίζομαι, εὐαγγέλιον, κτλ," *TDNT* 2:707–37.
[71] Ando writes, "Under Claudius ... Paullus Fabius Persicus, as governor of Asia, wrote to the *koinon* of the province cautioning cities not to drain their resources by establishing new priesthoods 'as often as good news arrived from Rome'" (*Ideology*, 169).

course no self-evident phrase, and in attempting to understand this notion one must be careful to avoid simply locating instances of the phrase "kingdom of God" within Luke-Acts and building a "Lukan" conception from these occurrences.[72] Despite the phrase first occurring in 4:43, the developing story, with its royal and restoration themes, has already highlighted the establishment of God's kingdom (see, e.g., 1:33). For many, the primary question is temporal—when? Though much ink has been spilled over the extent to which the kingdom in Luke is a present or future reality, there is language that intimates both its present (6:20; 11:20; 16:16; 17:20; 22:29–30) and future nature (11:2; 13:28–9; 21:31; 22:16, 18).[73]

The priority of time over space, for many, is exacerbated by what appears to be direct disavowals of the kingdom's spatial presence. Thus, for instance, Jesus's final parable before entering Jerusalem, The Parable of the Pounds (19:11–27), is ostensibly a response to the crowd's belief that the kingdom of God was about to appear (ἀναφαίνω, v. 11). Traditionally, this parable has been understood as an attempt to mollify the crowds' temporal expectations, pushing the realization of the kingdom to

---

[72] This, e.g., is what we find with Alexander Prieur (*Die Verkündigung der Gottesherrschaft: Exegetische Studien zum lukanischen Verständnis von βασιλεία τοῦ θεοῦ*, WUNT 2/89 (Tübingen: Mohr Siebeck, 1996)). Not only does Prieur restrict himself to occurrences of the phrase, but he also designates a limited number of what he redaction-critically determines to be admissible Lukan uses of "kingdom of God."

[73] On the kingdom of God in Luke-Acts, Conzelmann proposed that Luke abandoned eschatology in favor of a "timeless" kingdom centered on Jesus's moral teachings (*Theology*, 104, 113–19; see also Helmut Flender, *St. Luke: Theologian of Redemptive History* (Philadelphia: Fortress, 1967)). For others, the kingdom is tied to Jesus's presence, so that with the ascension, the kingdom departs and is awaited (Otto Merk, "Das Reich Gottes in den lukanischen Schriften," in *Jesus und Paulus: Festschrift für Werner Georg Kümmel zum 70. Geburtstag*, eds. E. Earle Ellis and Erich Gräßer (Göttingen: Vandenhoeck & Ruprecht, 1975), 201–20; Alfons Weiser, "'Reich Gottes' in der Apostelgeschichte," in *Der Treue Gottes Trauen: Beiträge zum Werk des Lukas: Für Gerhard Schneider*, eds. Claus Bussmann and Walter Radl (Freiburg: Herder, 1991), 127–34; Michael Wolter, "'Reich Gottes' bei Lukas," NTS 41 (1995): 541–63. For the kingdom as solely future, see Erich Gräßer, *Forschungen zur Apostelgeschichte*, WUNT 137 (Tübingen: Mohr Siebeck, 2001), 294–5; Richard H. Hiers, "Delay of the Parousia in Luke-Acts," NTS 20 (1973–4): 145–55. More common, however, is a form of inaugurated eschatology that variously emphasizes both present and future elements (Carroll, *Response*, 17; E. Earle Ellis, *Christ and the Future in New Testament History*, NovTSup 97 (Leiden: Brill, 2000), 112–28; Maddox, *Purpose*, 132–7; Robert F. O'Toole, "The Kingdom of God in Luke-Acts," in *The Kingdom of God in 20th-Century Interpretation*, ed. Wendell Willis (Peabody, MA: Hendrickson, 1987), 147–62; Nolland, "Salvation-History," 68–70; Constantonio Antonio Ziccardi, *The Relationship of Jesus and the Kingdom of God according to Luke-Acts*, TGST 165 (Rome: Gregorian University Press, 2008)). Generally, for such formulations, the present kingdom is apolitical (Ziccardi, *Relationship*; Bruce, *Apostles*, 102; Michael A. Salmeier, *Restoring the Kingdom: The Role of God as the "Ordainer of Times and Seasons" in the Acts of the Apostles*, PrTMS (Eugene, OR: Pickwick, 2011), 83–4; Youngmo Cho, *Spirit and Kingdom in the Writings of Luke and Paul*, PBM (Waynesboro, GA: Paternoster, 2005), 110–95). Somewhat differently, James D. G. Dunn, ties the kingdom to the Spirit, so that the apostles are only brought into the kingdom at Pentecost (*The Christ and the Spirit: Pneumatology* (Grand Rapids: Eerdmans, 1998), 133–41; idem., "Spirit and Kingdom," ExpTim 82 (1970-1): 36–40). For others, there remains a present, ecclesiological, and sociopolitical element (Maston, "Kingdom," 169–78; Turner, *Power*, 319–33; Hahn, "Kingdom," 294–326; Kuhn, *Kingdom*; Rowe, *World*, 99–102).

some indeterminate future when Jesus will reward the faithful and judge the wicked.[74] Luke Timothy Johnson has rightly called this interpretation into question, noting, for one thing, that nothing in the parable or its introduction confirms or denies the temporal expectations of the kingdom.[75] Johnson argues instead that the parable is an allegory affirming the kingdom's immediate realization. Such a reading, for Johnson, makes sense of Jesus's affirming the present nature of the kingdom in 22:9. However, this interpretation might be taken a step further. R. Alan Culpepper, for one, maintains that the parable, which he entitles "The Parable of the Greedy and Vengeful King," parodies royal rule, in which the king serves as an "anti-type for Jesus."[76] The question is not so much *when*, but *how* the kingdom is manifest. Nothing in the parable suggests that it confronts an overzealous eschatological expectation. Rather, the focus is on the manner in which such expectation should be realized, how the kingdom should take up space. This is emphasized later in Jesus's contrasting of worldly authorities with the kingdom conferred on the twelve (22:24–30).

The parable comes as a response to another iteration in which Jesus teaches the disciples (e.g., 9:43–5; 18:31–4; 22:22–3) and they are unable to understand what he means (e.g., 9:46–8, 49–50, 51–6; 18:35–9; 22:24–7). Previously, the disciples had been rebuked for advocating violence, exclusion, and enforced hierarchy. Jesus's parodic presentation of this king exemplifies their misunderstanding of Jesus's kingship and God's kingdom. Jesus's primary objection is not that they are too concerned about time, but that their concern about immediacy (παραχρῆμα) is related to a certain violent imposition of the kingdom. This immediacy coheres, for example, with the impatience that encourages reigning fire down on Samaritans (9:51–6).

Nevertheless, Jesus certainly discusses time and the kingdom's fulfillment. There is a sense that the imminent reality of God's kingdom is not "fulfilled" and is to come (Lk. 11:2; 13:28–9; 21:31; 22:16, 18; Acts 3:21). Yet, Luke also utilizes temporal terminology to speak of the kingdom's proximity. At Jesus's crucifixion, one crucified with Jesus asks to be remembered when Jesus enters into his kingdom, and Jesus affirms that this man will be with him "today" (σήμερον) in paradise (23:42–3). This reference to "today" resonates with Jesus's Nazareth sermon (4:21) and highlights the *present* reality of God's kingdom, as well as victory over death.

---

[74] Conzelmann, *Theology*, 75, 113, 121; Bovon, *Luke*, 2:611; John T. Carroll, *Luke: A Commentary*, NTL (Louisville: Westminster John Knox, 2012), 379–82.

[75] L. T. Johnson, *Luke*, 292–4.

[76] R. Alan Culpepper, *The Gospel of Luke: Introduction, Commentary, and Reflections*, in *The Gospel of Luke, The Gospel of John*, NIB 9 (Nashville: Abingdon, 2002), 361–4. See also Tiede, *Prophecy*, 79; Richard B. Vinson, "The Minas Touch: Anti-Kingship Rhetoric in the Gospel of Luke," *PRSt* 35 (2008): 69–86; Curtis Hutt, "'Be Ye Approved Money Changers!': Reexamining the Social Contexts of the Saying and Its Interpretation," *JBL* 131 (2012): 589–609; Adam F. Braun, "Reframing the Parable of the Pounds in Lukan Narrative and Economic Context: Luke 19:11–28," *CurTM* 39 (2012): 442–8. Compare Laurie Guy, "The Interplay of the Present and Future in the Kingdom of God (Luke 19:11–44)," *TynBul* 48 (1997): 119–37. Craig L. Blomberg's critique that such parodic readings miss the "how much more" logic of the parables, though correct in naming this aspect, dismisses the context of the parable (*Interpreting the Parables*, 2nd ed. (Downers Grove, IL: IVP Academic, 2012), 280). There may be a "how much more" element, yet there remains contextually a critique of the disciples' conception of the kingdom.

God's kingdom is relegated to neither a temporally distant reality nor a present reality dependent on social progress. For Luke, God's kingdom is something sought (12:31), something given by God (12:32), something participated in (18:22–5), something invading mysteriously (13:18–21), and something by which one is overcome through God's salvific activity (10:9, 11; 11:20), though never grasped. Thus, the statement, "the kingdom of God is among (ἐντός) you (pl.)" (17:22), reflects a social and a dynamic spatial reality,[77] but that it should not be so reduced is made clear by emphasis on the kingdom's divine origin and activity (10:9, 11; 11:20). Bovon notes that the sense of the adverb ἐντός used as a preposition in 17:21 is "in the space of." Green writes of the kingdom as a "sphere" of "experiencing, identifying with, participating in, coming under the influence of, and joining the community formed in relation to God's kingdom."[78] God's kingdom is something that takes up space among us that has entered complex mundane space mysteriously (13:18–21). Indeed, to say that God's kingdom has come near (10:9, 11; cf. 11:20) is not so much a temporal statement about "any day now," but a proclamation about the invasion of kingdom space. God's kingdom, a heavenly originated and situated field of power and organization, comes near in Jesus and this Jubilee *today*, and the theopolitical body called by Jesus seeks to participate in and be ordered by this impressing spatial reality.

By contrast, Matthew's presentation of God's kingdom includes parables that portray God's kingdom as a mundane, earthly reality with mixed composition. So the kingdom is a field in which the enemy sows bad plants among the good (13:24–30), or it is a net that pulls the good and the bad (13:47–50). The bad will be sorted out at the eschaton. Luke does not include these parables. For Luke, God's kingdom is not the church or the world; it is not a mixture of the just and unjust, but a state and space of justness that disciples seek to participate in. It is a mystery that encounters and reorders existence. God's kingdom functions as a consistent cosmic thirdspace calling into question normalized place, animating the church as it strives to participate in God's kingdom. As the church does so, it is involved in the production of space, not producing the kingdom but a social-political space of participating in the kingdom.

3.4.2 Kingdom as Mystery

In some ways, this kingdom reality can be understood as a mystery (μυστήριον). Though this term μυστήριον is used only once in Luke-Acts (8:10), it helps to

---

[77] "Among you" remains the preferred reading of commentators (e.g., L. T. Johnson, *Luke*, 263; Ringe, *Luke*, 221; Bovon, *Luke*, 1:516). Though it is not the most common use of the preposition ἐντός, it does make the most sense in context. Jean Lebourlier has shown that both readings ("within you" and "among you") are possible, making the context the most determinative factor ("*Entos hymōn*: Le sens 'au milieu de vous' est-il possible?" *Bib* 73 (1992): 259–62).

[78] Joel B. Green, "Kingdom of God/Heaven," in *Dictionary of Jesus and the Gospels*, 2nd ed., eds. Joel B. Green, Jeannine K. Brown, and Nicholas Perrin (Downers Grove, IL: InterVarsity Press, 2013), 468.

conceptualize the spatial reality of the kingdom.[79] By mystery, I do not mean "secret" or "paradox"; rather, mystery (μυστήριον) is a *disclosure* of the true ordering of space and time, a disclosure that is never exhausted, because it is never completely perceived or conceived. It is an *other* space continually calling into question and re-forming mundane conceptions of space and normalized conceptual patterns of being, thinking, and doing. In simple terms, it is something other than the space in which the world has been living in the kingdoms of the "civilized world" (οἰκουμένη).[80]

In the NT, such a mystery (μυστήριον) can generally be understood as cosmic disclosure (cf. Eph. 1:9; 2 Thess. 2:7) that changes the apprehension of perceived realities (Rom. 11:25; 1 Cor. 15:51; Eph. 3:3–4). Indeed, Christ himself and the order to which he attests (as do the prophets) is a mystery (Rom. 16:25; 1 Tim. 3:16). The emphasis on disclosure is seen in how often the term occurs with verbs of saying and revealing (1 Cor. 2:1, 7; 15:51; Eph. 6:19; Col. 1:27; 4:3). Paul utilizes the term to indicate an apocalyptic revelation uncovered eschatologically, yet the sense is that, for Paul, *now* is the eschatological time, and the mystery reveals what is (Rom. 16:25; 2 Cor 2:7; Eph. 3:3, 5, 9–10; Col. 1:26–7; 2:2–3).

It is in this sense that Rowe identifies Acts as "apocalyptic."[81] God's kingdom is an uncovering of cosmically legitimated social space. Though the term μυστήριον (mystery) is not a key term for Luke, such cosmic disclosure is essential to spatial re-envisioning in Luke-Acts. Indeed, Luke-Acts is a narrative entry into this mystery, as the reader is privy to the Spirit-inspired reformulations of power relationships based on cosmic imagination in the Magnificat and the Benedictus (1:46–55, 68–79), the juxtaposition of Jesus's birth in a manger to Caesar's census and Roman authority over space (2:1–7), the encounter of shepherds with angels who unveil the universe's true political and cosmological structure (2:8–20), the explanations of Jesus's teaching to

---

[79] Focusing on μυστήριον (mystery) might seem strange given both that the term occurs only once in Luke-Acts (Lk. 8:10) and that Luke has traditionally been understood to remove apocalyptic imagery (e.g., Richard A. Horsley, "The Kingdom of God and the Renewal of Israel: Synoptic Gospels, Jesus Movements, and Apocalypticism," in *The Origins of Apocalypticism in Judaism and Christianity*, ed. John J. Collins, vol. 1, *The Encyclopedia of Apocalypticism*, eds. Bernard McGinn, John J. Collins, and Stephen J. Stein (New York: Continuum, 1998), 1:339–41). Regarding apocalyptic imagery, this redaction-critical estimation depends on assessing omissions but often ignores the substance of what remains. Pertinent for our investigation is Luke's apparent parallel to Mk 1:15, Lk. 4:15. Horsley argues that Luke has de-apocalypticized Mk 1:15 because Luke has omitted any discussion of the time being fulfilled and God's kingdom having come near. Nevertheless, it is precisely this message that is encapsulated in Lk. 4:16–21. If anything, Luke expands on these notions. Further, Luke utilizes the exact or similar language as Mk 1:15 in Lk. 10:9, 11; 11:20. One must assume that Luke omitted the language of Mk 1:15 with a clear head, while simply missing the apocalyptic implications of Lk. 10:9, 11; 11:20, which seems improbable.

[80] My use of mystery (μυστήριον) corresponds more with Jewish apocalyptic than Hellenistic thought. I am interested in something like Dunn's definition, "the mystery of how the cosmos functions, and particularly of how God's purpose will achieve its predetermined end" (James D. G. Dunn, "Mystery," *NIDB* 4:185–7). Notice both the spatial and temporal elements linked to the ultimate grounding of reality. Similarly, Markus Bockmuehl notes occurrence of both "cosmological" and "eschatological" mysteries. These "mysteries" point to the mystery of God's kingdom and the ordering of time and space (*Revelation and Mystery in Ancient Judaism and Pauline Christianity*, WUNT 2/36 (Tübingen: Mohr Siebeck, 1990), 33–7).

[81] Rowe, *World*, 137.

his disciples (e.g., 8:9–10), a hindsight perspective on the disciples' incomprehension (9:45; 18:34; 22:24–7, 38), and the witness to the resurrection and ascension (24:1–53), to name only a few elements. These are disclosures of the way the world "really is." God's kingdom itself is a *mystery* being disclosed.

The church's social space is embedded in a cosmic-comprehensive conception of reality that surpasses it, in a mystery that longs to be grasped. The social reality of the people participating in God's kingdom is much like that of the relationship of the iconic signifier (church) to signified (kingdom), in which the signifier never fully coincides with but continuously pursues the signified.[82] At points at which they align or overlap, the church participates in the reality of the kingdom (the signified).[83] But, it is not simple correspondence. Rather, foundational cosmic space overcomes (φθάνω) from without the one who encounters and lives within it (11:20), as a man digging a channel is overtaken by a flow of water in its flooding (Homer, *Il.* 257–62). God's rule, God's active salvific action, comes into complex mundane space. Such an organization of space defies attempts to map, define, and homogenize place; rather, the church seeks continually to live within and be overtaken by this outside space (thirdspace). This is no isolated reality, but by living into this kingdom space, people, who exist across a multiplicity of spaces within the world, transform those spaces by being and doing according to kingdom space. Perhaps this is what the Didache implies in its use of the phrase, "the earthly mystery of the church" (μυστήριον κοσμικὸν ἐκκλησίας, 11:11).

This discussion of mystery (μυστήριον) is important because it defines the good news itself. It is not Roman good news or even of some zealous Jewish revolt, but of God's kingdom, of a cosmic reality to which Jesus and Luke-Acts attest. Jesus's message is not a social project in simple space, but a declaration of a mystery, the reality of God's kingdom, the reality of what is. He does not proclaim, "Imagine the world *as if* this were the case." Rather, Jesus's message is that *this is*, and that what *remains*, ultimately *is not*, being hollowed out by the changing of time ("today") and the proximity of such cosmic space.[84] This does not nullify the need for deliverance; it is, rather, grounded in deliverance's assurance. Nor does it leave one blind to world realities. Rather, the

---

[82] I am referring specifically to Charles Sanders Peirce's notion of an iconic sign: "An *Icon* is a sign that refers to the Object that it denotes merely by virtue of characters of its own, and which it possesses, just the same, whether any such Object actually exists or not" in (*Collected Papers of Charles Sanders Peirce*, 8 vols., eds. Charles Hartshorne and Paul Weiss (Cambridge, MA: Belknap, 1960), 2:247, also 276, 279, 282). This is distinguished from an indexical or symbolic sign.

[83] Bruce Chilton's description of God's kingdom in Jesus's teaching as "neither a sign that points only to one referent nor … a concept within a theological system, but … a symbol that conveys a reality without exhausting it" is helpful, though it is of course not simply a symbol but an alternate space of action (*Pure Kingdom: Jesus' Vision of God* (Grand Rapids: Eerdmans, 1996), 11; cf. Norman Perrin, *Jesus and the Language of the Kingdom: Symbol and Metaphor in New Testament Interpretation* (Philadelphia: Fortress, 1976)). It is important not to situate this reality in the plane of ideas but as an alternate space of being and social embedding. Further, the notion of icon leaves room for the multivalence of mystery (μυστήριον). The kingdom is inexhaustible and sought after, but the church itself becomes an iconic mystery that can be understood only by those with eyes to see and ears to hear (cf. *Did.* 11.11). Analogously, for Paul, to the world, the church and the cross are foolishness, and thus a μυστήριον that veils the μυστήριον of God's kingdom (1 Cor. 2:1, 7).

[84] Cf. Giorgio Agamben, *The Time That Remains: A Commentary on the Letter to the Romans* (Stanford: Stanford University Press, 2006), 59–87.

re-envisioning of complex space changes one's relationship to those realities through a cosmic imaging that simultaneously de-authorizes, for instance, Roman cosmic legitimation;[85] it de-authorizes the tacit assumptions of normal space in societies Jewish, Greek, Roman, and beyond.

3.4.3 Good News for the Poor

Not only is the good news that this reality *is*, but also that it is *for the poor* (6:20; cf. 14:15–24; 18:16–17). This is explicit throughout Luke where the poor receive special attention[86] and almsgiving functions as a primary sign of discipleship.[87] Centering of the poor typifies this restructured social space.

The OT generally presents the poor sympathetically.[88] There we find the development of legislation that portrays God as defender and protector of the poor (Exod. 22:24; 23:6, 10–11; Deut. 15:4). This portrayal undergirds Jubilee legislation and aids its conceptual development. However, as noted above, Jubilee legislation also develops ties to Israel's restoration, and one might imagine that the "poor" here is Israel needing redemption, and not the literal poor (cf., e.g., Isa. 54:11).[89] Such a conclusion becomes problematic when one considers incorporation of Isa. 58:6 in Lk. 4:18, a passage focusing on worship as socioeconomic action for the least, and especially if Luke views Christology through a wider Isaianic lens (e.g., Isa. 11:4–5), where a Davidic savior will bring justice for the poor and meek.

Considering the use of πτωχός (poor) in Luke (4:18; 6:20; 7:22; 14:13, 21; 16:20, 22; 18:22; 19:8; 21:3), Green rightly notes that poverty is more properly identified in terms of "status honor" than restricted to economic poverty.[90] The poor are "them" or "outsiders" that exist in "a social state that may or may not have economic roots."[91] Luke associates poverty with diverse conditions such as being hungry, mournful, hated, excluded, reviled, cast out (6:20–3), blind, lame, leprous, deaf, dead (7:22–3),

---

[85] Steve Walton, referring to the ascension, writes, "[Lukan] cosmology critiques the claimed place of Caesar in the Roman empire. Rather than Caesar being the one with universal jurisdiction and worthy of worship, Jesus should receive the highest honors" ("'The Heavens Opened': Cosmological and Theological Transformation in Luke and Acts," in *Cosmology and New Testament Theology*, LNTS 355 eds. Jonathan T. Pennington and Sean M. McDonough (London: T&T Clark, 2008), 71). Our concern emphasizes social-space produced without de-emphasizing this important Christological element.

[86] Lk. 4:18; 6:20; 7:22; 14:13, 21; 16:20, 22; 18:22; 19:8; 21:3.

[87] Lk. 11:41; 12:21, 23, 33; 14:33; 18:22; Acts 3:2–3, 10; 9:36; 10:2, 4, 31; 24:17. See Timothy W. Reardon, "Cleansing through Almsgiving in Luke-Acts: Purity, Cornelius, and the Translation of Acts 15:9," *CBQ* 78 (2016): 447–66. On Lk. 12:21 and almsgiving, see Joshua A. Noble, "'Rich toward God': Making Sense of Luke 12:21," *CBQ* 78 (2016): 302–20.

[88] An exception to the positive presentation of the poor can be found in the wisdom tradition, e.g., Prov. 6:6–11; 21:17; 23:21; Sir. 25:2; 40:28; 41:1–4.

[89] So David P. Seccombe, *Possessions and the Poor in Luke-Acts*, SNTSU B6 (Linz: Fuchs, 1983).

[90] Joel B. Green, "Good News to Whom? Jesus and the 'Poor' in the Gospel of Luke," in *Jesus of Nazareth: Lord and Christ: Essays on the Historical Jesus and New Testament Christology*, eds. Joel B. Green and Max Turner (Grand Rapids: Eerdmans, 1994), 64; idem, *Luke*, 211; idem, "Good News to the Poor: A Lukan Leitmotif," *RevExp* 111 (2014): 173–9.

[91] Green, "Whom," 60.

crippled (14:13, 21), and widowed (21:3). In Lk. 4:18-19, the poor are particularized as the captive, blind, and oppressed. The poor might additionally be those ostracized as sinners, tax collectors, or demoniacs. Poverty is a social reality.

The poor receive God's unmerited forgiveness and debt-cancelation (forgiveness) and are beneficiaries of God's justice and release, while the rich are condemned as those who oppress the poor and who achieve salvation through repentance and turning to God's economy.[92] This dichotomy is seen, for example, in the Sermon on the Plain (6:20-6), the Magnificat (1:51-3), the Parable of the Great Banquet (14:15-24), and the Parable of Lazarus (16:19-31) (see also 12:13-21; 14:7-11, 12-14; 16:1-14; 19:1-10). God's forgiveness is offered freely, but it requires repentance and conformity to new Jubilee era life and release for the poor.

The intimate connection between forgiveness and debt cancelation (Jubilee) is highlighted in Luke's Lord's prayer (11:2-4), where God's forgiveness is assumed only as a result of having forgiven all those indebted to the one praying (v. 4). Reconciliation with God assumes participation in a forgiveness/Jubilee economy. It is seemingly impossible then to separate personal forgiveness with God and the manifestation of the social extension of Jubilee release. Forgiveness is available, but one must accept its implications. Who will receive the Jubilee economy? For the poor, this declaration of release, of the Jubilee era and reorganized social space, is good news. For the rich, its message of divestment and reformation is difficult (18:22-3).

3.4.4 Summary

As we continue to argue for an embodied, holistic, and political soteriology, God's kingdom plays an important role as the spatial reality to which the world is reconciled. God's kingdom is a mystery, an *other* space, that all are invited into, though never grasped or contained within mundane space. It is a thirdspace, spatially near, calling the world and its structures into question and, simultaneously, being for the world, a spatial reality that threatens mal-ordered space and celebrates new possibilities and release for the poor. This space revolves around Jesus, who invites all to participate in this soteriological reality, manifesting it himself in his ministry and authoritative forgiveness.

3.5 Release to the Captives: Jesus's Forgiveness

Jesus's claim "to proclaim good news to the poor" is particularized in a series of infinitive clauses. Two of these clauses include statements of release (ἄφεσις): for the prisoner (αἰχμάλωτος) and the oppressed (τεθραυσμένος). These statements, in their Isaianic context, indicate physical release. Isaiah 61:1 speaks of Israel's redemption from exile as release for the prisoner (αἰχμάλωτος). In Isa. 58:6, the focus is on unjust socioeconomic realities within Israel. Israel is depicted as oppressing workers,

---

[92] Giambrone, *Charity*, 268-71, 281-2.

quarreling, and striking the lowly on days of fasting and Sabbath.[93] The prophecy, in turn, calls for social reformation in which injustice is rooted out, oppressive contracts are torn up, encumbering debts are forgiven, the oppressed and weakened are released from their toil, bread is shared with the hungry, the poor (πτωχός) are invited into homes, the naked are clothed, and families reunited (vv. 7-8). The victims of Israel's unjust social economy are the oppressed (οἱ τεθραυσμένοι). In terms of Lk. 4:18-19, though Isa. 61:1-2 already intimates a social economy defined by release and care for the poor, the incorporation of 58:6 makes this explicit. The juxtaposition of these two passages in Lk. 4:18-19 encourages one to see the announcement of release in Isa. 61:1-2, and in Jesus's "today" (Lk. 4:21), as the eschatological realization of the exhortations in 58:6-14.

Nevertheless, reference to physical release causes some difficulty when occurrences of ἄφεσις (release/forgiveness) are encountered elsewhere in Luke-Acts, where the consistent use of ἄφεσις for forgiveness of sins (ἄφεσις ἁμαρτιῶν) (Lk. 1:77; 3:3; 24:47; Acts 2:38; 5:31; 10:43; 13:38; 26:18) might lead to the conclusion that, as with the Benedictus, the apparently political language of Jesus's Nazareth sermon has been subjectively compartmentalized. However, this is not so.[94] We have dealt sufficiently with forgiveness of sins in Chapter 2, demonstrating that it does not require such a reductive move. Similarly, use of the verb ἀφίημι (forgive, release, permit) with reference to forgiving sins (5:17-26; 7:36-50; 11:1-4; 17:1-4) and Jesus's forgiveness from the cross (23:34) legitimates the production of social space defined by reciprocal forgiveness and social restoration, stemming from Jesus's unique authority to bring reconciliation and release.[95]

Considering Jesus's authority to forgive, let us consider 5:17-26. There, Jesus declares a paralyzed man's sins forgiven (v. 20), drawing ire from the gathered Pharisees and Sadducees who accuse Jesus of blasphemy (v. 21). Jesus emphasizes his distinct authority (ἐξουσία) to forgive sins (v. 24). There has been debate about what exactly Jesus is declaring and why the Pharisees and Scribes were upset (cf. Mt. 9:1-8; Mk 2:1-12). For many, Jesus, as an intermediate agent, declares that God has forgiven, by way of a divine passive (ἀφέωνται),[96] and that such declarations of forgiveness would not be uncommon from priests and/or prophets. This interpretation then explains Jesus's forgiveness as perhaps extraordinary but not beyond the pale, and certainly not blasphemous. However, in v. 24, where it reads "the Human One has

---

[93] The theme of Sabbath is more than sufficiently addressed in Luke. It is not incidental that the Jubilee message of 4:18-19 occurs on the Sabbath (v. 16). Jesus often heals on the Sabbath and is involved in debate on the nature of the Sabbath (4:31-41; 6:6-11; 13:10-17; 14:1-6). Note in particular Lk. 13:10-17 where Jesus does not simply argue that healing on the Sabbath is not work, but rather that the Sabbath requires (δεῖ) such restoration (v. 16). It simply cannot be maintained that there is no Sabbath theology in Luke.

[94] See Koet, *Studies*, 34-5; Sloan, *Favorable*, 119.

[95] The other occurrences of ἀφίημι generally refer to basic release, leaving, or permission and not forgiveness (Lk. 4:39; 5:11; 6:42; 8:51; 9:60; 10:30; 12:39; 13:8, 35; 17:34-5; 18:16, 28-9; 19:44; 21:6; Acts 5:38; 14:17), yet see also Lk. 12:10; Acts 8:22. The occurrences of "forgiveness of sins" (ἄφεσις ἁμαρτιῶν) also account for nearly every reference to sin (ἁμαρτία) in Luke-Acts (cf. Acts 22:16).

[96] Nolland, *Luke*, 1:235; L. T. Johnson, *Luke*, 93; Bock, *Luke*, 1:487; Green, *Luke*, 241; Bovon, *Luke*, 1:182.

authority on the earth to forgive (ἀφιέναι) sins," the divine passive disappears. Here, the language is quite specific. The authority is not to *announce* forgiveness, that is, acting as a mouthpiece for God's decision; rather Jesus's authority is *to forgive* sins, a not inconsequential distinction.[97]

Is this language common to priests and prophets? Both James Dunn and Crispin Fletcher-Louis assume that Jesus exemplifies a priestly prerogative, which, Dunn argues, explains the Pharisees' vexation at a perceived attack on the temple establishment.[98] Dunn clarifies that the prerogative for forgiveness remains with God, but to pronounce sins forgiven "was the prerogative of the priest."[99] Dunn's primary evidence is the passive affirmation of sin forgiveness found in the description of the priests making atonement in Leviticus (4:20, 26, 31, 35; 5:10, 13, 16, 18, 26; 19:22; cf. Num. 15:25, 28; Jer. 5:1). However, these passages each relate simply that a priest offers atonement and that the offender's sins are forgiven (ונסלח להם, it will be forgiven to him/her). Klaus Koch was first to argue that the passive forgiveness formula was to be pronounced by the priest when making the sacrifice; thus, the priest declares sins forgiven.[100] Nevertheless, several critics have shown this to be erroneous.[101] Not only do these verses not say anything about the priests making such a declaration, there are no extant Jewish sources from Jesus's time or earlier indicating, even where one would most expect it (e.g., *Ep. Arist.* 92–5), that a priest declares forgiveness or does anything more than offer atonement; and even this was done in silence.[102] Further, the Pharisees' response is not that only God can forgive through the priest and the temple institution, but that only God can forgive. Jesus's statement on forgiveness, especially v. 24, does not mirror a priestly prerogative.

---

[97] Wolter notes that the forgiveness is by God, but based on the words of Jesus (*Lukasevangelium*, 222). The distinction is slight. Jesus does not forgive sins, but God forgives them based on Jesus's direct agency. In explicating this dynamic, Wolter cites Jn 20:23 in which Jesus relates the disciples' forgiveness to forgiveness as in heaven (cf. Mt. 16:19; 18:18). Nevertheless, this distinction is not made in this passage.

[98] James D. G. Dunn, *The Parting of the Ways: Between Christianity and Judaism and Their Significance for the Character of Christianity* (London: SCM, 1992), 44–6, 175; Crispin H. T. Fletcher-Louis, "Jesus as the High Priestly Messiah," *JSHJ* 4 (2006): 155–75; 5 (2007): 57–79. See also Gerhard Friedrich, "Beobachtungen zur messianischen Hohepriestererwartung in den Synoptikern," *ZTK* 53 (1956): 265–311; William H. Brownlee, "Messianic Motifs of Qumran and The New Testament," *NTS* 3 (1956-7): 195–210; David H. Wenkel, "Jesus at Age 30: Further Evidence for Luke's Portrait of a Priestly Jesus?" *BTB* 44 (2014): 195–201.

[99] Dunn, *Parting*, 175.

[100] Klaus Koch, "Sühne und Sündenvergebung um die Wende von der exilischen zur nachexilischen Zeit," *EvT* 26 (1966): 217–39.

[101] Otfried Hofius, "Vergebungszuspruch und Vollmachtsfrage: Mk 2,1–12 und das Problem priesterlicher Absolution im antiken Judentum," in *"Wenn nicht jetzt, wann dann?" Aufsätze für Hans Joachim Kraus zum 65. Geburtstag*, eds. Hans-Georg Geyer, Johann Michael Schmidt and Werner Schneider (Neukirchen-Vleuyn: Neukirchener, 1983), 115–27; idem, "Jesu Zuspruch der Sündenvergebung: Exegetische Erwägungen zu Mk 2,5b," in *Neutestamentliche Studien*, WUNT 132 (Tübingen: Mohr Siebeck, 2000), 59–60; E. P. Sanders, *Judaism: Practice and Belief 63 BCE-66 CE* (London: SCM, 1992), 109; Tobias Hägerland, *Jesus and the Forgiveness of Sins: An Aspect of His Prophetic Mission*, SNTSMS 150 (Cambridge: Cambridge University Press, 2012), 133–42; Daniel Johansson, "'Who Can Forgive Sins but God Alone?' Human and Angelic Agents, and Divine Forgiveness in Early Judaism," *JSNT* 33 (2011): 351–74.

[102] See E. P. Sanders, *Judaism*, 80–1.

A prophetic paradigm has also been suggested.[103] Yet, the difficulty, again, is in finding a prophet who has been given the authority to forgive, not simply to declare what God has done. Tobias Hägerland, who sees this as the lone paradigm for Jesus's declaration, argues for an understanding of such prophetic authority from two specific passages, one often cited (2 Sam. 12:13) and one he believes to have been overlooked (Josephus, *Ant.* 6.92).[104] Conversely, Daniel Johansson critiques this conclusions, maintaining that there are no clear examples of any human figures authorized to forgive sins directly.[105] Concerning *Ant.* 6.92, the issue is whether God or Samuel is the subject of forgiveness (ἀφίημι). Johansson argues that the plain translation and context indicate that God is the subject. Samuel is merely asked to petition God for others. Later, Samuel even attempts to make intercession for Saul and fails to secure forgiveness (*Ant.* 6.142–54; cf. 1 Sam. 15:10–31). Similarly, 2 Sam. 12:13, does not demonstrate Nathan's authority to forgive, but merely his reporting of God's forgiveness to David. This leaves no clear evidence that prophets were given such authority.

Indeed, the scandalized response of the Pharisees and scribes in v. 21 seems to indicate that Jesus was doing something more controversial than what prophets are simply expected to do. Further, if the objection is that Jesus is not really an authorized prophetic representative, the objection should be, "Who can declare sins forgiven, other than a *prophet*?"[106] The question, "Who is this who speaks blasphemy?" (v. 21), straightforwardly indicates, at least the Pharisees and scribes believe, that what Jesus has done in v. 20 is something that only God can do (and not a prophetic mediator or a priest in the temple).

Contentions made about the divine passive are questionable. Despite the popularity of recognizing ἀφέωνται (have been forgiven) as a divine passive, such a determination is not as clear as one might imagine.[107] Not all agentless passives, of course, are divine passives. Agentless passives appear in a variety of contexts. One pragmatic effect of agentless passives is to draw attention to the action or the receiver of the action rather than the subject, even if the actor is understood. Thus, if one hears a news report, "Two men were arrested last night," though the agent is assumed (the police), the construct places emphasis on the receivers of the action and what is happening to them.

Daniel Wallace's discussion of the divine passive is somewhat circumspect though instructive.[108] He begins with the assumption that the divine passive is a distinct category of agentless passive, but then begins to waver. He notes, with little commitment to the idea, that such a phenomenon supposedly resulted from a reluctance to say the divine

---

[103] Green, *Luke*, 242; Sellner, *Heil*, 184.
[104] Hägerland, *Forgiveness*, 142–67.
[105] Johansson, "Forgive."
[106] So Hofius, "Zuspruch," 40–1.
[107] Though the *passivum divinum* has broadly served NT criticism since Jeremias's popularizing of the concept (*New Testament Theology* (London: SCM, 1971), 9–14), there are both questions in this context (Beniamin Pascut, "The So-Called *Passivum Divinum* in Mark's Gospel," *NovT* 54 (2012): 313–33) and regarding its status as a category in general (E. M. Sidebottom, "The So-called Divine Passive in the Gospel Tradition," *ExpTim* 87 (1976): 200–4; Peter-Ben Smit and Toon Renssen, "The *passivum divinum*: The Rise and Future Fall of an Imaginary Linguistic Phenomenon," *FN* 27 (2014): 3–24).
[108] Daniel B. Wallace, *Greek Grammar beyond the Basics: An Exegetical Syntax of the New Testament* (Grand Rapids: Zondervan, 1996), 435–8.

name, but then rejects Jeremias's supporting reasoning, finding that "such expressions are not due to any reticence on the part of the author to utter the name of God."[109] Reversing course, he suggests subsuming such occurrences of agentless passives with God as subject under other categories.

Certainly, ἀφέωνται in v. 20 is an agentless passive, but it is not clear that God is the implied subject, at least as Jeremias understands it to the exclusion of Jesus. The emphasis is on the man and his forgiveness declared by Jesus. Other determinations, however, might influence one's interpretation. One might assume a low Christology, one that could be deemed, for instance, more historical, and this would lead one to conclude that Jesus's action does not transcend that of prophet. Nevertheless, the context itself and Jesus's assumption of the authority to directly forgive in v. 24 prohibit this interpretation of v. 20. His authority (ἐξουσία) may derive from God, but it is authority to dispense forgiveness himself, not mediate it—an authority that appears unprecedented.

Indeed, the portrayal of Jesus's direct activity of forgiveness from heaven in Acts or the tying of forgiveness to "Jesus's name" only furthers this impression (Acts 2:38; 5:31; 10:43; 13:38; 26:18). He does not simply communicate or announce forgiveness; he is integral to its reality and its associated social production in mundane space. There is room here, then, for a combined affirmation of the "divine passive"—or, more properly, the agentless passive with God as subject—and Jesus's direct agency, in that this places both God and Jesus as the subject of ἀφέωνται, intimating a unique relationship and unity that could draw a blasphemy charge.[110] Indeed, when read through a Trinitarian lens, there is ample room for a legitimate interpretation in which Jesus places himself within the divine subject of ἀφέωνται.[111]

Rowe notes the central issue is that "Jesus is accused of placing himself alongside God, not simply charged with encroaching upon the prerogative of God."[112] Thus, the formula, distinct to Luke, within the Pharisees' question, "God alone" (μόνος ὁ θεός) alludes to a recurrent Jewish affirmation of God's uniqueness (e.g., 2 Sam. 19:15; Ps. 86[85]:10; 2 Macc. 7:37; Jn 5:44; *Ep. Arist.* 132; *Sib. Or.* 3.760).[113] An indirect "agent," as with 2 Sam. 12:13, does not threaten God's uniqueness. John, for instance, functions as such an agent, declaring God's turning and offering a means of atonement in repentance (Lk. 1:77; 3:3). John mediates by offering an atonement ritual *for* forgiveness, which is proper to the priest's role, not himself forgiving. In forgiving sins, Jesus does something unique. He is the bringer of forgiveness and Jubilee release.

---

[109] Wallace, *Greek*, 438. Jeremias asserted that the divine passive was a characteristic element of Jesus's speaking (*Theology*, 13–14); however, Wallace maintains that "θεός as nominative subject occurs *more frequently* when Jesus is the speaker than otherwise" (*Greek*, 438).

[110] This relationship is on display in Lk. 23:34. There, the sense of the imperative ἄφες is open. Is it a request or an assertion of authority within this special relationship? Answering that question requires context. Luke 5:17–26 would seem to indicate that this is an assertion of particular authority within Jesus's relation to the Father. Indeed, Jesus's imperative reaffirms Jesus's authority amid the ridicule of crucifixion.

[111] Jesus is inserted directly into the divine action so that his functioning is defined by that relation. Indeed, as Luke would have it, the Father is known only through the Son (10:22), and distinctly here, the Son is authorized only through the Father (5:24), who is then made known in forgiveness, and only through the Son.

[112] Rowe, *Christology*, 102.

[113] Rowe, *Christology*, 98–105.

Here is the key point. Jesus is the authoritative bringer of forgiveness/release (ἄφεσις), and, here, forgiveness and release are not separable. Forgiveness is instrumental in properly ordering space, and Jesus, as the divine agent of release/forgiveness, not only declares God's initiatory forgiveness freely given but restructures the order of the social world by that forgiveness. Jesus repeats this same formula, "your sins have been forgiven," to the woman at the Pharisee's house (7:36–50). Here it is clear that forgiveness comes to this woman out of divine largess, as an unmerited debt forgiveness (vv. 41–3), from which her response is gratitude and love.[114] The formula, your sins have been forgiven (v. 48), is socially productive. The woman's shame is overcome (cf. vv. 37, 39), rewriting her social place, centering her agency and virtue, and impacting her engagement with the social world. She is honored by Jesus and becomes the major beneficiary of an economy of forgiveness, finally told that her fidelity has saved her and to go in peace (v. 50).

This social reality defined by cosmic forgiveness is witnessed in Jesus's teaching to his disciples in 17:3–4. The disciples are told to rebuke those who have sinned, sin being what disturbs the proper order of space.[115] Yet, what defines this forgiveness-space is not complete perfection or the eradication of sin, but, rather, repentance, social concern, and the offer of forgiveness and care. This costly and reordering forgiveness, requiring repentance and placing responsibility on those who cause the "least" to stumble (vv. 1–2), produces and is the foundation for a social reality of Jubilee release. In Jesus is the confluence of what has been conceived separately as forgiveness of sins and Jubilee release. In this Jubilee era, holistic reconciliation and Jubilee social-spatial atonement emanate from Jesus, the unique authority of release/forgiveness (ἄφεσις), who properly orders space.

3.6 Recovery of Sight to the Blind: Apprehending the Mystery

In between references to release, Jesus also declares his mission to pronounce recovery of sight to the blind (τυφλοῖς ἀνάβλεψιν). This sight imagery is similar to the Benedictus's light imagery. In Isa. 42:7, in particular, the concepts parallel each other in describing release: "to open the eyes that are blind, to bring out the prisoners from the dungeon, from the prison those who sit in darkness" (cf. 42:18; 43:8). In Isa. 61:1, the LXX renders ולאסורים פקח קוח (and release to the prisoners) as τυφλοῖς ἀνάβλεψιν (recovery of sight to the blind), further supporting the sociopolitical reading of this sight language,[116] and emphasis at home in Lk. 4:18, surrounded by declarations of release.

---

[114] See Giambrone, *Charity*, 95–118. On the importance of debt terminology more generally, see G. A. Anderson, *Sin*.

[115] Luke does not define sin, present sin as a power, or explicitly state that humanity is universally under sin. Sin (ἁμαρτία) is almost always related to ἄφεσις/ἀφίημι (1:77; 3:3; 5:20–1, 23–4; 7:47–9; 11:4; 24:47; Acts 2:38; 5:31; 10:43; 13:38; 26:18). Exceptions include Acts 3:19 (ἐξαλείφω, wipe away; cf. Dan. 9:24, ἀπαλείφω), 7:60 (ἵστημι, stand/place), 22:16 (ἀπολούω, washed).

[116] See Shalom M. Paul, "Deutero-Isaiah and Cuneiform Royal Inscriptions," in *Essays in Memory of E. A. Speiser*, AOS 53 ed. W. W. Hallo (New Haven: American Oriental Society, 1968), 180–6, esp. 182; J. A. Sanders, "From," 49.

Nevertheless, proper vision in Luke-Acts includes and exceeds physical or sociopolitical phenomena (e.g., 2:30; 3:6). Sight, in Luke, functions similarly to how "knowledge" functions in Acts (2:36; 3:17; 8:30; 13:27, 38; 17:23, 30; 22:14; 28:28), with a concern for conceptual reformation (e.g., Lk. 9:28–36; 18:35–43; 24:31–2; Acts 9:18–19), or as Green puts it, "an opening of the mind to understand what was previously incomprehensible"[117] (Lk. 5:26; 12:54–7). Luke's appropriation of sight language directly relates to the concept of *mystery* already developed.

The continual culprits of incomprehension are the disciples (9:45; 18:34; 24:16, 31), despite the fact that they are those to whom "it has been given to know the mysteries" of God's kingdom (8:10). Part of their conceptual inability relates to the social economy within which their identity is shaped. Thus, for example, Joshua Strahan argues that the greatest inhibiting factor in understanding Jesus's passion predictions (9:43–5; 18:31–4; 22:14–23) is not incorrect data but an incorrect social framework within which to process this data, and in particular Strahan points to the disciples' understanding of "status and greatness."[118]

Proper vision requires not a new ideology or symbolic framework but a space of being and doing where sight is appropriated through discipleship, through imitation of Jesus (see, e.g., 6:39–49; 9:23–4; 14:27).[119] Such space can be stylized as a journey centered on following Jesus (5:11, 27–8; 7:9; 9:11, 23, 57, 59, 61; 18:22, 28, 43).[120] The relation of vision and discipleship is made explicit in the Sermon on the Plain (6:20–49). In 6:39–42, Jesus indicates that a person must pick their teacher wisely, for a disciple is not above her teacher, and the blind guide will only lead another blind person into a pit. Sight requires following the one who can see, Jesus, and putting into action what he says (vv. 46–9). Jesus is the *mystagogue*, guiding in kingdom practices, which are themselves revelatory. Cleopas and his companion in Lk. 24:13–35, for instance, though walking with Jesus, are unable to recognize him, not even in the exposition of Scripture (v. 27), until they practice hospitality and break bread together; only then are their eyes opened (vv. 30–1, 35; cf. 5:29–32; 9:10–17; 14:15; Acts 2:42).[121]

---

[117] Green, *Body*, 127. See also Dennis Hamm, "Sight to the Blind as Metaphor in Luke," *Bib* 67 (1986): 457–77.

[118] Joshua Marshall Strahan, *The Limits of a Text: Luke 23:34a as a Case Study in Theological Interpretation*, JTISup 5 (Winona Lake, IN: Eisenbrauns, 2012), 73. Strahan notes how Jesus's passion predictions are juxtaposed to the disciples' failure to grasp issues of status in kingdom social space (9:46–8; 18:39; 22:24–7).

[119] On Lukan discipleship, cf. Isak J. du Plessis, "Discipleship according to Luke's Gospel," *R&T* 2 (1995): 58–71; Dennis M. Sweetland, *Our Journey with Jesus: Discipleship according to Luke-Acts* (Collegeville, MN: Liturgical Press, 1990); idem, "The Journey of Discipleship in Luke," *TBT* 41 (2003): 277–82.

[120] On the journey metaphor in Luke-Acts, see Green, *Conversion*, 99–105.

[121] Cf. Green, *Luke*, 841–4; Arthur A. Just Jr., *The Ongoing Feast: Table Fellowship and Eschatology at Emmaus* (Collegeville, MN: Liturgical Press, 1993), 254–61; D. Brent Laytham, "Interpretation on the Way to Emmaus: Jesus Performs His Story," *JTI* 1 (2007): 101–15; Tannehill, *Unity*, 1:289–90. See also J. Bradley Chance, "The Journey to Emmaus: Insights on Scripture from Mystical Understandings of Attachment and Detachment," *PRSt* 38 (2011): 363–81.

Implicitly, imitation of Jesus, God's Son,[122] enables one to become God's child among a community of God's children (6:36; cf. 10:22), thus creating a social economy defined by mutual kinship with others and God (6:37–8). This journey extends with Jesus in solidarity and fidelity/obedience, practicing the kingdom even when threatened by state violence (exemplified by the cross) and the powers of death (14:27). One sees in this shared journey; one is saved in this solidarity (9:23–4).

Sight is enmeshed in a cosmic drama. The seventy(-two), for example, are told to rejoice at their return because their eyes have seen what many prophets and kings have wanted to see but did not (10:17–24). This "seeing" amounts to a cosmic revelation that corresponds to the eschatological era of release. Jesus recounts Satan falling from heaven like lightning (v. 18), which is directly related to the cosmic authority that Jesus imparts (v. 19) and is integral to the proclamation of the kingdom and peace (vv. 5, 9).

Many connect Jesus's saying here to Isa. 14:12.[123] The political elements of the passage from which this verse derives are important for understanding its relation to Jesus's words. Note that, in Isaiah, the specific reference is not to Satan, but to the king of Babylon (v. 4), the paradigmatic example of an oppressing king. Further, this is part of a taunt that the people will raise when they have conquered his oppression. Given what we know of the cosmic legitimation of worldly authority and the indelible association of worldly and cosmic powers in Luke (e.g., 4:6), it should not be too surprising that an allusion to the fall of the Babylonian king would be made in this context. Jesus's vision is a witness to God's kingdom conquering Satan's authority, though this revelation remains a mystery (10:21–4). Jesus's ministry establishes a kingdom that is opposed to mundane oppressive systems. To see Satan fall as lightning is surely not an abstract spiritual reality, and Jesus's continuous victory over the soldiers of this cosmic reality continues to support this notion that Jesus's kingdom is battling the evil forces of the world.[124]

This reality is summed up well in Acts 26:17–18. There, Paul relates his revelation from Jesus and how he is to go to the gentiles to "open their eyes." This eye-opening involves a transition from one space to another defined by light and darkness. If it was unclear that these light-based spaces are to be defined by cosmic rule, Paul explicitly clarifies that the transition is from Satan's power to God's power. In this transition, the gentiles receive "forgiveness of sins." Paul describes the incorporation of a political reality defined by its place within cosmic space. This cosmic space is understood dualistically, but the primary metaphor for the salvation imagined here is recovery of sight and is prefigured by Lk. 4:18. This recovery of sight is comparable to "knowledge" in the Irenaean scheme (*Haer.* 5.16.3, 21.2–3; *Epid.* 34). Acquiring knowledge is not so much the product of attaining information, but of (1) being freed from the (demonic) lies that shape one's world and (2) discipleship and fidelity to Jesus. Jesus will soon find that his audience in Nazareth will also not "see."

---

[122] Luke 1:32, 35; 2:49; 3:22; 3:38; 4:3, 9, 41; 8:28; 9:35; 22:70.

[123] Susan R. Garrett, *The Demise of the Devil: Magic and the Demonic in Luke's Writings* (Minneapolis: Fortress, 1989), 46–57; L. T. Johnson, *Luke*, 169; Green, *Luke*, 418.

[124] Lk. 4:33–6, 41; 6:18; 7:21; 8:2, 12, 26–39; 9:37–43, 49–50; 10:17–20; 11:14–26; 13:12, 16. This cosmic drama is further developed in Chapter 4.

The Nazareth scene is itself framed by demonic activity, Jesus's temptation (4:1–13) and Jesus's encounter with a demon-possessed man after leaving Nazareth (4:31–5). Given the proximity of Jesus's temptation scene, it would be appropriate to compare the Nazareth pericope to Jesus's temptation. Jesus has overcome the devil (*Haer.* 5.21.3), having recapitulated Israel's past, responding positively where it had failed,[125] and thusly is able to proclaim an alternate social-political vision (restoring Israel), a Jubilee time and space not beholden to the devil's authority (4:6). Nevertheless, his Jubilee message is rejected in Nazareth. Though Jesus has conquered the devil, it would not be wrong to see this audience as those still bound by the devil, disobedience, and the exploitative structures of the world, lacking "knowledge" and "sight." The demon encountered after Jesus leaves Nazareth (4:31–5) echoes what is, perhaps, implicit in the Nazareth crowd's response to Jesus, though the demon demonstrates deeper insight about Jesus's identity: "Let us alone! What have you to do with us (τί ἡμῖν καὶ σοί), Jesus of Nazareth? Have you come to destroy us [or our way of living!]? I know who you are, the Holy One of God" (4:34). The framing of the Nazareth pericope encourages us to see those in Nazareth as blinded by and submitting to demonic authority.

To summarize, the theme of sight permeates Luke's narrative, functioning at multiple levels. In particular, this discussion has noted the importance of elements integral as well to the Irenaean scheme, such as knowledge, discipleship, and cosmic bondage. Sight involves turning from darkness to light, from Satan's authority to God's (Acts 26:18). In this way, attaining sight is part of a cosmological conflict, overcoming Satan and finding freedom in conformity to God's purposes. Thus, in this theme, we see the importance of release from demonic bondage, but also how Lukan soteriology links demonic bondage with political and conceptual bondage. To see properly is to participate in the new era of Jubilee, which involves a comprehensive release.

3.7 The Lord's Acceptable Year: Jesus and Time

The final clause of Jesus's quotation situates the reader within a specific time, an eschatological era. Luke-Acts witnesses to the qualitative changing of time itself, characterized not by pure extension, but its relation to space, the imminent and impending kingdom, and the Christological journey. *Today* (σήμερον, v. 21) is the day of prophetic and Christological fulfillment (cf. 2:11; 5:26; 12:28; 13:32–3; 19:5, 9; 22:34, 61; 23:43). For Luke's audience, this announcement reverberates throughout their own conceptions of time, as Bovon maintains: "The σήμερον becomes 'today' for each hearer and reader to the extent that they rightly understand the proclamation."[126] Compare this Lukan *today* with Mk 1:14–15, where Jesus preaches the gospel (εὐαγγέλιον) of God, claiming that the time has been fulfilled (πεπλήρωται ὁ καιρός) and the kingdom of God has drawn near (ἤγγικεν; cf. Lk. 10:9, 11; 11:20). In Mark, the

---

[125] Green, *Luke*, 192–3; L. T. Johnson, *Luke*, 76; Marshall, *Luke*, 166–7; David B. Sloan, "Interpreting Scripture with Satan? The Devil's Use of Scripture in Luke's Temptation Narrative," *TynBul* 66 (2015): 231–50.

[126] Bovon, *Luke*, 1:154.

qualitative feature of this time is the kingdom's spatial nearness. Similarly, Luke's time is infused with the kingdom's spatial nearness in Jesus's preaching. Luke's expectation is, however, more developed, elaborating on this nearness in terms of Jubilee and Christocentric orientation.[127] In Jesus, salvation and God's kingdom concerns the nearness of a heavenly derived and ordered field of power influencing the organization of mundane space.

This is a new era within complex space and time. As Karl Barth describes the era of the church as a period of grace in which the time of Christ, the eternal lasting time that becomes manifest in the incarnation, persists with other fallen times, so also this time exists as what Barth calls "the time between," or, similarly, what Giorgio Agamben calls the "time that remains."[128] Yet, this proclamation places particular emphasis on fulfillment, the reality of this space that changes the color of time itself. This spatial relationship to time is important. This is not "as if" time, imagining how things can be and pushing progressively forward.[129] Rather, this time *is* because this spatial reality *is*, though, in God's grace, it simultaneously holds back (13:6–9). This is the Lord's acceptable year (ἐνιαυτὸν κυρίου δεκτόν), an eschatological era ordering space in terms of Jubilee release,[130] where Jubilee release emanates from Jesus outward. Jesus's forgiveness is representative of an eschatological turning point inaugurated by God's own turning to *accept* Israel (cf. Isa. 49:8–13).[131]

This time is not one of totalizing simple space. Here, Barth's time of God's grace remains pertinent. The spatial reality *is*, and God's kingdom *is near*, but it is not totalizing. For now, this time remains one simultaneously of participation and anticipation (12:35–50). Though our passage focuses on *today*, reference to the coming complete instantiation of God's kingdom and the upheaval associated with its impending judgment (and just-making/rectifying) has not thus far been absent (3:7–9), and it will continue to be emphasized (e.g., 10:14; 13:6–8; Acts 3:20–1; 17:31). Indeed, the "present evil generation" remains, if also a passing reality (Lk. 7:31; 17:25; Acts 2:40). Even with Jesus's crucifixion, the *today* is not pushed to the future as if the crucifixion defeated the original hope of the *today*;[132] it is not revoked as if the *today* depended on human action. Indeed, *today* hope is victorious even in crucifixion (23:43). The church lives into this *today* in the present, and the spatial nearness of the kingdom that the church participates in is not subverted by Jesus's death; rather, the crucifixion, resurrection, and ascension only defeat the best attempts of authority under Satan's control to stave off God's kingdom.

Conzelmann's claims about Luke's delay of the Parousia projected an austere time of disappointment in which hope merely encourages capitulation to mundane reality

---

[127] On this Christocentric orientation, see Strauss, *Messiah*, 218.
[128] Karl Barth, *The Doctrine of Reconciliation*, vol. 4.1 of *Church Dogmatics*, eds. G. W. Bromiley and T. F. Torrance, trans. G. W. Bromiley (Peabody, MA: Hendrickson, 2010), §62.3; Agamben, *Time*, 59–87. See also Andrew Burgess, *The Ascension in Karl Barth* (London: Routledge, 2004), 53–73.
[129] On the notion of "as if" time versus "as not" time, see Agamben, *Time*, 35–42.
[130] Pao, *Exodus*, 74; Hanks, *God*, 103; Danker, *Luke*, 59; Sloan, *Favorable*, 35.
[131] Bovon, *Luke*, 1:154.
[132] Cf. Robert C. Tannehill, "Israel in Luke-Acts: A Tragic Story," *JBL* 104 (1984): 69–85.

while waiting for eternal life. Nevertheless, as Carroll has argued, for Luke, now is the time of imminent and unpredictable expectation.[133] It is this time that influences the makeup of space in Luke-Acts. Indeed, the temporal expectation and the spatial nearness of the kingdom implicate a telos, but it does not function simply to foster speculation and docility; rather, it "reconfigures those who permit themselves to be drawn by it."[134] The spatial reality of God's kingdom is *now*, though waiting to unite creation and kingdom. In this complex reality, the church lives within multiple spaces. The space produced by participation in the kingdom permeates, influences, and disseminates within complex space, spread by the church's existence in multiple spaces. Living into the kingdom changes the space around it. Yet, simultaneously, the cosmic reality of the kingdom hollows out other authoritative spaces of their significance, leaving those spaces open for use.

A couple of examples are worth mentioning. First is Paul's invocation of Roman citizenship in Acts (16:37; 22:28). Though Paul on two occasions invokes his Roman citizenship, this appears only strategic since elsewhere he specifically mentions only his Jewish lineage (e.g., 22:3). Paul exists within Roman space, though utilizing it for the manifestation of God's kingdom. Such utilization relates somewhat to Agamben's notion of living in the world "as not," utilizing but hollowing out the time of the world (which Agamben relates to the time of domination, acquisition, and capitalism).[135]

We might read Jesus's teaching on paying taxes to Caesar in terms of the "as not" as well (20:20-6). Refusing to choose between revolt and allegiance, Jesus instead advocates giving to God the things that are God's and to Caesar the things that are Caesar's. Here, Caesar makes a demand on the things of his space, and existence within that space demands the payment of taxes. When queried on the matter, Jesus does not advocate open revolt; rather, he hollows out the authority and reality of Caesar's authoritative space itself. The coin for this tax, a denarius (v. 24), containing Caesar's image, represents idolatry, and the false creations of such space are to be given back to Caesar.[136] It is well recognized that Jews had an aversion to images,[137] but these images represented a distinct power within Greco-Roman society as well. Clifford Ando notes, "Roman law's insistence on the sacrosanctity of the imperial portrait had its counterpart in the popular belief that imperial portraits were numinous, that they somehow shared in and were animated by that 'double in another sphere of being' that connected the emperor to forms of existence beyond the human and to regions beyond himself."[138] Indeed, a coin with the emperor's image was so sacrosanct it was illegal to take these coins into bathrooms or brothels (Seutonius, *Tib.* 58). Philostratus even recounts a

---

[133] Carroll, *Response*.
[134] Paul J. Griffiths, "The Cross as the Fulcrum of Politics: Expropriating Agamben on Paul," in *Paul, Philosophy, and the Theopolitical Vision: Critical Engagements with Agamben, Badiou, Žižek, and Others*, ed. Douglas Harink (Eugene, OR: Cascade, 2010), 187. This quotation concerns Agamben's assessment of Pauline time, though it relates to our context as well.
[135] Agamben, *Time*, 19-34.
[136] On the power of images in the Roman Empire, see Zanker, *Images*; Ando, *Ideology*, 206-73.
[137] See Paul Corby Finney, "The Rabbi and the Coin Portrait (Mk 12:15b, 16): Rigorism Manqué," *JBL* 112 (1993): 629-44.
[138] Ando, *Ideology*, 369.

story of a slave owner charged with impiety (ἀσέβεια, a serious offense) after beating his slave with a coin bearing Tiberius's image in the slave's pocket (*Vit. Apoll.* 1.15). These ubiquitous coins represented a dispersion of power tied to numinous veneration of the emperor, solidifying the emperor's place within a hierarchical cosmic space.

Jesus's response, which has often been understood to distinguish neatly delineated religious and political spheres (sacred and secular), serves, rather, to redefine space. Give the idolatrous coins back to Caesar, and give back that which belongs to God, which is certainly all creation. The use of the verb ἀποδίδωμι (give back) is important. Bovon notes that the coin itself represented and even brought with it submission to Rome, but Jesus's response, with its use of ἀποδίδωμι rather than simply δίδωμι (give), represents a sort of dis-integration from Roman authority.[139] It is preferable to conceptualize this action as a hollowing out of those spaces (i.e., Roman authoritative space); it is not a separation from that space but a reformulation of existence within complex space. Jesus's words hollow out the space and social/cosmic construction represented by the denarius, and, by extension, the authority of Caesar, without trivializing the weight experienced by those under Roman *imperium*. In the context of Luke-Acts, both the proximity of the kingdom and the shape of time legitimate this strategy. Indeed, where Caesar demands the idolatrous products of his space, he can take them; where, however, such unjust mammon (τοῦ μαμωνᾶ τῆς ἀδικίας, 16:9) can be utilized to make friends and eternal dwellings (τὰς αἰωνίους σκηνάς) (i.e., the production of space that participates in God's kingdom), do so (16:1–13).

The shape of time and space itself, as we have seen in Jesus's opening vision, impacts the makeup of social space and the life of the church and how it relates to and functions within the world. The focus is not on some future detached time, but on a reality that finds implementation now. Jesus announces that today that time has come and it is the acceptable year of the Lord, an eschatological Jubilee era.

3.8 Conclusion

In Lk. 4:16–30, the Davidic king promised in the Benedictus arrives in Nazareth to proclaim release from captivity, yet he does not advocate violent revolt as a means of liberation; he proclaims the reality of God's kingdom and Jubilee release; he declares it present, inviting all to share in this kingdom *today*. The *beginning* of Luke's soteriological narrative expressed here echoes the themes of Luke's early chapters— Israel's restoration, concern for the poor, and holistic embodied release (cf. 1:53–4). The *end* toward which this salvation moves is a spatial reorganization commensurate with an eschatological Jubilee era.

Jubilee is important for this scheme because Jubilee, more than simply a socioeconomic addendum to Israel's life, conceptualizes a social-spatial extension of atonement. Indeed, as with our Irenaean *Christus Victor* scheme, there is a focus on

---

[139] Bovon, *Luke*, 3:54.

release and restoration, not exactitude in balanced reciprocity. That is, the focus is not on affecting God, and there is no payment, restitution, or equivalence given to restore the balance of God's honor or the demands of justice for past disobedience. Instead, atonement comes as God's activity *for* the world in reordering mal-ordered (bound-by-Satan) realities and space, establishing God's justness in the world and among people (and for the poor) through a cosmic-comprehensive and social-political salvation. Release and justness comes in deliverance from economic, social, and demonic enslavement (mal-ordering) and reconciliation of the world to God's kingdom. This is a comprehensive salvation that reshapes both the time and space that God's people occupy. Forgiveness, in this scheme, is not simply a declaration of personal absolution. Rather, forgiveness is a social reality requiring repentance and responsive participation, manifesting a reordered existence. Thus, satisfaction of God's justice comes not through affecting God, but God's being in Jesus reconciling the world to God, God's justness, and God's kingdom.

This kingdom is not simply a socially constructed or imposed reality; rather, Jesus declares that it already is. It has come (spatially) near. It is a *mystery* in proximity within which Jesus calls his followers to share. Partaking in this kingdom space requires repentance, guidance, discipleship, and fidelity to God. Here, we find further emphasis on the importance of obedience, knowledge, and the imitation of Jesus found in our Irenaean scheme. Jesus comes as the *mystagogue* to teach the people to walk the way of discipleship, true knowledge, and peace (cf. 1:78–9) and to truly *see*, so that "recovery of sight" is part of release from bondage to deceptive and demonic mal-ordered realities. Overcoming that bondage requires *knowledge* and *sight* that is not primarily cognitive but comes through participating in kingdom practices and discipleship.

Jesus's narrative moves forward dethroning Satan. Jesus comes to Nazareth, having already conquered, through fidelity to God, the temptations of the devil, who holds authority over the world's kingdoms. Thus, Jesus is uniquely able to declare an *other* kingdom, reconciled to God and not bound to demonic idolatry. This cosmic drama is further developed in Chapter 4. Here, release is defined as more than just liberation from worldly political powers and social realities; it simultaneously involves freedom from cosmic oppression.

God visits, in Jesus, to bring release, overcoming the worldly kingdoms and social-economies of oppression under Satan's authority. Liberation comes through discipleship; fidelity to God; deconstructing ideologies of injustice and exploitation; and participating in an *other*, ultimately enduring and victorious, personal, social-political, and cosmic reality. The economy of God's kingdom is not characterized by domination, violence, and exploitation, but the way of peace and persuasion. Salvation involves sharing in new life together in the theopolitical body of God's kingdom, centered around Jesus, in fidelity to God. However, Jesus's path also leads through the cross, resulting in both his death and cosmic enthronement, matters taken up in.

4

Heaven Invading: The Holy Spirit, Church, and Salvific Space (Acts 2)

Thus far, Luke's salvation narrative has emphasized God's gracious invitation, turning to offer forgiveness, reconciliation, and holistic release from oppression and blindness (Lk. 4:18–19); however, we were also prepared for opposition (2:34–5; 4:28–30). Chapter 3 concerned Jesus's inaugural pronouncement of the Jubilee era. Yet, as we come to Acts, Jesus's invitation to join in God's kingdom has largely been rejected. On the road to Emmaus, Jesus's crucifixion demonstrates to Cleopas and his companion that Jesus's mission was a failure (24:19–21), exposing their blindness. Nevertheless, they come to understand that Jesus and the kingdom are victorious—that is, their eyes are opened—by participating in kingdom practices. The kingdom has not been thwarted. How will it be fully realized? This is where we find ourselves at the beginning of Acts.

This chapter continues to focus on salvation's spatial manifestation, conceptualizing it now in relation to an enthroned king and communities empowered by the Spirit. This chapter proceeds in four parts. The first two concern cosmic-comprehensive and social-political space. Regarding cosmic-comprehensive space, I focus on heaven, Jesus's ascent, and the Spirit's descent (or outpouring). With respect to social-political space, attention is given to Jerusalem, Luke's mapping (2:9–11), and, in the first part, the missional trajectory that unfolds under heaven. The third part attends specifically to Peter's Pentecost address. Finally, the fourth part shows the effect of the Spirit's arrival in the church's response and participation in soteriological space.

The cosmic victory of the crucified Christ makes clear the order of the world. God's gracious invitation through forgiveness is to enter into this kingdom, to be baptized, turning from former allegiances, to align under Jesus's authority, joining the community of those "being saved" (2:47). This is the story of Israel's victorious king, in whom God is reconciling the world to God's self and sending the Spirit as heaven (God's domain) invading mundane space. The *end* of salvation, then, is the reconciliation of heaven and earth, the times of refreshment from the Lord,[1] an anticipation of "universal

---

[1] The sense of "times of refreshment" (καιροὶ ἀναψύξεως) is unclear. Hans F. Beyer argues that καιροὶ ἀναψύξεως refers to "any divine intervention ... which would relieve and refresh from the world's burdens ... as a result of repentance and forgiveness of sins" ("Christ-centered Eschatology in Acts 3:17–26," in *Jesus of Nazareth: Lord and Christ: Essays on the Historical Jesus and New Testament Christology*, eds. Joel B. Green and Max Turner (Grand Rapids: Eerdmans, 1994), 245–9). Beyer

restoration" (ἀποκατάστασις, 3:19–21; cf. Eph. 1:10).² This is a picture of a cosmic atonement through the victorious Christ, made manifest within mundane space.

4.1 Heaven and Cosmic-Comprehensive Space (Acts 2:1–4)

The Pentecost event opens in Acts 2:1–4 with the Spirit being poured out in fiery tongues on some 120 women and men (1:15) waiting covertly for the Father's promise. The event is a dramatic cosmic revelation. The sound of a "mighty wind" comes from heaven. This "from heaven" is important. The reader is confronted with the cosmic-comprehensive space within which this narrative unfolds. As the wilderness, a boundary space, threatened the stability of normalized order, so too the Spirit's invasion offers a similar threat, a disruption testified to throughout Acts.³ As Steve Walton writes, the Spirit's descent is "heaven invading earth."⁴ The focus on heaven, however, is not new, being informed by Jesus's ascension in 1:9–11. This section focuses on the presentation of cosmic space that prepares for the Spirit's arrival and its connection to Luke-Acts' salvation narrative.

4.1.1 Heavenly Orientation and the Ascension

Heaven, as Matthew Sleeman has aptly demonstrated, functions as thirdspace within Acts, exercising "an unceasing influence over the whole narrative and its theology."⁵ The Spirit invades from heaven (ἐκ τοῦ οὐρανοῦ, 2:2) and witnesses to "all the nations under heaven" (ὑπὸ τὸν οὐρανόν, 2:5; cf. 4:12). Heaven orients Acts' world, much as we saw with God's kingdom, governing and influencing, though not wholly accessible. It discloses, while remaining hidden. Nevertheless, this thirdspace is part of cosmic-comprehensive space, and, as an object of orientation—that is, as an object that demands attention and influences one's view of all other things—it guides the

---

argues that both refreshment and restoration, though tied to the Parousia, also concern present events (e.g., Acts 3:13). See similarly Göran Lennartsson, "Refreshing & Restoration: Two Eschatological Motifs in Acts 3:19–21" (PhD diss., Lund University, 2007).

2   Restoration (ἀποκατάστασις) need not be punctiliar. The sense of ἀποκατάστασις is moving into proper order (see Ilaria L. E. Ramelli, *The Christian Doctrine of Apokatastasis: A Critical Assessment from the New Testament to Eriugena*, VCSup 120 (Leiden: Brill, 2013), 1–10). The term ἀποκατάστασις was used astronomically of an orbit or return to proper order or alignment (Geminus, *Astr.* 18.1–3, 10, 18), medically to refer to restoration to health (Hippocrates, *Artic.* 30.38), and in Stoic thought of a cosmic cycle (SVF 2.599, 625). Hellenistic Jewish use is particularly interesting. Though Philo utilized ἀποκατάστασις for spiritual restoration (*Rev. Div. Her.* 293), he also uses it for Jubilee legislation (*Dec.* 164). Josephus uses it for return from exile (*Ant.* 11.63; cf. *Ep. Arist.* 123.4). On the Jubilee sense of Acts 3:19–21, see K. Stalder, "Der Heilige Geist in der lukanischen Ekklesiologie," *US* 30 (1975): 287–93.

3   E.g., Acts 4:1–31; 5:17–42; 6:8–15; 7:54–8:1; 9:23–5, 28; 12:1–2; 13:44–6, 50; 14:5, 19; 16:16–24; 17:1–8; 18:12–17; 19:23–41; 21:27–8.

4   Walton, "Heavens," 68.

5   Sleeman, *Geography*, 257. See also idem, "The Ascension and Spatial Theory," in *Ascent into Heaven in Luke-Acts: New Explorations of Luke's Narrative Hinge*, eds. David K. Bryan and David W. Pao (Minneapolis: Fortress, 2016), 157–74.

shaping of and participation in social-political space. For the model reader, heaven, in its authority, rightfully ought to determine the order of the world.[6]

Early in Acts, heaven and Jesus are reciprocally defining. Jesus's exaltation to God's right hand (1:9–11; 2:33; 5:31; 7:55) within heaven confirms his authority and legitimates Jesus's kingdom vision, simultaneously defining heaven in terms of this ethical vision. Heaven legitimates Jesus's authority; Jesus explicates what structure heaven authorizes. All nations, whether they recognize it or not, are under *this* heaven (2:5; 4:21), which is defined by *this* Jesus. This mutual association is emphatically presented in 1:10–11 where οὐρανός (heaven) is repeated, somewhat inelegantly, four times (cf. Lk. 24:51). After Jesus ascends, the disciples remain staring *into heaven* (εἰς τὸν οὐρανόν), when two men wearing white appear, asking why the disciples are staring *into heaven* since this Jesus who ascended *into heaven* will come back the same way that he went *into heaven*.

Heaven is now characterized by Jesus's presence, and Jesus by heaven. Nevertheless, the import of this assertion depends on how heaven is conceived within cosmic-comprehensive space. For some, the dynamic here is one of separation and absence. Heaven is where Jesus goes "off stage," leaving us with an "absentee Christology."[7] Yet, others have argued that Jesus remains active through direct guidance, his name, his Spirit, and so on, and have taken issue with the passive implications of "absentee Christology."[8]

Some confusion results from conceiving of heaven as a simple geographic location to which Jesus goes, usually within a three-tiered universe (heaven-earth-hell), assuming a naïve cosmology. Simultaneously, there is a modern tendency to assume simple, flattened space while requiring spiritual or metaphysical space to be distinctly

---

[6] See David K. Bryan, "A Revised Cosmic Hierarchy Revealed: Apocalyptic Literature and Jesus's Ascent in Luke's Gospel," in *Ascent into Heaven in Luke-Acts: New Explorations of Luke's Narrative Hinge*, eds. David K. Bryan and David W. Pao (Minneapolis: Fortress, 2016), 61–82.

[7] The phrase "absentee Christology" is generally attributed to C. F. D. Moule ("The Christology of Acts," in *Studies in Luke-Acts: Essays Presented in Honor of Paul Schubert*, eds. Leander E. Keck and J. Louis Martyn (Nashville: Abingdon, 1966), 179–80), but see also Conzelmann (*Theology*, 186) and Haenchen (*Acts*, 151–2). More recently, an absentee Christology has been argued by Arie W. Zwiep (*The Ascension of the Messiah in Lukan Christology*, NovTSup 87 (Leiden: Brill, 1977); idem, "Assumptus est in caelum: Rapture and Heavenly Exaltation in Early Judaism and Luke-Acts," in *Christ, the Spirit and the Community of God*, WUNT 2/293 (Tübingen: Mohr Siebeck, 2010), 38–67.

[8] Most recently, see the helpful synopsis by Steve Walton, "Jesus, Present and/or Absent? The Presence and Presentation of Jesus as a Character in the Book of Acts," in *Characters and Characterization in Luke-Acts*, eds. Frank E. Dicken and Julia A. Snyder, LNTS 548 (London: Bloomsbury T&T Clark, 2016), 123–40. See also the sources in Robert F. O'Toole, "Activity of the Risen Jesus in Luke-Acts," *Bib* 62 (1981): 471–98; Steve Walton, "Ascension," in *Dictionary of Jesus and the Gospels*, 2nd ed., eds. Joel B. Green, Jeannine K. Brown, and Nicholas Perrin (Downers Grove, IL: InterVarsity Press, 2013), 61. Responding to criticism about Jesus's inactivity in his assessment, Zwiep asserts that he affirms only the "bodily" absence of Jesus who still remains active ("Assumptus," 67). His monograph, however, is ambiguous. He notes that the rapture Christology he associates with the ascension is dominated by both physical absence and the "present inactivity of the exalted Lord," though later referring to Jesus's "active though distant rulership" (*Ascension*, 182, 198). See also Zwiep's response to Sleeman: "Ascension Scholarship," in *Ascent into Heaven in Luke-Acts: New Explorations of Luke's Narrative Hinge*, eds. David K. Bryan and David W. Pao (Minneapolis: Fortress, 2016), 18.

separate from material or physical space.⁹ This can exacerbate the temporal separation between Jesus and the present, pushing Jesus's return to the indeterminate future and leaving only persistence in the Spirit for those remaining.

Nevertheless, heaven, in ancient cosmology, rather than a compartmentalized other space, is intimately related to mundane space. Heaven and earth, which are cited in tandem by Luke to note the totality of existence (Lk. 10:21; 12:56; Acts 4:24; 14:15; 17:24), are not disconnected realms; they are "parallel and interlocking universes inhabited by the creator god on the one hand and humans on the other."¹⁰ Heaven and earth form a cosmological whole, so that the structure of heaven impacts the structure of earth. That is, one's understanding of her embeddedness within a cosmic-comprehensive space in which heaven is the seat of God's authority (Lk. 3:22; 11:13, 15; 15:18, 21; 18:13; Acts 7:49, 55–6; cf. Lk. 9:54; 11:16; 17:29) impacts how one understands and participates in mundane space.

Heaven is not a simple spatial container. It is a space of significance that interacts with, forms, and is in tension with the mundane world. Often, in Luke-Acts, heaven is the source of disclosure giving prominence to the metaphor of vision (Lk. 2:25; Acts 9:3; 10:11, 16; 11:5, 9–10; 22:6; see Chapter 3). The explicit tie between heavenly disclosures and proper sight reveals heaven as a source of true vision. Heavenly orientation does not focus simply on "spiritual," subjective, or personal realities; it discloses the "proper" ordering of the world. Heaven does not bring focus on *another* world but on the true nature of *this* world.¹¹

Still, mundane and heavenly space remain distinct, if only because heaven is the location of God (Lk. 10:21; 11:13; Acts 7:55–6), who by virtue of God's own holiness is distinct from the world. Yet, this distinction is maintained by an ordering tension, the same tension apparent between God's kingdom and the world, a tension typified in Jesus's crucifixion (cf. Acts 5:29–32).¹² Heaven is a space that both forms and repels, an *other* space characterized by its tensive and transformational social ordering disclosed in Jesus's ministry and legitimated by Jesus's resurrection and ascension. Jesus appeals to heaven as a locus of other-ordering in legitimating his ethic (Lk. 6:23; 10:21; 12:33; 18:22). The centering of the poor, hungry, weeping, and persecuted is assured because heaven's ordering is more authoritative than the ordering of worldly social-political space.¹³

---

⁹ See Milbank, "Space," 275.
¹⁰ N. T. Wright, *The Resurrection of the Son of God*, vol. 3 of *Christian Origins and the Question of God* (Minneapolis: Fortress, 2003), 655.
¹¹ Note the sight language in Acts 1:10–11: Jesus is taken from their *sight* "while staring" (ἀτενίζω), and they will *see* Jesus return the way he left.
¹² See Timothy W. Reardon, "'Hanging on a Tree': Deuteronomy 21.22–23 and the Rhetoric of Jesus' Crucifixion in Acts 5.12–42," *JSNT* 37 (2015): 407–31.
¹³ Note the tendency to present heaven as "opening" and disclosing or descending into mundane space, e.g., Lk. 3:21–2; Acts 7:56. On the narrative movement from disorder to cosmic order, see Charles Anderson, "Lukan Cosmology and the Ascension," in *Ascent into Heaven in Luke-Acts: New Explorations of Luke's Narrative Hinge*, eds. David K. Bryan and David W. Pao (Minneapolis: Fortress, 2016), 175–212.

Heaven, the location of God's throne (Lk. 7:49, 55–6; cf. Isa. 66:1–2). is authoritative. So, the prodigal son confesses that he has sinned against heaven (15:18, 21) or Jesus asks the Pharisees in their dispute over authority whether John's baptism derived from heaven or human beings (20:4–5). Further, this heavenly authority is tied to space in the metaphor of verticality,[14] "up" signifying authority, power, blessing, and honor. Thus, Jesus breaks bread and lifts his eyes to heaven (Lk. 9:16; cf. 18:13), or God is called Most High (Lk. 1:32, 35, 76; 6:35; 8:28).[15] The narration of Jesus's ascension utilizes this spatial significance to characterize Jesus's relation to both mundane and heavenly reality.[16]

This space, then, which Jesus occupies, is not simply where God happens to be located; it is space produced, so to speak, by God's habitation, God's throne, and tension and interaction with mundane space, a tension that calls the mundane world to account and exhorts transformation and reordering. Heaven is the imposing sphere that brings release, and salvific reordering, and the place of Jesus's ascension to God's right hand (Acts 2:34; 7:55–6; cf. Ps. 110:1), the Davidide, who proclaims God's kingdom, Jubilee era, and was crucified by the prevailing authorities.

4.1.2 The Cosmic Drama, the Cross, and the Davidide's Victory

Though heaven is a place of disclosure and authority, it is not static. It is a dynamic space of cosmic struggle. Understanding Lukan soteriology and its theopolitical implications requires grasping how this cosmic drama unfolds throughout Jesus's life, death, and resurrection. One place where this drama is particularly notable is Luke 10, where, after the seventy(-two) return from preaching the kingdom, healing, and exorcising demons, Jesus claims to have seen Satan falling from heaven as lightning (v. 18).[17]

---

[14] George Lakoff and Mark Johnson, *Metaphors We Live By* (Chicago: University of Chicago Press, 1980), 14–21; Joel B. Green, "'He Ascended into Heaven': Jesus' Ascension in Lukan Perspective, and Beyond," in *Ears That Hear: Explorations in Theological Interpretation of the Bible*, eds. Joel B. Green and Tim Meadowcroft (Sheffield: Sheffield Phoenix, 2013), 147–8.

[15] The verticality metaphor's pervasiveness can be seen both in discussions of heaven and general assertions of honor, authority, social ordering, and so on. See, e.g., table-seating and honor (Lk. 14:7–10; cf. 20:46), submissiveness through lowering one's body position (5:8; 8:35; 10:39; 17:15; 22:41), and God's social reordering by raising and lowering in the Magnificat (1:52–3; cf. 3:4–6; 14:11; 18:14; Isa. 4:3–5).

[16] On background, form, and reliance on other traditions, such as Elijah's ascension (2 Kgs 2:1–12), see Andy Johnson, "Resurrection, Ascension, and the Developing Portrait of the God of Israel in Acts," *SJT* 57 (2004): 146–62; Steve Walton, "Jesus's Ascension through Old Testament Narrative Traditions," in *Ascent into Heaven in Luke-Acts: New Explorations of Luke's Narrative Hinge*, eds. David K. Bryan and David W. Pao (Minneapolis: Fortress, 2016), 31–9; Gerhard Lohfink, *Die Himmelfahrt Jesu: Untersuchungen zu den Himmelfahrts- und Erhöhungstexten bei Lukas*, SANT 26 (München: Kösel, 1971); Alan F. Segal, "Heavenly Ascent in Hellenistic Judaism, Early Christianity and Their Environment," *ANRW* 2.23.2: 1333–94; Mary Dean-Otting, *Heavenly Journeys: A Study of the Motif in Hellenistic Jewish Literature*, JU 8 (Frankfurt am Main: Peter Lang, 1984); D. W. Palmer, "The Literary Background of Acts 1.1–14," *NTS* 33 (1987): 432–4; Martha Himmelfarb, *Ascent to Heaven in Jewish and Christian Apocalypses* (Oxford: Oxford University Press, 1993); Zwiep, *Ascension*, 36–79; idem, "Assumptus."

[17] On Lk. 10:17–24, see Chapter 3.

The precise nature of Satan's fall has been understood variously as a primordial event,[18] a previous event in the life of Jesus (whether the temptation[19] or baptism[20]), a metaphorical reflection on the disciples' mission,[21] an actual event resulting from the disciples' mission,[22] a look forward to the resurrection and ascension,[23] or as the future eschatological event of Satan's final defeat.[24] The argument that Jesus is prophesying a future event usually references Satan's continual presence (e.g., Acts 13:4–12; 26:18). Yet, this misses the function of the *down*-ward movement from heaven. Bovon notes, "Satan's expulsion from heaven did not mean that he was slain once and for all."[25] Satan still exercises power in the time remaining.[26] This revelation is an apocalyptic uncovering of cosmic events.[27] Satan's dethroning results from the ministry of the seventy(-two), but also from Jesus's soteriological program more generally. Nevertheless, narratively, as the opposite spatial and authoritative movement of Satan's downfall, Jesus's ascension is the ultimate countermovement to Satan's dethroning.[28]

Readers will recognize that Satan's occupation of heavenly authoritative space coheres with the devil's assertion of authority (ἐξουσία) over the kingdoms of the "civilized world" (οἰκουμένη) (4:5–7). As the narrative progresses, Jesus, who is born Davidic Messiah, Lord, and savior (2:11), goes forth preaching God's kingdom, fighting demonic forces, and attacking Satan's authority. Amid this, in response to the disciples' mission characterized by exorcism (battle with these forces), Jesus sees Satan fall (10:18). Where earlier, the devil claims that he had been bestowed (παραδίδωμι) ruling authority (4:6), Jesus now claims that all things have been given (παραδίδωμι) to him by his Father (10:21–2). Even the intimacy of kinship language suggests a superiority to Jesus's authority. Jesus's whole life and ministry, culminating in his death, resurrection, and ascension, is a process of dethroning Satan and ascending to his rightful place as Lord and Savior (Acts 2:36).[29] In Luke, this process comes to a head in Jerusalem, where Satan makes a final attack, entering Judas (22:3), "sifting" Jesus's disciples (22:31), and setting in motion the events leading to his execution (22:53). Jesus's resurrection and ascension represent victory over the best efforts of the corrupt powers, Satan and the earthly authorities (Acts 4:26).

---

[18] Gerhard Kittel, "λέγω, λόγος, κτλ," *TDNT* 4:130.
[19] Sydney H. T. Page, *Powers of Evil: A Biblical Study of Satan and Demons* (Grand Rapids: Baker, 1995), 109–10; Geldenhuys, *Luke*, 302.
[20] Joel Marcus, "Jesus' Baptismal Vision," *NTS* 41 (1995): 512–21.
[21] Fitzmyer, *Luke*, 2:860; Marshall, *Luke*, 1978.
[22] Bock, *Luke*, 2:1007.
[23] Garrett, *Demise*, 51.
[24] Green, *Luke*, 419; Simon Gathercole, "Jesus' Eschatological Vision of the Fall of Satan: Luke 10,18 Reconsidered," *ZNW* 94 (2003): 143–63.
[25] Bovon, *Luke*, 2:31.
[26] See Garrett, *Demise*, 61–99.
[27] The apocalyptic sense is heightened by the inclusion of ἐθεώρουν in v. 18, used similarly throughout Daniel 7 to begin apocalyptic visions (vv. 2, 4, 6, 7, 9, 11, 13).
[28] To see this as an apocalyptic uncovering of the way things really are is to make sense of the transition from Lk. 10:17–20 to 10:21–4.
[29] Garrett avers that the same cosmic struggle between the Davidide and Belial in 11QMelchizedek is exhibited in Lk. 10:17–24 (Garrett, *Demise*, 52–5).

Here we see the cosmic battle characteristic of the *Christus Victor* narrative.[30] Irenaeus himself cites Lk. 10:19 to highlight the cosmic struggle that has persisted since Eden (*Haer.* 3.23.7).[31] One might, however, argue that Luke-Acts' presentation of the cross lacks the centrality one would expect in a *Christus Victor* narrative. Here, Irenaeus proves instructive. For Irenaeus, the cross is not singularly effective for salvation; it is an important part in the greater movement of recapitulation, generally paired with incarnation.[32] The cross is both the ultimate expression of Jesus's obedience and fidelity and a revelation of justice (*Haer.* 3.18.6, 21.10; *Epid.* 69).[33] J. Kameron Carter notes that, for Irenaeus, Jesus's fidelity, exemplified in his birth and life, imprints "a new modality of existence on [humankind], a modality of the cross, the ascetical model of life that refuses to tyrannically possess the world" (*Haer.* 5.18.3; *Epid.* 34).[34] This fidelity is not simply a moral example[35] but an effective weapon against the bondage of Satan, injustice, and the demonic means of domination, working through *persuasion* (*suadela*, *Haer.* 5.1.1) rather than violent imposition.[36] Jesus's crucifixion defeats Satan by culminating Jesus's fidelity to God's justness even to death, a process which began in the temptation (*Haer.* 5.21.2), fidelity/obedience of which no other human was capable, exposing Satan as a liar and undoing the power that has bound humanity (*Haer.* 3.18.2; 5.16.3; *Epid.* 34). Jesus's death and resurrection reveal demonic injustice and the victory of Jesus's way of fidelity/obedience, persuading humanity to pledge their fidelity to Jesus, following him in formational imitation, turning humans from Satan to God (cf. Acts 26:18). Similarly, at the cross, violence is met with forgiveness (*Haer.* 3.16.9; Lk. 23:34).[37] In this way, the cross is a place of contestation and revelation, demonstrating Christ's justness (*Haer.* 5.21.3; Lk. 23:47) and the unjustness of those crucifying him and the cross itself (*Epid.* 69, 97).

Irenaeus's presentation of the cross is nuanced and intimately tied to the incarnation. Though imagery of sacrifice and ransom from slavery are present, how this imagery functions requires comment. Regarding ransom from slavery, mention

---

[30] See the preliminary discussion of the Irenaean *Christus Victor* model in Chapter 1.
[31] Irenaeus also emphasizes Christ's importance as Davidic Messiah in this scheme (*Epid.* 29–31, 36, 38, 49, 56, 59, 62–4).
[32] On recapitulation, see Eric Osborn, *Irenaeus of Lyons* (Cambridge: Cambridge University Press, 2001), 97–140; Minns, *Irenaeus*, 103–10. See Kathryn Tanner's articulation of a *Christus Victor* model that emphasizes incarnation (*Christ*, 247–73).
[33] See Wanke, *Irenäus*.
[34] Carter, *Race*, 28.
[35] Boersma rightly notes that Irenaeus utilizes multiple atonement models in an overlapping manner. Nevertheless, I am less convinced that Irenaeus utilizes propitiation in the way Boersma asserts ("Hospitality," 207–26; idem, *Violence*, 119, 161–2; idem, "Eschatological Justice and the Cross: Violence and Penal Substitution," *ThTo* 60 (2003): 186–99). Boersma does, however, at points, indicate that this theme is marginal. Cf. Joshua Schendel, "'That Justice Might Not Be Infringed Upon': The Judgment of God in the Passion of Christ in Irenaeus of Lyons," *SJT* 71 (2018): 212–25.
[36] Irenaeus emphasizes persuasion (*Haer.* 5.1.1; cf. 4.20.10; 4.37.1–4); i.e., Jesus persuades humanity through obedience, uncovering Satan as a liar. See Osborn, *Irenaeus*, 198; Boersma, *Violence*, 129–31. Humanity is no longer bound by Satan's deception, and conversely, Satan is now bound by his own lies (*Haer.* 3.23.7; 5.21.1–2).
[37] On the authenticity of Lk. 23:34, see Strahan, *Limits*; Nathan Eubank, "A Disconcerting Prayer: On the Originality of Luke 23:34a," *JBL* 129 (2010): 521–36.

of Jesus's redeeming blood is, at most, subdued when speaking of ransom payment specifically or, more likely, focused on Jesus's death generally as a means of deliverance (e.g., *Haer.* 3.5.3, 16.9; 4.20.2).[38] One passage that might appear to highlight a ransom payment is *Haer.* 5.1.1. Neil Forsyth rightly argues that slavery imagery is palpable, yet his conclusion that redemption must come by a ransom payment to Satan misses the primary logic by which Irenaeus describes attaining redemption in this passage.[39] Redemption comes by "persuasion," where persuasion is of human beings not Satan (see also *Haer.* 4.20.10, 37.1–4). Further, whereas Gregory of Nyssa saw God's justice as only fulfilled by paying a ransom payment to Satan (*Great Catechism* 5.22), Irenaeus highlights the *injustice* of the captivity (*Haer.* 5.1.1; cf. 4.5.4). Jesus's blood is persuasive and purifying (cf. *Haer.* 3.5.3, 12.7), not a payment.

Regarding sacrifice, though sacrificial language is sparse, it is present. Irenaeus's understanding of "propitiation" (*propitio*) requires context. One key text is *Haer.* 4.8.2, where Irenaeus, speaking of Jesus's ministry, states, "He did not make void, but fulfilled the law, by performing the offices of the high priest, propitiating God for men [*sic*], and cleansing the lepers, healing the sick, and Himself suffering death, that exiled man might go forth from condemnation, and might return without fear to his own inheritance" (*ANF* 1:471). Hans Boersma sees this as perhaps the clearest example of Irenaeus interpreting Christ's death as "a sacrifice that propitiates the Father."[40] However, there is no clear link between propitiation and Jesus's death; rather, Irenaeus ties this propitiation to Jesus's ministry, where he performs priestly functions, such as propitiation (forgiveness of sins), cleansing, healing, and so on. Likely, propitiation, here, refers to Jesus's mediatory role and declarations of forgiveness within his ministry such as we find in Luke (5:21–4; 7:47–9). Indeed, Irenaeus's focus in this passage is Jesus's ministry of healing and release from Satan, citing Lk. 13:16. Thus, when Irenaeus refers to Jesus's death allowing exiled (*exiliatus*) humans to escape/pass over (*exeo*) from condemnation to inheritance, overcoming discord fits largely in the context of release from Satan.

Jesus's crucifixion, manifesting the world's opposition to God's justness, not only exposes and binds Satan (revealing his injustice and deception), but also exemplifies the obedience that reconciles us to God.[41] It is in solidarity with and fidelity to this Jesus that humanity overcomes this discord. Thus, in *Haer.* 5.17.1—perhaps a better passage from which to argue for propitiation—though Irenaeus notes that humans have discord with God, God overcomes this hostility, not by assuaging God's wrath,[42] but by bringing humanity into reconciliation and obedience through Christ's persuasion and release from demonic injustice and captivity. Indeed, this bringing into fidelity (reconciling) is called "propitiation," and this propitiation is, here, notably, not linked

---

[38] See the discussion of λύτρωσις in Chapter 2.
[39] Forsyth, *Enemy*, 335–8.
[40] Boersma "Hospitality," 218; See also idem, *Violence*, 161–2; Andrew J. Bandstra, "Paul and an Ancient Interpreter: A Comparison of the Teaching of Redemption in Paul and Irenaeus," *CTJ* 5 (1970): 58–61.
[41] Not that the cross itself is desirable, rather the just life that is ultimately victorious over the forces of death and injustice revealed at the cross.
[42] Indeed, Irenaeus highlights God's love.

to Jesus's death, but specifically to Jesus's incarnation. Compare this to God's initiatory offer of participatory and liberating forgiveness/release in Jesus's life within Luke's Gospel as discussed in previous chapters.

For Irenaeus, it is not primarily Jesus's death that sets things right, but rather his life, a life facing opposition and death within a world of hostility. The cross brings this conflict to a head, exposing and defeating it, but it is Christ's incarnate obedience— that is, his life—that reveals and enables life overcoming discord with God. The cross manifests the obedience of the new Adam, in whom hostility is reconciled, friendship with God attained, and participation in new humanity made available (*Haer.* 4.13.4).

Indeed, this is God's merciful act *for us*. Certainly, Christ's obedience and human participation in that obedience can be said to "satisfy" God's justness, but not by undergoing divine punishment for injustice, but by God embodying, instantiating, and reconciling to God a just reality that satisfies (makes right) the unreconciled state between humanity and God evident in the cross. William Loewe maintains of Irenaeus's understanding of Jesus's death, "Far from acting on God to change his mind or allay his wrath, the sacrifice of the cross is first of all the Father's gift to humankind for its redemption, while what gives the cross its redemptive significance is the obedience unto death on the part of the Son that it incarnates."[43] Thus, were it that Irenaeus described the cross as propitiation in a few cases, it would not be problematic as Christ's obedience manifests order cohering to God's justness, reveals unjustness, and is an incarnational revelation in which humanity is invited to participate.

Though not as theologically developed as Irenaeus, the Lukan drama moves similarly through the temptation (Lk. 4:1-13); Jesus's life in conflict with powers of evil; Jesus's arrival in Jerusalem as king (19:38); and to Satan's appearance in Judas, in "sifting" the disciples, and in the worldly powers (22:3, 31, 53), to whose violence Jesus responds with forgiveness and righteousness (23:34, 46-7). The cross is a site of contestation where justness/righteousness (δίκαιος) is revealed both in displaying Jesus's own justness/righteousness and as a demonstration of the unjustness/unrighteousness of those opposing Jesus.[44] This valuation is clear in the apostles' rhetoric of the cross that

---

[43] Loewe, "*Christus*," 8-9. See also Aulén, *Christus*, 27, 33; Andrew P. Klager, "Retaining and Reclaiming the Divine: Identification and the Recapitulation of Peace in St. Irenaeus of Lyons' Atonement Narrative," in *Stricken by God? Nonviolent Identification and the Victory of Christ*, eds. Brad Jersak and Michael Hardin (Grand Rapids: Eerdmans, 2007), 449-52; Lawson, *Irenaeus*, 193-4. Elsewhere, Irenaeus compares God to Abraham sacrificing his son for humanity's redemption (*redemptio*, λύτρωσις, *Haer.* 4.5.4; cf. Lk. 1:68).

[44] Note *persuasion* uncovering injustice within the crucifixion scene: the daughters of Jerusalem mourning (22:26-32), the cosmological phenomenon of darkness, the temple curtain tearing (v. 45), the centurion's response (v. 47), and the crowd's mourning (v. 48). Further, multiple responses demonstrate blindness: e.g., the Jerusalem leadership's disinterestedness in Jesus's actual status, simply looking for an accusation (22:66-71); Pilate's declarations of innocence, which only emphasize the injustice of allowing Jesus's execution (23:4, 14-15, 22-5; cf. 13:1); the Jerusalem leadership's concern about perversion against Caesar, not God (23:2; cf. Deut. 13:1-11); Herod and the soldiers mocking Jesus (v. 11); the crowd's demand for the release of a murderer and insurrectionist (vv. 18-25; Acts 3:14-15); and Jesus's unmerited forgiveness from the cross (v. 34) amid continued mocking (vv. 35-9). On the use of δίκαιος in Lk. 23:47, see Sylva, *Reimaging*. See also, Frank J. Matera, "The Death of Jesus According to Luke: A Question of Sources," *CBQ* 47 (1985): 469-85. *Contra* Dibelius, *Tradition*, 201; B. Beck, "*Christi*"; Sterling, "Death," 398-9.

contests common perception (Acts 2:22–4; 3:13–15; 4:10; 5:30; 10:39–40; 13:27–30), utilizing the cross as a means of persuasion, uncovering injustice and opposition to God.[45] Jesus's crucifixion and exaltation unmasks as a lie the evil that brought his death, and his obedience/fidelity to God leads to vindication and enthronement (Lk. 22:69; Acts 2:34–5; 7:56),[46] incorporating a people allied under his authority rather than Satan's authority.[47]

Further, the cross is a site of God's forgiveness amid hostility (Lk. 23:34). God has turned to visit, to offer (atoning) forgiveness, reconciliation, and deliverance, to usher in a new Jubilee era (e.g., Lk. 1:77; 3:3; 4:18–19). This revelation of justness at the cross overcomes the powers of evil, exposes *their* unjustness and the people's complicity, and calls Israel to God's kingdom and covenant fidelity through *persuasion*, not violent domineering.

Though this is not vicarious expiatory sacrifice, it need not be understood as non-sacrificial. Irenaeus, for example, compares God's sacrifice of Jesus to Abraham's sacrifice of Isaac (*Haer.* 4.5.4).[48] This is God's sacrifice of covenant fidelity, and Jesus's death confirms God's initiatory and unwavering covenant commitment to Israel (Lk. 22:19–20), revealing God to all who can see (cf. 10:22).[49] God, in Jesus's life of covenant fidelity *for* Israel, affirms a new (renewed) covenant, leaving room amid the world's injustice in unmerited mercy for a participatory life of fidelity (Lk. 9:21–6; 14:27; cf. Irenaeus, *Haer.* 3.18.5; 5.1.1, 16.3).[50]

An exhaustive appraisal of the cross in Luke is not necessary. Without making comprehensive claims about Luke's presentation of the cross, these elements demonstrate a *Christus Victor* form. Jesus's victory affords cosmic reconciliation and salvation. The cross, whereby the cross exposes injustice, reveals God's covenant

---

[45] See Reardon, "Crucifixion."
[46] Repeated use of δεῖ emphasizes Jesus's obedience and the necessary results of such obedience (Lk. 9:22; 13:33; 17:25; 22:37; 24:7, 26, 44). God does not desire Jesus's crucifixion as a ransom or as an expiation. God desires Jesus's prophetic mission, which results in his execution (13:33). Note that Jesus's "necessity" is, more broadly, proclamation of the kingdom and the Father's "things" (2:49; 4:43).
[47] Compare Irenaeus's emphasis on participation in Christ's obedience, whereby a new human existence is available, overcoming Adam's disobedience (*Haer.* 3.18.5; 5.1.1, 16.3).
[48] Hochban, "Irenaeus," 547; Loewe, "*Christus*," 9.
[49] On scholarly interpretation of Luke's cross, see Chapter 1. Note generally that Jesus's death is marked by divine necessity (δεῖ, 9:22; 13:33; 17:25; 22:37; 24:7, 26, 44) and linked to the prophets (13:31) with no explicit expiatory significance. Nevertheless, see Lk. 22:19b–20. Yet, apart from expiatory sacrifice, Jesus's life committed to the prophetic declaration of God's kingdom, Jubilee mission, "opening eyes," and so on, which culminates in death, an act of uncompromising self-giving and service for others, gives sufficient sense to Jesus's claim that his body and blood is given "for you" (ὑπὲρ ὑμῶν). On Jesus's death as covenant establishing, see Francis Giordano Carpinelli, "'Do This as *My* Memorial' (Luke 22:19): Lucan Soteriology of Atonement," *CBQ* 61 (1999): 74–91.
[50] On the imitation of Jesus in Acts, see C. K. Barrett, "Theologia Crucis—in Acts?" in *Theologia Crucis—Signum Crucis: Festschrift für E. Dinkler*, eds. G. Anderson and G. Klein (Tübingen: Mohr, 1979), 73–84; Robert F. O'Toole, *The Unity of Luke's Theology: An Analysis of Luke-Acts*, GNS 9 (Wilmington, DE: Michael Glazer, 1984), 62–96. Marguerat identifies a process of *syncrisis* by which Paul and Peter are modeled on each other and Jesus (*Historian*, 56–9). See also Barrett's later essay where he, unfortunately, reverses course ("*Imitatio Christi* in Acts," in *Jesus of Nazareth: Lord and Christ: Essays on the Historical Jesus and New Testament Christology*, eds. Joel B. Green and Max Turner (Grand Rapids: Eerdmans, 1994), 251–62).

fidelity, and defeats Satan through obedience to God, calling all to true knowledge of cosmic order in which this crucified servant-king is enthroned in heaven at God's right hand. The ascension cannot be understood without the crucifixion.

4.1.3 Spatial Trajectories and the Missional Journey

So, again, our attention returns to how this configuration of cosmic-comprehensive space impacts mundane space and the manifestation of a spatial salvation. First, we must distinguish between the narrative's spatial orientation and trajectory. Though heaven provides the *orientation* that forms and structures social-political space, the narrative *trajectory* of Acts has two major movements, the first defining the second. The first is the "vertical" movement of heaven invading mundane space, particularly the Spirit. The second movement is the outward, "horizontal" missional movement of the church empowered by the Spirit (1:8).[51]

The ascension might lead us to conclude that the primary vertical movement is upward and away. Yet, even in 1:10–11, with its fourfold focus on going "into heaven" (1:10–11), the disciples are told that the ultimate movement is Jesus's return *from* heaven. With Jesus's ascension, the trajectory is still from heaven to mundane space. The ascension is the catalyst for the bestowal (*de*-scension) of the Spirit (2:33), the opposite movement, which provokes the church's social-political life (1:3, 6; 8:12; 14:22; 19:8; 20:25; 28:23, 31). Rightly, this should focus the reader's attention not away from but toward fulfillment in the world.

The second movement finds programmatic expression in Acts 1:8. This is the movement of salvation spreading from Jerusalem to Judea and Samaria, and the end of the earth. The emphasis, here, is less on the center, Jerusalem, than the goal, the end of the earth. For Loveday Alexander, Acts has two "mental maps" at play, "one centered on Jerusalem and one centered on the Mediterranean," where the shift in the journey toward the Mediterranean represents the shift in "early Christianity."[52] However, we should emphasize that this narrative shift is not to a new "center" but outward. That is, the focus is not the Mediterranean, Rome, Ethiopia, or Spain as a new center, but a *trajectory to* the end of the earth, its telos, implying that all mundane space sits within

---

[51] Loveday C. A. Alexander identifies this outward movement with Paul's invading "Greek cultural territory" ("'In Journeyings Often': Voyaging in the Acts of the Apostles and in Greek Romance," in *Luke's Literary Achievement: Collected Essays*, JSNTSup 116 ed. C. M. Tuckett (Sheffield: Sheffield Academic, 1995), 38–9).

[52] Alexander, "Acheivement," 30. See also ead., "Narrative Maps: Reflections on the Toponymy of Acts," in *The Bible in Human Society: Essays in Honour of John Rogerson*, JSOTSup 200 eds. M. Daniel Carroll R., David J. A. Clines and Philip R. Davies (Sheffield: Sheffield Academic, 1995), 17–57. Parsons rightly notes that Jerusalem is neither degraded nor the center of the symbolic universe, but is, in Acts, the beginning place of mission ("The Place of Jerusalem on the Lukan Landscape: An Exercise in Symbolic Cartography," in *Literary Studies in Luke-Acts: Essays in Honor of Joseph B. Tyson*, eds. Richard P. Thompson and Thomas E. Phillips (Macon, GA: Mercer University Press, 1998), 167–8). On negotiating central space, see also James M. Scott, *Geography in Early Judaism and Christianity: The Book of Jubilees*, SNTSMS 113 (Cambridge: Cambridge University Press, 2002), 56–7; Peter-Ben Smit, "Negotiating a New World View in Acts 1.8? A Note on the Expression ἕως ἐσχάτου τῆς γῆς," *NTS* 63 (2017): 1–22.

the formative path of a journey that continues until the time of universal restoration (3:21). We might see this instead as a movement of decentralization, a key element of which is orientation toward heaven, not Jerusalem or Rome. This phrase, "the end of the earth," is an undefined reality, a goal with little specific form, characterizing Israel's vocation (Isa. 49:6).[53] That is, the end of the earth is not an objectively mapable place, but the extent to which Israel's "light" must go forth.

This spatial trajectory is outlined by Jesus in 1:7–8 as a response to the disciples' question, "Lord, will you in this time return the kingdom to Israel?" (v. 6). This question has often been viewed as based on a misunderstanding of Jesus's kingdom vision,[54] a failure to transcend "Judaism," which led the disciples to falsely assume a political rather than (reductively) spiritual kingdom,[55] adopt nationalistic rather than universal concerns,[56] and expect a present, rather than future, fulfillment.[57] As Fitzmyer writes, for example, "Though the disciples who pose the question are Christians, they speak as Judean Jews on behalf of 'Israel.'"[58] This line of thinking implies a certain anti-Jewishness, emphasizing a transcending of national particularity, ethnicity, and embodiedness. Nevertheless, despite these commentators' assertions, Jesus's response makes no critique of their concern for restoration, focus on Israel, or uncouth broaching of politics.

Far from an abrupt and ignorant interruption, the disciples' question derives directly from Jesus's teaching to remain in Jerusalem, to wait for the Father's promise, and to expect baptism in the Spirit (vv. 4–5).[59] Expectation for Israel's restoration

---

[53] I discuss the importance of Isa. 49:6 in defining Israel's vocation in Luke-Acts below. See also Peter Mallen, *The Reading and Transformation of Isaiah in Luke-Acts*, LNTS 367 (London: T&T Clark, 2008), 182–4; Koet, *Studies*, 106–10, 144–5; James A. Sanders, "Isaiah in Luke," *Int* 36 (1982): 150.

[54] John Calvin, *The Acts of the Apostles 1–13* (Grand Rapids: Eerdmans, 1965), 29; William Barclay, *Acts of the Apostles* (Philadelphia: Westminster, 1976), 11; John R. W. Stott, *The Spirit, the Church, and the World: The Message of Acts* (Downers Grove, IL: InterVarsity Press, 1990), 40–5; David J. Williams, *Acts*, NIBCNT (Peabody, MA: Hendrickson, 1995), 23; Pervo, *Acts*, 41; Derek W. H. Thomas, *Acts*, REC (Phillipsburg, NJ: P&R, 2011), 10. Conversely, Loveday C. A. Alexander characterizes Jesus's response to the disciples as "yes," though noting the issue of timing (*Acts*, PBC (Oxford: Bible Reading Fellowship, 2006), 24). See also Wall, *Acts*, 41–2; Beverly Roberts Gaventa, *Acts*, ANTC (Nashville: Abingdon, 2003), 65.

[55] See D. J. Williams, *Acts*, 23; F. F. Bruce, *The Acts of the Apostles: The Greek Text with Introduction and Commentary*, 3rd ed. (Grand Rapids: Eerdmans, 1990), 115; Stott, *Spirit*, 41; C. K. Barrett, *The Acts of the Apostles*, 2 vols., ICC (New York: T&T Clark, 1994–8), 1:71, 76; Luke Timothy Johnson, *The Acts of the Apostles*, SP 5 (Collegeville, MN: Liturgical, 1992), 29; Carl R. Holladay, *Acts: A Commentary*, NTL (Louisville: Westminster John Knox, 2016), 74.

[56] Stott, *Spirit*, 41; Barrett, *Acts*, 1:76; Thomas, *Acts*, 10–11.

[57] On these three criticisms, see Stott, *Spirit*, 40–5. Conversely, Buzzard, "Eclipse," 197–215; Maston, "Kingdom," 169–78. Both Buzzard and Maston see temporal confusion as the main misunderstanding, in agreement with Conzelmann (*Theology*, 163) and Haenchen (*Acts*, 143). See also Pao, *Exodus*, 95; Hilary Le Cornu and Joseph Shulam, *A Commentary on the Jewish Roots of Acts* (Jerusalem: Academon, 2003), 15.

[58] Fitzmyer, *Acts*, 205.

[59] There is a dialogical quality to vv. 4–8 (vv. 4–5, Jesus; v. 6, the apostles; vv. 7–8 Jesus), though the transition from vv. 4–5 to v. 6 is obscured by some commentators' assertion that v. 6 marks the beginning of a "discrete scene" (e.g., I. Howard Marshall, *The Acts of the Apostles*, TNTC (Grand Rapids: Eerdmans, 1980), 55; Gaventa, *Acts*, 62). Pao notes "the specifically Lukan phrase οἱ μὲν οὖν marks division" (*Exodus*, 91). Nevertheless, this construct often occurs within blocks of material (e.g., 5:41; 15:3; 23:18, 22; 28:5).

is a reasonable response to these instructions. Notably, there is ample precedent for assuming that the Spirit's bestowal would result in Israel's restoration[60] and that Jerusalem would be central.[61] The apostles' question is not based on a failure, but it does provide opportunity for further clarification concerning the movement of salvation. Among the areas of clarification in vv. 7–8, note specifically aspects of geography, agency, and time.[62]

First, Jesus clarifies the geography of the disciples' mission as a journey moving from Jerusalem, to Judea and Samaria, and to the end of the earth. The exact phrase ἕως ἐσχάτου τῆς γῆς (end of the earth) occurs only five times throughout ancient Greek literature other than Acts, and four of these are in Isaiah (Isa. 8:9; 48:20; 49:6; 62:11). Of particular importance is Isa. 49:6, which most commentators agree is alluded to in Acts 1:8 and elsewhere in Luke-Acts (Lk. 2:32; Acts 13:47; cf. 26:16–18). David L. Tiede claims that Isa. 49:6 "might well be regarded as a thematic statement of Luke's entire narrative."[63] In Isaiah 49, YHWH's servant is identified first as Israel (v. 3), yet as the passage progresses, the servant's mission is to bring Jacob back, to restore Israel (vv. 5–6). This shift allows for the interpretation of the servant as a righteous remnant that will act on behalf of Israel for its salvation.[64] Further, this servant will bring light to the gentiles and salvation to the end of the earth (v. 6).[65]

The implication for Acts is not that the disciples have wrongly assumed a parochial nationalism, but that they have rightly identified Israel's centrality in God's soteriological scheme. Their calling is that of the remnant/servant, to restore Jacob and bring light to the gentiles (cf. Lk. 24:47).[66] The movement outward is a missional trajectory that moves from Jerusalem to restore divided Israel (Judea and Samaria, cf. Jer. 50:17–20) and to the gentiles (cf. Acts 3:26; 13:46).[67] These are not simply locations on a map, but the manifestation of a restoration geography. Acts 1:8 is not so much a summary of the

---

[60] Isa. 11:1–16; 32:9–20; 42:1–9; 44:1–5; 48:16; 61:1–11; Ezek. 11:17–19; 18:30–2; 36:24–32; 37:1–14; Joel 2:28–32. See specifically the parallels between Isa. 32:15 and Lk. 24:49 and Acts 1:5.

[61] Isa. 2:1–4; 24:23; 27:13; 33:20–2; 40:9–11; 52:1–10; 60:1–7 LXX; 62:6–7; 66:20; Jer. 3:17; 17:25–6; Mic. 4:2; Joel 2:32; 3:1; Zeph. 3:14–20; Zech. 1:16–17; 8:1–8; 9:9–13.

[62] Sleeman, *Geography*, 68–70.

[63] Tiede, *Prophecy*, 31. See also idem, "The Exaltation of Jesus and the Restoration of Israel in Acts 1," *HTR* 79 (1986): 278–86; Koet, *Studies*, 113, 142–5; J. A. Sanders, "Isaiah in," 150; Mallen, *Reading*, 182–4; Pao, *Exodus*, 91–6.

[64] Beers (*Following*, 38) argues that the Isaianic servant provides a substructure for Luke-Acts. On the importance of the Isaianic servant for Luke-Acts, see also Glöckner, *Verkündigung*, 171–4; Joel B. Green, *The Death of Jesus: Tradition and Interpretation in the Passion Narrative* (Eugene, OR: Wipf & Stock, 2011), 317–18; idem, "Servant," 1–28; idem, "Necessary," 71–85; H. Douglas Buckwalter, *The Character and Purpose of Luke's Christology*, SNTSMS 89 (Cambridge: Cambridge University Press, 1996), 231–72; O'Toole, "Servant," 328–46; Rouven Genz, *Jesaja 53 als theologische Mitte der Apostelgeschichte: Studien zu ihrer Christologie und Ekklesiologie im Anschluss an Apg 8,26–40*, WUNT 2/398 (Tübingen: Mohr Siebeck, 2015).

[65] Childs, *Isaiah*, 385; Goldingay, *Isaiah*, 2:166; Paul, *Isaiah*, 327.

[66] See Beers, *Followers*, 130–33; David W. Pao, "Jesus's Ascension and the Lukan Account of the Restoration of Israel," in *Ascent into Heaven in Luke-Acts: New Explorations of Luke's Narrative Hinge*, eds. David K. Bryan and David W. Pao (Minneapolis: Fortress, 2016), 145.

[67] Seeing here a restoration itinerary does not necessitate stages of restoration as in a check list. Restoration has begun, as has gentile inclusion, yet we need not assert that Israel's restoration is complete by Acts 15 (*contra* Jervell, *People*, 56).

movement of Acts—and if it were, it would be a poor one, given that Paul arguably does not reach the end of the earth.[68] It is not the movement to a new center, but a program for the church's mission empowered by the Spirit, oriented by heaven.[69] The end of the earth is the telos of their vocation,[70] which is also *Israel's* vocation (Isa. 49:3).[71]

Second, the apostles assume *Jesus's* agency in restoration; Jesus, however, shifts their attention to *their* missional movement through the Spirit's empowerment. They will be Jesus's witnesses (μάρτυρες). Holly Beers argues that Jesus here passes the role of servant to his disciples.[72] Though the disciples are often identified as witnesses of the resurrection (1:22; 2:32–3; 3:15; 13:31), "resurrection" is metonymic for the totality of Jesus's life, death, exaltation, and the composition of eschatological cosmic-comprehensive space (2:32–3; 5:30–2; 10:39–43; 28:23).[73]

Finally, Jesus addresses whether "now" is the time of restoration. Rather than moving the restoration to the future, Jesus obscures that question. It is not for them to know the times or seasons (χρόνους ἢ καιρούς) (cf. 1 Thess. 5:12). *Contra* Conzelmann, this reply does not nullify Parousia expectation.[74] Jesus's impending return still qualitatively impacts narrative time, which is in "the last days" (Acts 2:17).[75] The focus shifts from "now" to the *time that remains*. Much as the "today" of Lk. 4:21, this is a qualitatively different time impacted by Jesus's impending return and missional mandate. However, the apostles' initial invocation of "now," of a moment of imposition, potentially expresses not only a time when, but also a manner. Though Jesus does not directly critique a violent impulse, we are reminded of Lk. 19:11–27. There, the disciples

---

[68] For the end of the earth as Ethiopia, see Herodotus, *Hist.* 3.25; Strabo, *Geogr.* 1.1.6, 2.31, 4.6; 3.1.8; as Rome, see Ign., *Rom.* 2.2. In the LXX, the end of the earth is a more general idea (Deut. 28:49; Ps. 134:6–7; Isa. 8:9; 14:21–2; 48:20; 49:6; 62:11; Jer. 6:22; 10:12; 16:19; 1 Macc. 3:9; *Pss. Sol.* 1.4; 8.15). E. Earle Ellis conjectures that the end of the earth refers to Spain ("'The End of the Earth' [Acts 1:8]," in *History and Interpretation in New Testament Perspective*, BibInt 54 ed. E. Earle Ellis (Leiden: Brill, 2001), 54–63). See also James S. Romm, *The Edges of the Earth in Ancient Thought* (Princeton: Princeton University Press, 1992).

[69] Sleeman argues heaven rather than Jerusalem provides the narrative's orientation (*Geography*, 58–9; *contra* J. M. Scott, *Geography*, 56–7), adding, "Rather than a fixed element of a 'tradition', Jerusalem needs to be read as one part of a dynamic restructuring of place and geography in Acts resulting from Christ's ascension" (*Geography*, 33–4).

[70] Beers, *Followers*, 132–3.

[71] Tiede writes, "The promise of God's reign is not simply the restoration of the preserved of Israel, but the renewal of the vocation of Israel to be a light to the nations to the end of the earth" ("Exaltation," 286).

[72] Beers, *Following*, 118–25, 179.

[73] Acts 2:32–33 explicitly notes the relationship between witness and exaltation/resurrection. However, more generally, witness also relates to salvation from this generation (2:40), the word of the Lord (8:25), that Jesus is the Christ (18:5), and the advent of repentance, faith, and the gospel of God's grace (20:21, 24). There are several instances as well where the message of these witnesses is God's kingdom (Acts 8:12; 19:8; 20:25; 28:23).

[74] Conzelmann, *Theology*, 95–136. See also Haenchen, *Acts*, 95–6; Grässer, *Forschungen*, 48–58, 292–320; François Bovon, *Luke the Theologian: Fifty Years of Research (1950-2005)*, 2nd ed. (Waco, TX: Baylor University Press, 2006), 11–33.

[75] See, e.g., S. G. Wilson, "Lukan Eschatology," *NTS* 16 (1970): 330–47; Kevin Giles, "Present-Future Eschatology," *RTR* 41 (1982): 11–18; Gaventa, "Eschatology," 27–42; Carroll, *Response*; Nolland, "Salvation-History," 65–7. See the *Forschungsbericht* in Bovon, *Theologian*, 33–85.

concern for immediacy (παραχρῆμα) was not simply an objective temporal concern but belied their expectation of the kingdom's nature and imposition.[76]

The disciples are not simply to wait for the end of times and seasons. Temporal space is made now for Israel's restoration and gentile inclusion. How and when this restoration will be complete is not for the disciples to understand. Rather, they are simply to journey the missional trajectory. In this time remaining, the missional trajectory manifests salvation, taking up space in the world, a cosmic transformation, not brought in by divine fiat but by God's servants who establish salvific space not by violence (or the means of the world under Satan's authority) but by persuasion, witness, and the power of God's Spirit.

4.1.4 The Spirit, Producer of Salvific Space

On Pentecost, the Spirit enters, as heaven invading and empowering the church. There is, of course, much debate about the Spirit's function in Luke-Acts. Though few disagree that the Spirit enables prophetic speech, whether there are additional functions associated with the Spirit remains contested. For a number of scholars the Spirit is a *donum superadditum*, a gift that is given subsequent to "salvation" and prior to "restoration."[77] Robert Menzies insists that the Spirit in Luke-Acts is missiological and not soteriological. This, however, requires a restricted definition of salvation, one primarily focused on the inner person, justification, and adoption, distinct from the social, economic, and political life of the community.[78]

Conversely, James Dunn argues that Lukan pneumatology is soteriological, largely adopting the same restricted soteriology.[79] The Spirit offers inner transformation and

---

[76] Willie James Jennings identifies a "tragic" quality to the question in its assumed violence, as the disciples pose it to Jesus, who has overcome the world's violence and death (*Acts*, Belief (Louisville: Westminster John Knox, 2017), 16–17).

[77] Robert P. Menzies, *The Development of Early Christian Pneumatology with Special Reference to Luke-Acts*, JSNTSup 54 (Sheffield: JSOT Press, 1991), 47–9; idem, *Empowered for Witness: The Spirit in Luke-Acts*, JPTSup 6 (Sheffield: Sheffield Academic Press, 1994), 202–35; idem, "Luke's Understanding of Baptism in the Holy Spirit: A Pentecostal Dialogues with the Reformed Tradition," *JPT* 16 (2008): 86–101. See also Roger Stronstad, *The Charismatic Theology of St. Luke: Trajectories from the Old Testament to Luke-Acts*, 2nd ed. (Grand Rapids: Baker Academic, 2012), 55–69; F. F. Bruce, "The Holy Spirit in the Acts of the Apostles," *Int* 27 (1973): 178; Marshall, *Historian*, 199–202; Cho, *Spirit*. For further references, see William H. Shepherd Jr., *The Narrative Function of the Holy Spirit as a Character in Luke-Acts*, SBLDS 147 (Atlanta: Scholars Press, 1994), 11–23; Bovon, *Theologian*, 225–72; Craig S. Keener, *Acts: An Exegetical Commentary*, 5 vols. (Grand Rapids: Baker Academic, 2012–17), 1:689. The most significant rebuttals to Menzies are Turner, *Power*; Matthias Wenk, *Community-Forming Power: The Socio-Ethical Role of the Spirit in Luke-Acts*, JPTSup 19 (Sheffield: Sheffield Academic Press, 2000).

[78] Note those instances where the Spirit appears not only to induce speech, but also to transform: Lk. 1:41, 67; 4:18–19; 12:12; Acts 1:2, 16; 2:4, 17–18, 33; 4:8, 25, 31; 6:10; 10:44–5; 19:6; 28:25.

[79] James D. G. Dunn, *Baptism in the Holy Spirit: A Re-examination of the New Testament Teaching on the Gift of the Spirit in Relation to Pentecostalism Today* (Philadelphia: Westminster, 1970), 38–54; idem, "Baptism in the Holy Spirit: A Response to Pentecostal Scholarship on Luke-Acts," *JPT* 3 (1993): 2–27; idem, "Baptism in the Holy Spirit—Yet Once More," *JEPTA* 18 (1998): 3–25; idem, "Baptism in the Holy Spirit: Yet Once More—Again," *JPT* 19 (2010): 32–43. See also J. H. E. Hull, *The Holy Spirit in Acts of the Apostles* (London: Lutterworth, 1967), 44.

the "experience" of salvation in terms of justification and what Dunn calls "sonship." So, for Dunn, the disciples do not experience salvation until Pentecost.[80] Nevertheless, occurrences of adoption and justification language are few and far between (cf. Acts 13:38–9). When becoming God's children does arise, it appears largely social and ethical (e.g., Lk. 6:35). Dunn's specific inward, transformative soteriology is not the primary focus of Luke-Acts, nor is it directly apparent in the Spirit's work according to the Lukan narrative (cf. Jn 4:14; 7:37–9; 20:22; Rom. 8:9, 14; Gal. 3:2–3). Though these interpretations are ostensibly diametrically opposed, in fact, they share an erroneous personalist soteriology.

For those who emphasize the Spirit's role in inward soteriological transformation, texts such as Jer. 31:31–4 and Ezek. 36:22–32 play a key role. In these texts, God promises an eschatological Spirit event in which the law is placed in people's hearts (Ezek. 36:26). A connection between Pentecost and Sinai is emphasized, where Jesus, as a Moses-figure, ascends on high to bring forth God's covenant. It should be noted, however, that nowhere else in the NT is Pentecost associated with such an event (cf. Acts 20:16; 1 Cor. 16:8).[81] Further, though there are later associations made between Pentecost and Sinai in Rabbinic literature (*m. Meg.* 3:5; *b. Meg.* 31a) and earlier references to Pentecost and renewal of the Noahic covenant (*Jub.* 6.15–18),[82] there is no evidence for a direct link between Sinai and Pentecost in the first century CE.[83] Additionally, though the story includes repeated emphasis on sound, noise, and fire, elements of the Sinai theophany (Exod. 19:19; 20:18; Deut. 4:24, 33, 36; 5:22–7; cf. Philo, *Dec.* 33, 46),[84] these are not restricted to Sinai and are more generic.[85] For instance, Ps. 29:7 (28:7 LXX), which states "the voice of the Lord flashes forth flames of fire," speaks of the Lord's revelation with no reference to Sinai (see also 2 Sam. 22:9–16). Further, there are no references to indwelling law or Sinai in Peter's speech or to Jer. 31:31–4 or Ezek. 36:22–32. Instead, Peter focuses exclusively on the prophetic Spirit as expressed in Joel 2:28–32 and the Davidic

---

[80] Dunn, *Baptism*, 41. See Turner's response (*Power*, 318–41).

[81] Bent Noack, "The Day of Pentecost in Jubilees, Qumran, and Acts," *ASTI* 1 (1962): 72–95. Luke will at times use Jewish festivals as chronological markers (e.g., Lk. 22:1–2; cf. 2:41; Acts 12:3–4; 20:6).

[82] J. M. Scott maintains that Luke utilizes Jubilees and may be similarly alluding to the Noahic covenant (*Geography*, 63–4).

[83] Those noting this and other arguments against the association include Strauss, *Messiah*, 145–7; Eduard Lohse, "πεντηκοστή," *TDNT* 6:48–9; Haenchen, *Acts*, 172; I. Howard Marshall, "The Significance of Pentecost," *SJT* 30 (1977): 348–9; Jürgen Roloff, *Die Apostelgeschichte: Übersetzt und erklärt* (Göttingen: Vandenhoeck & Ruprecht, 1981), 40; Menzies, *Development*, 231–9; Bock, *Proclamation*, 182. See the discussion in Keener, *Acts*, 1:784–7.

[84] Those seeing Sinai allusions include Jacques Dupont, "La nouvelle Pentecôte (Ac 2, 1–11)," in *Nouvelle études sur les Actes des Apôtres*, LD 118 (Paris: Cerf, 1984), 193; Joseph A. Fitzmyer, *To Advance the Gospel: New Testament Studies* (New York: Crossroad, 1991), 280–5; idem, *Acts*, 233–4; Turner, *Power*, 279–89; J. M. Scott, *Geography*, 63–4; Le Cornu and Shulam, *Acts*, 1:59; L. T. Johnson, *Acts*, 46.

[85] See, e.g., Exod. 3:2–3; 13:21; 14:24; Deut. 4:24, 33; 18:16–18; 2 Sam. 22:9–16; 1 Kgs 18:38; Pss. 18:8; 29:7; Isa. 66:15; Ezek. 1:13, 27.

covenant. While one might fill the gaps with material from Jeremiah 31 and Ezekiel 36, there is little direct evidence for that connection.[86]

Perhaps the key critic of both Menzies and Dunn is Max Turner, who simultaneously critiques Menzies' relegation of the Spirit to a *donum supereadditum* as well as the restricted soteriology of both Dunn and Menzies. For Turner, the Spirit's primary role is to empower prophetic speech, but the prophetic Spirit in Second Temple Jewish writing is also often portrayed with expected ethical effects.[87] This is not a secondary but a primary attribute, a non-distinguishable element of the prophetic Spirit, and these ethical effects are directly related to Israel's restoration. In making this connection, Turner obscures the bifurcation between mission and salvation.[88] Salvation is no longer reduced to inward transformation, and the church's mission is not to speak of a *coming* restoration distinguished from inner salvation. The church's mission is to proclaim and enact a developing salvation that is part of that restoration *now*. Salvation unfolds in space as "participation in God's dynamic, liberating, restoring, and transforming eschatological reign."[89]

Turner's student, Matthias Wenk, develops the "social-ethical" aspect of the Spirit's work, arguing that the Spirit impacts the community's common life and moves consistently throughout Acts to guide, expand, define, and enable conflict resolution within the community.[90] The Spirit impacts the community's social space and an expansion of Jesus's mission announcing the Lord's favorable year through the church. In Acts, on receiving baptism and the Spirit (2:38–41), the church does not spread out in proclamation as receiving the Spirit of prophecy *simpliciter*; rather, the immediate response is the creation of a community.

The Spirit is the power of the production of soteriological space. This requires a shift in soteriological focus from inward transformation, personally centered, to the restoration of a people, a salvation that impacts social structure, political interaction, and community existence. Salvation is participation in the "sphere" of the realization of God's reign. This is what is declared when the apostles announce God's forgiveness (2:38; 3:19; 5:31; 10:43; 13:38; 26:18), an invitation to participate in God's kingdom and restoration. As this kingdom space is centered on the Spirit-filled Jesus in Luke, so now it is centered on the Spirit sent from Jesus. Though the phrase "kingdom of God" does not appear in Acts to the degree that it did in Luke, it still plays a significant

---

[86] Denying that Pentecost parallels Sinai does not mitigate the importance of the Isaianic New Exodus theme. See, esp., Acts 3:22. See also G. K. Beale's argument that Acts presents the church as the new temple utilizing a Sinai typology ("The Descent of the Eschatological Temple in the Form of the Spirit at Pentecost," *TynBul* 56, no. 1 (2005): 73–102; 56, no. 2 (2005): 63–90). See also Richard Bauckham, "James and the Jerusalem Church," in *The Book of Acts in Its Palestinian Setting*, BAFCS 4, ed. Richard Bauckham (Grand Rapids: Eerdmans, 1994), 452–62.

[87] Turner, *Power*, 119–37.

[88] Turner, though, emphasizes that the speech at Pentecost is doxological and not missiological (*Power*, 271–2).

[89] Turner, *Power*, 331.

[90] Wenk, *Community*.

role.[91] God's kingdom brackets Acts (1:3, 6; 28:23, 31) and is the central element of Jesus's instruction to the disciples (1:3–8). There is no sense that the disciples' initial restoration hope (1:6) has faded from subsequent kingdom preaching (8:12; 19:8; 20:25; 28:23). Even Paul's later declaration about entering the kingdom through many sufferings (14:22) expresses an important present aspect of the kingdom.[92] The kingdom is a reality within which the church strives to participate, and, in this participation, the church aligns to the ultimate structure of the cosmos to which it is being reconciled.

As the narrative continues, the Spirit guides the church beyond Israel's boundaries and acceptable proselytes. The Spirit sends Philip to the Ethiopian eunuch (8:29, 39; cf. Deut. 23:2 LXX; Isa. 56:3–5) and Peter to Cornelius (10:19), where she falls as a witness of Cornelius's cleanliness (10:44–8; 15:7, 9),[93] determines the essentials for gentile inclusion (15:28), selects Paul and Barnabas (13:2, 4), and shows where Paul will go (16:6–7; 19:21; 20:22; cf. 21:4). The Spirit directs the church's mission, the community's make-up, the mission's geography, and, as I argue below, the social and political dynamics of that space.[94]

4.1.5 Summary

In Acts 2:1–4, a phenomenon of wind and fire invades from heaven. The reader is drawn to the structure of cosmic-comprehensive space within which the world is embedded. God's salvation unfolds within this world. Key to Luke's soteriology is heaven, not as a location but as a space of cosmic conflict and authority, which is inhabited by God and Jesus, the Davidic Messiah. This space invades in the Spirit, who drives the church forward in mission, participating in and promulgating the restoration of all things. Heaven changes the way one with "knowledge" understands the mundane world, its authorities, and organization.

4.2 Mapping the World (Acts 2:5–13)

In this section, I continue to attend to movements in and presentations of space, the place of Jerusalem, the movement toward and away from this perceived center, and the mapping of the world, envisioning the world through the revelation of Jesus's ascension to heaven.

---

[91] Weiser points to God's kingdom at key moments in Acts' narrative (1:3, 6; 8:12; 14:22; 19:18; 20:25; 28:23, 31), demonstrating its continued programmatic importance ("Reich," 127–8). See also Ziccardi, *Relationship*, 37–8; Rudolf Schnackenburg, *God's Rule and Kingdom* (Freiberg: Herder, 1963), 259–70; Wolter, "Reich," 541–4.

[92] Maddox, *Purpose*, 136–7.

[93] Reardon, "Cleansing," 476.

[94] Note also how the Spirit influences the community's economic reciprocity. The Spirit's prophecy through Agabus concerning the coming famine (Acts 11:28) leads the church in Antioch to send aid to Jerusalem (v. 29), extending the economic fellowship from an intra-communal to inter-communal reality.

4.2.1 Jerusalem: Ingathering to Decentralization

Pentecost unfolds in Jerusalem (v. 5), a cosmopolitan city with Jews from a multitude of nations (cf. 6:9).[95] Those present, likely both residents and pilgrims,[96] are characterized as devout Jews from every nation "under heaven." Jerusalem is a place of ingathering, central to the geographic imagination of many Jews,[97] having a historically economic and political centrality.[98] An element of this centrality is on display in this pilgrimage festival. Pilgrimage festivals, such as Pentecost, brought Jews from thousands of cities who took up residence in Jerusalem (Philo *Spec. Leg.* 1.69).[99]

At first glance, one might assume that the invocation of Pentecost conveys support for a centralizing movement, especially given the role of and movement toward Jerusalem exhibited in Luke-Acts (e.g., Lk. 1:5–23; 24:52; Acts 1:4). Nevertheless, the primary narrative trajectory is outward (1:8). Symbolically represented in the rending of the temple curtain (Lk. 23:45) and manifest distinctly in Pentecost, the Spirit is no longer centralized in Jerusalem or the temple (not that it ever necessarily was—cf. Acts

---

[95] On the cosmopolitan nature of Jerusalem, see Martin Hengel, *Between Jesus and Paul: Studies in the Earliest History of Christianity* (London: SCM, 1983), 17–18, 57; Josephus, *War* 1.397, 437, 672.

[96] Whether these people were simply pilgrims or diaspora Jews who have taken up residence in Jerusalem is somewhat unclear. Most critics conclude that they were permanent residents. E.g., Gerhard Schneider, *Die Apostelgeschichte*, 2 vols., HTKNT 5 (Freiberg: Herder, 1980), 251; Gerhard A. Krodel, *Acts*, ACNT (Minneapolis: Augsburg, 1986), 78; L. T. Johnson, *Acts*, 43 (yet, cf. p. 381); James D. G. Dunn, *Acts of the Apostles*, EpComm (Peterborough: Epworth, 1996), 26; Charles H. Talbert, *Reading Acts: A Literary and Theological Commentary on the Acts of the Apostles* (New York: Crossroad, 1997), 42; Jervell, *Apostelgeschichte*, 134–5; Daniel Marguerat, *Les Actes des Apôtres*, 2 vols., CNT 5 (Genève: Labor et Fides, 2007), 1:75; Keener, *Acts*, 1:833–5. Those who understand these Jews as pilgrims include Bruce, *Apostles*, 115; J. M. Scott, *Geography*, 66. The term κατοικέω (v. 5) often indicates residence and not visitation (e.g., Lk. 13:4; Acts 1:19; 7:4; 9:22, 32, 35; 11:29; 13:27; 19:10, 17; 22:12), though more ambiguous are Acts 1:20; 4:16. There are, however, exceptions. For the Festival of Booths, Leviticus LXX uses κατοικέω twice in one verse to describe those dwelling in booths (23:42 LXX), and a related term κατοικίζω in v. 43. The length of this dwelling is seven days. The notion of temporary dwelling is within the semantic range of κατοικέω. See Acts 2:5, 9, 14. In v. 9, some of those "dwelling" in Jerusalem "dwell" in Mesopotamia. The imperfective participle in v. 9 implies a continuing reality, indicating their temporary presence in Jerusalem. Nevertheless, this group is categorized simultaneously as Jews/Judeans dwelling (imperfective participle again) in Jerusalem. The easiest explanation is that there are different senses within the semantic range of κατοικέω being employed. Similarly, what of "those visiting from Rome" (οἱ ἐπιδημοῦντες Ῥωμαῖοι, v. 10). Does this phrase distinguish these visitors from residents, or does it further enforce the temporary nature of all of the pilgrims?

[97] J. M. Scott argues that, "Jerusalem is the *omphalos* connecting heaven and earth, a veritable axis mundi" (*Geography*, 56–7; cf. Ezek. 5:5; 38:12; *Jub.* 8.12–21). See also Bauckham, "James," 417–27.

[98] On Judea's economy centered in Jerusalem, see Douglas E. Oakman, *Jesus and the Economy of His Day*, SBEC 8 (Lewiston, NY: Edwin Mellen, 1986), 78. See also Halvor Moxnes, *The Economy of the Kingdom: Social Conflict and Economic Relations in Luke's Gospel*, OBT (Philadelphia: Fortress, 1988), 70–2; William R. Herzog II, *Jesus, Justice, and the Reign of God: A Ministry of Liberation* (Louisville: Westminster John Knox, 2000), 112–23; Philip A. Harland, "The Economy of First-Century Palestine: State of the Scholarly Discussion," in *Handbook of Early Christianity: Social Science Approaches*, eds. Anthony J. Blasi, Jean Duhaime and Philip-Andre Turcotte (Walnut Creek, CA: Alta Mira, 2002), 515.

[99] Martin Goodman, "The Pilgrimage Economy of Jerusalem in the Second Temple Period," in *Judaism in the Roman World: Collected Essays*, AJEC 66 ed. Martin Goodman (Leiden: Brill, 2007), 61. See also, idem, *The Ruling Class of Judaea: The Origins of the Jewish Revolt against Rome A.D. 66–70* (Cambridge: Cambridge University Press, 1987), 56.

7:48–50).¹⁰⁰ Now, the Spirit fills the church, and spurs it forward and outward. The church's missiological goal appears not as an "ingathering," but an outward movement, guided by the Spirit. Whereas pilgrimage is a move *inward*, the Pentecost event demands a move *outward* (1:8; cf. 22:17–21).

This decentralization and dispersal is on display in the community as well. There is an interesting word play in Acts 2 between the economic koinonia of the community formed by the Spirit and the arrival of the fiery tongues, where the same word (διαμερίζω) is used to speak of the Spirit's *dispersal* (v. 3) and the community's *distribution* of resources after having sold their possessions (v. 45), the only two times διαμερίζω is used in Acts (cf. Lk. 22:17).¹⁰¹ The community's economic koinonia functions as Spirit moved distribution, influenced by heaven's authoritative imaging of social-political organization.

This wordplay's aptness is demonstrated by the decentralizing role of tongues in Acts 2. The Spirit embraces difference rather than flattening centralization, reaching each in the audience's native tongues, not, for example, Hebrew, Greek, or Aramaic, the last two being languages of conquest.¹⁰² This is particularly significant given that a common language, Aramaic or Greek, was likely available (21:37). Though some have seen this event as a reversal of Babel's punishment through recentralization (Gen. 11:1–9; cf. Zeph. 3:9; *T. Jud.* 25.3),¹⁰³ the opposite proves to be true, affirming Babel and the multiplicity of native languages (2:8).¹⁰⁴ Here can be heard at least an implicit critique of empire, centralization, and Rome, whose imperial destiny (so it was said) was to "form one body under the name of Romans" (Tacitus, *Ann.* 11.24 [Jackson, LCL]).¹⁰⁵ As Christoph Uehlinger has shown, the allusion to Babel references not a tragedy to be overcome, but an affirmation of God's provision against centralizing domination.¹⁰⁶ At Pentecost, heaven orders social-political space.

4.2.2 Mapping World Space

Jerusalem, as the origin point in this outward missional movement, is not inconsequential. Its centrality is evident in the map of 2:9–11. Barrett has suggested

---

[100] Joel B. Green, "'In Our Own Languages': Pentecost, Babel, and the Shaping of Christian Community in Acts 2:1–12," in *The Word Leaps the Gap: Essays on Scripture and Theology in Honor of Richard B. Hays*, eds. J. Ross Wagner, C. Kavin Rowe and A. Katherine Grieb (Grand Rapids: Eerdmans, 2008), 212. There is no direct critique of Jerusalem or the temple in Acts 2; however, Acts conveys an obvious antipathy for the Jerusalem aristocracy (Acts 4:8–11, 16–21; 5:17–18, 27–32; 13:27–9; see also Lk. 20:45–21:4).

[101] Though money is still centralized with the apostles (Acts 4:34–5), the emphasis is consistently on general redistribution and care for the poor (2:45; 11:27–30).

[102] On the relationship between language and centralized civilization and economic exploitation, see Roland Boer and Christina Petterson, *Time of Troubles: A New Economic Framework for Early Christianity* (Minneapolis: Fortress, 2017), 79–81.

[103] E.g., J. G. Davies, "Pentecost and Glossolalia," *JTS* 3 (1952): 228–31; J. M. Scott, *Geography*, 64–5; Wenk, *Community*, 256; C. R. Holladay, *Acts*, 94.

[104] See Conzelmann, *Acts*, 14; Green, "Languages," 198–213.

[105] Green, "Languages," 212.

[106] Christoph Uehlinger, *Weltreich und "eine Rede": Eine neue Deutung der sogenannten Turmbauerzählung (Gen 11,1–9)*, OBO 101 (Göttingen: Vandenhoeck & Ruprecht, 1990).

that this map represents a specific list of diaspora nations, though, as he recognizes, there is little evidence for dependence on such a list.[107] Nevertheless, this mapping of diverse diasporic inhabitants of Jerusalem has led some scholars to assert that Acts is portraying Israel's eschatological ingathering.[108] James M. Scott sees a pattern of centripetal ingathering and centrifugal mission,[109] yet there is little evidence for another ingathering at any stage in Acts outside of Paul's own visits to Jerusalem, which hardly amount to an ingathering.[110] Indeed, Paul's vision in the temple subverts its centrality, instructing Paul to leave because Jerusalem will not accept his witness and sending him outward to the nations (22:17–21). Others have suggested that the list of nations is reliant on astrological lists of nations[111] or a "table of nations" relating to Gen. 10.[112] Given the obvious allusions to Babel (Gen. 11:1–9), it is not out of the question that Luke appeals to the table of nations.

Gary Gilbert suggests that Acts' list represents a parody of Roman conquest lists.[113] Such lists were common features in Roman political propaganda, evoking the empire's glory and power, the most famous being the extended catalogue of conquests in Augustus's *Res gestae* (chs. 25–33) affixed in bronze to temples throughout the empire.[114] Gilbert appeals to Tertullian's interpretation of Acts 2 (*Adv. Jud.* 7), which

---

[107] Barrett, *Acts*, 1:122. Cf. Philo, *Leg. Gai.* 281–2; Josephus, *Apion* 2.282; *War* 2.398; *Ant.* 14.114–18.

[108] Jacob Kremer, *Pfingstbericht und Pfingstgeschehen: Eine exegetische Untersuchung zu Apg 2,1–13*, SBS 63/64 (Stuttgart: KBW, 1973), 156; Donald H. Juel, *Luke-Acts: The Promise of History* (Atlanta: John Knox, 1983), 58; Rebecca Denova, *The Things Accomplished among Us: Prophetic Tradition in the Structural Pattern of Luke-Acts*, JSNTSup 141 (Sheffield: Sheffield Academic Press, 1997), 173; Jervell, *Apostelgeschichte*, 136.

[109] James M. Scott, "Acts 2:9–11 as an Anticipation of the Mission to the Nations," in *The Mission of the Early Church to Jews and Gentiles*, WUNT 127, eds. Jostein Ådna and Hans Kvalbein (Tübingen: Mohr Siebeck, 2000), 108–9, 117. See also Robert L. Brawley, *Luke-Acts and the Jews: Conflict, Apology, and Conciliation*, SBLMS 33 (Atlanta: Scholars Press, 1987), 34–6; Eberhard Güting, "Der geographische Horizont der sogenannten Volkerliste des Lukas," ZNW 66 (1975): 149–69.

[110] There is perhaps justification for portraying Acts 2 as an ingathering such as in Sir. 36:13 where the tribes come to receive their inheritance and, subsequently, move outward manifesting God's kingdom. See Denova, *Things*, 172–3; Pao, *Exodus*, 130–1. Others questioning the idea include Steve Smith, *The Fate of the Jerusalem Temple in Luke-Acts: An Intertextual Approach to Jesus' Laments over Jerusalem and Stephen's Speech*, LNTS 553 (London: Bloomsbury T&T Clark, 2017), 175; Steve Walton, "A Tale of Two Perspectives? The Place of the Temple in Acts," in *Heaven on Earth*, eds. T. Desmond Alexander and Simon J. Gathercole (Carlisle: Paternoster, 2004), 135–50, esp. 144–9.

[111] Stefan Weinstock, "The Geographical Catalogue in Acts II, 9–11," JRS 38 (1948): 43–6; J. A. Brinkman, "The Literary Background of the 'Catalogue of the Nations' (Acts 2:9–11)," CBQ 25 (1963): 418–27. Cf. C. R. Holladay, *Acts*, 97–8. This notion has been thoroughly critiqued by Bruce M. Metzger ("Ancient Astrological Geography and Acts 2.9–11," in *Apostolic History and the Gospel: Biblical and Historical Essays Presented to F. F. Bruce on His 60th Birthday*, eds. W. Ward Gasque and Ralph P. Martin (Exeter: Paternoster, 1970), 123–33).

[112] Connection to the "table of nations" has been most thoroughly developed by J. M. Scott (*Geography*, 68–84; see also Le Cornu and Shulam, *Acts*, 1:84–5). However, the parallels that he draws showing dependence have led to critique. See Gary Gilbert, "The List of Nations in Acts 2: Roman Propaganda and the Lukan Response," *JBL* 121 (2002): 504; Darrell L. Bock, *Acts*, BECNT (Grand Rapids: Baker Academic, 2007), 102.

[113] Gilbert, "List," 497–529.

[114] Gilbert, "List," 509. See, e.g., Vergil, *Aen.* 6.781–2; 8.714–28; Pliny the Elder, *Nat.* 7.98; Augustus, *Res ges.* 25–33; Horace, *Carm.* 4.14; Quintus Curtius, *History of Alexander* 6.3.2–3; Strabo, *Geog.* 4.3.2.

mentions not an ingathering but a movement through the whole world under Jesus's lordship, recognizing rhetorical similarities with Roman propaganda. Yet, Gilbert does not suggest that Luke presents Jesus as a subduing king similar to Caesar; rather, Luke creatively consumes dominant cultural production to reimagine legitimating narratives.[115] In so doing, Luke delegitimizes Roman claims concerning the organization of space. The nations are "under heaven" (v. 5), a space of cosmic authority inhabited by the enthroned Lord Jesus, at God's right hand. The list then portrays nations under Jesus's cosmic authority, not Caesar or Rome.

It is also particularly notable that this map of nations extends beyond Roman authority, including Parthia, portraying, contrary to Roman self-presentation, not a uniform civilized world (οἰκουμένη) under Roman control, but a world in tension. Indeed, to begin this map with Parthia, Rome's bitter enemy is provocative.[116] While the list includes mostly social-geographic territories, these territories (and two people groups, Medes and Elamites)[117] are listed between these two distinct peoples, the Parthians and the Romans, conveying a world in tension.[118] This is the world inhabited by the Jewish diaspora. Nevertheless, this world is "under heaven" (v. 5), and these great empires are subordinated to the heaven that Luke-Acts articulates, inhabited by the ascended Jesus.

Thus, this mapping rightly occurs in relation to doxological speech concerning God's "great things" (τὰ μεγαλεῖα τοῦ θεου, v. 11; cf. 7:2–47; 10:46; 13:17–22). God's "great things" are often associated with acts of deliverance and salvation (Deut. 11:2–7; Sir. 36:7 LXX; 3 Macc. 7.22), while at other times speaking of God's control over and fashioning of all creation (Sir. 17:9 LXX; 18:4; 42:21). Texts such as Sir. 36:1–22 place these great deeds in direct contrast to the claims of human authorities (esp. vv. 2–5). Certainly, this should bring to mind and reinforce the tenor and claims of the Benedictus (Lk. 1:68–79). Those hopes have not been dashed nor deferred; rather, they are unfolding.

---

[115] See Rowe, *World*, 128; Walton, "Heavens," 71–2. See also Jervell, *Apostelgeschichte*, 434. On Caesar as "king," see Appian, *Bell. civ.* 2.86; Herodian 2.4.4; Josephus, *War* 3.351; Acts 17:7; 1 Pet. 2:13, 17.

[116] See, e.g., Josephus, *War* 2.379; Suetonius, *Jul.* 44.3; *Aug.* 8.2; Tacitus, *Hist.* 1.2; Horace, *Carm.* 3.5.1–4.

[117] The list begins with three peoples, Parthians, Medes, and Elamites. J. M. Scott suggests that the Elamites and Medes represent locations where the tribes of the Northern Kingdom were exiled (2 Kgs 17:6; 18:11; Isa. 11:11; Dan. 5:31) (*Geography*, 76). Here, at least, they represent the eastern edge of the map.

[118] Note that the phrase "Jews and proselytes" (v. 11) occurs outside the framing by imperial peoples (vv. 9–10). However, it is not likely that this phrase means to add "Jews" in v. 11 to the list as one nation among other nations. First, all of the people implicated by the list in vv. 9–10 are Jews (v. 5). Second, Judea is already listed in v. 9. More likely, the phrase indicates that all the aforementioned peoples are Jews and proselytes. This is perfectly permissible by the grammar and conforms to the apparent structure of vv. 9–10 in which territories are bookended by imperial peoples. One issue, however, is the final awkward inclusion of "Cretans and Arabs." Otto Eißfeldt has suggested that the reference here to Crete and Arabia serves as a synecdoche where islands and inland are a poetic expression for all places ("Kreter und Araber," *TLZ* 72 (1947): 207–12. See also Kremer, *Pfingstbericht*, 153; Metzger, "Geography," 132). See, e.g., Jer. 2:10–11; Philo, *Leg. Gai.* 283.

4.2.3 Summary

Luke's imaging of cosmic-comprehensive and social-political space under heaven disrupts normative conceptions of organization and power. The dispersion of tongues, connected to the community's dispersion of resources, emphasizes distribution and outward movement. Peter's speech too, which invites the hearer to a different "knowledge," suggests a different ordering of the world under heaven and Jesus's enthronement. Salvation pertains to this reorganization of the cosmos, impacting social-political space.

4.3 Peter's Speech (Acts 2:14–36)

Acts has confronted us to this point with a great reordering. Peter's speech (2:14–36) is designed to persuade and bring knowledge to those in Jerusalem concerning the shape of what is unfolding in time and space. Below, I attend, first, to Peter's citation of Joel, an apocalyptic vision placing the current events within a cosmic context (vv. 14–21), and, second, I address the remainder of Peter's speech, which identifies this Jesus as Christ and Lord who is enthroned in heaven pouring out the Spirit (vv. 22–36).[119] The implication of this persuasion is a shift in allegiance from the lawless ones who executed Jesus (v. 23) to God and his Messiah, resulting in the gathering community a political body participating in and manifesting space of God's kingdom within the world (vv. 37–47).

4.3.1 The Last Days (Acts 2:14–21)

Peter begins by rhetorically casting the current events in light of apocalyptic prophecy, citing Joel 2:28–32 (3:1–5 LXX) and inviting a reimagining of time and cosmic order. Beginning with time, where Joel 3:1 LXX has "after these things" (μετὰ ταῦτα), Acts reads "in the last days" (ἐν ταῖς ἐσχάταις ἡμέραις). "In the last days" situates the audience in an apocalyptic and eschatological "now," reorienting time much as Jesus's "today" in Nazareth (Lk. 4:21). Nevertheless, Peter's citation makes no reference to the northern army of desolation (Joel 2:2–11, 20) or gentiles being gathered for judgment (3:2), and though the reader may be well enough versed in Joel to import those elements, this omission appears calculated.[120] Joel is used in service to Luke-Acts' conception of Israel's restoration. Within the Lukan program, this "time that remains" is one of repentance, restoration, and Israel as a light to the nations. Even if the latter missiological focus is absent (though see "all flesh," v. 17),[121] reference to the

---

[119] The speech naturally divides into three major segments marked by vocative address (vv. 14–21, 22–8, 29–36).
[120] C. M. Blumhofer writes, "The fundamental difference between Joel 3 and Acts 2 is to be found in God's action to begin the restoration of Israel but not to usher in with it the final judgement" ("Luke's Alteration of Joel 3.1–5 in Acts 2.17–21," *NTS* 62 (2016): 513).
[121] L. T. Johnson, e.g., avers that "all flesh" includes the nations, as in Isa. 40:5 and Lk. 3:4–6 (*Acts*, 49).

destruction of the nations appears conspicuously culled. The focus is on Israel's Spirit empowered restoration, the first missiological prong of Isa. 49:6.

The phrase "all flesh" (v. 17) is clarified in a way that results in social leveling through the universal bestowal of God's Spirit to sons and daughters, young and old, and finally to "my male servants and my female servants." This reference, "all flesh," draws one back to John's announcement of salvation in Lk. 3:4–6, which occurs in a similar context of social leveling using topographical metaphors (Isa. 40:3–5). "My male and my female servants" functions as a comprehensive designation for those receiving the Spirit. Joel 3:2 LXX does not include the double use of the first-person pronoun "my," but with the emendation in Peter's speech, these are clearly *God's* servants. C. M. Blumhofer has linked the servant language here with a Jubilee social ordering, pointing to Lev. 25:42, 55, where the moral logic of Jubilee is substantiated by Israel's status as God's servant redeemed from the exodus.[122] The implication would be that this apocalyptic vision supposes a social reordering such as Jesus proclaims in Nazareth (Lk. 4:18–21) and in the Jerusalem community (Acts 2:41–7).

At v. 19, new time is imagined alongside cosmic events, signs, and wonders. Cosmic-comprehensive order is disrupted in conjunction with social-political ordering. Signs (σημεῖον) and wonders (τέρας), when coupled in the LXX, in more than half of occurrences, refer to the exodus event,[123] the archetypal deliverance and disruption event already invoked through Luke.[124] Stylistically, this pair joins other terminological pairs—heaven and earth, above and below—casting these signs and wonders within comprehensive space engaged in this apocalyptic event. This unfolding cosmic upheaval connotes eschatological judgment complete with blood, fire, and smoke. The effect is to reimage cosmic-comprehensive space in a way that calls into question assumptions about the order it legitimates (cf. Lk. 23:44–9).[125] In the era of God's inbreaking salvation, however, these signs and wonders occur through the church (Acts 2:22, 43; 4:30; 5:12; 6:8; 14:3; 15:12; cf. 4:16, 22, 8:6, 13).

Joel's prophecy decenters the audience's conception of time and space. They live in the time between the advent of the last days and "the great and glorious day of the Lord" (v. 20). In this time, everyone who calls on the Lord's name will be saved. Those incorporated into the community (vv. 41–7) are those "being saved." Indeed, it is there where the salvation rhetorically introduced through Joel's prophecy is being realized and made manifest. Salvation's condition is "calling on the name of the Lord" (v. 20). Certainly, this "Lord" (κύριος) in Joel is God, but Peter's speech culminates with a

---

[122] Blumhofer, "Alteration," 509.
[123] Exod. 7:3, 9; 11:9–10; Deut. 4:34; 6:22; 7:19; 11:3; 26:8; 29:2; 34:11; Pss. 77:43 LXX; 104:27 LXX; 134:9 LXX; Jer. 39:20–1; Bar. 2:11. Joel's prophecy (3:3 LXX) contains only wonders (τέρας). In Acts 2:19, "signs" (σημεῖον) is inserted.
[124] Casting these events in terms of exodus-like delivery is not enough to assert a Sinai typology. Though "signs and wonders" are used for the exodus, this coupling occurs in contexts with no reference to exodus (e.g., Deut. 13:2–3 LXX; 28:46; Est. 10:3 LXX; Isa. 8:8; 20:3; Mt. 24:24; Mk 13:22; Jn 4:8). Referring to "signs and wonders" conjures the exodus but simply because it is paradigmatic example of God's redemption.
[125] Caesar is often presented as cosmically legitimated (Horace, *Carm.* 1.12.49–57; Suetonius, *Jul.* 88; Vergil, *Ecl.* 4.46–9).

declaration of Jesus's lordship (v. 36) and a call to be baptized in Jesus's name (v. 38). Indeed, there is no other name under heaven by which people can be saved (4:17).

4.3.2 Knowledge of the Christ and Lord (Acts 2:22–36)

Following his citation of Joel, Peter shifts attention to Jesus's centrality to this unfolding time and space. He begins with what he assumes the crowd already understands, namely, Jesus was a man attested by God through power, wonders, and signs (v. 19). Immediately, we are drawn back to Joel's prophecy. The signs and wonders that God foretold through Joel are manifest through Jesus (v. 22). Nevertheless, those in Jerusalem sided with lawless ones (v. 23). God responds by overturning their violence, not with violence, but with life. Indeed, God raises this one, not to bring retribution for this manifest injustice, but to make available forgiveness and repentance (5:31). It is not that God foregoes justice, but that God's justice is not manifest in mimicking this violence. God's justice is revealed in forgiveness and the establishment of justness, a lived reconciling reality, brought by persuasion and fidelity through Jesus. Peter's speech uncovers the identity of this Jesus, calling them to true knowledge.

Through a series of citations from the Psalms (Pss. 16:8–11; 110:1, 132:11), Peter argues that Davidic prophecy applies to Jesus on account of the resurrection,[126] characterizing the resurrection in terms of Davidic enthronement (v. 30; Ps. 132:11; cf. 2 Sam. 7:11–16; 4Q174 I, 7–13).[127] In v. 33, Peter identifies this enthroned Messiah with the Lord spoken of in Joel 3:1–5 LXX, pouring out the Spirit. Jesus is not subordinated to his forefather David, but placed in a superior position as his Lord (vv. 34–5; Ps. 110:1).[128] The Christ is not simply the human progeny of the Davidic line; rather, the Christ is David's Lord, possessing an authority that supersedes human authorities.[129]

Peter's speech reaches its climax at v. 36. Pointedly, he identifies the audience for this message as the "whole house of Israel," reinforcing the disciples' mission to Israel and resonating with the Isaianic servant theme.[130] Israel is to know that God has made Jesus both Lord and Christ, and this knowledge is juxtaposed to Jesus's crucifixion and its injustice. The speech is epistemological, juxtaposing Jesus's identity as Lord and Christ with the false knowledge that led to his execution. Crucifixion and God's response of

---

[126] On David as prophet, see Yuzuru Miura, "David as Prophet: The Use of Ps 15 (LXX) in Acts 2:25–31," *Exeg* 18 (2007): 21–46.

[127] Strauss, *Messiah*, 139.

[128] Though the citation (Ps. 110:1) is clearly messianic in the NT, there is little evidence that it was used messianically elsewhere. See Adela Yarbro Collins, *Mark: A Commentary*, Hermeneia (Minneapolis: Fortress, 2007), 579–80.

[129] The concept "messiah," in Second Temple Judaism was variegated (see James H. Charlesworth, ed., *The Messiah: Developments in Earliest Judaism and Christianity* (Minneapolis: Fortress, 1992); Gerbern S. Oegema, *The Anointed and His People: Messianic Expectations from the Maccabees to Bar Kochba*, JSPSup 27 (Sheffield: Sheffield Academic Press, 1988); Joseph A. Fitzmyer, *The One Who Is to Come* (Grand Rapids: Eerdmans, 2007)).

[130] Pilgrimage festivals such as Pentecost were seen as an assembly of all Israel and opportunities to discuss issues that pertained to the whole nation (Daniel K. Falk, "Festivals and Holy Days," in *Eerdmans Dictionary of Early Judaism*, eds. John J. Collins and Daniel C. Harlow (Grand Rapids: Eerdmans, 2010), 636; cf. Philo, *Spec. Leg.* 1.68–70).

resurrection uncover the lie and ignorance of those opposing Jesus (cf. 3:15; 4:10; 5:30; 10:39–40; 13:29–30). Resurrection is a cosmic victory and an act of persuasion.

God raised Jesus in order to offer Israel repentance and forgiveness of sins (5:31), to turn from this rejection to God, from Satan's authority to God's authority (26:18). It is not that forgiveness of sins is not available prior to the resurrection (e.g., Lk. 5:21–4; 7:47–9). However, the people have partnered in Jesus's execution, and Jesus can offer no forgiveness from death. Indeed, the people and authorities have rejected this forgiveness, yet Jesus does not return with retribution and violence to slaughter his enemies (cf. Lk. 19:27). The resurrection overturns Israel's rejection, and demonstrates God's forgiving initiative and perseverance for the people despite their continued rejection. God chooses persuasion. Jesus's resurrection manifests God's covenant fidelity and mercy, the forgiveness economy, and exposes injustice.

The audience is given two ways: the way they had already chosen (and from which they are called to repent) that sees Jesus as one worthy of crucifixion and the way being made known by God, acknowledging Jesus as Lord and Messiah. Do they side with God or the "lawless hands" through whom they have already been implicated (v. 23)? The conclusion of Peter's speech throws this juxtaposition in stark relief. Let all Israel *know* (γινώσκω) *truly* (ἀσφαλῶς) that God presented this Jesus as Lord and Christ, the one whom *you* (those in Jerusalem) crucified.[131]

4.4 The Crowd Responds (Acts 2:37–47)

The remainder of Acts 2 tells of the community's response to Peter's speech. Deeply affected and persuaded, the crowd asks Peter and the apostles what they must do. Peter calls the audience to respond to God's graciousness and this revelation with repentance and baptism, an embodied participation, response, and entrance into salvific space.

4.4.1 Repent and Be Baptized

Peter's specific exhortation (vv. 38–40) is to repent and be baptized in Jesus's name for the forgiveness of sins, so that the Holy Spirit will be poured out. The precise relationship between the various elements of Peter's response in v. 38 has been parsed and debated. In particular, there has been a trend that isolates and separates baptism and repentance, so that "for the forgiveness of sins" relates only to repentance, and baptism functions parenthetically.[132] The motivation, in most cases, is to separate the "external" act of baptism from the "internal" element of forgiveness, prioritizing the latter. F. F. Bruce, for instance, declares that baptism is merely "an external token."[133]

---

[131] Importantly, this is not a condemnation of Israel. Peter does not make known to Israel that "you crucified" Jesus, but that God made him Lord and Christ. Those in Jerusalem, not all Israel, are then the subject of ἐσταυρώσατε in v. 26.

[132] See, e.g., Dunn, *Baptism*, 96–8. Cf. George R. Beasley-Murray, *Baptism in the New Testament* (Grand Rapid: Eerdmans, 1962), 102–3, 107–8, 120–2, 263–6, 271–9, 303–5, 393–5.

[133] Bruce, *Book*, 70.

This argument is made on at least two grammatical fronts. First, H. E. Dana and Julius R. Mantey advanced the idea that Acts 2:38 contains a rare "causal" εἰς (because of). In this way, baptism and forgiveness are severed by making baptism a causal response to forgiveness already declared, removing the significance of embodied action in favor of the reductively spiritual. They reject the standard purposive εἰς (for) because it implies that baptism is "a ceremonial means of salvation," doing "violence to Christianity as a whole, for one of its striking distinctions from Judaism and Paganism is that it is a religion of salvation by faith while others teach salvation by works"[134] Their theological bias is explicit and based on a problematic view of Christianity and Judaism. Nevertheless, this has view been roundly refuted in favor of the purposive εἰς.[135]

Second, Luther B. McIntyre, for one, has argued that the imperative βαπτισθήτω (be baptized) is grammatically subordinate because it switches to third-person singular, whereas μετανοήσατε (repent) and the pronoun attached to the prepositional phrase εἰς ἄφεσιν τῶν ἁμαρτιῶν ὑμῶν (for forgiveness of your sins) are both second-person plural.[136] McIntyre argues that according to the rule of concord forgiveness of sins must refer simply to repentance. Nevertheless, Ashby L. Camp has aptly demonstrated that McIntyre's grammatical argument does not demand the theological results he posits, and more to the point, the rule of concord does not apply here.[137] The rhetorical amendment of the subject to the singular ἕκαστος (each one) modified by a similar second-person plural pronoun, ὑμῶν, functions to intensify the exhortation with reference to baptism.[138]

There is nothing, grammatically speaking, that prompts one to subordinate baptism or sever the link between baptism and forgiveness of sins. Nevertheless, theological, anthropological, and epistemological biases influence the search for an interpretation that assumes a repentance that does not necessitate "physical" acts such as baptism. However, baptism is not the external act of an internal repentance, but the enactment of embodied repentance (see Chapter 2). The link between baptism and forgiveness

---

[134] H. E. Dana and Julius R. Mantey, *A Manual Grammar of the Greek New Testament* (New York: Macmillan, 1957), 104. See also Julius R. Mantey, "The Causal Use of Eis in the New Testament," *JBL* 70 (1951): 45–8; idem, "On Causal Eis Again," *JBL* 70 (1951): 309–11.

[135] See Mantey's primary interlocutor, Ralph Marcus, "On Causal Eis," *JBL* 70 (1951): 129–30; idem, "The Elusive Causal Eis," *JBL* 71 (1952): 43–4. J. C. Davis asserts, "A study of standard Greek lexicons, dictionaries, and grammars of the past two hundred years from throughout the entire theological spectrum shows, on the one hand, that 'causal' *eis* in Acts 2:38 is without a real grammatical foundation and, on the other hand, 'purposive' *eis* in Acts 2:38 is firmly established. An examination of all the New Testament passages that mention 'baptism' and 'forgiveness,' 'baptism' and 'salvation,' or 'baptism' and 'washing away of sins' shows that the order is always the same. Forgiveness, salvation, washing away of sins always follow baptism, never precede it" ("Another Look at the Relationship between Baptism and Forgiveness of Sins in Acts 2:38," *ResQ* 24 (1981): 80–8).

[136] Luther B. McIntyre Jr., "Baptism and Forgiveness in Acts 2:38," *BSac* 153 (1996): 53–62.

[137] Ashby L. Camp, "Reexamining the Rule of Concord in Acts 2:38," *ResQ* 39 (1997): 37–42.

[138] Carroll D. Osburn, "The Third Person Imperative in Acts 2:38," *ResQ* 26 (1983): 81–4; See also A. Andrew Das, "Acts 8: Water, Baptism, and the Spirit," *ConcJ* 19 (1993): 117–18.

is not surprising (Lk. 3:3; Acts 2:38), nor is the fact that baptism generally precedes reception of the Spirit,[139] since reception of the Spirit is a demonstration of cleanliness (cf. 15:8–9).[140] Similarly, neither should we reduce forgiveness to an internal principle. Forgiveness is a socially productive reality. God's forgiveness and the economy of forgiveness within which the church immerses itself in baptism instantiates a specific social order characterized by release.

This baptism, like John's baptism, is not simply an absolving ritual, but a participatory transformative event by which one enters into salvation. As Catherine Bell argues, rituals are transformative practices that shape one's place within the world and the space within which one exists.[141] She criticizes modern anthropological research for persistently replicating and deepening a subject-object dichotomy,[142] characterizing this intellectual and discursive activity as a distorting subordination of artificially manufactured spheres in otherwise irreducibly complex phenomena.[143] Bell argues that ritual, as practice, is an integrated reality, dependent on its specific location and contextual embeddedness, that forms one's place within a social and cosmic order. Enacting and participation in ritual serves to restructure bodies in the act of doing

---

[139] There is debate concerning the relationship between baptism and the Holy Spirit, particularly where the pattern exhibited in 2:38 is disregarded: 8:4–17; 10:34–48; 19:1–7. See, e.g., Anthony Ash, "John's Disciples: A Serious Problem," *ResQ* 45 (2003): 85–93; Friedrich Avemarie, *Die Tauferzählungen der Apostelgeschichte*, WUNT 139 (Tübingen: Mohr Siebeck, 2002), 129–74; Beasley-Murray, *Baptism*, 105–22; Schuyler Brown, "'Water Baptism' and 'Spirit Baptism' in Luke-Acts," *AThR* 59 (1977): 135–51; Ellen Juhl Christiansen, "Taufe als Initiation in der Apostelgeschichte," *ST* 40 (1986): 55–79; Das, "Acts," 108–34; Dunn, *Baptism*, 55–72, 90–102; Gordon D. Fee, "Baptism in the Holy Spirit: The Issue of Separability and Subsequence," *Pneuma* 7 (1985): 87–99; Lloyd David Franklin, "Spirit Baptism: Pneumatological Continuance," *RevExp* 94 (1997): 15–30; Green, "Baptism," 157–72; Heidrun Gunkel, *Der Heilige Geist bei Lukas*, WUNT 2/389 (Tübingen: Mohr Siebeck, 2015), 194–236; Menzies, *Empowered*, 202–28; Turner, *Power*, 352–400; Sarah Hinlicky Wilson, "Water Baptism and Spirit Baptism in Luke-Acts: Another Reading of the Evidence," *Pneuma* 38 (2016): 476–501.

[140] Cornelius provides the primary example of divergence from the baptismal pattern (2:38), receiving the Spirit prior to baptism. Cornelius was a special case, apparently more about witnessing to Peter (15:8) and the church about God's concern for border-crossing fellowship (Green, "Baptism," 166–7; Reardon, "Cleansing," 472–5). One might, in this scenario, see God overlooking the need for an embodied act of cleansing, yet this is not so. Cleansing is a particularly salient theme in the three recountings of the Cornelius event (10:1–48; 11:1–18; 15:7–9). The plain cause of God's declaration of cleanliness is Cornelius's acts of righteousness, typified by prayer and almsgiving (10:2, 4, 15, 34–35; 15:7–9; cf. Lk. 11:37–44). Baptism, as an embodied act of repentance, is not replaced by an internal act (e.g., faith), nor is it replaced by another external act (i.e., almsgiving); rather, the emphasis is on the embodied nature of repentance enacted in baptism and acts of righteousness (10:35).

[141] Catherine Bell, *Ritual Theory, Ritual Practice* (New York: Oxford University Press, 1992).

[142] Bell (*Ritual*, 25) indicates that this distinction between thought and action "runs particularly deep in the intellectual traditions of Western culture." Even in ritual studies, where, Bell notes, theorists have postulated ritual as an activity that overcomes the bifurcation of subject and object, these theorists conceptualize this activity in a way that privileges the subjective aspect of the ritual activity—the thought, intention, or emotion behind ritual—in such a way that makes the action itself superfluous.

[143] Bell, *Ritual*, 48–9: "Yet the more subtle and far-reaching distortion is not the obvious bifurcation of a single, complex reality into dichotomous aspects that can exist in theory only. Rather, it is the far more powerful act of subordination disguised in such differentiations, the subordination of act to thought, or actors to thinkers."

the ritual.¹⁴⁴ A baptism of repentance is the crowd's primary, embodied, and formative response to this epistemological and apocalyptic disclosure.

Peter's declaration—in development from John's baptism (Lk. 3:3)—that this baptism is now "in the name of Jesus Christ" (ἐπὶ τῷ ὀνόματι Ἰησοῦ Χριστοῦ; Acts 2:38; cf. 8:12, 16; 10:43, 48; 19:5; 22:16) brings with it several implications. First, baptism inaugurates one into the community where Jesus is Christ and Lord. The production of social-political space, the community's life within the world, is governed by this imaging of Jesus's place in cosmic space. Second, as a result, even if reluctantly, it is a community at odds. On one level, Jesus is Lord of all, not Caesar (10:38).¹⁴⁵ On another level, Peter juxtaposes this social reality—the present manifestation of kingdom space—to the present "crooked generation" (v. 40). The resultant conflict can be seen, for instance, where the Jerusalem leadership responds to the apostles primarily because they are preaching (in Jesus's name) in a way that brings the leadership's own authority into question (4:7, 17–18; 5:28, 40–1; 9:14–15).¹⁴⁶ Third, baptism into this name is baptism into salvation. Baptism in this Lord's name draws the reader back to Joel's prophecy (v. 21). Peter's identification of Jesus as Lord makes baptism in Jesus's name the fulfillment of Joel's prophecy that all who call on the Lord's name will be saved (σώθητε).

4.4.2 Salvific Space

Baptism inaugurates one into the community of salvation manifest at Pentecost. Max Turner notes that this community, serving God in holiness and justness/righteousness, looks a lot like the fulfillment of Lk. 1:71–5.¹⁴⁷ In v. 47, "those who are being saved" (τοὺς σῳζομένους), a substantive imperfective participle, describes a community experiencing this unfolding reality of salvation as people are added daily. Here, explicitly, *now* is the time of salvation. Salvation is not merely an existentially appropriated forgiveness mediated between the individual believer and God; "salvation is incorporation into the Christocentric community."¹⁴⁸

The link between baptism and the community is clear in the structure of the passage itself, where vv. 41 and 42 are linked by a μέν/δέ construction so that the development and life of the community itself is tied to the Pentecost event. Verse 42 offers something of a summary of vv. 43–7, containing two couplets joined by καί: they devote themselves

---

¹⁴⁴ Bell, *Ritual*, 93: "The strategies of ritualization are particularly rooted in the body, specifically, the interaction of the social body within a symbolically constituted spatial and temporal environment. Essential to ritualization is the circular production of a ritualized body which in turn produces ritualized practices. Ritualization is embedded within the dynamics of the body defined within a symbolically structured environment."

¹⁴⁵ See Rowe, *World*, 103–16.

¹⁴⁶ Notably, the Jerusalem leadership's concern is not with heresy, but their own authority. See Reardon, "Crucifixion," 420–3.

¹⁴⁷ Turner, *Power*, 406–15. Turner adds that both of the first community summaries in Acts (2:42–7; 4:32–7) immediately follow outpourings of the Spirit (2:1–4; 4:31), highlighting the Spirit's role in community formation. Wenk writes, "If in Luke's account the Spirit is mainly (or even exclusively) the Spirit of prophecy in the sense of proclamation or inspired speech, one would expect to find emphasis on the church's witness and preaching in the first two summaries, following the diffusion of the Spirit" (*Community*, 270).

¹⁴⁸ Green, "Saviour," 91–2. See Rowe, *World*, 101.

to (1) the apostles' teaching (v. 43) and the community (vv. 44–5) and (2) the breaking of bread (v. 46) and prayers (v. 46–47a). Though the precise relationship between these elements is not completely clear, each offers a distinct aspect of the community.

Those participating in this community are called "the faithful" (οἱ πιστεύοντες, v. 44). Significantly, at this juncture, faithfulness designates neither a cognitive ascent nor simply a personal quality. This is indicated by its connection with the actions of fellowship (κοινωνία) to which it is coupled (vv. 44–5). As Teresa Morgan has argued, this sort of faithfulness (πίστις) is an organizational component of the community:[149] "*Pistis* is not only part of, but is structural to, the kingdom or household of God, both earthly and eschatological. In imagining the divine-human relationship as creating a *politeia* structured by virtues, a new society through which, if it does not in practice replace all one's existing social relationships, all one's other relationships are reinterpreted."[150] This fidelity (πίστις) creates community and structures it according to a specific relational economy.

The term κοινωνία (fellowship) has a relatively broad semantic range centered around tangible fellowship and relationship. This could include a community of goods or business compacts, and although it could refer to the communal abolishing of private ownership (e.g., Plato, *Resp.* 449D, 550C), it need not necessarily.[151] Opinions vary regarding the precise nature of the community's fellowship and sharing presented in Acts 2, and we need not settle that matter here. Nevertheless, with this term comes not only a relationship but also mutual responsibility. This κοινωνία is not merely a "spirit" of communion and unity, the community's fellowship (κοινωνία) pertains to its whole life as a theopolitical body.[152] In vv. 44–5, the faithful are said to have all things

---

[149] Teresa Morgan, *Roman Faith and Christian Faith: Pistis and Fides in the Early Roman Empire and Early Churches* (Oxford: Oxford University Press, 2015), 477. Faith should not be understood in terms of a subject/object split: "[Faith] is, first and foremost, neither a body of beliefs nor a function of the heart or mind, but a relationship which creates community" (p. 14). Morgan adds that the interiority of faith is largely neglected by first-century writers in favor of a focus on relationality and community praxis, though she understands a full understanding of πίστις/*fides* is simultaneously cognitive, affective, and relational. For critiques of Morgan's work, see Francis Watson, "Roman Faith and Christian Faith," *NTS* 64 (2018): 243–7; Mark A. Seifrid, "Roman Faith and Christian Faith," *NTS* 64 (2018): 247–55; as well as Morgan's more-than-able response "Roman Faith and Christian Faith," *NTS* 64 (2018): 255–61.

[150] Morgan, *Faith*, 499. Notably the first few occurrences of πιστεύω in Acts include no object and appear in context of communal formation (2:44; 4:4, 32; 5:14; cf. 11:21).

[151] See, e.g., Seneca, *Ep.* 90.38; Plato, *Resp.* 420C–422D, 462B–464A; *Leg.* 679B–C; 684C–D; 744B–746C; 757C. See also Steve Walton, "Primitive Communism in Acts? Does Acts Present the Community of Goods (2:44–45; 4:32–35) as Mistaken?" *EvQ* 80 (2008): 103.

[152] Scholars perceive this economic fellowship in various ways. On κοινωνία as spiritual fellowship, see Heinrich Seesemann, *Der Begriff KOINΩNIA im Neuen Testament*, BZNW 74 (Giessen: Töpelmann, 1933), 87–92; Pervo, *Acts*, 92–3. Conversely, Reta Haltemann Finger rejects minimizing the material, economic fellowship associated with κοινωνία (*Of Widows and Meals: Communal Meals in the Book of Acts* (Grand Rapids: Eerdmans, 2007), 226–7). Brian Capper argues that the passage betrays a historical community modeled on Essene communism ("Community of Goods in the Early Jerusalem Church," *ANRW* 26.2:1730–74; idem, "The Palestinian Cultural Context of the Earliest Christian Community of Goods," in *The Book of Acts in Its Palestinian Setting*, ed. Richard Bauckham, BAFCS 4 (Grand Rapids: Eerdmans, 1995), 323–56; idem, "Holy Community of Life and Property amongst the Poor: A Response to Steve Walton," *EvQ* 80 (2008): 113–27). Barrett

in common (ἅπαντα κοινά), selling their property and possessions and distributing according to need. Without a doubt, there was economic communion that required using one's resources for the benefit of the community.[153]

Reference to "having all things in common" (ἅπαντα κοινά) echoes the topos of friendship found in both philosophical literature and general parlance,[154] and in the familiar proverb κοινὰ τὰ φίλων (friends hold all things in common).[155] The topos's frequent invocation in multiple situations gives it a semantic expansiveness that is tough to pin down outside of the context in which it appears. Luke appeals to this malleable notion of friendship, investing it with the specific economy of God's kingdom, though, rather than speaking of the community as friends, they are the faithful, those characterized by fidelity (πίστις).[156] That is, the friendship topos does not constrain the description of the community, but is rather a vehicle for explicating the nature of God's manifesting kingdom. Rhetorically, this common reference point, the friendship topos, functions as an exhortative characterization of the model community, presenting this reciprocity and economic community as an ideal, not a utopian ideal that appeals to some unreachable and never-to-be-repeated beginning, but a perlocutionary and rhetorical description of a communal way of being. In this economic fellowship, the Jubilee economy is manifest and salvific space participated in.

This presentation of the community, with its remarkable level of economic sharing, emphasizes what was a major theme of Jesus's teaching: God owns all things and the possessions of the community should be held lightly (e.g., Lk. 6:30; 12:13–34; 16:1–31).[157] Not all are equally in need; the poor are placed at the center.[158] Importantly, this is at odds with then standard formulations of the friendship topos, which tend to focus on relationships between social equals. Additionally, this dismantles any notion of reciprocity that would force the receiver of help to

---

has argued that Luke refers to a community of goods as a historical reality but does not himself advocate it (*Acts*, 1:167–9). Others see economic sharing emphasized but stop short of a community of goods (Luke Timothy Johnson, *Sharing Possessions: What Faith Demands*, 2nd ed. (Grand Rapids: Eerdmans, 2011), 109–34; idem, *The Literary Function of Possessions in Luke-Acts*, SBLDS 39 (Missoula, MT: Scholars Press, 1977), 183–90; Walton, "Communism," 99–111; Christopher M. Hays, *Luke's Wealth Ethics: A Study in Their Coherence and Character*, WUNT 2/275 (Tübingen: Mohr Siebeck, 2010), 200–1).

[153] Cf. Rom. 15:25–32; 1 Cor. 16:1–4; 2 Cor. 8–9; Gal. 2:10; Phil. 4:15–20; *Did.* 4.5–8; *Barn.* 19.8.

[154] On the topos of friendship in relation to the Acts community see C. M. Hays, *Wealth*, 50–4, 201–11; Walton, "Communism," 103; L. T. Johnson, *Literary*, 186–7; idem, *Sharing Possessions*, 111–27; Alan C. Mitchell, "The Social Function of Friendship in Acts 2:44–47 and 4:32–37," *JBL* 111 (1991): 255–72; John T. Fitzgerald, ed., *Greco-Roman Perspectives on Friendship*, SBLSBS 34 (Atlanta: Scholars Press, 1997). For an extensive listing of primary sources, see Talbert, *Reading*, 48–9.

[155] Diogenes Laertius maintains that Pythagoras was the one to coin the slogan "friends hold all things in common" (κοινὰ τὰ φίλων εἶναι, *Life of Pythagoras*, 9.10). Note also Plato, *Resp.* 424A, 449C. See also Acts 4:32.

[156] Mitchell rightly notes that Luke is more concerned with a general popular topos on friendship into which he invests a particular sense rather than absorbing a rigid philosophical distinction into his theology ("Social Function," 257).

[157] This logic undergirds the Lukan theme of almsgiving and divestment (e.g., Lk. 11:41; 12:23, 33; 14:33; 18:22; Acts 3:2–3, 10; 9:36; 10:2, 4, 31; 24:17).

[158] See, Eckhard Schnabel, *Early Christian Mission*, 2 vols. (Downers Grove, IL: InterVarsity Press, 2004), 1:413–14.

return in kind. As Alan C. Mitchell writes, "Friendship was doubtless a vehicle for wealth, status, and power for the ruling elite of Luke's day. Normally, it was formed within social orders, and its benefits were shared by people of the same status. Luke, however, uses friendship to equalize relationships in his own community."[159] Thus, though the language invokes familiar notions of friendship, Luke invests this concept with a distinct emphasis.

One of the most telling practices of this early community, however, is sharing food. Food, drink, and meals appear constantly throughout Luke-Acts,[160] and some of the most fundamental revelatory moments occur in relation to meals: the feeding of the 5,000 in the desert (9:10–17), the Last Supper (22:7–38), and Jesus's appearance to his disciples after his resurrection (24:28–35, 36–43).[161] In Acts, Jesus initially instructs the disciples while eating with them (1:4), the community is structured around feeding widows (6:1–7), and the acceptance of gentiles is understood saliently through the lens of table fellowship (10:9–16, 11:3; 15:20; see also 20:7, 11; 27:35–6).

Table-fellowship was an intimate affair tied directly to the order of the cosmos.[162] One's social standing, kin, and general honor played out in the performance of meals. The arrangement of persons, those excluded and included, purity rituals, and even the type of food act out the structure of the world, a structure that people both legitimate and are captive to. Deviations from the norm can serve to upset that cosmic ordering. Jesus's table fellowship helped produce social-political space that was in many ways at odds with and an affront to normative social ordering.[163] Robert J. Karris goes as

---

[159] Mitchell, "Social Function," 272.

[160] See, e.g., Lk. 5:27–39; 7:36–50; 9:10–17; 10:38–42; 11:37–54; 12:38; 13:29–30; 14:1–23; 15:1–2; 19:1–10; 22:7–38; 24:13–35, 36–53; Acts 2:42–7; 6:1–7; 11:2; 16:34. On table fellowship and hospitality in Luke-Acts, see Willi Braun, *Feasting and Social Rhetoric in Luke 14*, SNTSMS 85 (Cambridge: Cambridge University Press, 1995); Kathleen E. Corley, *Private Women, Public Meals: Social Conflict in the Synoptic Tradition* (Peabody, MA: Hendrickson, 1993), 108–46; Esler, *Community*, 71–109; R. H. Finger, *Widows*, 169–93; John Paul Heil, *The Meals Scenes in Luke-Acts: An Audience-Oriented Approach*, SBLMS 52 (Atlanta: Society of Biblical Literature, 1999); Joshua W. Jipp, *Saved by Faith and Hospitality* (Grand Rapids: Eerdmans, 2017), 17–34; Just, *Feast*; Robert J. Karris, *Luke: Artist and Theologian: Luke's Passion Account as Literature*, SCBTP (New York: Paulist, 1985), 47–78; idem, "Food in the Gospel," *TBT* 38 (2000): 357–61; Martin William Mittelstadt, "Eat, Drink, and Be Merry: A Theology of Hospitality in Luke-Acts," *WW* 34 (2014): 131–9; Moxnes, *Economy*; Jerome H. Neyrey, "Ceremonies in Luke-Acts: The Case of Meals and Table Fellowship," in *The Social World of Luke Acts: Models for Interpretation*, ed. Jerome H. Neyrey (Peabody, MA: Hendrickson, 1991), 361–87; David W. Pao, "Waiters or Preachers: Acts 6:1–7 and the Lukan Table Fellowship Motif," *JBL* 130 (2011): 127–44; William K. Poon, "Superabundant Table Fellowship in the Kingdom: The Feeding of the Five Thousand and the Meal Motif in Luke," *ExpTim* 114 (2003): 224–30; Dennis E. Smith, "Table Fellowship as a Literary Motif in the Gospel of Luke," *JBL* 106 (1987): 613–38; Santos Yao, "Dismantling Social Barriers through Table Fellowship: Acts 2:42–47," in *Mission in Acts: Ancient Narratives in Contemporary Context*, eds. Paul Hertig and Robert R. Gallagher (Maryknoll, NY: Orbis Books, 2004), 29–36.

[161] On hospitality: Lk. 4:39; 5:27, 29; 10:38; 19:5–7; Acts 16:14–15, 34; 18:7; 28:7, 14.

[162] On the cosmic ordering associated with table fellowship, see Mary Douglas, "Deciphering a Meal," in *Myth, Symbol, and Culture*, ed. Clifford Geertz (New York: Norton, 1971), 61; Neyrey, "Ceremonies," 366.

[163] Note specifically Jesus's boundary-breaking meals with tax-collectors and "sinners" (Lk. 5:30; 7:34; 15:1) and his emphasis on inclusion of the poor, crippled, lame, and blind (14:7–25).

far as to assert that "Jesus got himself crucified because of the way he ate."[164] This new community, formed by the boundary defying Spirit, embodies that way of eating,[165] and they accept it as eschatological joy (ἀγαλλίασις, v. 46; see also Lk. 1:14, 44; 15).[166]

It is fitting that the climax to the Pentecost event is community. The narrative reshaping of time and space that unfolds here results in a distinct body under heaven where Jesus is Christ and Lord. To this community, the Lord added to those being saved, those who are manifesting salvation in the world. By participating in this salvific space, "redemption from the hands of our enemies" (Lk. 1:71, 74) is not brought about through revolt, but through the recognition and participation in the true structure of the world and the movement of the Spirit producing space of salvation.

4.5 Conclusion

Salvation in Luke-Acts is a comprehensive reality unfolding not simply in believers' hearts, or between individuals and God, but within space organized around bodies, a reconciliation of heaven and earth. In this chapter, we saw how the salvation narrative unfolds in a dynamic cosmic drama, moving through Jesus's life, death, and resurrection and oriented by heaven, the location of God, divine authority, Jesus's ascension, and the source of the Spirit's descent. The dynamic of cosmic reconciliation advancing in Luke-Acts involves two spatial trajectories: (1) the "vertical" movement of heaven invading earth and (2) the "horizontal" movement outward from Jerusalem throughout the mundane world, sustained by God's Spirit, who empowers the production of salvific space and the community. These trajectories are, together, a movement *for* the world and the restoration of all things.

Cosmic-comprehensive space has, at its center, Jesus's ascension, the consummation of his journey as the one raised to restore Israel as the promised Davidic king. Jesus's enthronement as Lord in heavenly space demystifies and delegitimates the cosmic ideological claims of other reigning authorities, including Rome. Caesar is not Lord of all; Jesus is. The heavenly centering of *this* Jesus, opposed by worldly authorities, proclaiming and embodying an *other* kingdom governed by an alternate construction social-political space, critiques prevailing authorities who demonstrate their opposition against God's salvific intervention (cf. 4:25–7; 5:27–32).

---

[164] Karris, *Artist*, 70.
[165] C. M. Hays notes, the community here lives out Jesus's economic teaching and example, specifically in terms of hospitality, sharing food, personal divestiture and giving to the poor. The only major element missing in Acts 2 is restitution (Lk. 19:8), but this is because, at least as of yet, there has been no extortion in the community (*Wealth*, 210). See, e.g., the emphasis on giving to the poor and in need (Lk. 6:29–34; 10:25–37; 12:33; 14:7–14; 18:22), against the rich hoarding (12:16–21; 16:1–13, 19–31; 17:26–33), sharing meals (3:11; 14:12–24), and generosity and love (10:25–7; 16:29–31; 18:18–22).
[166] Note the theme of the eschatological banquet and its tie to status reversal (e.g., Isa. 25:6–8; Lk. 13:24–30; 14:15–24). Pao, "Waiters," 134.

This salvation narrative is one of cosmic conflict, which, as with our Irenaean scheme, involves God's movement to release humanity from bondage to Satan. Satan moves behind the scenes as worldly authorities align against Jesus; and the cross, at the "opportune time" (Lk. 4:13; 22:3, 53), becomes a stage of cosmic conflict. Jesus, in Jerusalem, forgoes the strategies of power utilized by mundane authorities, adopting what Irenaeus calls *persuasion* (*Haer.* 5.1.1), a posture that rejects the domination and imposed violence of worldly realities. In this way, crucifixion is a revelation that uncovers Jesus's own justness, preemptive forgiveness, and the injustice of involved authorities. The cross, in its grave unjustness, reveals Jesus's fidelity to God (and God's kingdom) as well as God's covenant fidelity to Israel—the Father sending his Son in covenant fidelity despite the world's rejection (cf. 20:13–15; Irenaeus, *Haer.* 4.5.4). This is God's consistent action *for* humanity, raising Jesus victoriously not to avenge injustice or to slaughter his enemies (Lk. 19:11–36), but to offer forgiveness and repentance (Acts 5:31).

The rhetoric of the cross is centrally important for Peter, exhorting the crowd to "know" the truth about this Jesus, juxtaposing what "you" (the Jerusalemites) did with God's affirmation of Jesus as Lord and Christ (Acts 2:23–4). The cross is an epistemological event. Saving *knowledge* is a revelation of the true structure of the cosmos that brings Peter's audience to repentance and exhorts them to saving participation in the enduring reality of God's community. Practically, this cosmic reimagining frees the community, empowered by the Spirit, to envision, reorder, and produce alternate spaces of social-political life, forming a social-political body organized around an economy of mutuality and common fidelity (2:41–7), in which there is social, economic, and spiritual release for those *being saved*. Though worldly authorities still exercise power, this power only prevails in the *time that remains*, the times and seasons of restoration (cf. 1:7; 3:21). The church's existence is not one of opposition, but of positive manifestation of an other, apocalyptically revealed order, in community within the world, for the world, and enmeshed in the world.

In the time that remains, the community participates in the social-political reality of salvation that is invading from heaven, impacting the space around it, while they are intimately enmeshed within it, witnessing to Jesus's resurrection and God's kingdom to the end of the earth. The *end* of the salvation narrative is God's restoration of all things, a comprehensive and spatial vision of salvation. However, this does not push salvation to the indeterminate future. Salvation involves an unfolding reconciliation, a cosmic atonement, conjoining heaven to earth by the Spirit, an extension of enduring atonement space. In our next chapter, Chapter 5, Paul and Barnabas go forth on the outward missional trajectory proclaiming this salvation to the end of the earth.

5

The Mission of Salvation and Historical Recurrence (Acts 13:16–52)

In Chapter 4, I discussed heaven invading and salvation taking up space in the world, a comprehensive, social, and political salvation involving the reconciliation of all things to God and impacting the organization of bodies and Jesus's body on earth. This spatial reality involves not only the production of social space oriented by heaven but also two trajectories: heaven's inbreaking salvific movement into mundane space and the church's outward missional trajectory from Jerusalem to the end of the earth. In Chapter 5, I discuss two such Spirit-inspired, missional agents, Paul and Barnabas, as they come to Pisidian Antioch. Their message continues Luke-Acts' comprehensive and political soteriology.

When standing to speak in the Antiochene synagogue, Paul's portrait of salvation is not one of personal forgiveness and reductively religious reconciliation; rather, he preaches an enthroned king and Israel's national restoration. Paul proclaims forgiveness of sins not as achieved by Jesus's death's satisfying God's need for just restitution for past sin; instead, as in previous chapters, forgiveness, God's initiatory disposition, is socially productive, gathering a people who participate in the manifestation of God's justness in fidelity to God's king. These are those who are faithful, as in the Jerusalem community, and by their fidelity they are justified. The gathering of this people, in keeping with Pentecost's remaking of space, spreads outward, overcomes boundaries, and includes gentiles.

Paul's synagogue sermon is structured by a story of *historical recurrence*, emphasizing God's continual faithfulness. God chooses and redeems Israel from captivity, and moves them toward God's ordering. Despite the recurrence of Israel's rejection of God's rule, God works through covenant mercy, manifesting enduring acts of faithfulness for Israel, including Jesus's ascension. It is a salvation narrative grounded in Israel. Understanding the embeddedness of this salvation story in God's covenant with Israel helps us understand further how salvation, forgiveness, and even the rare occurrence of justification language in Luke-Acts should be understood. As I conclude, I note some of the tensions that remain at the end of Luke's narrative, though not at the *end* of the *salvation narrative*.

5.1 Setting the Scene

After arriving in Pisidian Antioch, Paul and Barnabas go to the synagogue on the Sabbath where they are asked to offer a word of consolation (παράκλησις, v. 15; cf. Lk. 2:25; Acts 15:32).[1] Acts 13:16–52 presents the first instance of Paul's missionary preaching, and the only such example of diaspora synagogue preaching, a perpetual locale for Paul's mission (9:20; 13:5, 14; 14:1; 17:1–2, 10, 17; 18:4, 19, 26; 19:8), going first to Jews (cf. 1:8; 3:26; 13:46; cf. Rom. 1:16; 2:9–10). Much like Jesus's and Peter's inaugural addresses, this speech has programmatic significance, giving us a glimpse into Paul's standard synagogue address.[2]

Some have noted parallels between Jesus's Nazareth preaching (Lk. 4:16–30) and Paul's speech here.[3] Both speeches inaugurate Jesus's and Paul's respective missions at a synagogue (Lk. 4:16; Acts 13:14). Both Jesus and Paul find initial success (Lk. 4:22; Acts 13:42–3; cf. 2:37–47), speak of gentiles (Lk. 4:25–7; Acts 13:44–8; cf. 2:39; 3:25–6), are eventually rejected (Lk. 4:23–30; Acts 13:44–50; cf. 4:1–3; 6:8–15), and subsequently heal a lame man (Lk. 5:17–26; Acts 14:8–10; cf. 3:1–10). Further, Paul's speech is preceded by encountering and overcoming Satan in the figure of Bar-Jesus (Acts 13:6–12; cf. Lk. 4:1–13), who is called son of the devil (v. 10).[4] Paul's engagement with Bar-Jesus is done "full of the Holy Spirit" (v. 9; cf. Lk. 4:1). Whereas Paul and Barnabas are prophets (13:1; cf. Lk. 4:24), Bar-Jesus is a false prophet (v. 6). Though Paul's speech in Antioch does not directly address cosmic struggle and the manifestation of the demonic in mundane powers, the overarching cosmic drama remains in the background. Mundane events and the machinations of worldly powers continue to be intimately related to cosmological forces (Lk. 4:5–7; 22:3, 53) and the foundational struggle with Satan persists (Acts 26:18).

---

[1] Perhaps this phrase describes a sermon (cf. Heb. 13:22; 1 Tim. 4:13; 1 Macc. 10:24; 2 Macc. 15:11). See C. R. Holladay, *Acts*, 265; L. T. Johnson, *Acts*, 230; Keener, *Acts*, 2:2047. C. A. Joachim Pillai argues that this phrase refers to a technical tradition focusing on God's saving acts (*Early Missionary Preaching: A Study of Luke's Report in Acts 13* (Hicksville, NY: Exposition, 1979), 55).

[2] Denova, *Things*, 182; Strauss, *Messiah*, 149–50; Joseph B. Tyson, *The Death of Jesus in Luke-Acts* (Columbia: University of South Carolina Press, 1986), 39.

[3] See Tannehill, *Unity*, 2:160–1; Pervo, *Acts*, 331. See also Jacques Dupont, "Je t'ai établi lumière des nations," in *Nouvelle études sur les Actes des Apôtres*, LD 118 (Paris: Cerf, 1984), 343–9; L. T. Johnson, *Acts*, 23; Mikael C. Parsons, *Acts*, Paideia (Grand Rapids: Baker Academic, 2008), 191; Walter Radl, *Paulus und Jesus im lukanischen Doppelwerk: Untersuchungen zu Parallelmotiven im Lukasevangelium und in der Apostelgeschichte*, EH 23/49 (Bern: Lang, 1975), 82–102; Claire K. Rothschild, *Luke-Acts and the Rhetoric of History: An Investigation of Early Christian Historiography*, WUNT 2/175 (Tübingen: Mohr Siebeck, 2004), 131; Alfons Weiser, *Die Apostelgeschichte*, 2 vols., ÖTK 5 (Gütersloh: Gütersloh Verlaghaus, 1985), 2:339–40; Ben Witherington III, *The Acts of the Apostles: A Socio-Rhetorical Commentary* (Grand Rapids: Eerdmans, 1998), 128–9.

[4] See Pervo, *Acts*, 331; Hans-Josef Klauck, *Magic and Paganism in Early Christianity: The World of the Acts of the Apostles* (Edinburgh: T&T Clark, 2000), 54.

As a setting, Pisidian Antioch is interesting in that this city was essentially a little Rome. Pisidian Antioch, not technically in Pisidia but Phrygia (Strabo, *Geogr.* 12.557, 569, 577),[5] was the chief Roman colony in the region, officially known as "Colonia Caesarea" (Pliny, *Nat.* 5.94),[6] a status conferred in 25 CE.[7] The city was its own displaced piece of Rome. The people (*coloni*), many of whom were veterans, were of equal standing with Roman citizens, enjoying the same rights and privileges.[8] The city was heavily Latinized, including a publicly displayed Latin inscription of Augustus's *Res gestae*[9] and a temple to Augustus constructed during Tiberius's reign.[10] It was even topographically similar to Rome, being laid out on seven hills, divided in Roman-style neighborhoods (*vici*) with streets named resembling Roman streets.[11]

This setting is a fitting beginning for the public mission of a man whose life will find its completion in Rome. Given what we have said about the parallels between Jesus's and Paul's beginnings, we might also note the specter of Roman rule that attended Jesus's birth and John's appearance (Lk. 2:1; 3:1). Further, we should not miss that Paul comes to proclaim the Lord of all (cf. Acts 10:36), the Davidic Messiah, a king (cf. 2:25-36), a savior (cf. 5:31; 13:23), as part of a movement that has already made inroads into the Roman household (Acts 10; 13:5-12).[12] Paul does not directly address Caesar, but these elements are not anodyne. There is a tension between Caesar's self-claims and Jesus enthroned in heaven. The scene in Pisidian Antioch does not obviate this tension, but, rather, coming on the heels of cosmic struggle in 13:6-12, this tension remains implicit.

---

[5] Barrett, *Acts*, 1:627; Barbara Levick, *Roman Colonies in Southern Asia Minor* (Oxford: Oxford University Press, 1967), 18.

[6] Levick, *Colonies*, 34, 122.

[7] W. M. Ramsay, *The Cities of St. Paul: Their Influence on His Life and Thought* (New York: Hodder & Stoughton, 1907), 268.

[8] Ramsay, *Cities*, 269.

[9] Levick, *Colonies*, 90-1, 122; John McRay, *Archaeology and the New Testament* (Grand Rapids: Baker, 1991), 238; Ramsay, *Cities*, 262.

[10] McRay maintains that emperor worship was well established in Pisidian Antioch (*Archaeology*, 238-9). See also Benjamin Rubin, "Ruler Cult and Colonial Identity: The Imperial Sanctuary at Pisidian Antioch," in *Building a New Rome: The Imperial Colony of Pisidian Antioch (25 BC-AD 700)*, eds. Elaine K. Gazda and Diane Y. Ng (Ann Arbor: Kelsey Museum Publications, 2011), 33-60.

[11] Levick, *Colonies*, 78; McRay, *Archaeology*, 237; Stephen Mitchell, "Antioch of Pisidia," *ABD* 1:264-5; Ramsey, *Cities*, 277.

[12] Notably, Sergius Paulus came from Pisidian Antioch, receiving large estates there (Stephen Mitchell, "Population and the Land in Roman Galatia," *ANRW* 2.7.2:1073-4).

The speech itself is divided by threefold vocative address (vv. 16, 26, 38).[13] Though the structure of the passage is debated,[14] several scholars have argued for a rhetorical structure that coheres with this basic division:[15]

Proem/Exordium:	v. 16
Narratio:	vv. 17–25
Propositio:	v. 26
Probatio:	vv. 27–37
Epilogue:	vv. 38–41

I focus on a simple threefold division: vv. 16–25, 26–37, 38–41, with the central section subdivided as vv. 26–31, 32–7,[16] while also being attentive to this rhetorical structure.

5.2 Historical Recurrence (Acts 13:16–25)

Paul begins by tying the present moment into God's past covenant fidelity and attempts to establish God's providential rule among Israel. This narrative anchors God's present salvific work within Israel, from whom goes the light to the nations. Importantly, the historical logic that Paul establishes here (historical recurrence) structures the entire argument of his speech. Paul is drawing his audience into a history of Israel's interaction with God's providence, including its historical rejection of God's purpose, a reality played out in the present time in Jerusalem, exhorting them to avoid this pattern.

---

[13] See David A. deSilva, "Paul's Sermon in Antioch of Pisidia," *BSac* 151 (1994): 34–5; Christian Dionne, *L'Évangile aux Juifs et aux païens: Le premier voyage missionnaire de Paul (Actes 13–14)*, LD 247 (Paris: Cerf, 2011), 168–79; Odile Flichy, *La figure de Paul dans les Actes des Apôtres: Un phénomène de réception de la tradition paulinienne à la fin du 1er siècle*, LD 214 (Paris: Cerf, 2007), 186; Fitzmyer, *Acts*, 507; Gaventa, *Acts*, 196; George A. Kennedy, *New Testament Interpretation through Rhetorical Criticism* (Chapel Hill: University of North Carolina Press, 1984), 124–5; Pervo, *Acts*, 335; Rudolf Pesch, *Die Apostelgeschichte*, EKKNT 5 (Köln: Benziger, 1986), 2:30; Roloff, *Apostelgeschichte*, 202–3; Schneider, *Apostelgeschichte*, 2:130; Marion L. Soards, *The Speeches in Acts: Their Content, Context, and Concerns* (Louisville: Westminster John Knox, 1994), 79; Wenxi Zhang, *Paul among Jews: A Study of the Meaning and Significance of Paul's Inaugural Sermon in the Synagogue of Antioch in Pisidia (Acts 13:16–41) for His Missionary Work among the Jews* (Eugene, OR: Wipf & Stock, 2011), 122–3. Weiser is also correct to note the division at v. 32 (*Apostelgeschichte*, 322–3).

[14] E.g., Parsons argues that the speech does not fit a specific rhetorical category (*Acts*, 192), while Kennedy suggests epideictic rhetoric (*Interpretation*, 124–5). See also C. Clifton Black II, "The Rhetorical Form of the Hellenistic Jewish and Early Christian Sermon: A Response to Lawrence Wills," *HTR* 81 (1988): 10. Keener suggests the speech is deliberative (*Acts*, 2:2054–5).

[15] Black, "Form," 8–10; idem, *The Rhetoric of the Gospel: Theological Artistry in the Gospels and Acts*, 2nd ed. (Louisville: Westminster John Knox, 2013), 123–6; Marguerat, *Actes*, 2:39; Soards, *Speeches*, 79; Ben Witherington III, *New Testament Rhetoric: An Introductory Guide to the Art of Persuasion in and of the New Testament* (Eugene, OR: Cascade, 2009), 63; idem, *Acts*, 407. Kennedy's rhetorical breakdown is identical except that he shortens the epilogue to vv. 38–9, making no mention of vv. 40–1. Keener argues, conversely, for an extended *narratio* (vv. 17–31) (*Acts*, 2:2054–5). An alternate rhetorical breakdown can be found in Flichy, *Paul*, 187–90. Cf. Anon. Seg. 1.1.

[16] Note the distinction between how the word came "to us" (v. 26) and the shift to "us" proclaiming the promise (v. 32).

5.2.1 The Pattern of Paul's History

Paul first addresses his audience as Israelites and those fearing God (οἱ φοβούμενοι τὸν θεόν). Reference to Israelites is not surprising (2:22; 3:12; 5:35), and prepares the audience for an Israel-centric oration. More uncertain is the reference to those who fear God—identified variously as gentiles,[17] proselytes,[18] or a segment among the Jewish people.[19] Nevertheless the accent is on Israel.

Paul's *narratio* (vv. 17–25) begins by reciting Israel's history from Egypt, through David, and to Jesus, David's seed. It is a story of election and God's continual care that connects God's promise of redemption in the exodus to God's work through Jesus.[20] But it is generally missed that the narration is patterned by historical recurrence.[21] This historical recurrence draws the audience in, as Paul implicates them in this unfolding history.

Luke-Acts exhibits elsewhere a proclivity for the recurrence of event types and characters.[22] This patterning of current events and imitation in characters is based on the cyclical and recurrent quality of events and human nature, rhetorically providing the impression of truth.[23] G. W. Trompf writes, "[Luke] wrote as though established historical events, which were for him divinely guided, had their own inner relatedness, connections between events amounting to the virtual reenactment of special happenings or the repetition of an earlier stage of history in a later one, or even the recurrent operation of certain laws or principles."[24] Luke here presents a history not simply as a chain of events or back story but as historical recurrence in which events, characters, and actions can be understood in types and repetition of the past.

---

[17] Bruce, *Book*, 203; Matthäus Franz-Josef Buss, *Die Missionspredigt des Apostles Paulus im Pisidischen Antiochien: Analyse von Apg 13,16–41 im Hinblick auf die literarische und thematische Einheit der Paulusrede*, FzB 38 (Stuttgart: Katholisches Bibelwerk, 1980), 35; deSilva, "Sermon," 35; Flichy, *Paul*, 333–9; Fitzmyer, *Acts*, 449–50, 516, 514; Jervell, *Apostelgeschichte*, 303–4; Marguerat, *Actes*, 42–3; Pesch, *Apostelgeschichte*, 2:31.

[18] Barrett, *Acts*, 1:500, 630–1; John Eifion Morgan-Wynne, *Paul's Pisidian Antioch Speech (Acts 13)* (Cambridge: James Clark, 2014), 69–73, 101; Mikeal C. Parsons and Martin M. Culy, *Acts: A Handbook on the Greek Text* (Waco, TX: Baylor University Press, 2004), 252; Günter Wasserberg, *Aus Israels Mitte—Heil für die Welt: Eine narrative-exegetische Studie zur Theologie des Lukas*, BZNW 92 (Berlin: de Gruyter, 1998), 48–51.

[19] Bruce J. Malina and John J. Pilch, *Social-Science Commentary on the Book of Acts* (Minneapolis: Fortress, 2008), 93.

[20] See Dionne (*L'Évangile*, 180–9), who notes a series of narrative relationships within this section.

[21] On historical recurrence elsewhere in Luke-Acts, see G. W. Trompf, *The Idea of Historical Recurrence in Western Thought: From Antiquity to Reformation* (Berkeley: University of California Press, 1979), 116–78; Rothschild, *Rhetoric*, 99–141.

[22] See, e.g., Radl, *Paulus*; Rothschild, *Rhetoric*, 107–41; Charles H. Talbert, *Literary Patterns, Theological Themes, and the Genre of Luke-Acts*, SBLMS 20 (Missoula, MT: Scholars Press, 1974); Tannehill, *Unity*, 2:74–9. Such patterns might be noted as well in the echoes of the Genesis narrative in Luke 1 with Elizabeth's barrenness (Lk. 1:5–7; Gen. 11:30; 17:15–16), comparisons between Mary and Hannah (Lk. 1:46–55; 1 Sam. 2:1–10), or the recurrence of Elijah and Elisha as types in Luke (Lk. 1:17; 4:25–7; 7:1–17); see, e.g., Jonathan Huddleston, "What Would Elijah and Elisha Do? Internarrativity in Luke's Story of Jesus," *JTI* 5 (2011): 262–82; John S. Kloppenborg and Joseph Verheyden, eds., *The Elijah-Elisha Narrative in the Composition of Luke*, LNTS 493 (London: Bloomsbury, 2014).

[23] Rothschild, *Rhetoric*, 102–7.

[24] Trompf, *Recurrence*, 129. Thucydides appeals in particular to the stability of human nature (1.76.2–3; 3.39.5; 3.45.7; 3.83.2; 4.19.4).

Paul's recitation of history in vv. 17-25 displays recurrence in two specific, patterned cycles (vv. 17-19, 20-2)[25] that open up to a third cycle occurring contemporaneously with the audience so that the *narratio* ends at the beginning of a new cycle with Jesus's arrival as savior.[26] The pattern is as follows:

A God's faithful action for Israel (vv. 17, 20, [23-25]).
    v. 17 – God brought them out of Egypt.
    v. 20 – God gave them governance in the land, judges representing God's rule.

B Forty-year period of forbearance through opposition/rebellion (vv. 18, 21).
    Note common beginning conjunction καί and repetition of "forty years."
    v. 18 – God bore with them forty years in the wilderness.
        (<u>καὶ</u> ὡς **τεσσερακονταετῆ** χρόνον)
    v. 21 – God gave them Saul for forty years.
        (<u>κἀ</u>κεῖθεν … **ἔτη τεσσεράκοντα**)

C God's continued (initiatory) action after forbearance period (vv. 19a, 22a).
    Note aorist temporal participle (καθελών [v.19], μεταστήσας [v. 22]).
    v. 19a – after destroying the seven nations
        (<u>καὶ</u> **καθελὼν** ἔθνη ἑπτὰ ἐν γῇ Χανάαν)
    v. 22a – after removing Saul
        (<u>καὶ</u> **μεταστήσας** αὐτὸν)

D God's purpose realized (vv. 19b, 22b) Note aorist verb.
    v. 19b – he gave them the land as an inheritance
        (**κατεκληρονόμησεν** τὴν γῆν αὐτῶν)
    v. 22b – he raised David for them
        (**ἤγειρεν** τὸν Δαυὶδ αὐτοῖς)

---

[25] Also conceivable is the division, vv. 17-20a, 20b-22. The bulk of v. 20 serves as a transition between the two cycles, referencing a period of 450 years and "after these things." An issue is whether the 450 years refer to the previous events or the following. Advocating for the former, a number of scholars assert that the 450 years references time in Egypt (400 years; Gen. 15:13; Acts 7:6), the desert (40 years), and conquest (10 years) (e.g. Fitzmyer, *Acts*, 511; Marguerat, *Actes*, 2:44; Weiser, *Apostelgeschichte*, 319). Eugene H. Merrill has noted, however, that there are still a number of issues with this estimation ("Paul's Use of 'About 450 Years' in Acts 13:20," *BSac* 138 (1981): 246-57). The historical narration does not begin with the start of Israel's sojourn in Egypt, but with God's choosing their ancestors, a much longer period. If the benchmark is the exodus, this would be too short a period. The same could be said, nevertheless, for associating the 450 years with the period of judges. Merrill, however, argues that this number is reached by a simplistic addition of the dates in Judges and the period of Eli before Samuel. Dating for this period varies (see, e.g., Josephus, *Ant.* 11.112). Textually, the structure, indicating the duration of a period with ὡς followed by the activity of that period, is mirrored two verses earlier in v. 18, ὡς τεσσερακονταετῆ χρόνον ἐτροποφόρησεν αὐτούς. See also Acts 5:7; 7:23. Thus, v. 20 would read: "For about 450 years after these things, he gave judges until Samuel the prophet." On the view that 450 years refers to the later period, see Conzelmann, *Acts*; deSilva, "Sermon," 35-6; Pervo, *Acts*, 336. Pervo adds that there may be some significance to the figure 450 plus a 40-year period for David, situating David at the beginning of the "eighth week," pointing to eschatological restoration (Dan. 9:20-7).

[26] Philip E. Satterthwaite recognizes a similar structure, calling it "analogical patterning" ("Acts against the Background of Classical Rhetoric," in *The Book of Acts in Its Literary Setting*, eds. Bruce W. Winter and Andrew D. Clarke, BAFCS 1 (Grand Rapids: Eerdmans, 1994), 363-5).

This historical recurrence manifests throughout the remaining speech. God's faithful action (A) in Jesus is rejected by those in Jerusalem and their leaders (B) (vv. 27–9). God bore with this conduct, resurrecting Jesus and exalting him (vv. 30–7). Now is a time of both forbearance and realization (C). The final coming realization (D) is prepared for by Paul in both hopeful expectation (e.g., v. 34) and warning (vv. 40–1). Notably, the attention throughout the *narratio* is on God's action, a marked difference from Stephen's history, which emphasizes actions of people (7:2–53).[27] Emphasizing God's action, this is a story about God's saving covenant fidelity and Israel's election. As our salvific scheme has so far argued, God's faithful action is a presupposition of this history. Nevertheless, commentators have often been quick to overlook the place of the people's recalcitrance in the narration.

5.2.2 From Exodus to the Promised Land (vv. 17–19)

The first cycle speaks of God's delivering the people from Egypt. The exodus of course is the paradigmatic example of God's providence, delivering the people from a foreign power, taking a nation for God's self (Exod. 6:1, 6; 13:3, 9, 14, 16; 32:11; Deut. 1:31; 4:34, 37; 5:15; 9:26, 29; 10:15). With this cycle, Paul establishes both the persistence of God's covenant fidelity and the recurrence of the rejection of God's purposes. Nevertheless, God's covenant faithfulness supersedes this rejection, and through forbearance, God continues to act on the people's behalf.

For many, however, this *narratio* has no negative appraisal of Israel's conduct.[28] A key issue is determining the text of v. 18. Does it read ἐτροποφόρησεν, God "bore/put up with" (א B C² D 𝔐), or ἐτροφοφόρησεν, God "cared for" (𝔓74 A C* E 33 181)? The distinction is significant, and the textual evidence is inconclusive. Most commentators accept ἐτροποφόρησεν (bore with) as original, assuming it more likely that a later editor attempted to harmonize this passage with Deut. 1:31 LXX.[29] Nevertheless,

---

[27] Joachim Jeska, *Die Geschichte Israels in der Sicht des Lukas: Apg 7,2b-53 und 13,17-25 im Kontext antik-jüdischer Summarien der Geschichte Israels*, FRLANT 195 (Göttingen: Vandenhoeck & Ruprecht, 2001), 221-31.

[28] E.g., Barrett, *Acts*, 1:632; deSilva, "Sermon," 35-8; Fitzmyer, *Acts*, 507-8; Keener, *Acts*, 2:2058; Pervo, *Acts*, 336; Tannehill, *Unity*, 2:168; Jervell, *Apostelgeschichte*, 355; Witherington, *Acts*, 409-10.

[29] Bock, *Acts*, 452; Fitzmyer, *Acts*, 510; C. R. Holladay, *Acts*, 265-6; Jervell, *Apostelgeschichte*, 355; Marshall, *Acts*, 223; Parsons and Culy, *Acts*, 253-4; Schneider, *Apostelgeschichte*, 2:132. It should be noted that the same textual uncertainty exists for Deut. 1:31 LXX. The argument in favor of the alternate, ἐτροφοφόρησεν, is made almost always based on the sense of the passage. See Barrett, *Acts*, 1:632; Haenchen, *Acts*, 408; Jeska, *Geschichte*, 222-3; Keener, *Acts*, 2:2058; Marshall, *Acts*, 223; Morgan-Wynne, *Speech*, 74; Pillai, *Preaching*, 85; Strauss, *Messiah*, 158; Witherington, *Acts*, 410. Yet, this prematurely stifles other interpretive possibilities. See also, Marguerat, *Actes*, 2:44; Marcel Dumais, *Le langage de l'évangélisation: L'Annonce missionnaire en milieu juif (Actes 13,16-41)* (Tournai: Desclée & Cie, 1976), 143; Josef Pilcher, *Paulusrezeption in der Apostelgeschichte: Untersuchungen zur Rede im pisidischen Antiochien*, ITS 50 (Innsbrook: Tyrolia-Verlag, 1997), 145-6.

these commentators subsequently downplay any emphasis on wayward conduct.[30] The prevailing consensus is well represented by Metzger who notes that the committee for UBS[4] determined that the textual witnesses slightly favored the reading "bore with" (ἐτροποφόρησεν), though adds, citing internal sense, "One has the feeling that in the context it is more likely that reference should be made to God's interposition and efforts in behalf of the Israelites."[31] My contention is that Metzger's assessment that the external evidence favors "bore with" is correct. However, his assessment of the inner sense, that it mitigates this sense of bearing with Israel's conduct, is undermined by an alternate reading of the text. Indeed, a reading attuned to the recurrence in Paul's rhetoric suggests, rather, that Paul, through use of ἐτροποφόρησεν, is emphasizing God's forbearance through Israel's wayward conduct, cohering better with Metzger's preferred text.[32]

An unfavorable appraisal of the exodus experience would not be new to the Lukan narrative. Stephen has already emphasized this negative history (7:35–43; cf. Josh. 5:6; Ps. 95:10; Isa. 63:10; Amos 5:25) and its recurrence in the present (7:51), though in a more polemical context. Here, Paul's critique, though consistent, is indirect—of the ancestors, of the people and leadership in Jerusalem, not of his audience—serving not as deprecating speech, but as a warning to avoid repeating this cycle (vv. 40–1). Paul need not obscure the negative elements of a well-known common history in order to establish a sympathetic hearing. Narrating Israel's rebellion in the wilderness, a matter of biblical record, would not be shocking for Paul's audience nor alienating (e.g., Exod. 16:1–3; 17:1–7; 32; Num. 14:32–4).[33] Indeed, as a matter of recurrence, both the wilderness event and the demand for a king were seen as a rejection of God's rule over the people (e.g., Num. 14:11; 1 Sam. 8:7; 10:19), fitting well into an event type that provides historical warning concerning rejecting God's present work in Jesus.

5.2.3 From Judges to David, to Jesus (vv. 20–5)

The second cycle (vv. 20–2) concerns God's providing the judges until Samuel; Israel's request for a king, Saul; and God's eventual rejection of Saul (μεταστήσας αὐτόν) and selection of David. Most scholars agree that the request for a king is portrayed negatively. In the OT, this event is represented as the rejection of God as king (cf. 1 Sam. 8:7; 10:19).[34] Notably, this request is the only instance in which the people are the subject of a verb in this historical narration. God bears with them for another

---

[30] Barrett, *Acts*, 1:632; Bruce, *Book*, 255; Flichy, *Paul*, 192; Fitzmyer, *Acts*, 510; Jervell, *Apostelgeschichte*, 355; L. T. Johnson, *Acts*, 231; Krodel, *Acts*, 234; Marshall, *Acts*, 223. Nevertheless, on the negative emphasis here, see William S. Kurz, *Acts of the Apostles*, CCSS (Grand Rapids: Baker Academic, 2013), 210; Marguerat, *Actes*, 2:44.
[31] Metzger, *Commentary*, 357. See also Barrett, *Acts*, 1:632.
[32] This is the reading preferred by many standard translations, e.g., CEB, KJV, RSV, NRSV, NIV, NASB.
[33] Marguerat, *Actes*, 2:44.
[34] On the negative appraisal, see, e.g., Barrett, *Acts*, 1:635; Jeska, *Geschichte*, 231; Keener, *Acts*, 2:2061; Parsons, *Acts*, 194; Soards, *Speeches*, 82–3.

forty-year period, giving Saul (see Josephus, *Ant.* 6.378), a king who fails to meet God's expectations (e.g., 1 Sam. 15:10–35; 16:1) and is eventually removed in favor of David.

David represents God's renewed action on Israel's behalf and a foreshadowing of God's recurrent action in the present. The Lukan link between David and Jesus has been firmly established (Lk. 1:27, 32–3, 69; 2:4, 11, 26; 6:3–5; 18:38; 20:41–4; Acts 2:25–36; 13:33–7; 15:15–17). Moreover, several scholars have argued that Paul's speech as a whole appears to be a midrashic exposition of 2 Sam. 7:4–7 (cf. 22:50–1), Nathan's oracle to David concerning building the temple and the eternal endurance of the Davidic line.[35] There, God speaks to David of Egypt (v. 6), judges (v. 11 LXX), and one of his lineage (σπέρμα, v. 12) whose kingdom will be established forever (vv. 13–16).[36]

God's endorsement of David in v. 22, a composite allusion to 1 Sam. 13:14; Ps. 89:20; and Isa. 44:28, further encourages an eschatological reading.[37] While 1 Sam. 13:14 LXX has Samuel tell Saul of a king after God's heart (κατὰ τὴν καρδίαν αὐτοῦ) who will replace Saul, Isa. 44:28 LXX speaks of Cyrus as God's anointed (χριστός, Isa. 45:1) and the rebuilding of Jerusalem. Yuzuru Miura maintains that this language is specifically eschatological, that the reference to the son of Jesse additionally alludes to Isa. 11:1 LXX, and that the reference to Ps. 89 links David to the messianic righteous suffer.[38] Jesus fulfills this type as David's seed raised in incorruptibility (cf. Acts 13:34–5). He will restore the nation.

The typology, however, extends beyond David and Jesus. The second cycle brings to the fore specific characters that make their own recurrence in the present:

- David (v. 22) ≈ Jesus (v. 23)
- Samuel (v. 20) ≈ John (v. 24)[39]
- Saul (v. 21) ≈ Jerusalem's wayward leadership (v. 27)
- the people (then) (v. 21) ≈ the people in Jerusalem (now) (v. 27)

We have already noted the typological link between Samuel and John (see Chapter 2).[40] However, the emphasis on Saul implies as well that this occurs in conjunction with a critique of Israel's current wayward leadership, which coheres with the later critique in

---

[35] J. W. Bowker, "Speeches in Acts: A Study in Proem and Yelammedenu Form," *NTS* 14 (1967): 103–4; J. W. Doeve, *Jewish Hermeneutics in the Synoptic Gospels and Acts* (Assen: Van Gorcum, 1954), 172–3; Dumais, *Langage*, 135–7; Dave Goldsmith, "Acts 13:33–37: A Pesher on 2 Samuel 7," *JBL* 87 (1968): 321–4; Evald Lövestam, *Son and Saviour: A Study of Acts 13,32-37 with an Appendix: "Son of God" in the Synoptic Gospels*, ConBNT 18 (Lund: Gleerup, 1961), 7; Pesch, *Apostelgeschichte*, 2:34; Strauss, *Messiah*, 150–74.

[36] Later eschatological interpretations of this passage can be found in 4QFlorilegium, which speaks of a Davidic messianic figure and Tg. Neb. 2 Sam. 7:20, which speaks of "the age that is coming." Similarly, the LXX helps this interpretation by shifting the pronouns in v. 16 from *your* (David's) house and your throne to *his* house and his throne. In Acts 13, this prophecy applies eschatologically to Jesus, David's offspring (σπέρμα, v. 23).

[37] Strauss, *Messiah*, 158.

[38] See esp. Miura, *David*, 181–3.

[39] The judges are represented by Samuel (cf. Sir. 46:11–20).

[40] Jeska notes that similar historical summaries rarely reference Samuel (*Geschichte*, 225). Here, Samuel's rare appearance where few specific historical figures are noted strengthens the association of Samuel and John (as well as David and Jesus and Saul and current wayward leadership).

vv. 27–9. This critique of course is not new. It pervades Jesus's appearance in Jerusalem (see esp. Lk. 20:9–19). Further, the critique is not simply of Saul, but of the people asking for a king.[41] Their rejection of God's kingship (1 Sam. 8:7; 10:19) and Saul's leadership is then parallel to the leadership and people of Jerusalem of v. 27.

5.2.4 The Promise and a Savior

All of this is done according to "the promise" (ἐπαγγελία, vv. 23, 32). This idea's repetition indicates its importance. Here, the immediately apparent referent of the promise is 2 Sam. 7:16, concerning the continuation of the Davidic line and restoring the kingdom (cf. Acts 1:6).[42] This association is not wrong, but the promise is also the climax of a historical process that has begun with the election of the people's ancestors (πατέρας, v. 17).[43] Luke refers in different ways to the "promise" (Lk. 24:29; Acts 1:4; 2:33, 39; 7:17; 13:23, 32; 26:6), yet it is grounded singularly in God's covenant faithfulness. God's covenant faithfulness is the stable foundation of the historical recurrence in Paul's speech.[44] Here the continuity between the Davidic and Abrahamic promises is emphasized,[45] while the beginning of Acts focused on the promise of the Holy Spirit (Lk. 24:49; Acts 1:4; 2:33, 39), the dynamic power of restoration.[46] This is not a different promise but part of God's continued faithfulness. In Peter's speech, the promise of the Spirit is tied directly to the ascension of the Davidic Messiah (2:33), who brings national restoration and forgiveness of sins (2:38; 13:38). Nothing in this *narratio* suggests a reductive spiritualization of this promise; rather, the history encourages a reading in which political deliverance and God's reign through the eternal Davidide is at the forefront.

The foundational promise to Abraham is political as well, not only to establish a nation and to bless the gentiles (Gen. 22:16–18; Lk. 1:55, 73; Acts 3:25; cf. Rom. 2:13–17), but, explicitly in Acts 7:7, for God to "judge those who enslaved the Hebrews, and that afterward they would 'come out and worship me in this place'" (see also

---

[41] Jeska, *Geschichte*, 229–31.

[42] Fitzmyer, *Acts*, 512–13; John J. Kilgallen, "Acts 13,38–39: The Culmination of Paul's Speech in Pisidia," *Bib* 69 (1988): 490; Strauss, *Messiah*, 159.

[43] See Buss, *Missionspredigt*, 49. Jervell rightly reminds that Israel's history is not simply Jesus's prehistory; rather, Jesus is the culmination of Israel's history (*Apostelgeschichte*, 354).

[44] On the continuity of covenants and God's purpose, see Robert L. Brawley, "Abrahamic Covenant Traditions and the Characterization of God in Luke-Acts," in *The Unity of Luke-Acts*, ed. Joseph Verheyden, BETL 142 (Leuven: Leuven University Press, 1999), 131–2. This is related to the themes of necessity and the stability of God's purpose and foreknowledge in Luke-Acts (Lk. 2:49; 4:43; 7:30; 9:22; 13:16; 17:25; 19:5; 21:9; 22:22, 37; 24:7, 26, 44; Acts 1:16, 21; 2:23; 3:21; 4:28; 9:16; 10:42; 13:17, 36; 14:22; 15:7; 17:3, 31; 19:21; 20:27; 23:11; 25:10; 27:24).

[45] This continuity is noted as well in rabbinic literature, e.g., in Gen. Rab. 49:8, where the Davidic Messiah is an answer to the Abrahamic covenant. Abraham is referenced throughout Luke-Acts as a basis of national "mercy," by which we may understand God's covenant faithfulness toward the people (Lk. 1:55, 73; Acts 3:13, 25) and intercommunal solidarity and mercy for the least (Lk. 13:16, 28; 16:24–31; 19:9). On Abraham in Luke-Acts, see Brawley, "Covenant," 109–32; Chrupcała, *Everyone*, 55–77.

[46] Isa. 11:1–16; 32:9–20; 42:1–9; 44:1–5; 48:16; 61:1–11; Ezek. 11:17–19; 18:30–2; 36:24–32; 37:1–14; Joel 2:28–32.

Lk. 1:54–5, 68–75).⁴⁷ Paul, before Agrippa, summarizes the basis for his persecution from other Jews as his hope in the promise God has made to the ancestors (26:6–7). This hope has rightly been defined as resurrection (cf. 24:14, 21), but note also that it is a promise to the twelve tribes; it is the hope of national restoration. As Tannehill argues, if one were to perceive here that Paul is making much ado about nothing, arguing about a strictly religious and eschatological reality, resurrection, this likely derives from "ignoring the full range of meaning of hope and promise in Luke-Acts, under the assumption that resurrection of the dead simply means life after death for individuals."⁴⁸ Nevertheless, this resurrection is linked with the rise of the Davidic Messiah and the people's communal and national hopes.⁴⁹

It is notable then that Luke continues to describe Jesus as "savior" (Lk. 2:11; Acts 5:31; 13:23) in connection to national restoration (Acts 5:31) and the hoped-for Davidic Messiah (Lk. 2:11). We should not forget the palpable specter of Roman authority in the Roman colony, Antioch. Gary Gilbert writes, "Beginning with Augustus, the title [Savior], usually, *salus* in Latin or σωτήρ in Greek became a staple designation for the Roman emperor." He adds, "By the early principate ... public recognition of Roman officials as savior was almost exclusively confined to the emperor himself."⁵⁰ To declare Jesus savior in this context harkens to the atmosphere of Lk. 2:1–20, amid the disruptive demand for a census and the assumed authority of Augustus. Here, again, Luke utilizes the language of imperial authority and applies it to Jesus, allowing it to be filled with specific meaning from its new Davidic referent.

The first segment of Paul's speech, the *narratio*, concludes with the inauguration of a new cycle of God's continued faithfulness. God once again acts for the people, and John the Baptist has announced the coming of this savior appearing before his face (πρὸ προσώπου, cf. Mal. 3:1 LXX; Lk. 1:76), proclaiming a baptism of repentance,⁵¹ a realignment of behavior and allegiance, in preparation for the rise of the promised Davidide who will fulfill God's covenant faithfulness to Israel. The question is whether the people will align to this movement of God—which is not a new movement but the continuation of God's faithfulness to their ancestors—or whether they will again reject God's rule (vv. 17, 20; Num. 14:11; 1 Sam. 8:7; 10:19). The audience has been drawn into a story about Israel's salvation, a national salvation for a people under the Davidic king. The subsequent section, however, appeals to the recurrence of Israel's rejection of God's leadership. It functions, in juxtaposition to God's action, to reveal injustice and exhort allegiance to God's true king.

---

⁴⁷ Susan R. Garrett, "The Meaning of Jesus' Death in Luke," *WW* 12 (1992): 11–16.
⁴⁸ Tannehill, *Unity*, 2:319.
⁴⁹ On the resurrection as political/communal, see K. L. Anderson, *Resurrection*, 280–4; Klaus Haacker, "Das Bekenntnis des Paulus zur Hoffnung Israels nach der Apostelgeschichte des Lukas," *NTS* 31 (1985): 437–51; Keener, *Acts*, 4:3500; Tannehill, *Unity*, 2:319–20.
⁵⁰ Gilbert, "Propaganda," 238–9.
⁵¹ This baptism of repentance (13:24) should be understood within the continual emphasis on repentance and Israel's restoration (Isa. 40:1–2; Lk. 3:3; Acts 1:5, 22; 11:16).

5.3 Those Dwelling in Jerusalem and Their Leaders (Acts 13:26–31)

Paul turns to the present happenings in Jerusalem. Addressing his audience again, those fearing God are referenced, but now, rather than Israelites, there is mention of children of Abraham. This language ties us back to the beginning of the *narratio* and the reference to "our fathers" (τοὺς πατέρας ἡμῶν, v. 17).[52] The audience is characterized as beneficiaries of God's election, continued covenant faithfulness, and God's new salvific movement in Jesus. Simultaneously, however, they are bearers of a tradition in which their ancestors rebelled against God's purposes.

Following the address, Paul sets forth his claim (*propositio*) in v. 26b based on the narration of vv. 17–25: "the word of this salvation was sent to us." The near demonstrative (ταύτης) points the reader to that which has been presented in the *narratio*, finding its climax in Jesus. Indeed, Paul is here making an assertion about a *savior* (v. 24) who brings *salvation*. Further, the aorist verb "was sent" (ἐξαπεστάλη) signals an event that has concluded. Notably this event is not the speaking or announcement of the word, but the *sending* of the word, pointing to the Christ event just outlined by Paul (v. 23), the pinnacle of God's covenant faithfulness. This salvific word is then the foundational content of Paul's missionary message,[53] and it is sent to them.

This claim, however, leaves certain questions to be answered. The most basic question is how we know that Jesus is this eschatological Davidic king. Additionally, derived from the *propositio*, why has this word come *to us*? That is, why has it not been first accepted by those in Jerusalem? Why are Paul and Barnabas delivering this message, rather than the recognized leadership? Further, if Jesus is the eschatological Davidide, why was he not enthroned in Jerusalem (cf. Lk. 1:32)? The spatial assumption is that Jerusalem is the center (cf. Acts 9:1–3), but as we have seen from Acts 2, the spatial trajectory of Acts is outward. In terms of orientation, the shift has been from a Jerusalem-centered orientation to a heavenly orientation, which, at its center, is found the resurrected and ascended Jesus, an important element of Paul's proclamation (vv. 31–7).

It would be too simplistic to say that Paul neatly divides these two major issues—(1) why this message is not delivered from the Jerusalem leadership and (2) the enthronement of Jesus in heaven, not Jerusalem—into the two segments of the *probatio* (vv. 27–31, 32–7). Nevertheless, each section moves along these two basic themes. For both, Paul asserts that this outcome was according to God's plan. The proof thus serves throughout to demonstrate, not simply defend, that this is Israel's savior.[54]

---

[52] Flichy, *Paul*, 190–1.

[53] Most scholars maintain that this returns Paul to the word of exhortation (λόγος παρακλήσεως, v. 15) after his historical turn (Dumais, *Langage*, 68–9; Fitzmyer, *Acts*, 514; G. Walter Hansen, "The Preaching and Defense of Paul," in *Witness to the Gospel: The Theology of Acts*, eds. I. Howard Marshall and David Peterson (Grand Rapids: Eerdmans, 1998), 297–8; Soards, *Speeches*, 84; Witherington, *Acts*, 411). However, Dionne is right in noting that the reference refers to what has been sent (salvation, i.e., the savior, Jesus) and *la Bonne Nouvelle* associated with this savior (*L'Évangile*, 197–8).

[54] Black demonstrates how Paul, in his *probatio*, utilizes all four *a priori* "certainties" outlined by Quintilian in making his argument, including sense perception (witnesses, v. 31), things of shared agreement (God's power and providence (vv. 32–3, 37), things established by law/Scripture (vv. 27, 29, 33–5), and that which all involved parties admit (Jesus's innocence and execution by Pilate, v. 28; Jesus and David's death and burial, vv. 29, 36) ("Form," 9).

Paul begins by answering: Why to us? Why not to the designated rulers and the geographic center of the people in Jerusalem (cf. 28:21-2)? The simple answer is that they have rejected Jesus (vv. 27-9). The Jerusalemites and their leadership demonstrate their failure in at least three ways: (1) being ignorant of God's prophets, though being without excuse, (2) aligning with foreign powers over God's chosen regent, and (3) utilizing Scripture for injustice and against its purpose. However, Paul does not simply see the Jerusalemites' rejection as an impediment along the way but as a proof of fulfillment. This rejection is a proof replicating the pattern of historical recurrence in the *narratio* and fulfilling the prophets, who both anticipate this rejection and proclaim Jesus's true nature.

The syntax of v. 27 is muddled. Certainly "this one" (τοῦτον) refers to Jesus and is the object of "being ignorant (of)" (ἀγνοήσαντες). "The voices of the prophets" could conceivably be the object of ἀγνοήσαντες or "they fulfilled" (ἐπλήρωσαν). Here, a comparison to 3:17-18 is helpful.[55] There, Peter refers to the Jerusalemites and their leaders as acting according to ignorance (ἄγνοια), and of God as fulfilling (πληρόω) that which was proclaimed by the prophets, namely, that the Messiah would suffer. Thus, the word of the prophets in 13:27 is likely the object of fulfillment and Jesus is the object of ignorance specifically. The participle (judging, κρίναντες) dangles but obviously refers to judging Jesus. Despite the demonstrable culpability, none of this occurs outside of God's knowledge and control (Lk. 24:25-7, 44-7; Acts 2:23; 4:27-8; 13:29; 17:3); nevertheless, the Jerusalemites are not absolved.

Ignorance and knowledge are not new themes (e.g., 2:36; 3:17; 8:30; 13:27, 38; 17:23, 30; 22:14; 28:28). It is tempting to see Paul's attribution of ignorance to the Jerusalemites as exculpatory.[56] In 13:37, there is an expectation that they would hear the voices of the prophets and read the times properly. Such is the emphasis placed on the reading of the prophets every Sabbath.[57] Tzvi Novick, arguing that the ignorance that Paul identifies is *in*-culpatory, appeals to traditions in early Jewish literature emphasizing the importance of public Scripture reading as a means of educating so that the hearers will have no excuse for violating it (cf. 15:21).[58] Further, Paul ends his speech with an appeal to his audience, "Let it be known to you" (γνωστὸν οὖν ἔστω ὑμῖν, v. 38). Seemingly, Paul warns them not to succumb to the same ignorance. This later appeal includes Hab. 1:5, which Novick ties to a similar warning to listen to

---

[55] Eldon Jay Epp, *The Theological Tendency of Codex Bezae Cantabrigiensis in Acts* (Cambridge: Cambridge University Press, 1966), 46-8.

[56] *Pace* Epp (*Tendency*, 46-8), it is not necessary or even likely that the actions of the Jerusalemites and their leaders are somehow made less culpable by the fact that they were foreseen by the prophets, nor does 3:17 "clearly provide an excuse." See also Keener, *Acts*, 2:2067; C. A. Joachim Pillai, *Apostolic Interpretation of History: A Commentary on Acts 13:16-41* (Hicksville, NY: Exposition, 1980), 34; Witherington, *Acts*, 411. For ignorance as implying culpability, see Conzelmann, *Theology*, 158; C. R. Holladay, *Acts*, 269; Larry W. Hurtado, *Lord Jesus Christ: Devotion to Jesus in Earliest Christianity* (Grand Rapids: Eerdmans, 2003), 185; Jervell, *Apostelgeschichte*, 357-8.

[57] The specific texts that are fulfilled are not identified. Nevertheless, the scripturally testified historical recurrence is fulfilled, so that this rejection of God's governance was to be expected and fits the noted pattern. This appeal to general fulfillment is made by Luke elsewhere (Lk. 24:25-7, 44-7; Acts 4:11, 24-8; 13:29; 17:3; cf. Jn 1:45; Rom. 3:21; 16:26; 1 Pet. 1:10-12).

[58] Tvzi Novick, "Eschatological Ignorance and the *Haftarah*: On Acts 13:27," *NovT* 54 (2012): 168-75. On the law, see, e.g., Philo, *Hypoth.* 7.11-12; Josephus, *Apion* 2.175-8.

prophecy found at Qumran (1QpHab II, 6–10). Likewise, in Acts 3:17–19, the appeal to the Jerusalemites' ignorance is not meant to assuage their guilt but to intensify their need for repentance. Their ignorance has led them to crucify an innocent man (Lk. 23:4, 14–15, 22, 47)—indeed, the Messiah. Whether they knew what the prophets had proclaimed about Jesus, they were agents of injustice.

Specifically, these Jerusalemites committed this injustice by aligning with foreign powers. Here, this collusion is marked by Pilate's inclusion (v. 28). Acts has already noted this collusion explicitly, casting Jesus as the suffering Davidic servant persecuted by the kings of the earth (4:25–6; Ps. 2:1–2), identified as Herod and Pilate (4:27; cf. 2:23). In Jesus's trial scene (Lk. 23:1–5), the Jerusalem leadership, in presenting Jesus to Pilate, ironically characterizes him as a prophet perverting the people as in Deut. 13.[59] However, ironically, where one would expect their accusation against a false prophet to condemn his misleading Israel from *God*, Jesus's accusers indicate that Jesus is perverting the nation against *Caesar*. They accuse Jesus of (1) commanding others not to pay taxes to Caesar (Lk. 20:20–6) and (2) declaring himself a king, as opposed to Caesar.[60] The effect is to show that the true idolaters misleading the people against God are those currently in leadership over the nation. The Lukan narrative of opposition from powers and lack of knowledge continues in Pisidian Antioch.[61]

Importantly, Paul portrays the Jerusalemites and their leaders not just committing a wayward act of injustice nor simply ignoring Scripture, but as misappropriating Scripture resulting in opposition to God's purpose (cf. Lk. 4:10–11). Specifically, the leadership is presented as misusing scriptural provisions for capital punishment in Deut. 21:22–3.[62] Acts 13:29 is the third reference to Jesus's cross as a tree (ξύλον) in Acts (5:30; 10:39; cf. Gal. 3:13; 1 Pet. 2:24; 4QpNahum; 11QTemple LXIV, 6–13),[63] each juxtaposed to Jesus's offering "forgiveness of sins"—that is, national restoration (5:31; 10:43; 13:38), a phrase occurring only two other times in Acts with contrast formulas

---

[59] See Raymond E. Brown, *The Death of the Messiah: From Gethsemane to the Grave: A Commentary on the Passion Narratives in the Four Gospels*, 2 vols., ABRL (New Haven, CT: Doubleday, 1994), 1:739; Green, *Luke*, 800; Scot McKnight, *Jesus and His Death: Historiography, the Historical Jesus, and Atonement Theory* (Waco, TX: Baylor University Press, 2005), 96. On Jesus as false prophet, see Graham N. Stanton, "Jesus of Nazareth: A Magician and a False Prophet Who Deceived God's People?" in *Jesus of Nazareth: Lord and Christ: Essays on the Historical Jesus and New Testament Christology*, eds. Joel B. Green and Max Turner (Grand Rapids: Eerdmans, 1994): 164–80.

[60] Regarding the latter charge, compare Acts 17:3, 7. Here, such an accusation would be read as a threat to Caesar's sovereign authority.

[61] When the Jews of Pisidian Antioch turn on Paul and Barnabas (v. 50), they appeal to the leading men of the city, who were very likely Roman officials. See Jan N. Bremmer, "Magic, Martyrdom and Women's Liberation in the Acts of Paul and Thecla," in *The Apocryphal Acts of Paul and Thecla*, ed. Jan N. Bremmer (Kampen: Kok Pharos, 1996), 41 n. 24), and the devout women who were likely gentile women attracted to Judaism (cf. Josephus, *Ant.* 20.34, 38; see Gaventa, *Acts*, 203).

[62] On Acts' rhetorical use of "hanging on a tree," see Reardon, "Crucifixion."

[63] The first two allusions speak more fully of "hanging on a tree" (5:30; 10:39). Despite the volume of the allusion's decreasing to the singular use of ξύλον for cross in 13:29, the allusion's recurrence, its consistent context and application, and its coherence with historical interpretation of Deut. 21:22–3 indicate that the connection to Deut. 21:22–3 is emphasized here (see Reardon, "Crucifixion," 409–15).

of their own (2:38; 26:18).[64] These provisions from Deut. 21:22-3 had come to refer to crucifixion and the punishment of those who were a threat to the Israel's stability.[65] In particular, such a punishment was suited for one deemed a perverter of the people (Deut. 13:1-11), as the leadership wrongly presented Jesus amid their own idolatry.[66]

Were Jesus such a false prophet, "hanging on a tree" would be an appropriate execution according to Deut. 21:22-3. This sort of death is a public demonstration of his status as a curse to be rooted out of the people. However, God overturned this judgment. Thus, Paul's reference to Deut. 21:22-3, here, is not an appeal to Jesus's accursedness—or some elaborate soteriological scheme that depends on Jesus's substitutionary accursedness for us—but to the extent of the antagonists' ignorance and its destructive force. Paul uses this allusion to characterize the antagonists' false evaluative judgment. They have wrongly judged Jesus as an enemy of the people worthy of capital punishment.

This sense is found in the early church as well. For example, in Justin's *Dialogue with Trypho*, Trypho rejects the idea that Jesus could be Messiah because of his encountering God's curse in crucifixion (*Dial*. 32). However, Justin responds not that Jesus has taken that curse on for us, but that Jesus's death *unmasks* the sin and ignorance of those who executed him and judged Jesus as cursed (*Dial*. 96; see also *Barn*. 5.11-13; Tertullian, *Adv. Jud*. 10.1-5).[67] Jesus's resurrection demonstrates his *un-cursedness*.

Acts 13:29 adds an additional element that does not occur in the two previous allusions to Deut. 21.22-23. Paul refers specifically to Jesus's burial. It is mandated in Deut. 21:23 that a body must not remain on the tree/stake overnight but must be buried that day. Though this may seem like an unremarkable observation, note that Luke's passion account attributes the burial to Joseph of Arimathea specifically (23:50-3). Nevertheless, here, Paul attributes this burial to the Jerusalemites, who enact the execution of Jesus as a cursed corrupter of Israel. The Jerusalemites are completing the provisions for capital punishment. Within Paul's rhetoric, this prepares for Paul's later hermeneutical argument that "the law of Moses" cannot of itself justify/demonstrate justness/righteousness (v. 38), because, here, the Jerusalemites have falsely appropriated the law against God's messiah.

Nevertheless, despite the actions of the Jerusalemites and their leaders, God perseveres, raising Jesus from the dead (v. 30). Once again Luke employs a contrast schema (2:24; 3:13-15; 4:10; 5:30-1; 10:38-40), juxtaposing the actions of antagonists and God. Here, we find ourselves amid a new historic cycle as laid out in the *narratio*, representing Israel's rejection of God's providence and perseverance in covenant faithfulness. The *narratio* gives legitimacy to Paul's argument, demonstrating stable

---

[64] That this should be understood in terms of *national* wellbeing is furthered by the fact that this allusion always appears attributed to *Jewish* antagonists, supporting what Alexander has called the "intra-communal" nature of this contestation ("Apologetic," 43).

[65] Reardon, "Crucifixion," 409-15. See, e.g., 4QpNah 3-4 I, 7-8; 11QTa LXIV, 6-13.

[66] Caryn Reeder argues that Jesus is portrayed quite early in Luke-Acts as this false prophet in Lk. 4:14-30 (*The Enemy in the Household: Family Violence in Deuteronomy and Beyond* (Grand Rapids: Baker Academic, 2012), 132). See also Green, *Luke*, 218.

[67] Reardon, "Crucifixion," 408.

historical precedence for this pattern.⁶⁸ The *narratio* and the *probatio* serve together as an implicit exhortation to avoid rejection of God's faithfulness.

With the failure of Jerusalem and its leadership, Paul appeals to another authority, a group whose source is extrinsic to Jerusalem, those who came to Jerusalem from Galilee with Jesus and who saw him for many days after his resurrection. These are now the witnesses to the people. This emphasis on such authoritative witnesses (to whom has been covenanted a kingdom, Lk. 22:28–30), specifically those from Galilee (cf. Lk. 13:1; 22:59; 23:5–6, 49, 55; 24:6; Acts 1:11; 2:7; 5:37; 10:37), serves to decenter traditional authority. As we move into the next section, we return again to the ascension and the centrality of heaven.

5.4 Good News of the Promise (Acts 13:32–7)

There is a marked shift at v. 32. Paul moves from explaining Jesus's rejection by the recognized authorities in Jerusalem to explaining his own gospel attested by God and the witnesses from Galilee. The emphatic inclusion of ἡμεῖς (we) highlights this shift, furthering the overall sense of an extended contrast formula (vv. 27–9, 30–6). In opposition to those judging Jesus as corrupter of the people, Paul and Barnabas (we) proclaim good news (εὐαγγελίζω) about the promise made to the ancestors.⁶⁹ This is the same promise as v. 23, highlighting the Davidic covenant but within the context of God's continual covenant faithfulness. In the face of the rejection of the promised eschatological Davidic king and savior who brought the hopes of national blessing for which the people pray night and day (Lk. 2:25, 36–8; Acts 26:6–7), Paul invokes language of announcements of political victory (εὐαγγελίζω, see, e.g., Josephus, *War* 4.618).⁷⁰

Citing Ps. 2:7, a Davidic enthronement psalm (cf. Lk. 3:22; Rom. 1:3–4; Heb. 1:5; 5:5),⁷¹ Paul makes clear that this Jesus was not a corruptor of the people, but was raised by God and enthroned as a Davidic king (cf. 2 Sam. 7:12). There is some disagreement

---

⁶⁸ For Quintilian, the *narratio* is not simply a preamble but a foundation for the argument, not only instructing but persuading (*Inv.* 3.8.12; 4.2.1–3). See also *Rhet. Alex.* 30; Aristotle, *Rhet.* 3.16; Cicero, *De or.* 2.326–30; *Inv.* 1.27–30; Black, *Rhetoric*, 125–6. On the intimate relationship between *narratio* and *probatio* in Quintilian, see John O'Banion, "Quintilian on *Narratio* as the Heart of Rhetorical Thinking," *Rhet* 5 (1987): 325–51.

⁶⁹ It is possible as well that the "we" here is inclusive of the Galilean witnesses (v. 31), referring to a common gospel.

⁷⁰ Luke-Acts includes nearly half the uses of εὐαγγελίζω in the NT, and all the uses in the Synoptic Gospels except Mt. 11:5: Lk. 1:19; 2:10; 3:18; 4:18, 43; 7:22; 8:1; 9:6; 16:16; 20:1; Acts 5:42; 8:4, 12, 25, 35, 40; 10:36; 11:20; 13:32; 14:7, 15, 21; 15:35; 16:10; 17:18; cf. 1 Sam. 31:9; 2 Sam. 4:10; 18:19, 20, 31; 1 Kings 1:42; 1 Chron. 10:9; Ps. 67:12 LXX; Isa. 52:7–10; 61:1. Compare this, e.g., to the Priene inscription (*OGIS* 458). See also Chapter 3.

⁷¹ John Bright, *A History of Israel* (Philadelphia: Westminster, 1959), 225–6; Roland de Vaux, *Ancient Israel: Its Life and Institutions* (Grand Rapids: Eerdmans, 1961), 108–10; Nancy deClaissé-Walford, Rolf A. Jacobson, and Beth LaNeel Tanner, *The Book of Psalms*, NICOT (Grand Rapids: Eerdmans, 2014), 65; Hermann Gunkel, *Introduction to Psalms: The Genres of the Religious Lyric of Israel* (Macon, GA: Mercer University Press, 1998), 102. Rabbinic literature ties this Psalm to the Davidic Messiah (*b. Sukkah* 52a; *Gen. Rab.* 44:8; *Midr. Pss.* 2.9).

about whether this "raising" refers to bringing Jesus to be king, either in his birth or baptism (cf. Lk. 1:69; 7:16; Acts 3:22, 26; 13:22; 17:18, 37),[72] or to his resurrection and ascension (cf. Lk. 9:22; 24:6, 7, 34, 46; Acts 2:24, 32; 3:15; 4:10; 5:30; 10:41, 49; 13:34, 37; 17:3, 31).[73] For those arguing that this references resurrection, the argument continues the resurrection theme broached in v. 30. This may be correct, yet Paul's rhetorical shift from Jesus's rejection to Paul's gospel does not preclude beginning positively with Jesus's appearance as king.[74] Nevertheless, what is of primary importance in this instance is not when Jesus has become God's Son but that Jesus has been "raised" in *this* manner, as God's Son, in opposition to the Jerusalem authorities' judgment. The resurrection, whether the moment in question, functions here and elsewhere as a moment of uncovering, "making known," revealing Jesus's true nature and the authoritative structure of cosmic-comprehensive space.

The benefit of this enthronement is restoration blessing: God will give "to you" (ὑμῖν) the holy and faithful things of David (δώσω ὑμῖν τὰ ὅσια Δαυὶδ τὰ πιστά; Isa. 55:3). This affirmation is substantiated by Jesus's raising from the dead as the eschatological Davidide no longer returning to decay (διαφθορά, v. 34). The logical connection between the holy things and Jesus's resurrection is demonstrated rhetorically by way of *gezerah shewah* in the lexical links between Isa. 55:3 and Ps. 15:10 LXX (v. 34; cf. 2:25–8). Psalm 15:10 LXX, cited by Paul in (v. 35), claims that God will not let God's "holy one" (τὸν ὅσιόν; compare τὰ ὅσια in Isa. 55:3 LXX) see decay (διαφθορά; compare v. 34). It is inferred that David, in Ps. 15:10 LXX, is referring not to himself but to the eschatological Davidic Messiah, Jesus, whose resurrection by God demonstrates a fulfillment of David's expectation.[75]

The benefit of Jesus's resurrection, as this eschatological Davidic Messiah, is understood in terms of Isa 55.3. Yet, there is debate about how the "faithful holy things"

---

[72] E.g., Barrett, *Acts*, 1:645–6; Bruce, *Book*, 259–60; idem, *Apostles*, 309; Halladay, *Acts*, 272. Note that Luke seems not to distinguish between ἀνίστημι and ἐγείρω. See, Strauss, *Messiah*, 162.

[73] K. L. Anderson, *Resurrection*, 245; Conzelmann, *Acts*, 105; Fitzmyer, *Acts*, 517; Morgan-Wynne, *Speech*, 119; Robert F. O'Toole, "Christ's Resurrection in Acts 13,13–52," *Bib* 60 (1979): 366; Roloff, *Apostelgeschichte*, 207; Walter Schmithals, *Die Apostelgeschichte des Lukas*, ZBK 3.2 (Zürich: TVZ, 1982), 128; Eduard Schweizer, "The Concept of the Davidic 'Son of God' in Acts and Its Old Testament Background," in *Studies in Luke-Acts: Essays Presented in Honor of Paul Schubert*, eds. Leander E. Keck and J. Louis Martyn (Nashville: Abingdon, 1966), 186. Some have argued that this passage conveys an adoptionist Christology. See, e.g, Morgan-Wynne, *Speech*, 120; Pervo, *Acts*, 388–9; Eduard Schweizer, "υἱός, υἱοθεσία," *TDNT* 8:367. One might affirm that the passage refers to resurrection and not that Jesus becomes "Son" at the resurrection (see, e.g., Conzelmann, *Acts*, 105).

[74] Strauss argues for a hybrid view, maintaining that v. 32 refers to the resurrection, but that "Luke introduces the verse primarily to prove that Jesus is the Son of God, and hence the Messiah, who fulfills the promises of David in his whole life, death, and resurrection." The citation is primarily epistemological, keeping the whole Jesus event in view while emphasizing resurrection (*Messiah*, 164–6).

[75] Though not essential, the argument's logical coherence is tightened by taking οὕτως (thusly) in v. 34 as modifying ἀνέστησεν (raised) rather than εἴρηκεν (said). This puts emphasis retrospectively on being raised in the manner of a Davidic coronation, rather than simply asserting that Isa. 55:3 applies because Jesus does not experience corruption. The assertion in v. 33 of Jesus's sonship and Davidic status would then be integrated into the argument of vv. 34–6 as well as be a precursor to the Davidic promises in v. 34. Either way, the connection between the resurrection and national hopes is made explicit.

of David (τὰ ὅσια Δαυὶδ τὰ πιστά) should be understood. The MT discusses the mercy/covenant fidelity *of* David (חסדי דוד), referring to the covenant made with David and its eschatological realization for the people.[76] Strauss outlines four particular ways that "the holy things" might be understood here.[77] First, τὰ ὅσια has been understood as David's own piety, though this attributes the activity to David rather than God, which is out of step with the OT context and does not seem to make the best sense of the passage.[78] Second, the holy things have been understood as the resurrection of the Messiah in particular.[79] Third, Dupont has argued that the primary referent is not simply the resurrection but the salvific significance of the resurrection soon to be explicated in vv. 38–39, namely forgiveness and justification.[80] Fourth, Strauss—rightly, in my estimation—notes that it is more properly God's favor toward David that is under consideration, arguing that the "holy things" are the manifold elements of the covenant promise to David, simultaneously implying the benefits this will have for a restored Israel.[81] This is preferable because it coheres with the original context and fits with Paul's speech and an understanding of the Davidic promise as linked to God's continual covenant faithfulness stretching from Abraham for the people.

Importantly, this emphasis on the salvific blessings afforded by this Davidic king, Jesus, should not be reduced to discrete and personal forgiveness and justification, or even of individually acquiring eternal life through resurrection. The Isaianic context (55:1–5) has a sociopolitical tone, speaking of an era characterized by eschatological abundance, feasting, and Israel's political superiority. This occurs in the context of an "everlasting covenant" (διαθήκην αἰώνιον) centered on the Davidic promises, with the consequence of gentile inclusion. Paul's speech anticipates this sense. The benefits to the people are not merely personal salvation, but something more substantial, manifest in economic and political reordering.[82] Though the promises are given to David, the benefits are for all the people, fulfilling the era of God's purpose that has been rejected repeatedly through history (vv. 18, 21, 27–9). Here, again, is emphasized a political salvation, a restoration of a social order for a people. Where the leadership and those

---

[76] Jacques Dupont ("ΤΑ ὍΣΙΑ ΔΑΥΙΔ ΤΑ ΠΙΣΤΑ: Actes 13,34 = Isaïe 55,3," in *Études sur les Actes des Apôtres*, LD 45 (Paris: Cerf, 1967), 343–4) and Lövestam (*Son*, 75) associate this use of ὅσιος (see also Deut. 29:18) with a use more at home in Greek worship referring to the favors pledged to humans from a deity.

[77] Strauss, *Messiah*, 166–72.

[78] Alfred Loisy, *Les Actes des Apôtres* (Paris: Émile Nourry, 1920), 534–5; Hans Hinrich Wendt, *Die Apostelgeschichte*, KEK 5 (Göttingen: Vandenhoeck & Ruprecht, 1913), 213–15.

[79] Kirsopp Lake and Henry J. Cadbury, *The Acts of the Apostles: English Translation and Commentary*, vol. 4 of *The Beginnings of Christianity: Part I: The Acts of the Apostles*, eds. F. J. Foakes Jackson and Kirsopp Lake (London: Macmillan, 1933), 155. This is problematic simply because ὅσια is plural.

[80] Dupont, "ὍΣΙΑ," 352, 358–9. See also Kilgallen, "Culmination," 497–501.

[81] Strauss, *Messiah*, 170–2. See also Darrell L. Bock, "Scripture and the Realization of God's Promises," in *Witness to the Gospel: The Theology of Acts*, eds. I. Howard Marshall and David Peterson (Grand Rapids: Eerdmans, 1998), 50; Fitzmyer, *Acts*, 517; L. T. Johnson, *Acts*, 235; Keener, *Acts*, 2:2072.

[82] *Contra* Kilgallen, who asserts that Isaiah LXX and its subsequent appropriation in Paul's sermon refer to a spiritual inheritance ("Culmination," 497).

in Jerusalem partnered with political powers to execute Jesus, God has resurrected this one for the national hopes and communal blessing of Israel in keeping with God's covenant fidelity, and for blessing to the nations (cf. Isa. 55:5).

5.5 The Epilogue (Acts 13:38–41)

Paul finishes his speech with a summary (vv. 38-9) and a warning (vv. 40-1) in a unified epilogue.[83] Malcolm Heath notes, "The chief functions of the epilogue are to recapitulate the main points of our argument and to incite the emotional response which will finally carry the audience along with us."[84] Here, Paul provides both a summary and an emotionally charged call.[85]

Appropriately, he begins with an appeal to knowledge (γνωστὸν οὖν ἔστω ὑμῖν). This again is not a mere call to intellectual ascent, but to conceptualizing the times that are unfolding through a specific narrative. The content of this knowledge is presented in two parts: forgiveness of sins (v. 38b) and justification (vv. 38c-39). The prepositional phrase "from all that you were unable to be justified by in the law of Moses" modifies δικαιοῦται (to be justified) in v. 39 (cf. Rom. 6:7), rather than the verbal noun ἄφεσις (forgiveness, v. 38), so that the summary involves two positive statements. They are to understand that (1) through this one, forgiveness of sins is proclaimed to them, and (2) in this one, each one who is faithful is proven to be just. The prepositional phrase modifies this latter clause.

As already noted, forgiveness of sins is something of a Lukan theme, and its invocation appeals not simply to personal forgiveness but to Israel's restoration more broadly (Lk. 24:47; Acts 2:38; 5:31; 10:43; 26:18).[86] Forgiveness itself is socially productive, and I discussed in Chapter 3 the intimate connection between forgiveness and release as part of the Jubilee economy preached and lived out by Jesus. By bringing forgiveness and repentance, Jesus answers Israel's hope (cf. 26:6-7). Justification,

---

[83] Though Paul's epilogue can be split into two distinct sections, Black argues that rhetoricians from antiquity would consider this a single epilogue (*Rhetoric*, 126-7).

[84] Malcolm Heath, "Invention," in *Handbook of Classical Rhetoric in the Hellenistic Period 300 B.C.- A.D. 400*, ed. Stanley E. Porter (Boston: Brill Academic, 2001), 117. This coheres with Quintilian's dissection of the epilogue (*Inst.* 6.1-2). See also Cicero, *Inv.* 1.98-109; *Ret. ad Her.* 2.47-50; Anon. Seg. 198-253; Aspines, *Rh.* 10.

[85] Seeing this epilogue as a summary coheres with Dupont's ("ΟΣΙΑ," 358-59) and Kilgallen's ("Culmination," 480-1) approaches to the integration of "forgiveness of sins" and "justification" (vv. 38-9) as central elements of the speech and as goal and benefit of Davidic blessing. However, their definitions of these elements are unnecessarily restrictive. Dupont sees them as "essentiellement religieuse" ("ΟΣΙΑ," 349).

[86] The importance of emphasizing a non-reductive understanding of forgiveness can be seen by attending to Heikki Räisänen's argument concerning Luke's Paul (*Marcion, Muhammed and the Mahatma: Exegetical Perspectives on the Encounter of Cultures and Faiths* (London: SCM, 1997), 63). Räisänen laments the reduction of religion to forgiveness as the base of a supersessionist religion. Nevertheless, Räisänen evidences the same reductive approach, dependent on a thin interpretation of "forgiveness of sins," with the Benedictus where he claims that Lk. 1:76-7 introduces a different meaning of salvation where the spiritual supersedes the political (p. 51).

however, is not a common concept in Luke-Acts, and given its occurrence in a Pauline speech, commentators have debated the degree to which this correctly portrays Pauline theology.[87] However, the degree of correspondence to Pauline thought is not our primary concern.

Though there is likely at least an attempt at *prosopopoiea*, it is worth asking, what if we were to read this language of justification as Lukan and in alignment with Lukan theology?[88] On the surface, this may seem problematic because language of justification is so Pauline[89] and so not Lukan. The term employed for "justify," δικαιόω, appears nowhere else in Acts. Nevertheless, an operative notion of justness can be discerned throughout Luke-Acts, both in attending to δικ- language and, importantly, when looking beyond the level of a word search to Luke's critique of injustice masquerading as justness, a theme that has already played a key role (see Chapter 4).[90]

In Luke's Gospel, δικαιόω does appear on a few occasions, and its use is instructive. Generally, there is an element of demonstration and public recognition tied to δικαιόω so that even God (7:29) and Wisdom (7:35) are "justified," that is, publicly acknowledged as just/right. Others seek justification/recognition of rightness (wrongly) from people (10:29; 16:15); this attitude is juxtaposed to the tax collector in the temple who is justified by God in his humility (18:14).[91]

From this perspective, justification in Acts 13:38–39 would pertain to a recognition/demonstration of justness. Rather than simply a resultant benefit of Jesus's resurrection,

---

[87] An important study in this regard is Vielhauer, "Paulinism." On Paulinism in Acts, see the *Forschungsberichten* on the Lukan Paul by Odile Flichy, "The Paul of Luke: A Survey of Research," in *Paul and the Heritage of Israel: Paul's Claim upon Israel's Legacy in Luke and Acts in the Light of the Pauline Letters*, vol. 2 of *Luke the Interpreter of Israel*, eds. David P. Moessner, Daniel Marguerat, Mikeal C. Parsons and Michael Wolter, LNTS 452 (London: T&T Clark, 2012), 18–34; Paul-Gerhard Müller, "Der 'Paulinismus' in der Apostelgeschichte: Ein forschungsgeschichtlicher Überblick," in *Paulus in den neutestamentlichen Spätschriften*, QD 89 ed. Karl Kertelge (Freiburg: Herder, 1981), 157–201. See also, Joseph A. Fitzmyer, "Pauline Justification as Presented by Luke in Acts 13," in *Transcending Boundaries: Contemporary Readings of the New Testament: Essays in Honor of Francis J. Moloney*, eds. Rekha M. Chennattu and Mary L. Coloe (Rome: LAS, 2005), 249–63; Richard B. Hays, "The Paulinism of Acts, Intertextually Reconsidered," in *Paul and the Heritage of Israel: Paul's Claim upon Israel's Legacy in Luke and Acts in the Light of the Pauline Letters*, vol. 2 of *Luke the Interpreter of Israel*, eds. David P. Moessner, Daniel Marguerat, Mikeal C. Parsons, and Michael Wolter, LNTS 452 (London: T&T Clark, 2012), 35–48.

[88] The speech is generally recognized as a Lukan construction. See Eduard Schweizer, "Concerning the Speeches in Acts," in *Studies in Luke-Acts: Essays Presented in Honor of Paul Schubert*, eds. Leander E. Keck and J. Louis Martyn (Nashville: Abingdon, 1966), 208–16; Tannehill, *Unity*, 2:160–1.

[89] Rom. 2:13; 3:20, 24, 26, 28, 30; 4:2, 5; 5:1, 9; 6:7; 8:30, 33; 1 Cor. 4:4; 6:11; Gal. 2:16–7; 3:8, 11, 24; 5:4; Tit. 3:7.

[90] For many, Luke collapses justification into forgiveness, making both essentially negative (e.g., Fitzmyer, *Acts*, 518; Morgan-Wynne, *Speech*, 141; Vielhauer, "Paulinism," 41). However, though they are obviously related, justification in this passage has its own sense that is important to preserve. As we have argued that forgiveness of sins entails more than acquittal (thus the negative assessment), justification similarly requires more nuance.

[91] Fitzmyer argues that only in Acts 13:38–9 do we find justification terminology used in the "technical sense," yet this assessment leads him to discount what can be gleaned from Luke's use of δικαιόω elsewhere ("Justification," 256). See also other δικ- terminology in Luke-Acts: Lk. 1:6, 17, 75; 2:25; 5:32; 12:57; 14:14; 15:7; 18:9; 20:20; 23:41, 47, 50; Acts 3:14; 4:19; 7:52; 10:22, 35; 13:10; 17:31; 22:14; 24:15, 25; 28:4.

justness is manifest in one's response to God's providence. Throughout the speech, a salient contrast has been demonstrated between how those in Jerusalem treated Jesus and what Paul is exhorting from his audience. Those in Jerusalem are not justified by their behavior. They are directly implicated in conspiring with a Roman official to execute God's Son, and their action is portrayed in terms of the provisions for executing an Israelite deserving capital punishment (Deut. 21:22–3).[92] Luke demonstrates the antagonists' evaluative viewpoint in the way they are portrayed as executing Jesus in this manner (Acts 5:30; 10:39).[93] In this way, they have utilized and misappropriated Mosaic law to reject God's providence, demonstrating plainly that they were unable to exhibit justness by implementing Mosaic law. Rather, they have demonstrated unjustness, which is made explicit by God's vindication and resurrection of Jesus.

Verses 38–9 are not a clumsy Pauline flourish, then, but a summary of the material that has come before. It recapitulates the contrast formula evident in Jesus's execution and, even more deeply, in the aforementioned historical recurrence, assigning justification and forgiveness to active fidelity to God's providence and national restoration, respectively. Thus, the exegetical debate concerning a law that cannot justify at all[94] and a law that can justify in part but needs supplementation through faith[95] misses the point. The problem is magnified by the relatively positive assessment of the law in Luke-Acts.[96] However, the issue is not whether practicing the law will justify or only partially justify, but *how* one practices the law and the foundation of πίστις (fidelity). The law is insufficient when enacted through false fidelity (for example, fidelity to Caesar or demonic idolatry and grasping for power). It then cannot justify.

Paul has exposed a hermeneutical problem.[97] Rightly, one might assert that it is a conceptual failure that binds the unfaithful, and more than that, there is a certain idolatrous reliance on fidelity to worldly powers (Lk. 23:2; Acts 4:25–7; 13:28), a symptom of submission to the devil's authority and that which works against Jesus's Jubilee economy (Lk. 4:1–13; see Chapter 3). The crucifixion and resurrection then function as revelatory, persuading events, exposing this idolatry and injustice, enabling

---

[92] Reardon, "Crucifixion," 409–15.
[93] Reardon, "Crucifixion," 416–20.
[94] E.g., Bruce, *Book*, 262–3; Fitzmyer, *Acts*, 518–19; Haenchen, *Acts*, 412. This is often thought to be the more Pauline position (cf. Gal. 2:16; Rom. 8:13).
[95] Witherington argues that Luke could have in mind sacrifices that deal with unwillful sin, whereas faith justifies that for which the law does not offer forgiveness (*Acts*, 413). See Benjamin Wisner Bacon, *The Story of St. Paul: A Comparison of Acts and Epistles* (Boston: Houghton Mifflin, 1904), 103.
[96] In Luke, Jesus himself indicates that the law is sufficient for salvation (10:25–8) and, in Acts, Stephen praises the law (7:38, 53) and Paul attempts to refute accusations that he undermines the law (Acts 21:21, 28; cf. 25:8), has Timothy circumcised (16:1–3), takes a religious vow (18:18), and joins young Jewish Christians in a purification rite, paying for their heads to be shaved (21:23–4, 26). See also Lk. 2:22; 24:44; Acts 15:5; 28:23. The two traditional outliers to this presentation are 13:39 and 15:10. However, it is conceivable that the "burden" in both is this hermeneutical problem and the necessity of proper fidelity as a base.
[97] Gaventa remarks that notions of hermeneutical error are not foreign to Acts (*Acts*, 201). For example, Stephen, though expressing no complaint against the law, "surely indicts some of the law's supposed interpreters" (7:2–53).

release and proper perception through fidelity to God (rather than to Satan, Caesar, or authority and power in general). Paul does not reject the law, but exposes the law's inadequacy when appropriated through idolatrous allegiances.

Uncovering true justness is an important part of Luke's narrative. The spectacle of Jesus's crucifixion and his obviously unjust execution (Lk. 23:4, 14–15, 22, 41) is capped by the centurion's ironic revelation of Jesus's justness (δίκαιος, v. 47). More generally, Rowe has argued that the political strategy of Acts is to critique Roman application of its own law. Roman law has a correct interpretation, which, Rowe maintains, Luke legitimates while simultaneously uncovering and critiquing Roman unjustness by the standard of its own law.[98] Nevertheless, in light of the current passage, it might be more appropriate to appeal to an overarching sense of justice to which Luke holds both Roman and Jewish law. If Rowe is correct that Luke does not reject the justness of Roman law, but holds Romans to its standards, then something similar could be said here of Mosaic law, whereby the Jerusalemites' actions, in implementing the Mosaic law, demonstrate their unjustness as determined by God, the arbiter or justness and the vindicator of Jesus. Here, Paul is not critiquing the law *qua* law but a reading of the law. As discussed in Chapter 4, this comes to a head in the cross, which lays bare true justness and ignorance, where true allegiances are revealed and Satan is exposed.

Paul's subsequent warning (vv. 40–1) builds directly from this summarization. Citing Hab. 1:5, he enjoins his audience to hear the prophets as the Jerusalemites had not.[99] The original context of the citation is important. Habakkuk 1:5 is God's response to Habakkuk's first prayer (vv. 2–4), where the prophet mourns that the law has been broken/scattered (διασκεδάζω)—a term often found in relation to breaking covenant, commands, the law, or allegiance and justice (κρίμα)—and the law is being perverted (διαστρέφω; cf. Lk. 23:2, 14).[100] The ungodly (ἀσεβής), Habakkuk claims, oppress the "the righteous/just one" (ὁ δίκαιος), a term used almost titularly for Jesus in Acts

---

[98] See Rowe, *World*, 148–9.
[99] Notably, Luke's citation of Hab. 1:5 LXX includes an extra reference to work (ἔργον) and is amended with "to you" (ὑμῖν). This work is unfolding for them now, a work that they may not currently "believe" (πιστεύω). But, what precisely is that work? For some, it is Paul's preaching itself (cf. 5:38; 13:2; 14:26; 15:38) (e.g., Fitzmyer, *Acts*, 519; Gaventa, *Acts*, 202). However, the citation clearly portrays God as the agent of this work. Rather, the work is that which is described in Paul's gospel, not simply the resurrection, or the restoration of the Davidic line, but the complex of what is unfolding. Based on one's situatedness in relation to this proclamation, this could be either positive or negative. Negatively, there remains an element of judgment. If we are to work from the context of Habakkuk, this work is coming judgment (Hab. 1:6–11), and Luke-Acts allows for that possibility (Lk. 19:42–4; 21:6, 20–4; Acts 13:46). Nevertheless, this is also a promise, the establishment of justness by judgment in the face of oppression (Hab. 1:4). There is no contradiction in the assertion of God's establishment of justness and the positive work now of participating in kingdom space. Thus, Robert Wall is likely right that the work that they will not believe is the current mission ("The Function of LXX Habakkuk 1:5 in the Book of Acts," *BBR* 10 (2000): 247–58). This mission, we find out later, includes gentiles as well. Notably, the nations do not come for violence, as in Hab. 1:6–11, but as a people chosen by God (Acts 15:17).
[100] Gen. 17:14; Lev. 26:15, 44; Num. 15:31; Deut. 31:16, 20; Jdg 2:1; 1 Kgs 15:19; 2 Chron. 16:3; Ezra 9:14; Ps. 118(119):126; Zech. 11:10–11; Jer. 14:21; Dan. 3:34.

(3:14; 7:52; 22:14). Habakkuk 1:5 then speaks to this injustice, promising God's answer. In Paul's context, the Jerusalemites have contorted the law in order to bring about injustice and execute God's righteous one. But God promises an answer. This serves as a warning to his audience to not follow the footsteps of the Jerusalemites.

Paul is not making an argument about how one individually appropriates faith and is justified. Paul is making an argument about Israel's restoration and the incorporation of a people living under this Davidide in fidelity and justness. The focus is on a social restoration, an element exhibited in Paul's allusion to the "faithful" (τὰ πίστα) and holy things of David. Morgan has adroitly argued that πίστις/*fides* in antiquity, including the NT, is a quality that characterizes symbiotic relationships (cf. Cicero, *De or.* 2.343–4).[101] In relationships, the parties have faith together, in one another. Further, πίστις/*fides* and δικαιοσύνη/*iustitia* (justness/righteousness) are intimately related as "chief among the qualities which make human associations possible."[102] These qualities provide a foundation for societies and effective political institutions (Cicero, *Off.* 1.121; 2.21, 32, 38; *De or.* 1.85–6; Plutarch, *Mor.* 275A; cf. Horace, *Carm.* 1.24.5–8). This is an argument about the restoration of a people, the constitution of social space characterized by God's eschatological abundance, a benefit brought by faithful allegiance to God's king, Jesus.

5.6 The Next Sabbath (Acts 13:42–52)

Paul exits the synagogue with a seemingly positive response from the attendees (vv. 42–3). On the next Sabbath, however, nearly the whole city has come, and the Jews in attendance become zealous (ζῆλος), contradicting Paul (vv. 44–5).[103] Undoubtedly, it is Paul's preaching to a crowd of gentiles that vexes them.[104] It is clear that Paul and Barnabas are speaking the same message (v. 42); however, the message of promise and justification through faithfulness to Jesus is now preached to "the whole city" (πᾶσα ἡ πόλις, v. 44), certainly including gentiles.[105]

Such a zealous response is not new to Acts, nor does "jealousy" adequately describe it. Zeal is an intense commitment to God's law and to Israel's fidelity to God. The paradigm for such zeal was Phinehas, who slayed an Israelite man who was with a Midianite woman (Num. 25:6–11; 1 Macc. 2:24–6, 54; see also Ps. 106:30; Sir. 45:23; 4 Macc. 18.12). In Acts, as it was with Phinehas, zeal is applied by Jews within intra-Jewish contexts.[106] Some express zeal (ζῆλος, ζηλόω) in the face of gentile conversion

---

[101] Morgan, *Faith*.
[102] Morgan, *Faith*, 118.
[103] As Tannehill notes, here, these Jews have become the scoffers (v. 40) (*Unity*, 2:172).
[104] Buss (*Missionspredigt*, 135) and Schneider (*Apostelgeschichte*, 102) assert that these Jews are zealous because the Christian mission is more successful; however, this does not account for how zeal is used in Acts. See below.
[105] Koet, *Studies*, 98–106.
[106] See Reardon, "Crucifixion," 423–4. In fact, the only place in Acts where zeal might express jealousy alone is the use of ζηλόω in reference to Joseph's brothers' jealousy (7:9). Still, Stephen is possibly using this term rhetorically to associate the actions of Joseph's brothers with the actions of those opposing the church.

(13:45; 17:5), and some are zealots (ζηλωτής) for the law (21:20) or for God (22:3). In 5:17, the Jerusalem leadership expresses zeal amid a controversy over their own authority. In most cases this zealousness is perceived negatively, but Paul himself claims to be a "zealot (ζηλωτής) for God" (22:3); and the same noun is used to identify the apostle Simon (Lk. 6:15; Acts 1:13). Rightly then, in this context, zeal is directed toward Paul and Barnabas, not against the gentiles. Paul, by this active evangelization of gentiles, may be perceived as compromising God's people or their fidelity by speaking of God's promises through faithfulness to Jesus to the uncircumcised (cf. 15:1).

If zeal is a reaction directed toward offenders among the people who are deemed to be a threat to the nation's fidelity to God, then this further corroborates our understanding of Acts' appropriation of Deut. 21:22–3, in which the people zealously react to Jesus as a false prophet. With Paul and Barnabas this cycle continues. Jesus's death is a miscarriage and misappropriation of justice and law, and the rejection of Paul and Barnabas is similarly such a misguided rejection of God's purpose through an assumed but misguided zeal for God's law.

Paul and Barnabas respond by invoking Isa. 49:6, a text that has already substantiated Jesus's and the church's mission (Lk. 2:32; Acts 1:8; 26:17–18, 23; see Chapter 4). However, it is important to recognize that Isa. 49:6 and its context are not primarily about a gentile mission but about Israel's restoration. It is with this restoration that Israel's mission to the gentiles is employed. Notably, the passage has some ambiguity concerning the "servant" and Israel. In 49:3, Israel is explicitly identified as the servant; nevertheless, in the following verses, the servant's role is to restore Jacob (vv. 5–6). Israel is both the servant and the object of the servant's mission, a mission that incorporates both aspects of Israel's restoration and being a light to the gentiles. Commentators who have assessed Paul and Barnabas's appropriation of this text have identified the servant variously as Israel,[107] Jesus,[108] and Paul and Barnabas.[109] The distinction between the three is unnecessary.[110]

From the outset, the servant's mission is Israel's mission (cf. Isa. 49:8),[111] and in Luke, Jesus takes on this mission (2:25, 32). In Acts, proclamation of the light, which is both the content and goal of the gospel (26:17–18), comes from both the disciples and Jesus (1:8; 26:23). The citation in 13:47 situates Paul and Barnabas within this mission commissioned by Jesus (vv. 31–2), a servant role that enacts Israel's mission. Thus, in this sense, Jervell is correct to identify this citation as appealing to Israel's mission, specifically noting that the mission to the gentiles is not simply a secondary plan after

---

[107] Jervell, *People*, 61.
[108] Dionne, *L'Évangile*, 269–70; Dupont, "Lumière," 347–8; P. Gerlot, "Note sur Actes, XIII, 47," *RB* 88 (1981): 368–72; David Seccombe, "Luke and Isaiah," *NTS* 27 (1982): 252–9; Strauss, *Messiah*, 175.
[109] Jordan Daniel May, "Is Luke a Reader-Response Critic? Luke's Aesthetic Trajectory of Isaiah 49.6 in Acts 13.47," in *Trajectories in the Book of Acts: Essays in Honor of John Wesley Wyckoff*, eds. Paul Alexander, Jordan Daniel May and Robert G. Reid (Eugene, OR: Wipf & Sock, 2010), 59–86. May argues for Paul and Barnabas as the servant in this specific context (13:47), though he sees the citation as multivalent depending on context.
[110] Koet, *Studies*, 114. See also Beers, *Followers*, 163–4; Buss, *Missionspredigt*, 138; Mallen, *Reading*, 86.
[111] See Thompson, *Acts*, 118–20.

Israel refuses the gospel making the gentiles a "new Israel,"[112] but is rather an integral component to Israel's mission from the beginning.[113]

Jervell's formulation, however, argues a view of Israel not supported by the text. Though denying the notion that the Jews are rejected and superseded by "new Israel," Jervell maintains an irrevocable exclusion of certain Jews, redefining Israel solely by the faithful with the inclusion of an associate gentile people.[114] He argues that, in Luke-Acts, there is both historic Israel and restored Israel, yet Luke's use of Israel (Ἰσραήλ) is consistent; there is only a single historic Israel.[115]

As David Moessner maintains, "neither 'replacement' (Haenchen) nor 'restoration-exclusion' (Jervell)" does justice to Luke-Acts' presentation of Israel.[116] Instead, Luke-Acts testifies to a tension within Israel that finds no resolution by the narrative's end. This tension between Israel's rebellion against God's purpose and God's covenant faithfulness to and election of Israel (as well as the responsive among Israel) is emphasized from the beginning (Lk. 2:34–5), through the historical narrative of Paul's Antioch speech (Acts 13:17–25), through the present, and to Rome (28:23–8). Both Jervell's and Haenchen's formulations necessitate closure where the text maintains tension. For Haenchen, Israel is rejected in favor of a new Israel, there is no tension with God's election, and the Jewish period of history has closed. Similarly, Jervell requires that Israel be defined, and unrepentant Israel be irrevocably rejected before there may be gentile inclusion.

Both streams of thought point to instances of Jewish rejection and Paul's turning to the gentiles (esp. 13:44–52; 18:5–6; 28:23–8), assuming a logical order of operations in which mission to Jews and mission to gentiles are treated in distinct stages. Rightly, it is noted that the mission goes first to the Jews (v. 46; cf. 3:19–26); however, in neither Isa. 49 nor Luke-Acts does this require an identification of discrete stages such as that advocated by Jervell[117] or the complete rejection of Jews resulting in a turn to the gentiles as with Haenchen et al.[118]

---

[112] E.g., Conzelmann, *Theology*, 162–3; Haenchen, *Acts*, 100–3; idem, "The Book of Acts as Source Material for the History of Early Christianity," in *Studies in Luke-Acts: Essays Presented in Honor of Paul Schubert*, eds. Leander E. Keck and J. Louis Martyn (Nashville: Abingdon, 1966), 278.

[113] Lk. 2:32; 3:6; 24:45–8; Acts 1:8; 9:15; 13:47; 22:15; 26:16–18.

[114] Jervell, *People*, 64.

[115] Ethnicity and nationalism as conceived by moderns is foreign to the first century. However, something that approximates nationalism and ethnicity is observable in antiquity, which is the sense I intend here, and which Martin Goodblatt defines thusly: "By national identity I mean a belief in a common descent and shared culture available for mass political mobilization. By shared culture I mean that certain cultural factors are seen as criteria for, or indications of, membership in the national group" (*Elements of Jewish Nationalism* (Cambridge: Cambridge University Press, 2006), 26). Cf. Lk. 1:16, 54, 68, 80; 2:25, 32, 34; 4:25, 27; 7:9; 22:30; 24:21; Acts 1:6; 2:36; 4:10, 27; 5:21, 31; 7:23, 37, 42; 9:15; 10:36; 13:17, 23–4; 28:20.

[116] David P. Moessner, "Paul in Acts: Preacher of Eschatological Repentance to Israel," *NTS* 34 (1988): 96.

[117] Jervell, *People*, 41–3, 62; idem, *Apostelgeschichte*, 353; idem, "Church,"11–20.

[118] Conzelmann, *Theology*, 162–3; Haenchen, *Acts*, 100–3; idem, "Material," 278; Jantsch, *Jesus*, 35; Nordgaard, *Possessions*, 44–56; J. C. O'Neill, *The Theology of Acts: In Its Historical Setting* (London: SPCK, 1970), 95; Räisänen, *Marcion*, 49–63; Jack T. Sanders, *The Jews in Luke-Acts* (Philadelphia: Fortress, 1987); idem, "The Jewish People in Luke-Acts," in *Luke-Acts and the Jewish People: Eight Critical Perspectives*, ed. Joseph B. Tyson (Minneapolis: Augsburg, 1988), 51–75; idem, "Who Is a Jew and Who Is a Gentile in the Book of Acts," *NTS* 37 (1991): 434–55.

One problem is that the situation in Antioch is rather the opposite. Paul does not go to the gentiles *because* of the rejection of resident Jews, or after gathering all the faithful Jews. The resident Jews first reject Paul and Barnabas because the gentiles are *already* hearing this gospel; that is, these Jews reject Israel's Isaianic mission. Their rejection of the message causes Paul and Barnabas to turn their attention to those gentiles. David Ravens writes: "Perhaps Paul's statements of turning to the gentiles contain at least an element of 'if you will not, we will.'"[119] One might note that Paul and Barnabas cite only the portion of Isa. 49:6 referring to gentile mission. Yet, this is not surprising given that this message is to Jews concerning the validity of the gentile mission. It should not be taken as a rejection of the element of Israel's restoration emphasized at the outset of Acts (1:6–8). Notably, in 1:6–8, the disciples are told to engage in this light-mission while waiting on full restoration.

Further, it is not at all logically necessary or apparent that going first to Jews and then gentiles necessitates distinct stages in which God's restoration/rejection of the Jews, or unrepentant Israel, must be assured first. Priority is given to Israel, but in both Isa. 49:1–6 and Acts more generally, there is no sense that these missions cannot overlap. In fact, the ambiguity in defining the servant leaves room for both Israel's mission and the servant's mission *to Israel* continuing simultaneously. The rebuilt Davidic tent,[120] for instance, may allow for the inclusion of a chosen gentile people (Acts 15:14–17);[121] nevertheless, this need not imply that Israel's restoration has been completed.[122] Israel is not itself the tent, but a people who finds refuge and restoration there.

A primary issue, then, is the finality of Paul's pronouncements. In Acts 13:41, the warning of judgment from Hab. 1:5 does not necessitate irrevocable rejection, nor does it overcome the explicit tension between Israel's response to God and God's covenant faithfulness and Israel's election. Further, when Paul pronounces judgment on the

---

[119] Ravens, *Restoration*, 251.

[120] Concerning the Davidic tent as a space including multiple peoples in the messianic kingdom rather than as Israel (*pace* Jervell, *People*, 51–4, 92–3), Strauss notes, "It is not the church or the nation Israel but the Davidic dynasty (or 'kingly reign') that is here said to be re-built. When Christ re-established the Davidic reign, both Jews and Gentiles were offered a place in the messianic community of salvation" (*Messiah*, 190).

[121] God's calling (ἐπικαλέω) in Acts 15:14–17 to take a people for his name should draw the reader back as well to Peter's Pentecost speech where he declares both that whoever calls (ἐπικαλέω) on the name of the Lord will be saved (2:21) and that the promise (ἐπαγγελία) is for everyone whom the Lord calls (προσκαλέω).

[122] The use of λαός (people, Acts 15:14), which functions generally to identify God's people, Israel, is significant. In only two places do we find it referring to gentiles (Acts 15:14; 18:10; see also Nils Dahl, "'A People for His Name' (Acts XV.14)," *NTS* 4 (1958): 324). This term is generally singular, excluding Lk. 2:31; Acts 4:25, 27. The occurrence in Lk. 2:31 alludes to Isa. 49:6 and seems to refer beyond just Israel, switching back to the singular in v. 32, speaking of the singular people Israel. The first reference to gentiles as a λαός, in Acts 15:14, is in the context of the Jerusalem church's affirmation of gentile inclusion without circumcision. They are identified as a people God calls (ἐπικαλέω) alongside the Jewish λαός within the rebuilt Davidic tent (15:16–17; Amos 9:11–12). This, then, prepares for the other mention of a gentile λαός in 18:10. This is important because J. T. Sanders' argument that gentiles have replaced Jews as God's chosen people depends on a supersessionist reading of Acts 15:14 (*Jews*, 48–9). However, this argument is countered by the continual reference to Israel as ὁ λαός. While Israel remains solely utilized for singular Israel, by the end of Acts we can speak of multiple λαοί, though the term is most prominently used for the Jews.

crowd, he recognizes how the crowd has identified themselves as unworthy of eternal life (v. 46), but still there is no pronouncement of God's final rejection or the removal of God's covenant faithfulness. Paul's turning in mission does not require God's turning in exclusion.

The same issues occur with Acts 28:23–8. There is little clear evidence for Israel's exclusion and the revocation of God's covenant faithfulness within the text other than inference from Paul's declaration that he is turning to the gentiles. Paul certainly cites Isa. 6:9–10 as a negative appraisal of the Roman Jews' response, yet there is no reason to conclude that this citation is any more anti-Jewish than when Isaiah uttered it. Notably, there is no mention of Israel's rejection, only an affirmative statement of Paul's turning to the gentile mission (v. 28). Pervo, however, appeals to the "rule of threes," asserting that now, the third time is the final straw. There will be no turning back to the Jews, and they have finally been rejected.[123] However, this is not explicit. As in Pisidian Antioch and in Corinth, Paul turns away from preaching to the Jews there, but an assertion of God's rejection and ending God's covenant faithfulness must be imported by the exegete.

Dunn rightly states, "The mistake of those who see here the account of an irretrievable breakdown between Christianity and Judaism has been to assume that the third report of such a denunciation by Paul of his fellow Jews was intended to be final. On the contrary, Luke was well aware that the real history continued beyond the limits of his narrative."[124] The attempt to find closure here and in God's relationship with Israel trivializes the tension that remains prevalent through the ending of Acts. This is not to say that Acts does not promote a notion of a faithful remnant.[125] Peter clearly articulates that those who call on Lord's name will be saved from this corrupt generation (Acts 2:21, 38–40), and Paul claims that justification comes through fidelity to Jesus (13:38–9). However, the time that remains awaits closure, as does Jacob's restoration.

Indeed, the way that Acts 13:17–41 narrates history helps us to understand Israel's place in this scheme. It is a history that emphasizes election and God's covenant faithfulness in spite of recurrent opposition. This does not negate judgment, but it does not imply final rejection either. The history is a tension and an exhortation to situate one's self in right relation to this tension. This position does not "trivialize" the ending of Acts;[126] it takes seriously the development of the narrative; Luke's presentation of history; the complexity of God's relationship with Israel; and the clear textual indicators

---

[123] Pervo, *Acts*, 681. See also Jervell, *People*, 64; Marguerat, *Historian*, 224–5.
[124] Dunn, *Acts*, 353. See also Matthias Blum, "Antijudaismus im lukanischen Doppelwerk? Zur These eines lukanischen Antijudaismus," in *"Nun steht aber diese Sache im Evangelium ...": Zur Frage nach den Anfängen des christlichen Antijudaismus*, ed. Rainer Kampling (München: Ferdinand Schöningh, 1999), 107–49; Brawley, *Luke-Acts*, 119–39; Moessner, "Paul," 96–104; Tannehill, *Unity*, 2:350–1; idem, "Israel," 82–3; idem, "Rejection by Jews and Turning to Gentiles: The Pattern of Paul's Mission in Acts," in *Luke-Acts and the Jewish People: Eight Critical Perspectives*, ed. Joseph B. Tyson (Minneapolis: Augsburg, 1988), 83–101; David L. Tiede, "'Glory to Thy People Israel': Luke-Acts and the Jews," in *Luke-Acts and the Jewish People: Eight Critical Perspectives*, ed. Joseph B. Tyson (Minneapolis: Augsburg, 1988), 28–9.
[125] See David Seccombe, "The New People of God," in *Witness to the Gospel: The Theology of Acts*, eds. I. Howard Marshall and David Peterson (Grand Rapids: Eerdmans, 1998), 352–3.
[126] *Pace* Marguerat, *Historian*, 224.

that conclude Acts' narrative within this tension between God's salvific movement, the many unpersuaded among Israel, and election.[127] The servant's mission to Jacob has not been abrogated. Salvation is still anchored in God's covenant fidelity and election of Israel. The time that remains evinces a salvation in the making and in tension, while the church participates in this salvation space together in a complex world.

5.7 Conclusion

Paul's argument in his address to the synagogue in Pisidian Antioch depends on a narrative of historical recurrence that tells of God's providence and covenant faithfulness to Israel. Paul's rhetoric embeds his audience in a salvation narrative unfolding in their time, where God is the primary actor, who, despite Israel's wayward conduct, remains faithful to God's covenant, acting to bestow on Israel corporate blessing and salvation.

In this address, the primary matter of deliberation is Jesus's identity. Whereas the leadership and those in Jerusalem have crucified Jesus, ostensibly marking him a threat to national stability, God raises Jesus and exalts him as the Davidic Messiah. Thus, there are two conflicting evaluative viewpoints. The audience is invited to side in faithfulness with God. The cross, here, becomes an epistemological event, revealing injustice and the false allegiance of those who would crucify Jesus. This is typified in the leadership's misuse of law, characterizing Jesus as national threat requiring capital punishment. This is not a fault in the law but of human blindness and false allegiance, where the law is used to accomplish something that seemingly conflicts with its intent, opposing God's providence and legitimating Jesus's execution. In this way, the law on its own is unable to guide one in just action if one is aligned to false powers and idolatry.

Proper faithfulness is required, and fidelity to Jesus results in being proven just. Thus, justice is not overlooked in this scheme. However, it is not conceived primarily, for example, in terms of payment or restitution for past sins (as one might find in certain satisfaction models), but in the production of justness, an end state of just ordering, into which bodies are organized in an economy of fidelity around the exalted Jesus, in whom is found David's faithful things, the socioeconomic benefit tied to this political reality. This comes as a result of proper *knowledge*, a proper conceptual appropriation of the Jesus narrative and Israel's history, and this knowledge is not disembodied, but results in the present manifestation of Jesus's corporate body in mundane space.

Such world affirming and embodied salvific knowledge fits an Irenaean *Christus Victor* mold. The victorious Christ organizes a social-political and cosmic-comprehensive salvation, where fidelity involves participating in God's putting the

---

[127] See Tannehill, "Israel"; idem, "Rejection," 83–101. Tannehill rightly notes that there is something tragic about beginning with the Benedictus and ending as we do in Rome; nevertheless, we leave not with the rejection of these promises but the hope of fulfillment with Acts' open ending.

world to right, to establishing justness. The cross functions as a site of revelation, exposing its supposed justice as a travesty. Allegiance to false powers and idolatry produces blindness, but God lays bare injustice and idolatry masquerading as justice and fidelity by conquering over false powers with life and persuasion. God raises Jesus victorious, offering forgiveness, repentance, and new life. In Luke-Acts' salvation narrative, this is portrayed as a conceptual awakening within a cosmic drama, enabling a movement from Satan's authority to God and God's forgiveness (Acts 26:18).

Paul's message is initially well received, but when gentiles begin to accept the message, there is backlash from the Jews in Antioch (cf. Lk. 4:22–30). However, the outward missional trajectory on which the Spirit drives the church anticipates this, gathering a people under the Davidic tent as well from among the nations (Acts 15:14–18). The Spirit's decentering, border-crossing mission incorporates the world into Jesus's cosmic kingdom, ordering the world around this king. Still, this is Israel's mission—and, in Acts, led mostly by those from Israel—and it is grounded in God's historical work through this people.

Nevertheless, God's patience, covenant faithfulness, and strategy of persuasion leave tensions. By the end of Luke-Acts, neither the *temporal* tension between the world as it is and the promised world of universal restoration, nor the *spatial* tension between heaven—the just cosmic order inhabited by the enthroned Messiah—and earth—the mundane order of complex space, overlapping authorities, and unjust systemic, demonic, and exploitative economies—nor the tension between God's *election* of Israel and Israel's division concerning Jesus is overcome. The audience is left with these tensions, living in a world of conflict, knowing that these are the last days (cf. 2:17), and organizing around an alternate order of authority enthroned in heaven, trusting that God will resolve these tensions according to God's character, fidelity, mercy, and justness.

6

Conclusion

This study has argued that *Luke-Acts offers a complete, holistic, embodied, and political soteriology, cosmic in scope, that takes up space in the world and includes both the* what *and* how *of salvation, taking* Christus Victor *form*. Indeed, this is, in a sense, a spatial soteriology. Salvation pertains not simply to persons as individuals, but to social realities, communities, political structures, and so on in the social-political and cosmic-comprehensive space in which persons are embedded. Nevertheless, as I demonstrated in Chapter 1, Lukan soteriology has generally been understood as lacking. Some have imposed theological criteria foreign to Luke-Acts that Luke-Acts does not and cannot live up to. Some have argued that Luke presents the *what* of salvation, pointing repeatedly to the forgiveness of sins, though lacking a *how* achieving such forgiveness. I have argued that this is not the case, that Luke-Acts does offer such a complete picture of salvation.

At the same time, overtly political presentations of salvation, such as the Benedictus (Lk. 1:68–79), are downplayed by some as un-Lukan and ultimately cast in narrowly religious or eschatological terms. Certainly, the Lukan Jesus does not call his disciples to take up arms against the Jerusalem authorities or Rome; he does not frame his message as direct conflict with or utilize the strategies of worldly kingdoms. Nevertheless, this does not mean that Luke-Acts is apolitical. God's kingdom is not a political space in competition; it does not seek to dominate place. It simply is and need not compete for such space, producing its own social-political space that does not dominate territory, though impinging on normative place and impacting it all the same. Kingdom space is constituted by participation as a theopolitical body within an *other*, disturbing, and enduring kingdom *within* complex space, taking up space within the world, influencing the spaces that it encounters, and calling into question violent, dominating, and exploitative systems and authorities. As I argued in Chapter 3, those sharing in God's kingdom exist in a world of complex, overlapping space, in which they traverse multiple spaces of authority. Participation in God's kingdom affects one's participation in and utilization of those other spaces, as we saw for example with Paul's Roman citizenship (Acts 16:37; 22:25–9). The political reality of God's kingdom manifests as a body, an alternate ordering, while also seeping into and influencing other spaces within which Jesus's theopolitical body is engaged—like yeast hidden in three measures of flour (Lk. 13:20–1).

Ultimately, salvation appears as a movement of reconciling not simply people to God, but earth to heaven, of heaven invading and aligning this world to God's kingdom. Now is *the time that remains* in which God's kingdom has come near and manifests in mundane space moving from Jerusalem to the end of the earth, from Israel to the nations. This soteriological scheme is best understood, not as a system, but as a story.

6.1 Summarizing the Story

Luke-Acts begins with Israel waiting for restoration and for God to bring them salvation (see Chapter 2). This salvation pertains to them as a people, a communal and political body, and, appropriately, God's response is visitation through a Davidic savior who will restore Israel and teach God's people to walk the journey of peace (1:79). John comes to announce this salvation, making known that, at this moment in history, God is turning in gracious covenant fidelity and offering forgiveness. This forgiveness is the presupposition for salvation, not the outcome of this salvific movement. God does not send a savior to achieve forgiveness from God, but to gather and reconcile the world to God's already extended forgiveness. Forgiveness is not simply personal absolution. It is a responsive, relational reality, requiring repentance, turning, and participation in social space of the economy of forgiveness and release (cf. 11:4) that reorders social-political space. Forgiveness entails the production of social realities of release/forgiveness that relieve from social, political, economic, religious, and spiritual captivity and, in characteristic reversal, that center those made marginal. That is God's kingdom (cf. 6:20).

As Luke's Gospel proceeds, the Benedictus's salvific picture does not fade from view, but rather finds partial fulfillment as the promised Davidic savior, Jesus, is born, baptized, anointed, and tested, all in preparation for the announcement of a new, eschatological "today" in Nazareth (4:16–21). Filled with the Spirit, Jesus enters into a cosmic battle with the devil, to whose temptations *all* the kingdoms of the world have succumbed (4:1–13). Nevertheless, Jesus, God's faithful Son, through obedience (cf. Irenaeus, *Haer.* 3.18.6; 5.16.3, 21.2–3; *Epid.* 34), defeats the devil, who goes away for an "opportune time" (v. 13). Jesus, as the king who has overcome the demonic idolatry that animates the kingdoms of the "civilized world" (vv. 5–8), comes to Nazareth proclaiming an *other* kingdom, that can then rightly be called *God's* kingdom. This *other* kingdom is a mystery having come near and longing to be disclosed that does not compete for or dominate space, but produces space amid mundane authorities.

At Nazareth, Jesus, the Spirit-filled king, proclaims the reality of his kingdom through a royal declaration of the eschatological era of God's favor and Jubilee, asserting release from oppression, captivity, and blindness (vv. 18–19, 43; see Chapter 3). Jubilee is a social-spatial extension of atonement ordering, reconciling the world to God's way of being (God's kingdom, heaven). Jesus embarks on a ministry of reordering forgiveness/release, calling all Israel to participate in the kingdom through discipleship, imitation, and obedience, teaching all to walk the journey of peace (cf. 1:79). It is in obedience to this *other* economy and kingdom that one gains sight. Jesus invites all to align to a kingdom that is ordered in heaven and now manifest in the world, a political space with Jesus at its center and inhabited by the community of disciples practicing the kingdom of service, forgiveness, and neighbor-love.

Eventually, Jesus takes this message to Jerusalem, where he is rejected and crucified. Here is the opportune time for which Satan was waiting. Behind the scenes, Satan enters Judas to set in motion the events leading to Jesus's death (22:3), Satan sifts Peter (v. 31), and the Jerusalem authorities come in the power of darkness (v. 53). Satan, however, is not victorious, and the cross itself reveals Jesus's identity, the identity of the kingdom he preaches, and the injustice of the world, unmasking Satan's lies. Luke presents this well in the irony of his crucifixion scene. The cross reveals Jesus's own justness, which is attested to by a presiding centurion (23:47). In Jesus's justness, the cross also reveals the primacy of forgiveness (v. 34). This is not the king who responds by destroying all his enemies (cf. 19:27), but by forgiving. Thus, on the one hand, this reveals not so much Jesus's sacrifice to God, but sums up the Father's sacrifice *for* Israel, sending the Son to establish the kingdom. God's political strategy is *persuasion*, not violence. The cross, though demanded by the people and their leaders, expresses and solidifies God's covenant fidelity in the face of rejection, a theme that Paul will later emphasize in Pisidian Antioch, telling the story of God's historical and continuous work of salvation for Israel.

On the other hand, the cross reveals the world's injustice, unmasking Satan, the Jerusalem leadership in their concern with fidelity to Caesar (and not God), and Roman "justice." The cross is not necessary because God demands it, but because the world bound by demonic idolatry would demand it (cf. 13:33). God sent the Son, rather, to be about the Father's things (2:49), to preach the kingdom to the poor (4:18, 43), and to make known true fidelity to God. The cross is the culmination of a life in opposition to the injustice summed up in crucifixion. In the cross, Jesus implicitly identifies to death with those for whom he came to preach good news, the poor who are under the domination of worldly authorities and those bound in complicity to and blinded by demonic idolatry. Jesus's death is not just; it is unjust, though revealing justness. It is the revelation of this injustice/justness that is centered in the rhetoric of the Acts church.

Jesus overcomes these powers and Satan through fidelity to God's kingdom and *other* ordering—not succumbing to strategies of demonic idolatry, violence, and dominance—being raised and enthroned at God's right hand. The kingdom that Jesus declares is cosmically legitimated. Yet, this kingdom does not attempt to dominate space, but manifests socially constituted space within the world, conceived on the margins, placing at the center this crucified Jesus and the "poor" (cf. Lk. 4:18; Acts 4:32–5), a great reversal. This is the cosmic reality in which the world is embedded requiring new vision and new patterns of conceiving the world, and so, the passages I attended to in Acts emphasize *knowledge*. Peter's speech testifies to this cosmic reality, to this vision of social-political space, and to the salvation available when calling on the Lord's name. Thousands in Jerusalem respond, being baptized into the Lord Jesus's name, incorporating themselves into the political body of God's kingdom, and producing space within the world governed by Jubilee forgiveness/release. This community is identified as "those *being* saved" (Acts 2:47).

From there, the church moves on a missional trajectory from Jerusalem to the end of the earth, empowered by the Spirit, to bring light to the nations. Paul (see Chapter 5), beginning his participation in this outward movement, preaches at a synagogue in Pisidian Antioch, an outpost of Rome, declaring another king (cf. 17:6–7). He speaks of an eschatological reality of socioeconomic blessing, exhorting Israel to fidelity to God's king and this movement of salvation. Nevertheless, this community repeats the historical rebellion against God's purposes, though certain gentiles do respond, joining Israel in the Davidic tent as another called people (15:14–18). Paul continues his missional movement to the nations, to open their eyes, to turn them from darkness to light and from Satan's authority to God's (26:18), yet the story ends with tension, with salvation unfinished and Israel divided. Nevertheless, this is the story of God's redemption of Israel, Israel's blessing to the nations, the victory of God's kingdom, and the reconciliation of the world, and Luke-Acts leaves us in hopeful anticipation amid the tension.

The *beginning* of Luke's salvation narrative is comprehensive, involving people needing release from captivity. This captivity is to mal-ordered space. Beginning with Israel, the people are thrown into a world of social, political, economic, and cosmic captivity. This mal-ordering is tied to demonic authority and idolatry, exploitative systems, and blindness. Release from captivity involves not simply recovery of sight and personal *knowledge* gained through discipleship, but also the reordering of space that delivers those captive to this mal-ordered space, overcoming Satan. That is, salvation is not an individualistic reality, but new social and communal patterns of being for those oppressed by the demonic organization of power that orders the world. Salvation is embodied and affects the organization of bodies in space. Further, this is not a universal, departicularized program, but a work of salvation that unfolds through Israel and its restoration for the world.

The means or *middle* of this salvation is achieved by God's socially productive forgiveness and the revelation of fidelity in Jesus, which overcomes Satan and inaugurates disciples into the mystery of God's kingdom. Notably, while God's forgiveness is integral to reconciliation, this forgiveness is offered as a presupposition of the soteriological movement, not Jesus's achievement though some form of satisfaction or vicarious expiation. Jesus's cross displays, rather than achieves, forgiveness. Salvation is God's continuous act *for* Israel, the nations gathered to Israel under the Davidic tent, and the world. Jesus's life, death, resurrection, and ascension conquer Satan, exposing the mundane authorities and their injustice, releasing from blindness and the assumed normativity of the mal-ordered structures of mundane space governed by demonic idolatry, and enabling the production of alternate spaces of release. The church exists in the time that remains, awaiting the consummation of God's cosmic reconciliation of heaven and earth (the *end*).

6.2 Luke-Acts and *Christus Victor*

Different elements of the above presentation cohere with a particularly Irenaean *Christus Victor* model. First, the primary source of salvation is God's initiative, and God's presupposed forgiveness attests to God's mercy as key in establishing justice (a state of justness). This is grounded in God's covenant fidelity to Israel. Atonement is not needed to affect God. Certainly discord between God and people is a reality, but the primary issue is removing the boundary that keeps humanity from accepting God's forgiveness in repentance and reconciliation, and thereby overcoming that discord.

Salvation from captivity, including world powers, Satan, and blindness, is necessary. These realities are indelibly intertwined. World powers are under Satan's authority. The implication is that they have bowed and accepted the devil's temptations. Blindness and complicit ignorance appear part of the quotidian existence of the people, and this relates to false allegiance, which is demonstrated, for instance, in the Jerusalem leadership's concern for the people's fidelity to Caesar rather than God. The people find themselves bound by demonic idolatry manifest in social-political space. Not only are human beings personally bound, needing "sight" and "knowledge," but the "poor" are captive to the demonic systems of the "rich" that oppress them. Release is not simply personal but a cosmic undertaking, effecting the social-political order of the world. Satan lurks behind the scenes in Luke-Acts, so that Paul will succinctly sum up his mission as opening eyes and turning the nations from Satan's authority to God's (26:18). Luke's soteriology cannot be reduced to a moral exemplar presentation, though, as with Irenaeus, this is a component.

Release involves freedom for the poor who are subject to the machinations of worldly powers and systems bound by idolatry as well as release for those who are blindly allied to those demonic systems. Thus, the poor, for instance, may gladly flock to Jesus's new kingdom and the tangible release it affords, producing social spaces of forgiveness, inclusion, and economic release and mutuality. However, the rich, who are bound by systems of exploitation, blindly reject or seek half measures to participate in God's kingdom. In this way, Jesus's death at the hands of the powers and those complicit with this demonic authority is an identification with those who are dominated by that same power and authority. It reveals the injustice of those systems that exploit the poor and God's identification through the Son with those poor, bringing them victory through resurrection and new life now in the reordered social-political space of God's kingdom (cf. Lk. 18:29–30).

The release Jesus offers comes through fidelity to this God, whose Messiah is counted among the rejected, dominated, and exploited (and those enemies of the "state"; 22:37), yet who reveals the injustice and ultimate futility of these powers aligned under demonic authority. Jesus's obedience defeats Satan, exposing his lies and the unjustness of the world allied with him, and participation in that fidelity to God and new life overcomes allegiance to the false idolatry of the world. The role the cross plays in this has been discussed above. Nevertheless, obedience—learning to see as Jesus's disciples (6:39–49)—involves forsaking those social, economic, and political realities that are bound by Satan's temptation to exploitation. Release comes in allegiance to another kingdom. Thus, this "release" is not simply libertarian freedom, but it is a binding to Jesus and God's kingdom that establishes new life, new community, and new social patterns.

This kingdom is characterized by the strategies it employs. God's kingdom advances by persuasion, not through violent imposition. This is exemplified in the cross. God does not impose the kingdom, but sends the Son to establish this kingdom amid the rejection typified by crucifixion. Crucifixion reveals the discord between the world and God, yet, despite rejection, Jesus is not raised declaring retribution, but further extending forgiveness (cf. Acts 5:31). However, crucifixion exposing the nature of God's kingdom does not make this a passive kingdom of suffering. Rather, it is a kingdom where Jesus's disciples, in imitation of their king and empowered by the Spirit, go forward making known God's justice, establishing spaces of Jubilee release, and refusing to succumb to the demonic temptations of the world's violence and exploitation, knowing that the world's injustice will be met with God's victory. In this way, God's kingdom overcomes Satan. This is a vision of cosmic restoration that takes place now, spreading through space, anchored in Israel, and anticipating and participating in God's restoration of all things (3:21).

6.3 Contributions and Further Study

As would be expected of an investigation into one of the central themes of the largest portion of the NT, work remains to be done. This investigation attempted to narratively discern Luke-Acts' political salvation by attending to key waypoints along Luke-Acts' journey. However, there is room to extend this further through attention to other waypoints that may offer additional insight. Further, my approach to the cross was not meant to be exhaustive or to exclude other possibilities of interpretation. Though giving attention to Luke's passion scene, a more singularly focused study on the cross in these terms would be beneficial, including the oft-noted texts, Lk. 22:19–20; Acts 20:28. Additionally, I note salvation's cosmic scope, yet more could be said about Creation's place in this scheme.

The primary contribution of this study is in offering another paradigm for understanding Lukan salvation, one that does not posit a reductively spiritual mode or assess Lukan soteriology as deficient in explicating the means of this salvation. It is an atonement that draws one not up to heaven but heaven down to earth in cosmic reconciliation. This, I believe, contributes not only to the study of Lukan soteriology but to the appraisal of Luke-Acts' relation to politics. This may, nevertheless, still be unsatisfying for some, given my contention that Luke-Acts does not make satisfaction of justice through vicarious sacrifice primary. Additionally, it may be judged that I have not sufficiently attended to personal reconciliation. I do not wish to obscure personal forgiveness, but to see it as part of a greater whole, indeed, to incorporate persons and forgiveness into a social ontology. Personal transformation and new life are a part of this more social-political idiom. Although not emphasizing sanctification explicitly, neither do most satisfaction theories, for example, without an addendum. Certainly, this study does not satisfy all the inquiries of modern systematicians, but such has not been my goal. Rather, it is enough that it should no longer be acceptable to claim that Luke offers the *what* of salvation and reconciliation without the *means*.

I have presented here a political Lukan soteriology. My choice of the term "political" was not intended to reduce the scope of this soteriology to modern delineations of the political sphere, but to shift the conversation out of its compartmentalization in the religious sphere. I could have, perhaps, spoken primarily of a "holistic" or "cosmic" salvation (of which I do speak), but such emphases run the risk of leaving unchallenged modern divisions of space. Luke's soteriology envisions a cosmic reordering, and the means of this reordering is a release effected by Jesus and a new (political) life available in participation. *Today*, the church participates in complex space as the socially constituted political body of Christ, citizens of a kingdom within a world of competing authorities. Yet, only Christ, in this estimation, has claim to true cosmic legitimation. Only in this king are true sight, knowledge, and release from that which enslaves and oppresses. *Solus Christus divina nos docere, ac redimere potuit* (Irenaeus, *Haer.* 5.1.1).[1]

---

[1] "Only the divine Christ is able to teach us and set us free."

Bibliography

Abraham, M. V. "Good News to the Poor in Luke's Gospel." *BiBh* 14 (1988): 65–77.
Ackroyd, Peter R. *Exile and Restoration: A Study of Hebrew Thought of the Sixth Century B.C.* OTL. Philadelphia: Westminster, 1968.
Agamben, Giorgio. *The Time That Remains: A Commentary on the Letter to the Romans.* Stanford: Stanford University Press, 2006.
Ahn, Yong-Sung. *The Reign of God and Rome in Luke's Passion Narrative: An East Asian Global Perspective.* BibInt 80. Leiden: Brill, 2006.
Alexander, Loveday C. A. "'In Journeyings Often': Voyaging in the Acts of the Apostles and in Greek Romance." In *Luke's Literary Achievement: Collected Essays*, edited by C. M. Tuckett, 17–49. JSNTSup 116. Sheffield: Sheffield Academic, 1995.
Alexander, Loveday C. A. "Narrative Maps: Reflections on the Toponymy of Acts." In *The Bible in Human Society: Essays in Honour of John Rogerson*, edited by M. Daniel Carroll R., David J. A. Clines, and Philip R. Davies, 17–57. JSOTSup 200. Sheffield: Sheffield Academic, 1995.
Alexander, Loveday C. A. "The Acts of the Apostles as an Apologetic Text." In *Apologetics in the Roman Empire: Pagans, Jews, and Christians*, edited by Mark Edwards, Martin Goodman, and Simon Price, 15–44. Oxford: Oxford University Press, 1999.
Alexander, Loveday C. A. *Acts.* PBC. Oxford: Bible Reading Fellowship, 2006.
Allison, Dale C., Jr. "Was There a 'Lukan Community'?" *IBS* 10 (1988): 62–70.
Anderson, Charles. "Lukan Cosmology and the Ascension." In *Ascent into Heaven in Luke-Acts: New Explorations of Luke's Narrative Hinge*, edited by David K. Bryan, and David W. Pao, 175–212. Minneapolis: Fortress, 2016.
Anderson, Gary A. *Sin: A History.* New Haven: Yale University Press, 2009.
Anderson, Kevin L. *"But God Raised Him from the Dead": The Theology of Jesus' Resurrection in Luke-Acts.* PBM. Waynesboro, GA: Paternoster, 2006.
Ando, Clifford. *Imperial Ideology and Provincial Loyalty in the Roman Empire.* Berkeley: University of California Press, 2000.
Armstrong, Karen. *Islam: A Short History.* New York: Modern Library, 2002.
Arndt, William F. *The Gospel according to St. Luke.* St. Louis: Concordia, 1956.
Asad, Talal. "The Construction of Religion as an Anthropological Category." In *Genealogies of Religion: Discipline and Reasons of Power in Christianity and Islam*, 27–54. Baltimore: Johns Hopkins University Press, 1993.
Asad, Talal. "Reading a Modern Classic: W. C. Smith's *The Meaning and End of Religion*." *HR* 40 (2001): 205–22.
Asad, Talal. *Formations of the Secular: Christianity, Islam, Modernity.* Stanford: Stanford University Press, 2003.
Ash, Anthony. "John's Disciples: A Serious Problem." *ResQ* 45 (2003): 85–93.
Atkinson, Kenneth. *I Cried to the Lord: A Study of the Psalms of Solomon's Historical Background and Social Setting.* JSJSup 84. Leiden: Brill, 2004.
Aulén, Gustav. *Christus Victor: An Historical Study of the Three Main Types of the Idea of Atonement.* London: SPCK, 1931.

Avemarie, Friedrich. *Die Tauferzählungen der Apostelgeschichte*. WUNT 139. Tübingen: Mohr Siebeck, 2002.
Bacchiocchi, Samuele. *From Sabbath to Sunday: A Historical Investigation of the Rise of Sunday Observance*. Rome: Pontifical Gregorian University, 1977.
Bacon, Benjamin Wisner. *The Story of St. Paul: A Comparison of Acts and Epistles*. Boston: Houghton Mifflin, 1904.
Bakhtin, Mikhail M. "Forms of Time and the Chronotope in the Novel." In *The Dialogic Imagination: Four Essays by M. M. Bakhtin*, edited by Michael Holquist, 84–258. Austin: University of Texas Press, 2002.
Baltzer, Klaus. "Liberation from Debt Slavery after the Exile in Second Isaiah and Nehemiah." In *Ancient Israelite Religion: Essays in Honor of Frank Moore Cross*, edited by Patrick D. Miller Jr., Paul D. Hanson, and S. Dean McBride, 477–84. Philadelphia: Fortress, 1987.
Bandstra, Andrew J. "Paul and an Ancient Interpreter: A Comparison of the Teaching of Redemption in Paul and Irenaeus." *CTJ* 5 (1970): 43–63.
Barclay, William. *Acts of the Apostles*. Philadelphia: Westminster, 1976.
Barrett, C. K. *Luke the Historian in Recent Study*. Philadelphia: Fortress, 1961.
Barrett, C. K. "Theologia Crucis—in Acts?" In *Theologia Crucis—Signum Crucis: Festschrift für E. Dinkler*, edited by G. Anderson, and G. Klein, 73–84. Tübingen: Mohr, 1979.
Barrett, C. K. "*Imitatio Christi* in Acts" In *Jesus of Nazareth: Lord and Christ: Essays on the Historical Jesus and New Testament Christology*, edited by Joel B. Green, and Max Turner, 251–62. Grand Rapids: Eerdmans, 1994.
Barrett, C. K. *The Acts of the Apostles*. 2 vols. ICC. New York: T&T Clark, 1994–8.
Barth, Karl. *Church Dogmatics*. Vol. 4.1, *The Doctrine of Reconciliation*, edited by G. W. Bromiley, and T. F. Torrance, translated by G. W. Bromiley. Peabody, MA: Hendrickson, 2010.
Barton, Stephen C. "Can We Identify Gospel Audiences?" In *The Gospels for All Christians: Rethinking the Gospel Audiences*, edited by Richard Bauckham, 173–94. Grand Rapids: Eerdmans, 1998.
Bauckham, Richard. "James and the Jerusalem Church." In *The Book of Acts in Its Palestinian Setting*, edited by Richard Bauckham, 415–80. BAFCS 4. Grand Rapids: Eerdmans, 1995.
Bauckham, Richard. "The Restoration of Israel in Luke-Acts." In *Restoration: Old Testament, Jewish, and Christian Perspectives*, edited by James M. Scott, 435–88. JSJSup 72. Leiden: Brill, 2001.
Beale, Gregory K. "The Descent of the Eschatological Temple in the Form of the Spirit at Pentecost." *TynBul* 56, no. 1 (2005): 73–102; 56, no. 2 (2005): 63–90.
Beard, Mary, and Michael Crawford. *Rome in the Late Republic*. Ithaca, NY: Cornell University Press, 1985.
Beard, Mary, John North, and Simon Price. *Religions of Rome*. 2 vols. Cambridge: Cambridge University Press, 1998.
Beasley-Murray, George R. *Baptism in the New Testament*. Grand Rapid: Eerdmans, 1962.
Beck, Brian E. "'*Imitatio Christi*' and the Lucan Passion Narrative." In *Suffering and Martyrdom in the New Testament: Studies Presented to G. M. Styler by the Cambridge New Testament Seminar*, edited by William Horbury, and Brian McNeil, 28–47. Cambridge: Cambridge University Press, 1981.
Beck, Norman. *Anti-Roman Cryptograms in the New Testament: Hidden Transcripts of Hope and Liberation*, Rev ed. StBibLit 127. New York: Peter Lang, 2010.

Beers, Holly. *The Followers of Jesus as the Servant: Luke's Model from Isaiah for the Disciples in Luke-Acts*. LNTS 535. New York: Bloomsbury T&T Clark, 2015.
Bell, Catherine. *Ritual Theory, Ritual Practice*. New York: Oxford University Press, 1992.
Benoit, Pierre. "L'enfance de Jean-Baptiste selon Luc I." *NTS* 3 (1957): 169–94.
Berger, Klaus. *Die Gesetzesauslegung Jesu: Ihr historischer Hintergrund im Judentum und im Alten Testament*. WMANT 40. Neukirchen-Vluyn: Neukirchener Verlag, 1972.
Bergsma, John. Sietze. *The Jubilee from Leviticus to Qumran: A History of Interpretation*. VTSup 115. Leiden: Brill, 2007.
Beyer, Hans F. "Christ-centered Eschatology in Acts 3:17–26." In *Jesus of Nazareth: Lord and Christ: Essays on the Historical Jesus and New Testament Christology*, edited by Joel B. Green, and Max Turner, 236–50. Grand Rapids: Eerdmans, 1994.
Billings, Drew W. *Acts of the Apostles and the Rhetoric of Roman Imperialism*. Cambridge: Cambridge University Press, 2017.
Bird, Michael F. "The Unity of Luke-Acts in Recent Discussion." *JSNT* 29 (2007): 425–48.
Black, C. Clifton, II. "The Rhetorical Form of the Hellenistic Jewish and Early Christian Sermon: A Response to Lawrence Wills." *HTR* 81 (1988): 1–18.
Black, C. Clifton, II. *The Rhetoric of the Gospel: Theological Artistry in the Gospels and Acts*, 2nd ed. Louisville: Westminster John Knox, 2013.
Blomberg, Craig L. "The Gospel for Specific Communities *and* All Christians." In *The Audience of the Gospels: The Origin and Function of the Gospels in Early Christianity*, edited by Edward W. Klink III, 111–33. LNTS 353. London: T&T Clark, 2010.
Blomberg, Craig L. *Interpreting the Parables*, 2nd ed. Downers Grove, IL: IVP Academic, 2012.
Blum, Matthias. "Antijudaismus im lukanischen Doppelwerk? Zur These eines lukanischen Antijudaismus." In *"Nun steht aber diese Sache im Evangelium …": Zur Frage nach den Anfängen des christlichen Antijudaismus*, edited by Rainer Kampling, 107–49. München: Ferdinand Schöningh, 1999.
Blumenthal, Christian. "Elija bei Lukas." *BZ* 61 (2017): 86–103.
Blumhofer, C. M. "Luke's Alteration of Joel 3.1–5 in Acts 2.17–21." *NTS* 62 (2016): 499–516.
Bock, Darrell L. *Proclamation from Prophecy and Pattern: Lucan Old Testament Christology*. JSNTSup 12. Sheffield: Sheffield Academic Press, 1987.
Bock, Darrell L. *Luke*. 2 vols. BECNT. Grand Rapids: Baker Academic, 1994.
Bock, Darrell L. "Scripture and the Realization of God's Promises." In *Witness to the Gospel: The Theology of Acts*, edited by I. Howard Marshall, and David Peterson, 41–62. Grand Rapids: Eerdmans, 1998.
Bock, Darrell L. *Acts*. BECNT. Grand Rapids: Baker Academic, 2007.
Bockmuehl, Markus. *Revelation and Mystery in Ancient Judaism and Pauline Christianity*. WUNT 2/36. Tübingen: Mohr Siebeck, 1990.
Boer, Roland, and Christina Petterson. *Time of Troubles: A New Economic Framework for Early Christianity*. Minneapolis: Fortress, 2017.
Boersma, Hans. "Redemptive Hospitality in Irenaeus: A Model for Ecumenicity in a Violent World." *ProEccl* 11 (2002): 207–26.
Boersma, Hans. "Eschatological Justice and the Cross: Violence and Penal Substitution." *ThTo* 60 (2003): 186–99.
Boersma, Hans. *Violence, Hospitality, and the Cross: Reappropriating the Atonement Tradition*. Grand Rapids: Baker Academic, 2004.
Bonz, Marianne Palmer. *The Past as Legacy: Luke-Acts and Ancient Epic*. Minneapolis: Fortress, 2000.

Bovon, François. *Luke*. 3 vols. Hermeneia. Minneapolis: Fortress, 2002–13.
Bovon, François. *Luke the Theologian: Fifty Years of Research [1950–2005]*, 2nd ed. Waco, TX: Baylor University Press, 2006.
Bowker, J. W. "Speeches in Acts: A Study in Proem and Yelammedenu Form." *NTS* 14 (1967): 96–111.
Boyarin, Daniel. *Border Lines: The Partition of Judaeo-Christianity*. Philadelphia: University of Pennsylvania Press, 2004.
Braun, Adam F. "Reframing the Parable of the Pounds in Lukan Narrative and Economic Context: Luke 19:11–28." *CurTM* 39 (2012): 442–8.
Braun, Willi. *Feasting and Social Rhetoric in Luke 14*. SNTSMS 85. Cambridge: Cambridge University Press, 1995.
Brawley, Robert L. *Luke-Acts and the Jews: Conflict, Apology, and Conciliation*. SBLMS 33. Atlanta: Scholars Press, 1987.
Brawley, Robert L. "Abrahamic Covenant Traditions and the Characterization of God in Luke-Acts." In *The Unity of Luke-Acts*, edited by Joseph Verheyden, 109–32. BETL 142. Leuven: Leuven University Press, 1999.
Bremmer, Jan N. "Magic, Martyrdom and Women's Liberation in the Acts of Paul and Thecla." In *The Apocryphal Acts of Paul and Thecla*, edited by Jan N. Bremmer, 36–59. Kampen: Kok Pharos, 1996.
Brent, Allen. "Luke-Acts and the Imperial Cult in Asia Minor." *JTS* 48 (1997): 411–38.
Bright, John. *A History of Israel*. Philadelphia: Westminster, 1959.
Brinkman, J. A. "The Literary Background of the 'Catalogue of the Nations' (Acts 2:9–11)." *CBQ* 25 (1963): 418–27.
Brown, Raymond E. *The Birth of the Messiah: A Commentary on the Infancy Narratives in Matthew and Luke*. Garden City, NY: Doubleday, 1979.
Brown, Raymond E. *The Death of the Messiah: From Gethsemane to the Grave: A Commentary on the Passion Narratives in the Four Gospels*. 2 vols. ABRL. New Haven, CT: Doubleday, 1994.
Brown, Schuyler. "'Water Baptism' and 'Spirit Baptism' in Luke-Acts." *AThR* 59 (1977): 135–51.
Brownlee, William H. "Messianic Motifs of Qumran and The New Testament." *NTS* 3 (1956-7): 195–210.
Bruce, F. F. "The Holy Spirit in the Acts of the Apostles." *Int* 27 (1973): 166–83.
Bruce, F. F. *The Book of Acts*, 2nd ed. NICNT. Grand Rapids: Eerdmans, 1988.
Bruce, F. F. *The Acts of the Apostles: The Greek Text with Introduction and Commentary*, 3rd ed. Grand Rapids: Eerdmans, 1990.
Brückner, Martin. *Der sterbende und auferstehende Gottheiland in den orientalischen Religionen und ihr Verhältnis zum Christentum*. RV 1/16. Tübingen: Mohr, 1908.
Brueggemann, Walter. *Isaiah*. 2 vols. WC. Louisville: Westminster John Knox, 1998.
Bryan, Christopher. *Render to Caesar: Jesus, the Early Church and the Roman Superpower*. Oxford: Oxford University Press, 2005.
Bryan, David K. "A Revised Cosmic Hierarchy Revealed: Apocalyptic Literature and Jesus's Ascent in Luke's Gospel." In *Ascent into Heaven in Luke-Acts: New Explorations of Luke's Narrative Hinge*, edited by David K. Bryan, and David W. Pao, 61–82. Minneapolis: Fortress, 2016.
Bryan, Steven M. "The End of Exile: The Reception of Jeremiah's Prediction of a Seventy-Year Exile." *JBL* 137 (2018): 107–26.
Buckwalter, H. Douglas. *The Character and Purpose of Luke's Christology*. SNTSMS 89. Cambridge: Cambridge University Press, 1996.

Bultmann, Rudolf. *Theology of the New Testament*. 2 vols. New York: Charles Scribner's Sons, 1955.
Bultmann, Rudolf. "γινῶσκω, γνῶσις, ἐπιγινῶσκω, ἐπίγνωσις." In *Theological Dictionary of the New Testament*, 10 vols. translated by Geoffrey W. Bromiley, 689–714. Grand Rapids: Eerdmans, 1964.
Burgess, Andrew. *The Ascension in Karl Barth*. London: Routledge, 2004.
Burkert, Walter. *Ancient Mystery Cults*. Cambridge, MA: Harvard University Press, 1987.
Buss, Matthäus. Franz-Josef. *Die Missionspredigt des Apostles Paulus im Pisidischen Antiochien: Analyse von Apg 13,16–41 im Hinblick auf die literarische und thematische Einheit der Paulusrede*. FzB 38. Stuttgart: Katholisches Bibelwerk, 1980.
Buzzard, Anthony. "Acts 1:6 and the Eclipse of the Biblical Kingdom." *EvQ* 66, no. 3 (1994): 197–215.
Cadbury, Henry J. "The Purpose Expressed in Luke's Preface." *Exp* 21 (1921): 431–41.
Cadbury, Henry J. "Some Foibles of New Testament Scholarship." *JAAR* 26 (1958): 213–16.
Cadbury, Henry J. *The Making of Luke-Acts*, 3rd ed. London: SPCK, 1968.
Caird, G. B. *The Gospel of St. Luke*. PNTC. New York: Seabury, 1963.
Calvin, John. *The Acts of the Apostles 1–13*. Grand Rapids: Eerdmans, 1965.
Camp, Ashby L. "Reexamining the Rule of Concord in Acts 2:38." *ResQ* 39 (1997): 37–42.
Campenhausen, Hans von. *Der Kriegsdienst der Christen in der Kirche des Altertums*. Stuttgart: Wissenschaftliche, 1957.
Capper, Brian. "Community of Goods in the Early Jerusalem Church." *ANRW* 2, no. 26.2 (1995a): 1730–74.
Capper, Brian. "The Palestinian Cultural Context of the Earliest Christian Community of Goods." In *The Book of Acts in Its Palestinian Setting*, edited by Richard Bauckham, 323–56. BAFCS 4. Grand Rapids: Eerdmans, 1995b.
Capper, Brian. "Holy Community of Life and Property amongst the Poor: A Response to Steve Walton." *EvQ* 80 (2008): 113–27.
Carpinelli, Francis Giordano 'Do This as *My* Memorial' (Luke 22:19): Lucan Soteriology of Atonement." *CBQ* 61 (1999): 74–91.
Carroll, John T. *Response to the End of History: Eschatology and Situation in Luke-Acts*. SBLDS 92. Atlanta: Scholars Press, 1988.
Carroll, John T. *Luke: A Commentary*. NTL. Louisville: Westminster John Knox, 2012.
Carter, J. Kameron. *Race: A Theological Account*. Oxford: Oxford University Press, 2008.
Carter, Warren. "Singing in the Reign: Performing Luke's Songs and Negotiating the Roman Empire (Luke 1–2)." In *Luke-Acts and Empire: Essays in Honor of Robert L. Brawley*, edited by David Rhoads, David Esterline, and Jae Won Lee, 23–43. PrTMS 151. Eugene, OR: Pickwick, 2011.
Cassidy, Richard J. *Jesus, Politics, and Society: A Study of Luke's Gospel*. Maryknoll, NY: Orbis Books, 1978.
Cassidy, Richard J. *Society and Politics in the Acts of the Apostles*. Maryknoll, NY: Orbis Books, 1987.
Cassidy, Richard J. *Christians and Roman Rule in the New Testament: New Perspectives*. New York: Crossroad, 2001.
Cassidy, Richard J. "Paul's Proclamation of *Lord* Jesus as a Chained Prisoner in Rome: Luke's Ending Is in His Beginning." In *Luke-Acts and Empire: Essays in Honor of Robert L. Brawley*, edited by David Rhoads, David Esterline, and Jae Won Lee, 142–53. PrTMS 151. Eugene, OR: Pickwick, 2011.
Cassidy, Richard J., and Philip Scharper., eds. *Political Issues in Luke-Acts*. Maryknoll, NY: Orbis Books, 1983.

Cavanaugh, William T. *The Myth of Religious Violence: Secular Ideology and the Roots of Modern Conflict*. Oxford: Oxford University Press, 2009.
Cavanaugh, William T. *Migrations of the Holy: God, State, and the Political Meaning of the Church*. Grand Rapids: Eerdmans, 2011.
Certeau, Michel de. *The Practice of Everyday Life*. Berkeley: University of California, 1984.
Chance, J. Bradley. "The Journey to Emmaus: Insights on Scripture from Mystical Understandings of Attachment and Detachment." *PRSt* 38 (2011): 363–81.
Charlesworth, James H., ed. *The Messiah: Developments in Earliest Judaism and Christianity*. Minneapolis: Fortress, 1992.
Childs, Brevard S. *Isaiah*. OTL. Louisville: Westminster John Knox, 2001.
Chilton, Bruce. *Pure Kingdom: Jesus' Vision of God*. Grand Rapids: Eerdmans, 1996.
Cho, Youngmo. *Spirit and Kingdom in the Writings of Luke and Paul*. PBM. Waynesboro, GA: Paternoster, 2005.
Christiansen, Ellen Juhl "Taufe als Initiation in der Apostelgeschichte." *ST* 40 (1986): 55–79.
Chrupcała, L. Daniel. *Everyone Will See the Salvation of God: Studies in Lukan Theology*. SBFA 83. Milan: Edizioni Terra Santa, 2015.
Clark, David George. "Elijah as Eschatological High Priest: An Examination of the Elijah Tradition in Mal 3:24–25." PhD diss., University of Notre Dame, 1975.
Cohen, Shaye J. D. *The Beginnings of Jewishness: Boundaries, Varieties, Uncertainties*. HCS 31. Berkeley: University of California Press, 1999.
Coleridge, Mark. *The Birth of the Lukan Narrative: Narrative as Christology in Luke 1–2*. JSNTSup 88. Sheffield: JSOT Press, 1993.
Collins, Adela Yarbro. *Mark: A Commentary*. Hermeneia. Minneapolis: Fortress, 2007.
Collins, John J. *Daniel*. Hermeneia. Minneapolis: Fortress, 1993.
Collins, John J. *The Scepter and the Star: The Messiahs of the Dead Sea Scrolls and Other Ancient Literature*. ABRL. New York: Doubleday, 1995.
Collins, John J. "A Herald of Good Tidings: Isaiah 61:1–3 and Its Actualization in the Dead Sea Scrolls." In *The Quest for Context and Meaning: Studies in Biblical Intertextuality in Honor of James A. Sanders*, edited by Craig Evans, and Shemaryahu Talmon, 225–40. Leiden: Brill, 1997.
Constantelos, Demetrios J. "Irenaeos of Lyons and His Central Views on Human Nature." *SVTQ* 33 (1989): 351–63.
Conzelmann, Hans. *The Theology of St. Luke*. New York: Harper & Row, 1961.
Conzelmann, Hans. *Acts of the Apostles*. Hermeneia. Philadelphia: Fortress, 1987.
Corley, Kathleen E. *Private Women, Public Meals: Social Conflict in the Synoptic Tradition*. Peabody, MA: Hendrickson, 1993.
Crisp, Oliver D. "Is Ransom Enough?" *JAT* 3 (2015). Doi:10.12978/jat.2015-3.141117021715a.
Culpepper, R. Alan. "*The Gospel of Luke*: Introduction, Commentary, and Reflections." In *The Gospel of Luke, The Gospel of John*. NIB 9, 1–409. Nashville: Abingdon, 2002.
Cumont, Franz. *Oriental Religions in Roman Paganism*. Chicago: Open Court, 1911.
Dahl, Nils. "'A People for His Name' (Acts XV.14)" *NTS* 4 (1958): 319–27.
Dana, H. E., and Julius R. Mantey. *A Manual Grammar of the Greek New Testament*. New York: Macmillan, 1957.
Danker, Frederick W. *Jesus and the New Age according to St. Luke: A Commentary on the Third Gospel*. St. Louis: Clayton, 1972.
Danker, Frederick W. *Benefactor: Epigraphic Study of a Greco-Roman and New Testament Semantic Field*. St Louis: Clayton, 1982.

Darr, John A. *On Character Building: The Reader and the Rhetoric of Characterization in Luke-Acts*. LCBI. Louisville: Westminster John Knox, 1992.

Das, A. Andrew. "Acts 8: Water, Baptism, and the Spirit." *ConcJ* 19 (1993): 108–34.

Davies, Jason P. *Rome's Religious History: Livy, Tacitus, and Ammianus on Their Gods*. Cambridge: Cambridge University Press, 2004.

Davies, J. G. "Pentecost and Glossolalia." *JTS* 3 (1952): 228–31.

Davis, J. C. "Another Look at the Relationship between Baptism and Forgiveness of Sins in Acts 2:38." *ResQ* 24 (1981): 80–8.

Dean-Otting, Mary. *Heavenly Journeys: A Study of the Motif in Hellenistic Jewish Literature*. JU 8. Frankfurt am Main: Peter Lang, 1984.

DeClaissé-Walford, Nancy, Rolf A. Jacobson, and Beth LaNeel Tanner. *The Book of Psalms*. NICOT. Grand Rapids: Eerdmans, 2014.

Denova, Rebecca. *The Things Accomplished among Us: Prophetic Tradition in the Structural Pattern of Luke-Acts*. JSNTSup 141. Sheffield: Sheffield Academic Press, 1997.

DeSilva, David A. "Paul's Sermon in Antioch of Pisidia." *BSac* 151 (1994): 32–49.

Destro, Adriana, and Mauro Pesce "Forgiveness of Sins without a Victim: Jesus and the Levitical Jubilee." In *Sacrifice in Religious Experience*, edited by Albert I. Baumgarten, 151–74. SHR 93. Leiden: Brill, 2002.

Dibelius, Martin. *Studies in the Acts of the Apostles*. New York: Scribner's Sons, 1956.

Dibelius, Martin. *From Tradition to Gospel*. Cambridge: James Clarke, 1971.

Dillon, Richard J. "The Benedictus in Micro- and Macrocontext." *CBQ* 68 (2006): 457–80.

Dillon, Richard J. *The Hymns of Saint Luke: Lyricism and Narrative Strategy in Luke 1–2*. CBQMS 50. Washington, DC: Catholic Biblical Association of America, 2013.

Dionne, Christian. *L'Évangile aux Juifs et aux païens: Le premier voyage missionnaire de Paul (Actes 13–14)*. LD 247. Paris: Cerf, 2011.

Doble, Peter. *The Paradox of Salvation: Luke's Theology of the Cross*. SNTMS 87. Cambridge: Cambridge University Press, 1996.

Doeve, J. W. *Jewish Hermeneutics in the Synoptic Gospels and Acts*. Assen: Van Gorcum, 1954.

Douglas, Mary. "Deciphering a Meal." In *Myth, Symbol, and Culture*, edited by Clifford Geertz, 61–81. New York: Norton, 1971.

Driver, John. *Understanding Atonement for the Mission of the Church*. Scottsdale, PA: Herald Press, 1986.

Du Plessis, Isak J. "Discipleship according to Luke's Gospel." *R&T* 2 (1995): 58–71.

Du Plessis, Isak J. "The Lukan Audience—Rediscovered? Some Reactions to Bauckham's Theory." *Neot* 34 (2000): 243–61.

Dumais, Marcel. *Le langage de l'évangélisation: L'Annonce missionnaire en milieu juif (Actes 13,16–41)*. Tournai: Desclée & Cie, 1976.

Dungan, David Laird. *A History of the Synoptic Problem: The Canon, the Text, the Composition, and the Interpretation of the Gospels*. New York: Doubleday, 1999.

Dunn, James D. G. *Baptism in the Holy Spirit: A Re-examination of the New Testament Teaching on the Gift of the Spirit in Relation to Pentecostalism Today*. Philadelphia: Westminster, 1970.

Dunn, James D. G. "Spirit and Kingdom." *ExpTim* 82 (1970–1): 36–40.

Dunn, James D. G. *The Parting of the Ways: Between Christianity and Judaism and Their Significance for the Character of Christianity*. London: SCM, 1992.

Dunn, James D. G. "Baptism in the Holy Spirit: A Response to Pentecostal Scholarship on Luke-Acts." *JPT* 3 (1993): 2–27.

Dunn, James D. G. *Acts of the Apostles*. EpComm. Peterborough: Epworth, 1996.

Dunn, James D. G. "Baptism in the Holy Spirit—Yet Once More." *JEPTA* 18 (1998a): 3–25.
Dunn, James D. G. *The Christ and the Spirit: Pneumatology*. Grand Rapids: Eerdmans, 1998b.
Dunn, James D. G. "Baptism in the Holy Spirit: Yet Once More—Again." *JPT* 19 (2010): 32–43.
Dunn, James D. G. "Mystery." In *New International Dictionary of the Bible*, 5 vols. 4 edited by, Katherine Doob Sakenfeld, 185–7. Nashville: Abingdon, 1987.
Dupont, Jacques. "ΤΑ ὍΣΙΑ ΔΑΥΙΔ ΤΑ ΠΙΣΤΑ: Actes 13,34 = Isaïe 55,3." In *Études sur les Actes des Apôtres*, 337–59. LD 45. Paris: Cerf, 1967.
Dupont, Jacques. "Je t'ai établi lumière des nations." In *Nouvelle études sur les Actes des Apôtres*, 343–9. LD 118. Paris: Cerf, 1984a.
Dupont, Jacques. "La nouvelle Pentecôte (Ac 2, 1–11)." In *Nouvelle études sur les Actes des Apôtres*, 193–8. LD 118. Paris: Cerf, 1984b.
Dyson, Stephen L. "Native Revolt Patterns in the Roman Empire." *ANRW* 2, no. 3 (1975): 138–75.
Easton, Burton Scott. *Early Christianity: The Purpose of Acts and Other Papers*. Greenwich, CT: Seabury, 1954.
Eißfeldt, Otto. "Kreter und Araber." *TLZ* 72 (1947): 207–12.
Ellis, E. Earle. *The Gospel of Luke*, 2nd ed. NCB. London: Oliphants, 1974.
Ellis, E. Earle. *Christ and the Future in New Testament History*. NovTSup 97. Leiden: Brill, 2000.
Ellis, E. Earle. "'The End of the Earth' (Acts 1:8)." In *History and Interpretation in New Testament Perspective*, edited by Earle Ellis, 53–64. BibInt 54. Leiden: Brill, 2001.
Epp, Eldon Jay. *The Theological Tendency of Codex Bezae Cantabrigiensis in Acts*. Cambridge: Cambridge University Press, 1966.
Erdmann, Gottfried. *Die Vorgeschichten des Lukas- und Matthäus- Evangeliums und Vergils vierte Ekloge*. Göttingen: Vandenhoeck & Ruprecht, 1932.
Esler, Philip Francis. *Community and Gospel in Luke-Acts*. SNTSMS 57. Cambridge: Cambridge University Press, 1987.
Eubank, Nathan. "A Disconcerting Prayer: On the Originality of Luke 23:34a." *JBL* 129 (2010): 521–36.
Evans, C. F. *Saint Luke*. TPINTC. London: SCM, 1990.
Evans, Craig A. "Aspects of Exile and Restoration in the Proclamation of Jesus and the Gospels." In *Exile: Old Testament, Jewish, and Christian Conceptions*, edited by James M. Scott, 299–328. JSJSup 56. Leiden: Brill, 1997.
Evans, Craig A. "Jesus and the Continuing Exile of Israel." In *Jesus and the Restoration of Israel: A Critical Assessment of N. T. Wright's Jesus and the Victory of God*, edited by Carey C. Newman, 77–100. Downers Grove, IL: InterVarsity Press, 1999.
Falk, Daniel K. "Festivals and Holy Days." In *Eerdmans Dictionary of Early Judaism*, edited by John J. Collins and Daniel C. Harlow, 636–45. Grand Rapids: Eerdmans, 2010.
Farris, Stephen. *The Hymns of Luke's Infancy Narratives: Their Origin, Meaning and Significance*. JSNTSup 9. Sheffield: JSOT Press, 1985.
Farrow, Douglas. "St. Irenaeus of Lyons: The Church and the World." *ProEccl* 4 (1995): 333–55.
Fears, J. Rufus. "The Cult of Virtues and Roman Imperial Ideology." *ANRW* 2, no. 17.2 (1981a): 827–948.
Fears, J. Rufus. "The Theology of Victory at Rome: Approaches and Problems." *ANRW* 2, no. 17.2 (1981b): 736–826.

Fee, Gordon D. "Baptism in the Holy Spirit: The Issue of Separability and Subsequence." *Pneuma* 7 (1985): 87–99.
Festugière, André Jean. *Personal Religion among the Greeks*. Berkeley: University of California Press, 1954.
Finger, Reta Haltemann. *Of Widows and Meals: Communal Meals in the Book of Acts*. Grand Rapids: Eerdmans, 2007.
Finger, Thomas. "Christus Victor and the Creeds: Some Historical Considerations." *MQR* 72 (1998): 31–51.
Finney, Paul Corby. "The Rabbi and the Coin Portrait (Mark 12:15b, 16): Rigorism Manqué." *JBL* 112 (1993): 629–44.
Fitzgerald, John T., ed. *Greco-Roman Perspectives on Friendship*. SBLSBS 34. Atlanta: Scholars Press, 1997.
Fitzgerald, Timothy. *The Ideology of Religious Studies*. Oxford: Oxford University Press, 2000.
Fitzgerald, Timothy. "Encompassing Religion: Privatized Religions and the Invention of Modern Politics." In *Religion and the Secular: Historical and Colonial Formations*, edited by Timothy Fitzgerald, 211–40. London: Routledge, 2007.
Fitzmyer, Joseph A. "Further Light on Melchizedek from Qumran Cave 11." *JBL* 86 (1967): 25–41.
Fitzmyer, Joseph A. *The Gospel According to Luke*. 2 vols. AB 28. Garden City, NY: Doubleday, 1981–5.
Fitzmyer, Joseph A. *To Advance the Gospel: New Testament Studies*. New York: Crossroad, 1991.
Fitzmyer, Joseph A. "Pauline Justification as Presented by Luke in Acts 13." In *Transcending Boundaries: Contemporary Readings of the New Testament: Essays in Honor of Francis J. Moloney*, edited by Rekha M. Chennattu, and Mary L. Coloe, 249–63. Rome: LAS, 2005.
Fitzmyer, Joseph A. *The One Who Is to Come*. Grand Rapids: Eerdmans, 2007.
Flanagan, Neal. "The What and How of Salvation in Luke-Acts." In *Sin, Salvation, and the Spirit*, edited by Daniel Durken, 203–13. Collegeville, MN: Liturgical Press, 1979.
Flender, Helmut. *St. Luke: Theologian of Redemptive History*. Philadelphia: Fortress, 1967.
Fletcher-Louis, Crispin H. T. "Jesus as the High Priestly Messiah: Part 1." *JSHJ* 4 (2006): 155–75.
Fletcher-Louis, Crispin H. T. "Jesus as the High Priestly Messiah: Part 2." *JSHJ* 5 (2007): 57–79.
Flichy, Odile. *La figure de Paul dans les Actes des Apôtres: Un phénomène de réception de la tradition paulinienne à la fin du 1er siècle*. LD 214. Paris: Cerf, 2007.
Flichy, Odile. "The Paul of Luke: A Survey of Research." In *Paul and the Heritage of Israel: Paul's Claim upon Israel's Legacy in Luke and Acts in the Light of the Pauline Letters*. Vol. 2 of *Luke the Interpreter of Israel*, edited by David P. Moessner, Daniel Marguerat, Mikeal C. Parsons, and Michael Wolter, 18–34. LNTS 452. London: T&T Clark, 2012.
Foakes-Jackson, F. J., and Kirsopp Lake. *The Beginnings of Christianity: Part I: The Acts of the Apostles*. 5 vols. London: Macmillan, 1920.
Foerster, Werner. "σωτήρ." *TDNT* 7 (1971): 1003–12.
Foerster, Werner, and Gerhard von Rad "εἰρήνη." *TDNT* 2 (1965): 400–17.
Ford, J. Massyngbaerde. "Zealotism and the Lukan Infancy Narratives." *NovT* 18 (1976): 280–92.
Ford, J. Massyngbaerde. *My Enemy Is My Guest: Jesus and Violence in Luke*. Maryknoll, NY: Orbis Books, 1984.

Forsyth, Neil. *The Old Enemy: Satan and the Combat Myth*. Princeton: Princeton University Press, 1987.
Foucault, Michel. *The Order of Things*. New York: Vintage Books, 1971.
Foucault, Michel. *Power/Knowledge: Selected Interviews and Other Writings 1972-1977*. New York: Pantheon, 1980.
Franklin, Eric. *Christ the Lord: A Study in the Purpose and Theology of Luke-Acts*. Philadelphia: Westminster, 1975.
Franklin, Lloyd David. "Spirit Baptism: Pneumatological Continuance." *RevExp* 94 (1997): 15-30.
Fredriksen, Paula. "Mandatory Retirement: Ideas in the Study of Christian Origins Whose Time Has Come to Go." *SR* 35 (2006): 231-46.
Friedrich, Gerhard. "Beobachtungen zur messianischen Hohepriestererwartung in den Synoptikern." *ZTK* 53 (1956): 265-311.
Friedrich, Gerhard. "εὐαγγελίζομαι, εὐαγγέλιον, προευαγγελίζομαι, εὐαγγελιστής." *TDNT* 2 (1965): 707-37.
Fuller, Michael. *The Restoration of Israel: Israel's Re-gathering and the Fate of the Nations in Early Jewish Literature and Luke-Acts*. BZNW 132. Berlin: de Gruyter, 2006.
Fusco, Vittorio. "Luke-Acts and the Future of Israel." *NovT* 38 (1996): 1-17.
Galinsky, Karl. *Augustan Culture: An Interpretive Introduction*. Princeton: Princeton University Press, 1996.
Gane, Roy E. *Cult of Character: Purification Offerings, Day of Atonement, and Theodicy*. Winona Lake, IN: Eisenbrauns, 2005.
Garrett, Susan R. *The Demise of the Devil: Magic and the Demonic in Luke's Writings*. Minneapolis: Fortress, 1989.
Garrett, Susan R. "The Meaning of Jesus' Death in Luke." *WW* 12 (1992): 11-16.
Gasque, W. Ward. *A History of the Interpretation of the Acts of the Apostles*, 2nd ed. Peabody, MA: Hendrickson, 1975.
Gathercole, Simon. "Jesus' Eschatological Vision of the Fall of Satan: Luke 10,18 Reconsidered." *ZNW* 94 (2003): 143-63.
Gathercole, Simon. "The Heavenly ἀνατολή (Luke 1:78-9)." *JTS* 56 (2005): 471-88.
Gaventa, Beverly Roberts "The Eschatology of Luke-Acts Revisited." *Enc* 43 (1982): 27-41.
Gaventa, Beverly Roberts. *Acts*. ANTC. Nashville: Abingdon, 2003.
Gaventa, Beverly Roberts. *Our Mother Saint Paul*. Louisville: Westminster John Knox, 2007.
Geldenhuys, Norval. *Commentary on the Gospel of Luke*. NICNT. Grand Rapids: Eerdmans, 1956.
Genz, Rouven. *Jesaja 53 als theologische Mitte der Apostelgeschichte: Studien zu ihrer Christologie und Ekklesiologie im Anschluss an Apg 8,26-40*. WUNT 2/398. Tübingen: Mohr Siebeck, 2015.
Gerber, Daniel. *"Il vous est né un Sauveur": La construction du sens sotériologique de la venue de Jésus en Luc-Actes*. MdB 58. Geneva: Labor et Fides, 2008.
Gerlot, P. "Note sur Actes, XIII, 47." *RB* 88 (1981): 368-72.
Gerstenberger, Erhard. *Leviticus: A Commentary*. OTL. Louisville: Westminster John Knox, 1996.
Giambrone, Anthony. *Sacramental Charity, Creditor Christology, and the Economy of Salvation in Luke's Gospel*. WUNT 2/439. Tübingen: Mohr Siebeck, 2017.
Gilbert, Gary. "The List of Nations in Acts 2: Roman Propaganda and the Lukan Response." *JBL* 121 (2002): 497-529.

Gilbert, Gary. "Roman Propaganda and Christian Identity in the Worldview of Luke-Acts." In *Contextualizing Acts: Lukan Narrative and Greco-Roman Discourse*, edited by Todd C. Penner, and Caroline Vander Stichele, 233–56. SBLSymS 20. Leiden: Brill, 2004.

Gilbert, Gary. "Luke-Acts and the Negotiation of Authority and Identity in the Roman World." In *Multivalence of Biblical Texts and Theological Meanings*, edited by Christine Helmer, 83–104. SBLSymS 37. Atlanta: SBL, 2006.

Giles, Kevin. "Present-Future Eschatology." *RTR* 41 (1982): 11–18.

Glöckner, Richard. *Die Verkündigung des Heils beim Evangelisten Lukas*. WST 9. Mainz: Matthias Grunewald, 1975.

Gnilka, Joachim. "Der Hymnus des Zacharias." *BZ* 6 (1962): 215–38.

Goldingay, John. *A Critical and Exegetical Commentary on Isaiah 56–66*. ICC 24.4. London: Bloomsbury T&T Clark, 2014a.

Goldingay, John. *The Theology of the Book of Isaiah*. Downers Grove, IL: IVP Academic, 2014b.

Goldsmith, Dave. "Acts 13:33–37: A Pesher on 2 Samuel 7." *JBL* 87 (1968): 321–4.

Goodblatt, Martin. *Elements of Jewish Nationalism*. Cambridge: Cambridge University Press, 2006.

Goodman, Martin. *The Ruling Class of Judaea: The Origins of the Jewish Revolt against Rome A.D. 66–70*. Cambridge: Cambridge University Press, 1987.

Goodman, Martin. "The Pilgrimage Economy of Jerusalem in the Second Temple Period." In *Judaism in the Roman World: Collected Essays*, 59–68. AJEC 66. Leiden: Brill, 2007.

Gräßer, Erich. *Forschungen zur Apostelgeschichte*. WUNT 137. Tübingen: Mohr Siebeck, 2001.

Green, Joel B. "'The Message of Salvation' in Luke-Acts." *ExAud* 5 (1989): 21–34.

Green, Joel B. "The Death of Jesus, God's Servant." In *Reimaging the Death of the Lukan Jesus*, edited by Dennis D. Sylva, 1–28. BBB 73. Frankfurt am Main: Anton Hain, 1990.

Green, Joel B. "Good News to Whom? Jesus and the 'Poor' in the Gospel of Luke." In *Jesus of Nazareth: Lord and Christ: Essays on the Historical Jesus and New Testament Christology*, edited by Joel B. Green, and Max Turner, 59–74. Grand Rapids: Eerdmans, 1994.

Green, Joel B. *The Gospel of Luke*. NICNT. Grand Rapids: Eerdmans, 1997.

Green, Joel B. "'Salvation to the End of the Earth': God as the Saviour in the Acts of the Apostles." In *Witness to the Gospel: The Theology of Acts*, edited by I. Howard Marshall, and David Peterson, 83–106. Grand Rapids: Eerdmans, 1998.

Green, Joel B. "From 'John's Baptism' to 'Baptism in the Name of the Lord Jesus': The Significance of Baptism in Luke-Acts." In *Baptism, the New Testament and the Church: Historical and Contemporary Studies in Honor of R. E. O. White*, edited by Stanley E. Porter, and Anthony R. Cross, 157–72. JSNTSup 171. Sheffield: Sheffield Academic Press, 1999.

Green, Joel B. *Body, Soul, and Human Life: The Nature of Humanity*. STI. Grand Rapids: Baker Academic, 2008a.

Green, Joel B. "'In Our Own Languages': Pentecost, Babel, and the Shaping of Christian Community in Acts 2:1–12." In *The Word Leaps the Gap: Essays on Scripture and Theology in Honor of Richard B. Hays*, edited by J. Ross Wagner, C. Kavin Rowe, and A. Katherine Grieb, 198–213. Grand Rapids: Eerdmans, 2008b.

Green, Joel B. *The Death of Jesus: Tradition and Interpretation in the Passion Narrative*. Eugene, OR: Wipf & Stock, 2011a.

Green, Joel B. "Luke-Acts, or Luke and Acts? A Reaffirmation of Narrative Unity." In *Reading Acts Today: Essays in Honour of Loveday C. A. Alexander*, edited by Steve Walton, Thomas E. Philips, Lloyd K. Pietersen, and F. Scott Spencer, 101–19. LNTS 427. London: T&T Clark, 2011b.

Green, Joel B. "'Was It Not Necessary for the Messiah to Suffer These Things and Enter into His Glory?': The Significance of Jesus' Death for Luke's Soteriology." In *The Spirit and Christ in the New Testament and Christian Theology: Essays in Honor of Max Turner*, edited by I. Howard Marshall, Volker Rabens, and Cornelis Bennema, 71–85. Grand Rapids: Eerdmans, 2012.

Green, Joel B. "'He Ascended into Heaven': Jesus' Ascension in Lukan Perspective, and Beyond." In *Ears That Hear: Explorations in Theological Interpretation of the Bible*, edited by Joel B. Green, and Tim Meadowcroft, 130–50. Sheffield: Sheffield Phoenix, 2013.

Green, Joel B. "Good News to the Poor: A Lukan Leitmotif." *RevExp* 111 (2014): 173–9.

Green, Joel B. *Conversion in Luke-Acts: Divine Action, Human Cognition, and the People of God*. Grand Rapids: Baker Academic, 2015.

Green, Joel B. "Kingdom of God/Heaven." In *Dictionary of Jesus and the Gospels*, 2nd ed., edited by Joel B. Green, Jeannine K. Brown, and Nicholas Perrin, 468–81. Downers Grove, IL: InterVarsity Press, 2013.

Gregory, Andrew F. *The Reception of Luke and Acts in the Period before Irenaeus: Looking for Luke in the Second Century*. WUNT 2/169. Tübingen: Mohr Siebeck, 2003.

Gregory, Andrew F., and C. Kavin Rowe., eds. *Rethinking the Unity and Reception of Luke and Acts*. Columbia: University of South Carolina Press, 2010.

Gregory, Bradley C. "The Postexilic Exile in Third Isaiah: Isaiah 61:1–3 in Light of Second Temple Hermeneutics." *JBL* 126 (2007): 475–96.

Greimas, Algirdas Julian, and Joseph Courtés. *Semiotics and Language: An Analytical Dictionary*. Bloomington: Indiana University Press, 1982.

Grenz, Stanley J. *Theology for the Community of God*. Grand Rapids: Eerdmans, 1994.

Griffiths, Paul J. "The Cross as the Fulcrum of Politics: Expropriating Agamben on Paul." In *Paul, Philosophy, and the Theopolitical Vision: Critical Engagements with Agamben, Badiou, Žižek, and Others*, edited by Douglas Harink, 179–97. Eugene, OR: Cascade, 2010.

Gross, Michael B. *The War against Catholicism: Liberalism and the Anti-Catholic Imagination in Nineteenth-Century Germany*. Ann Arbor: University of Michigan Press, 2004.

Gunkel, Heidrun. *Der Heilige Geist bei Lukas*. WUNT 2/389. Tübingen: Mohr Siebeck, 2015.

Gunkel, Hermann. *Introduction to Psalms: The Genres of the Religious Lyric of Israel*. Macon, GA: Mercer University Press, 1998.

Güting, Eberhard. "Der geographische Horizont der sogenannten Volkerliste des Lukas." *ZNW* 66 (1975): 149–69.

Guy, Laurie. "The Interplay of the Present and Future in the Kingdom of God (Luke 19: 11–44)." *TynBul* 48 (1997): 119–37.

Haacker, Klaus. "Das Bekenntnis des Paulus zur Hoffnung Israels nach der Apostelgeschichte des Lukas." *NTS* 31 (1985): 437–51.

Haenchen, Ernst. "The Book of Acts as Source Material for the History of Early Christianity." In *Studies in Luke-Acts: Essays Presented in Honor of Paul Schubert*, edited by Leander E. Keck, and J. Louis Martyn, 258–78. Nashville: Abingdon, 1966.

Haenchen, Ernst. *The Acts of the Apostles: A Commentary*. Philadelphia: Westminster, 1971.

Hägerland, Tobias. *Jesus and the Forgiveness of Sins: An Aspect of His Prophetic Mission*. SNTSMS 150. Cambridge: Cambridge University Press, 2012.

Hahn, Scott W. "Kingdom and Church in Luke-Acts: From Davidic Christology to Kingdom Eschatology." In *Reading Luke: Interpretation, Reflection, and Formation*, edited by Craig G. Bartholomew, Joel B. Green, and Anthony C. Thistleton, 294–326. ScrH 6. Gloucesterschire: University of Gloucestershire Press, 2005.

Hamm, Dennis. "Sight to the Blind as Metaphor in Luke." *Bib* 67 (1986): 457–77.

Hanks, Thomas D. *God So Loved the Third World: The Bible, the Reformation, and Liberation Theologies*. Maryknoll, NY: Orbis Books, 1983.

Hansen, G. Walter. "The Preaching and Defense of Paul." In *Witness to the Gospel: The Theology of Acts*, edited by I. Howard Marshall, and David Peterson, 295–324. Grand Rapids: Eerdmans, 1998.

Harland, Philip A. "The Economy of First-Century Palestine: State of the Scholarly Discussion." In *Handbook of Early Christianity: Social Science Approaches*, edited by Anthony J. Blasi, Jean Duhaime, and Philip-Andre Turcotte, 511–27. Walnut Creek, CA: Alta Mira, 2002.

Harland, Philip A. *Associations, Synagogues, and Congregations: Claiming a Place in Ancient Mediterranean Society*. Minneapolis: Fortress, 2003.

Harris, Sarah. *The Davidic Shepherd King in the Lukan Narrative*. LNTS 558. London: Bloomsbury T&T Clark, 2016.

Hart, Trevor A. "Irenaeus, Recapitulation, and Physical Redemption." In *Christ in Our Place: The Humanity of God in Christ for the Reconciliation of the World*, edited by Trevor A. Hart, and Daniel P. Thimell, 152–81. Exeter: Paternoster, 1989.

Hays, Christopher M. *Luke's Wealth Ethics: A Study in Their Coherence and Character*. WUNT 2/275. Tübingen: Mohr Siebeck, 2010.

Hays, Richard B. "The Paulinism of Acts, Intertextually Reconsidered." In *Paul and the Heritage of Israel: Paul's Claim upon Israel's Legacy in Luke and Acts in the Light of the Pauline Letters*, edited by David P. Moessner, Daniel Marguerat, Mikeal C. Parsons, and Michael Wolter, 35–48. Vol. 2 of *Luke the Interpreter of Israel*. LNTS 452. London: T&T Clark, 2012.

Hays, Richard B. *Echoes of Scripture in the Gospels*. Waco, TX: Baylor University Press, 2016.

Heath, Malcolm. "Invention." In *Handbook of Classical Rhetoric in the Hellenistic Period 300 B.C.–A.D. 400*, edited by Stanley E. Porter, 89–119. Boston: Brill Academic, 2001.

Heil, John Paul. *The Meals Scenes in Luke-Acts: An Audience-Oriented Approach*. SBLMS 52. Atlanta: SBL, 1999.

Heitmüller, Wilhelm. *Taufe und Abendmahl im Urchristentum*. RV 1/22–3. Tübingen: Mohr, 1911.

Hendrickx, Herman. *The Third Gospel for the Third World*. 4 vols. Collegeville, MN: Liturgical Press, 1996.

Hengel, Martin. *Between Jesus and Paul: Studies in the Earliest History of Christianity*. London: SCM, 1983.

Herzog, William R., II. *Jesus, Justice, and the Reign of God: A Ministry of Liberation*. Louisville: Westminster John Knox, 2000.

Heumann, C. A. "Dissertatio de Theophilo, cui Lucas Historiam Sacram Inscripsit." In *Bibliotheca Historico-Philologico-Theologica*, edited by Johann Andreas Grimm, 483–505. Classis IV. Bremen: Hermanni Braueri, 1720.

Heusler, Erika. *Kapitalprozess im lukanischen Doppelwerk: Die Verfahren gegen Jesus und Paulus in exegetischer und rechtshistorischer Analyse*. NTAbh 38. Münster: Aschendorff, 2000.
Heywood, Andrew. *Politics*. New York: Palgrave Macmillan, 2007.
Hiers, Richard H. "Delay of the Parousia in Luke-Acts." *NTS* 20 (1973-4): 145–55.
Hill, Andrew E. *Malachi: A New Translation with Introduction and Commentary*. AB 25D. New York: Doubleday, 1998.
Himmelfarb, Martha. *Ascent to Heaven in Jewish and Christian Apocalypses*. Oxford: Oxford University Press, 1993.
Hochban, John I. "St. Irenaeus on the Atonement." *TS* 7 (1946): 543.
Hofius, Otfried. "Vergebungszuspruch und Vollmachtsfrage: Mk 2,1–12 und das Problem priesterlicher Absolution im antiken Judentum." In *"Wenn nicht jetzt, wann dann?" Aufsätze für Hans Joachim Kraus zum 65. Geburtstag*, edited by Hans-Georg Geyer, Johann Michael Schmidt, and Werner Schneider, 115–27. Neukirchen-Vleuyn: Neukirchener, 1983.
Hofius, Otfried. "Jesu Zuspruch der Sündenvergebung: Exegetische Erwägungen zu Mk 2,5b." In *Neutestamentliche Studien*, 57–69. WUNT 132. Tübingen: Mohr Siebeck, 2000.
Holladay, Carl R. *Acts: A Commentary*. NTL. Louisville: Westminster John Knox, 2016.
Holladay, William L. *Jeremiah*. 2 vols. Hermeneia. Minneapolis: Fortress, 1986–9.
Horn, Friedrich W. "Die Haltung des Lukas zum römischen Staat im Evanglium und in der Apostelgeschichte." In *The Unity of Luke-Acts*, edited by Joseph Verheyden, 203–24. BETL 142. Leuven: Leuven University Press, 1999.
Horsley, Richard A. *The Liberation of Christmas: The Infancy Narratives in Social Context*. New York: Crossroad, 1989.
Horsley, Richard A. "The Kingdom of God and the Renewal of Israel: Synoptic Gospels, Jesus Movements, and Apocalypticism." In *The Origins of Apocalypticism in Judaism and Christianity*, edited by John J. Collins, 303–44. Vol. 1 of *The Encyclopedia of Apocalypticism*, edited by Bernard McGinn, John J. Collins, and Stephen J. Stein. New York: Continuum, 1998.
Houston, Walter J. "'Today in Your Very Hearing': Some Comments on the Christological Use of the Old Testament." In *The Glory of Christ in the New Testament: Studies in Christology in Memory of George Bradford Caird*, edited by L. D. Hurst, and N. T. Wright, 37–47. Oxford: Clarendon, 1987.
Huddleston, Jonathan. "What Would Elijah and Elisha Do? Internarrativity in Luke's Story of Jesus." *JTI* 5 (2011): 262–82.
Hull, J. H. E. *The Holy Spirit in Acts of the Apostles*. London: Lutterworth, 1967.
Hurtado, Larry W. *Lord Jesus Christ: Devotion to Jesus in Earliest Christianity*. Grand Rapids: Eerdmans, 2003.
Hutt, Curtis. "'Be Ye Approved Money Changers!': Reexamining the Social Contexts of the Saying and Its Interpretation." *JBL* 131 (2012): 589–609.
Isasi-Díaz, Ada María. "Kin-dom of God: A Mujerista Proposal." In *In Our Own Voices: Latino/a Renditions of Theology*, edited by Benjamín Valentín, 171–89. Maryknoll, NY: Orbis, 2010.
Jantsch, Torsten. *Jesus, der Retter: Die Soteriologie des lukanischen Doppelwerks*. WUNT 381. Tübingen: Mohr Siebeck, 2017.
Jennings, Willie James. *The Christian Imagination: Theology and the Origins of Race*. New Haven: Yale University Press, 2010.
Jennings, Willie James. *Acts*. Belief. Louisville: Westminster John Knox, 2017.

Jeremias, Joachim. *New Testament Theology*. London: SCM, 1971.

Jervell, Jacob. *Luke and the People of God: A New Look at Luke-Acts*. Minneapolis: Augsburg, 1972.

Jervell, Jacob. *The Theology of the Acts of the Apostles*. NTT. Cambridge: Cambridge University Press, 1996.

Jervell, Jacob. *Die Apostelgeschichte: Übersetzt und erklärt*. KEK 3. Göttingen: Vandenhoeck & Ruprecht, 1998.

Jeska, Joachim. *Die Geschichte Israels in der Sicht des Lukas: Apg 7,2b-53 und 13,17–25 im Kontext antik-jüdischer Summarien der Geschichte Israels*. FRLANT 195. Göttingen: Vandenhoeck & Ruprecht, 2001.

Jipp, Joshua W. *Saved by Faith and Hospitality*. Grand Rapids: Eerdmans, 2017.

Johansson, Daniel. "'Who Can Forgive Sins but God Alone?' Human and Angelic Agents, and Divine Forgiveness in Early Judaism." *JSNT* 33 (2011): 351–74.

Johnson, Andy. "Resurrection, Ascension, and the Developing Portrait of the God of Israel in Acts." *SJT* 57 (2004): 146–62.

Johnson, Luke Timothy. *The Literary Function of Possessions in Luke-Acts*. SBLDS 39. Missoula, MT: Scholars Press, 1977.

Johnson, Luke Timothy. *The Gospel of Luke*. SP 3. Collegeville, MN: Liturgical Press, 1991.

Johnson, Luke Timothy. *The Acts of the Apostles*. SP 5. Collegeville, MN: Liturgical Press, 1992.

Johnson, Luke Timothy. *Sharing Possessions: What Faith Demands*, 2nd ed. Grand Rapids: Eerdmans, 2011.

Jones, Douglas. "The Background and Character of the Lukan Psalms." *JTS* 19 (1968): 19–56.

Jonge, M. de, and A. S. van der Woude "11Q Melchizedek and the New Testament." *NTS* 12 (1966): 301–26.

Juel, Donald H. *Luke-Acts: The Promise of History*. Atlanta: John Knox, 1983.

Jung, Franz. *ΣΩTHP: Studien zur Rezeption eines hellenistischen Ehrentitels im Neuen Testament*. NTAbh 39. Münster: Aschendorff, 2002.

Just, Arthur A., Jr. *The Ongoing Feast: Table Fellowship and Eschatology at Emmaus*. Collegeville, MN: Liturgical Press, 1993.

Kaiser, Walter C. "The Blessing of David: The Charter for Humanity." In *The Law and the Prophets: Old Testament Studies Prepared in Honor of Oswald Thompson Allis*, edited by John H. Skilton, Milton C. Fisher, and Leslie W. Sloat, 298–319. Nutley, NJ: Presbyterian and Reformed Press, 1974.

Karris, Robert J. *Luke: Artist and Theologian: Luke's Passion Account as Literature*. SCBTP. New York: Paulist, 1985.

Karris, Robert J. "Luke 23:47 and the Lukan View of Jesus' Death." In *Reimaging the Death of the Lukan Jesus*, edited by Dennis D. Sylva, 68–78. BBB 73. Frankfurt am Main: Anton Hain, 1990.

Karris, Robert J. "Food in the Gospel." *TBT* 38 (2000): 357–61.

Käsemann, Ernst. "The Beginnings of Christian Theology." In *New Testament Questions of Today*, 82–107. Philadelphia: Fortress, 1969.

Kaut, Thomas. *Befreier und befreites Volk*. BBB 77. Frankfurt am Main: Anton Hain, 1990.

Kawashima, Robert S. "The Jubilee Year and the Return of Cosmic Purity." *CBQ* 65 (2003): 370–89.

Keener, Craig S. *Acts: An Exegetical Commentary*. 5 vols. Grand Rapids: Baker Academic, 2012–17.

Kennedy, George A. *New Testament Interpretation through Rhetorical Criticism*. Chapel Hill: University of North Carolina Press, 1984.

Kilgallen, John J. "Acts 13,38–39: The Culmination of Paul's Speech in Pisidia." *Bib* 69 (1988): 480–506.

Kim, Seyoon. *Christ and Caesar: The Gospel and the Roman Empire in the Writings of Paul and Luke*. Grand Rapids: Eerdmans, 2008.

Kimbell, John. *The Atonement in Lukan Theology*. Newcastle upon Tyne: Cambridge Scholars, 2014.

Kinman, Brent. *Jesus' Entry into Jerusalem: In the Context of Lukan Theology and the Politics of His Day*. AGJU 28. Leiden: Brill, 1995.

Kittel, Gerhard. "λέγω, λόγος, ῥῆμα, λαλέω." *TDNT* 4 (1967): 100–37.

Klager, Andrew P. "Retaining and Reclaiming the Divine: Identification and the Recapitulation of Peace in St. Irenaeus of Lyons' Atonement Narrative." In *Stricken by God? Nonviolent Identification and the Victory of Christ*, edited by Brad Jersak, and Michael Hardin, 426–80. Grand Rapids: Eerdmans, 2007.

Klauck, Hans-Josef. *Magic and Paganism in Early Christianity: The World of the Acts of the Apostles*. Edinburgh: T&T Clark, 2000.

Klawans, Jonathan. *Impurity and Sin in Ancient Judaism*. Oxford: Oxford University Press, 2000.

Klein, Hans. *Das Lukasevangelium*. KEK 1/3. Göttingen: Vandenhoeck & Ruprecht, 2006.

Klein, Hans. "Jesus und der römiche Staat in der Sicht des Lukasevangeliums zugleich ein Beitrag zum Verhältnis von Kirche und Staat." *SacScr* 13 (2015): 139–52.

Kloppenborg, John S., and Joseph Verheyden., eds. *The Elijah-Elisha Narrative in the Composition of Luke*. LNTS 493. London: Bloomsbury, 2014.

Koch, Klaus. "Sühne und Sündenvergebung um die Wende von der exilischen zur nachexilischen Zeit." *EvT* 26 (1966): 217–39.

Koester, Helmut. "σπλάγχνον, σπλαγχνίζομαι, εὔσπλαγχνος, πολύσπλαγχνος, ἄσπλαγχνος." *TDNT* 7 (1971): 548–59.

Koet, B. J. *Five Studies on Interpretation of Scripture in Luke-Acts*. Leuven: Leuven University Press, 1989.

Koet, B. J. "Isaiah in Luke-Acts." In *Isaiah in the New Testament*, edited by Steve Moyise, and Maarten J. J. Menken, 79–100. London: T&T Clark, 2005.

Kort, Wesley A. *Place and Space in Modern Fiction*. Gainesville, FL: University Press of Florida, 2004.

Kotsko, Adam. *The Politics of Redemption: The Social Logic of Salvation*. London: Bloomsbury T&T Clark, 2010.

Kremer, Jacob. *Pfingstbericht und Pfingstgeschehen: Eine exegetische Untersuchung zu Apg 2,1–13*. SBS 63/64. Stuttgart: KBW, 1973.

Krodel, Gerhard A. *Acts*. ACNT. Minneapolis: Augsburg, 1986.

Kuhn, Karl Allen. *The Kingdom according to Luke and Acts: A Social, Literary, and Theological Introduction*. Grand Rapids: Baker Academic, 2015.

Kümmel, Werner Georg. "'Das Gesetz und die Propheten gehen bis Johannes': Lukas 16,16 im Zusammenhang der heilsgeschichtlichen Theologie der Lukasschriften." In *Verborum Veritas*, edited by Otto Böcher, and Klaus Haacker, 89–102. Wuppertal: Theologischer Verlag Rolf Brockhaus, 1970.

Kümmel, Werner Georg. "Current Theological Accusations against Luke." *ANQ* 16 (1975): 131–45.

Kurz, William S. *Acts of the Apostles*. CCSS. Grand Rapids: Baker Academic, 2013.

Lake, Kirsopp, and Henry J. Cadbury. *The Acts of the Apostles: English Translation and Commentary*. Vol. 4 of *The Beginnings of Christianity: Part I: The Acts of the Apostles*. Edited by F. J. Foakes Jackson, and Kirsopp Lake. London: Macmillan, 1933.

Lakoff, George, and Mark Johnson. *Metaphors We Live By*. Chicago: University of Chicago Press, 1980.

Lang, Friedrich Gustav "Abraham geschworen—uns geben Syntax und Sinn im Benediktus (1.68-79)." *NTS* 56 (2010): 491–512.

Lawson, John. *The Biblical Theology of Saint Irenaeus*. London: Epworth, 1948.

Laytham, D. Brent. "Interpretation on the Way to Emmaus: Jesus Performs His Story." *JTI* 1 (2007): 101–15.

Le Cornu, Hilary, and Joseph Shulam. *A Commentary on the Jewish Roots of Acts*. Jerusalem: Academon, 2003.

Lebourlier, Jean. "*Entos hymōn*: Le sens 'au milieu de vous' est-il possible?" *Bib* 73 (1992): 259–62.

Lefebvre, Henri. *The Production of Space*. Oxford: Blackwell, 1991.

Lennartsson, Göran. "Refreshing & Restoration: Two Eschatological Motifs in Acts 3:19–21." PhD diss., Lund University, 2007.

Levick, Barbara. *Roman Colonies in Southern Asia Minor*. Oxford: Oxford University Press, 1967.

Lindemann, Andreas. "*Orbis romanus* und οἰκουμένη: Römischer und urchristlicher Universalismus." In *Christ and the Emperor: The Gospel Evidence*, edited by Gilbert Van Belle, and Joseph Verheyden, 51–100. Leuven: Peeters, 2014.

Locke, John. *A Letter Concerning Toleration*. LLLA 22. New York: Liberal Arts, 1950.

Loewe, William P. "Irenaeus' Soteriology: *Christus Victor* Revisited." *ATR* 67 (1985): 1–15.

Lohfink, Gerhard. *Die Himmelfahrt Jesu: Untersuchungen zu den Himmelfahrts und Erhöhungstexten bei Lukas*. SANT 26. München: Kösel, 1971.

Lohse, Eduard. "πεντηκοστή." *TDNT* 6 (1969): 44–53.

Loisy, Alfred. *Les Actes des Apôtres*. Paris: Émile Nourry, 1920.

Lövestam, Evald. *Son and Saviour: A Study of Acts 13,32–37 with an Appendix: 'Son of God' in the Synoptic Gospels*. ConBNT 18. Lund: Gleerup, 1961.

Lundbom, Jack R. *Jeremiah: A New Translation with Introduction and Commentary*. 3 vols. AB 21–21C. New York: Doubleday, 1999–2004.

MacIntyre, Alasdair. "The Political and Social Structures of the Common Good." In *Dependent Rational Animals: Why Human Beings Need the Virtues*, 129–46. Chicago: Open Court, 1999.

MacMullen, Ramsay. *Paganism in the Roman Empire*. New Haven: Yale University Press, 1981.

Maddox, Robert. *The Purpose of Luke-Acts*. SNTW. London: T&T Clark, 1982.

Malina, Bruce J., and John J. Pilch. *Social-Science Commentary on the Book of Acts*. Minneapolis: Fortress, 2008.

Mallen, Peter. *The Reading and Transformation of Isaiah in Luke-Acts*. LNTS 367. London: T&T Clark, 2008.

Mantey, Julius R. "The Causal Use of Eis in the New Testament." *JBL* 70 (1951a): 45–8.

Mantey, Julius R. "On Causal Eis Again." *JBL* 70 (1951b): 309–11.

Marcus, Joel. "Jesus' Baptismal Vision." *NTS* 41 (1995): 512–21.

Marcus, Ralph. "On Causal Eis." *JBL* 70 (1951): 129–30.

Marcus, Ralph. "The Elusive Causal Eis." *JBL* 71 (1952): 43–4.

Marguerat, Daniel. *The First Christian Historian: Writing the "Acts of the Apostles."* SNTSMS 121. Cambridge: Cambridge University Press, 2002.

Marguerat, Daniel. *Les Actes des Apôtres*. 2 vols. CNT 5. Genève: Labor et Fides, 2007.
Marshall, I. Howard. "The Development of the Concept of Redemption in the New Testament." In *Reconciliation and Hope: New Testament Essays on Atonement and Eschatology*, edited by Robert Banks, 153–69. Exeter: Paternoster, 1974.
Marshall, I. Howard. "The Significance of Pentecost." *SJT* 30 (1977): 347–69.
Marshall, I. Howard. *The Gospel of Luke: A Commentary on the Greek Text*. NIGTC. Grand Rapids: Eerdmans, 1978.
Marshall, I. Howard. *The Acts of the Apostles*. TNTC 5. Grand Rapids: Eerdmans, 1980a.
Marshall, I. Howard. *Last Supper and Lord's Supper*. Grand Rapids: Eerdmans, 1980b.
Marshall, I. Howard. *Luke: Historian and Theologian*, 3rd ed. Downers Grove, IL: IVP Academic, 1998.
Marshall, I. Howard. "The Place of Acts 20.28 in Luke's Theology of the Cross." In *Reading Acts Today: Essays in Honour of Loveday C. A. Alexander*, edited by Steve Walton, Thomas E. Philips, Lloyd K. Pietersen, and F. Scott Spencer, 154–70. LNTS 427. London: T&T Clark, 2011.
Martin, Luther H. *Hellenistic Religions: An Introduction*. New York: Oxford University Press, 1987.
Marty, Martin. *Politics, Religion, and the Common Good: Advancing a Distinctly American Conversation about Religion's Role in Our Shared Life*. San Francisco: Jossey-Bass, 2000.
Martyn, J. Louis. *Theological Issues in the Letters of Paul*. Nashville: Abingdon, 1997.
Mason, Steve. "Jews, Judeans, Judaizing, Judaism: Problems of Categorization in Ancient History." *JSJ* 38 (2007): 457–512.
Maston, Jason. "How Wrong Were the Disciples about the Kingdom? Thoughts on Acts 1:6." *ExpTim* 126 (2015): 169–78.
Matera, Frank J. "The Death of Jesus according to Luke: A Question of Sources." *CBQ* 47 (1985): 469–85.
Mattill, A. J. Jr. "The Purpose of Acts: Schneckenburger Reconsidered." In *Apostolic History and the Gospel: Biblical and Historical Essays Presented to F. F. Bruce*, edited by W. Ward Gasque, and Ralph P. Martin, 108–22. Exeter: Paternoster, 1970.
May, Jordan Daniel. "Is Luke a Reader-Response Critic? Luke's Aesthetic Trajectory of Isaiah 49.6 in Acts 13.47." In *Trajectories in the Book of Acts: Essays in Honor of John Wesley Wyckoff*, edited by Paul Alexander, Jordan Daniel May, and Robert G. Reid, 59–86. Eugene, OR: Wipf & Sock, 2010.
McCutcheon, Russell T. "What Is Religion?" In *Introduction to World Religions*, edited by Christopher Partridge, 10–14. Minneapolis: Fortress, 2005.
McIntyre, Luther B. Jr. "Baptism and Forgiveness in Acts 2:38." *BSac* 153 (1996): 53–62.
McKnight, Scot. *Jesus and His Death: Historiography, the Historical Jesus, and Atonement Theory*. Waco: TX: Baylor University Press, 2005.
McRay, John. *Archaeology and the New Testament*. Grand Rapids: Baker, 1991.
Medina, Gilberto J. "The Lukan Writings as Colonial Counter-Discourse: Postcolonial Reading of Luke's Ideological stance of Duplicity, Resistance, and Survival." PhD diss., Vanderbilt University, 2005.
Meiser, Martin. "Lukas und die römische Staatmacht" In *Zwischen den Reichen: Neues Testament und Römische Herrschaft*, edited by Michael Labahn, and Jürgen Zangenberg, 175–93. TANZ 36. Tübingen: Francke, 2002.
Méndez-Moratalla, Fernando. *The Paradigm of Conversion in Luke*. JSNTSup 252. London: T&T Clark, 2004.
Menken, Maarten J. J. "The Position of σπλαγχνίζεσθαι and σπλάγχνα in the Gospel of Luke." *NovT* 30 (1988): 107–14.

Menzies, Robert P. *The Development of Early Christian Pneumatology with Special Reference to Luke-Acts*. JSNTSup 54. Sheffield: JSOT Press, 1991.
Menzies, Robert P. *Empowered for Witness: The Spirit in Luke-Acts*. JPTSup 6. Sheffield: Sheffield Academic Press, 1994.
Menzies, Robert P. "Luke's Understanding of Baptism in the Holy Spirit: A Pentecostal Dialogues with the Reformed Tradition." *JPT* 16 (2008): 86–101.
Merk, Otto. "Das Reich Gottes in den lukanischen Schriften." In *Jesus und Paulus: Festschrift für Werner Georg Kümmel zum 70. Geburtstag*, edited by E. Earle Ellis, and Erich Gräßer, 201–20. Göttingen: Vandenhoeck & Ruprecht, 1975.
Merrill, Eugene H. "Paul's Use of 'About 450 Years' in Acts 13:20." *BSac* 138 (1981): 246–57.
Metzger, Bruce M. "Ancient Astrological Geography and Acts 2.9–11." In *Apostolic History and the Gospel: Biblical and Historical Essays Presented to F. F. Bruce on His 60th Birthday*, edited by W. Ward Gasque, and Ralph P. Martin, 123–33. Exeter: Paternoster, 1970.
Metzger, Bruce M. *A Textual Commentary on the Greek New Testament*, 2nd ed. Stuttgart: Deutsche Bibelgesellschaft, 1994.
Meyer, Ben F. *The Aims of Jesus*. London: SCM, 1979.
Milbank, John. "On Complex Space." In *The Word Made Strange: Theology, Language, Culture*, 268–92. Oxford: Blackwell, 1997.
Milgrom, Jacob. "Israel's Sanctuary: The Priestly 'Picture of Dorian Gray.'" *RB* 83 (1976): 390–9.
Milgrom, Jacob. *Leviticus: A New Translation with Introduction and Commentary*. 3 vols. AB 3–3B. New York: Doubleday, 2000–2007.
Miller, Amanda C. *Rumors of Resistance: Status Reversals and Hidden Transcripts in the Gospel of Luke*. ESS. Minneapolis: Fortress, 2014.
Miller, Merril P. "The Function of Isa 61:1–2 in 11Q Melchizedek." *JBL* 88 (1969): 467–9.
Minear, Paul S. "Luke's Use of the Birth Stories." In *Studies in Luke-Acts: Essays in Honour of Paul Schubert*, edited by E. Keck Leander, and J. Louis Martyn, 111–30. Nashville: Abingdon, 1966.
Minns, Denis. *Irenaeus: An Introduction*, 2nd ed. London: T&T Clark, 2010.
Mitchell, Alan C. "The Social Function of Friendship in Acts 2:44–47 and 4:32–37." *JBL* 111 (1991): 255–72.
Mitchell, Stephen. "Population and the Land in Roman Galatia." *ANRW* 2, no. 7.2 (1980): 1053–81.
Mitchell, Stephen. "Antioch of Pisidia." In *The Anchor Bible Dictionary*, 1, edited by David Noel Freedman, 264–5. New York: Doubleday, 1992.
Mittelstadt, Martin William "Eat, Drink, and Be Merry: A Theology of Hospitality in Luke-Acts." *WW* 34 (2014): 131–9.
Mittmann-Richert, Ulrike. *Magnifikat und Benediktus: Die ältesten Zeugnisse der judenchristlichen Tradition von der Geburt des Messias*. WUNT 2/90. Tübingen: Mohr Siebeck, 1996.
Mittmann-Richert, Ulrike. *Der Sühnetod des Gottesknechts: Jesaja 53 im Lukasevangelium*. WUNT 220. Tübingen: Mohr Siebeck, 2008.
Miura, Yuzuru. "David as Prophet: The Use of Ps 15 (LXX) in Acts 2:25–31." *Exeg* 18 (2007a): 21–46.
Miura, Yuzuru. *David in Luke-Acts: His Portrayal in the Light of Early Judaism*. WUNT 2/232. Tübingen: Mohr Siebeck, 2007b.

Moehring, Horst R. "Census in Luke as an Apologetic Device." In *Studies in New Testament and Early Christian Literature: Essays in Honor of Allen P. Wikgren*, edited by David Edward Aune, 144–60. NovTSup 33. Leiden: Brill, 1972.

Moessner, David P. "Paul in Acts: Preacher of Eschatological Repentance to Israel." *NTS* 34 (1988): 96–104.

Molthagen, Joachim. "Rom als Garant des Rechts und als apokalyptiches Ungeheuer: Christliche Antworten auf Anfeindungen durch Staat und Gesellschaft im späten 1. Jahrhundert n. Chr." In *Gemeinschaft am Evangelium*, edited by Edwin Brandt, Paul S. Fiddes, and Joachim Molthagen, 127–42. Leipzig: Evangelische, 1996.

Montgomery, James A. *A Critical and Exegetical Commentary on the Book of Daniel*. ICC. Edinburgh: T&T Clark, 1927.

Moore, George Foot. *Judaism in the First Centuries of the Christian Era: The Age of the Tannaim*. 3 vols. Cambridge, MA: Harvard University Press, 1946–9.

Moralee, Jason. *"For Salvation's Sake": Provincial Loyalty, Personal Religion, and Epigraphic Production in the Roman and Late Antique Near East*. SClass. New York: Routledge, 2004.

Morgan, Teresa. *Roman Faith and Christian Faith: Pistis and Fides in the Early Roman Empire and Early Churches*. Oxford: Oxford University Press, 2015.

Morgan, Teresa. "Roman Faith and Christian Faith." *NTS* 64 (2018): 255–61.

Morgan-Wynne, John Eifion. *Paul's Pisidian Antioch Speech (Acts 13)*. Cambridge: James Clark, 2014.

Morris, Leon. *Luke: An Introduction and Commentary*. TNTC 3. Grand Rapids: Eerdmans, 1974.

Moule, C. F. D. "The Christology of Acts." In *Studies in Luke-Acts: Essays Presented in Honor of Paul Schubert*, edited by Leander E. Keck, and J. Louis Martyn, 159–85. Nashville: Abingdon, 1966.

Moxnes, Halvor. *The Economy of the Kingdom: Social Conflict and Economic Relations in Luke's Gospel*. OBT. Philadelphia: Fortress, 1988.

Moxnes, Halvor. "Kingdom Takes Place: Transformations of Place and Power in the Kingdom of God in the Gospel of Luke." In *Social Scientific Models for Interpreting the Bible: Essays by the Context Group in Honor of Bruce J. Malina*, edited by John J. Pilch, 176–209. BibInt 53. Leiden: Brill, 2001.

Müller, Paul-Gerhard. "Der 'Paulinismus' in der Apostelgeschichte: Ein forschungsgeschichtlicher Überblick." In *Paulus in den neutestamentlichen Spätschriften*, edited by Karl Kertelge, 157–201. QD 89. Freiburg: Herder, 1981.

Muñoz-Larrondo, Rubén. *A Postcolonial Reading of the Acts of the Apostles*. StBibLit 147. New York: Peter Lang, 2012.

Nave, Guy D., Jr. *The Role and Function of Repentance in Luke-Acts*. AcBib 4. Leiden: Brill, 2002.

Neagoe, Alexandru. *The Trial of the Gospel: An Apologetic Reading of Luke's Trial Narratives*. SNTSMS 116. Cambridge: Cambridge University Press, 2002.

Neyrey, Jerome H. "Ceremonies in Luke-Acts: The Case of Meals and Table Fellowship." In *The Social World of Luke Acts: Models for Interpretation*, edited by Jerome H. Neyrey, 361–87. Peabody, MA: Hendrickson, 1991.

Nielsen, Anders E. "The Purpose of the Lucan Writings with Particular Reference to Eschatology." In *Luke-Acts: Scandinavian Perspectives*, edited by Petri Luomanen, 76–93. FES 54. Göttingen: Vandenhoeck & Ruprecht, 1991.

Noack, Bent. "The Day of Pentecost in Jubilees, Qumran, and Acts." *ASTI* 1 (1962): 72–95.

Noble, Joshua A. "'Rich toward God': Making Sense of Luke 12:21." *CBQ* 78 (2016): 302–20.
Nolland, John T. *Luke*. 3 vols. WBC 35A–C. Dallas: Word, 1989–93.
Nolland, John T. "Salvation-History and Eschatology." In *Witness to the Gospel: The Theology of Acts*, edited by I. Howard Marshall, and David Peterson, 63–81. Grand Rapids: Eerdmans, 1998.
Nongbri, Brent. "Dislodging 'Embedded' Religion: A Brief Note on a Scholarly Trope." *Numen* 55 (2008): 440–60.
Nongbri, Brent. *Before Religion: A History of a Modern Concept*. New Haven: Yale University Press, 2013.
Nordgaard, Stefan. *Possessions and Family in the Writings of Luke*. Copenhagen: Museum Tusculanum Press, 2017.
Novick, Tzvi. "Eschatological Ignorance and the *Haftarah*: On Acts 13:27." *NovT* 54 (2012): 168–75.
O'Banion, John. "Quintilian on *Narratio* as the Heart of Rhetorical Thinking." *Rhet* 5 (1987): 325–51.
O'Neill, J. C. *The Theology of Acts: In Its Historical Setting*. London: SPCK, 1970.
O'Toole, Robert F. "Christ's Resurrection in Acts 13,13–52." *Bib* 60 (1979): 361–72.
O'Toole, Robert F. "Activity of the Risen Jesus in Luke-Acts." *Bib* 62 (1981): 471–98.
O'Toole, Robert F. *The Unity of Luke's Theology: An Analysis of Luke-Acts*. GNS 9. Wilmington, DE: Michael Glazer, 1984.
O'Toole, Robert F. "The Kingdom of God in Luke-Acts." In *The Kingdom of God in 20th-Century Interpretation*, edited by Wendell Willis, 147–62. Peabody, MA: Hendrickson, 1987.
O'Toole, Robert F. "Review of *Society and Politics in the Acts of the Apostles*, by Richard J. Cassidy." *Bib* 70 (1989): 424–8.
O'Toole, Robert F. "Jesus as the Christ in Luke 4,16–30." *Bib* 76 (1995): 498–522.
O'Toole, Robert F. "How Does Luke Portray Jesus as Servant of YHWH." *Bib* 81 (2000): 328–46.
O'Toole, Robert F. *Luke's Presentation of Jesus: A Christology*. SubBi 25. Rome: Pontifical Biblical Institute, 2004.
Oakman, Douglas E. *Jesus and the Economy of His Day*. SBEC 8. Lewiston, NY: Edwin Mellen, 1986.
Oegema, Gerbern S. *The Anointed and His People: Messianic Expectations from the Maccabees to Bar Kochba*. JSPSup 27. Sheffield: Sheffield Academic Press, 1988.
Osborn, Eric. *Irenaeus of Lyons*. Cambridge: Cambridge University Press, 2001.
Osburn, Carroll D. "The Third Person Imperative in Acts 2:38." *ResQ* 26 (1983): 81–4.
Page, Sydney H. T. *Powers of Evil: A Biblical Study of Satan and Demons*. Grand Rapids: Baker, 1995.
Palmer, D. W. "The Literary Background of Acts 1.1–14." *NTS* 33 (1987): 432–4.
Pao, David W. *Acts and the Isaianic New Exodus*. Grand Rapids: Baker Academic, 2002.
Pao, David W. "Waiters or Preachers: Acts 6:1–7 and the Lukan Table Fellowship Motif." *JBL* 130 (2011): 127–44.
Pao, David W. "Jesus's Ascension and the Lukan Account of the Restoration of Israel." In *Ascent into Heaven in Luke-Acts: New Explorations of Luke's Narrative Hinge*, edited by David K. Bryan, and David W. Pao, 136–56. Minneapolis: Fortress, 2016.
Parsons, Mikael C. "The Place of Jerusalem on the Lukan Landscape: An Exercise in Symbolic Cartography." In *Literary Studies in Luke-Acts: Essays in Honor of Joseph B.*

Tyson, edited by Richard P. Thompson, and Thomas E. Phillips, 155–72. Macon, GA: Mercer University Press, 1998.
Parsons, Mikael C. *Acts*. Paidea. Grand Rapids: Baker Academic, 2008.
Parsons, Mikael C., and Martin M. Culy. *Acts: A Handbook on the Greek Text*. Waco, TX: Baylor University Press, 2004.
Parsons, Mikael C., and Richard I. Pervo. *Rethinking the Unity of Luke and Acts*. Minneapolis: Fortress, 1993.
Pascut, Beniamin. "The So-Called *Passivum Divinum* in Mark's Gospel." *NovT* 54 (2012): 313–33.
Pattison, Stephen. "A Study of the Apologetic Function of the Summaries of Acts." PhD diss., Emory University, 1990.
Paul, Shalom M. "Deutero-Isaiah and Cuneiform Royal Inscriptions." In *Essays in Memory of E. A. Speiser*, edited by W. W. Hallo, 180–6. AOS 53. New Haven: American Oriental Society, 1968.
Paul, Shalom M. *Isaiah 40–66*. ECC. Grand Rapids: Eerdmans, 2011.
Peirce, Charles Sanders. *Collected Papers of Charles Sanders Peirce*. Edited by Charles Hartshorne, and Paul Weiss. 8 vols. Cambridge, MA: Belknap, 1960.
Perrin, Nicholas, and Joel B. Green "Jubilee." In *Dictionary of Jesus and the Gospels*, 2nd ed, edited by Joel B. Green, Jeannine K. Brown, and Nicholas Perrin, 450–2. Downers Grove, IL: InterVarsity Press, 2013.
Perrin, Norman. *Jesus and the Language of the Kingdom: Symbol and Metaphor in New Testament Interpretation*. Philadelphia: Fortress, 1976.
Pervo, Richard I. *Acts: A Commentary*. Hermeneia. Minneapolis: Fortress, 2009.
Pesch, Rudolf. *Die Apostelgeschichte*. EKKNT 5. Köln: Benziger, 1986.
Peterson, David. "Atonement Theology in Luke-Acts: Some Methodological Reflections." In *The New Testament in Its First-Century Setting: Essays on Context and Background in Honour of B. W. Winter on His 65th Birthday*, edited by P. J. Williams, Andrew D. Clarke, Peter M. Head, and David Instone-Brewer, 56–71. Grand Rapids: Eerdmans, 2004.
Pilcher, Josef. *Paulusrezeption in der Apostelgeschichte: Untersuchungen zur Rede im pisidischen Antiochien*. ITS 50. Innsbrook: Tyrolia-Verlag, 1997.
Pilgrim, Walter E. "The Death of Christ in Lukan Soteriology." ThD diss., Princeton Theological Seminary, 1971.
Pilgrim, Walter E. *Good News to the Poor: Wealth and Poverty in Luke-Acts*. Minneapolis: Augsburg, 1981.
Pillai, C. A. Joachim. *Early Missionary Preaching: A Study of Luke's Report in Acts 13*. Hicksville, NY: Exposition, 1979.
Pillai, C. A. Joachim. *Apostolic Interpretation of History: A Commentary on Acts 13:16–41*. Hicksville, NY: Exposition, 1980.
Pitre, Brant. *Jesus, the Tribulation, and the End of the Exile: Restoration Eschatology and the Origin of the Atonement*. Grand Rapids: Baker Academic, 2005.
Plummer, Alfred. *A Critical and Exegetical Commentary on the Gospel according to St. Luke*. ICC. New York: Scribner's Sons, 1902.
Poirer, John C. "Jesus as an Elijianic Figure in Luke 4:16–30." *CBQ* 71 (2009): 349–63.
Poon, William K. "Superabundant Table Fellowship in the Kingdom: The Feeding of the Five Thousand and the Meal Motif in Luke." *ExpTim* 114 (2003): 224–30.
Powell, Mark Allan "Salvation in Luke-Acts." *WW* 12 (1992): 5–10.
Price, Simon R. F. *Rituals and Power: The Roman Imperial Cult in Asia Minor*. Cambridge: Cambridge University Press, 1984.

Prieur, Alexander. *Die Verkündigung der Gottesherrschaft: Exegetische Studien zum lukanischen Verständnis von βασιλεία τοῦ θεοῦ*. WUNT 2/89. Tübingen: Mohr Siebeck, 1996.

Prior, Michael. *Jesus the Liberator: Nazareth Liberation Theology (Luke 4.16–30)*. BSem 26. Sheffield: Sheffield Academic Press, 1995.

Radl, Walter. *Paulus und Jesus im lukanischen Doppelwerk: Untersuchungen zu Parallelmotiven im Lukasevangelium und in der Apostelgeschichte*. EH 23/49. Bern: Lang, 1975.

Radl, Walter. *Der Ursprung Jesu: Traditionsgeschichtliche Untersuchungen zu Lukas 1–2*. HerdBS 7. Freiberg: Herder, 1996.

Räisänen, Heikki. *Marcion, Muhammed and the Mahatma: Exegetical Perspectives on the Encounter of Cultures and Faiths*. London: SCM, 1997.

Rajack, Tessa. "Was There a Roman Charter for the Jews?" *JRS* 74 (1984): 107–23.

Ramelli, Ilaria L. E. *The Christian Doctrine of* Apokatastasis: *A Critical Assessment from the New Testament to Eriugena*. VCSup 120. Leiden: Brill, 2013.

Ramsay, W. M. *The Cities of St. Paul: Their Influence on His Life and Thought*. New York: Hodder & Stoughton, 1907.

Ravens, David. *Luke and the Restoration of Israel*. JSNTSup 119. Sheffield: Sheffield Academic Press, 1995.

Reardon, Timothy W. "Recent Trajectories and Themes in Lukan Soteriology." *CBR* 12 (2013): 77–95.

Reardon, Timothy W. "'Hanging on a Tree': Deuteronomy 21.22–23 and the Rhetoric of Jesus' Crucifixion in Acts 5.12–42." *JSNT* 37 (2015): 407–31.

Reardon, Timothy W. "Cleansing through Almsgiving in Luke-Acts: Purity, Cornelius, and the Translation of Acts 15:9." *CBQ* 78 (2016): 447–66.

Reeder, Caryn A. *The Enemy in the Household: Family Violence in Deuteronomy and Beyond*. Grand Rapids: Baker Academic, 2012.

Reitzenstein, Richard. *Hellenistic Mystery-Religions*. PTMS 15. Pittsburgh: Pickwick, 1978.

Resseguie, James L. *Spiritual Landscape: Images of the Spiritual Life in the Gospel of Luke*. Peabody, MA: Hendrickson, 2004.

Ricoeur, Paul. *Time and Narrative*. 3 vols. Chicago: University of Chicago Press, 1984.

Rindoš, Jaroslav. *He of Whom It Is Written: John the Baptist and Elijah in Luke*. ÖBS 38. Frankfurt am Main: Peter Lang, 2010.

Ringe, Sharon H. *Jubilee, Liberation, and the Biblical Jubilee: Images for Ethics and Christology*. Eugene, OR: Wipf and Stock, 1985.

Ringgren, Helmer. *The Messiah in the Old Testament*. SBT 18. London: SCM, 1956.

Rive, James B. "Graeco-Roman Religion in the Roman Empire: Old Assumptions and New Approaches." *CBR* 8 (2010): 240–99.

Robbins, Vernon K. "Luke-Acts: A Mixed Population Seeks a Home in the Roman Empire." In *Images of Empire*, edited by Loveday C. A. Alexander, 202–21. JSOTSup 122. Sheffield: JSOT Press, 1991.

Robinson, Thomas A., and Hillary Rodrigues., eds. *World Religions: A Guide to the Essentials*. Peabody, MA: Hendrickson, 2006.

Roloff, Jürgen. *Die Apostelgeschichte: Übersetzt und erklärt*. Göttingen: Vandenhoeck & Ruprecht, 1981.

Romm, James S. *The Edges of the Earth in Ancient Thought*. Princeton: Princeton University Press, 1992.

Rossing, Barbara. "(Re)Claiming *Oikoumene*? Empire, Ecumenism and the Discipleship of Equals." In *Walk in the Ways of Wisdom: Essays in Honor of Elisabeth Schüssler*

Fiorenza, edited by Shelly Matthews, Cynthia Briggs Kittredge, and Melanie Johnson-DeBaufre, 74–87. Harrisburg: Trinity, 2003.
Rossing, Barbara. "Turning the Empire (οἰκουμένη) Upside Down." In *Reading Acts in the Discourses of Masculinity and Politics*, edited by Eric D Barreto, Matthew L. Skinner, and Steve Walton, 148–55. LNTS 559. London: Bloomsbury T&T Clark, 2017.
Rothschild, Claire K. *Luke-Acts and the Rhetoric of History: An Investigation of Early Christian Historiography*. WUNT 2/175. Tübingen: Mohr Siebeck, 2004.
Rowe, C. Kavin. "History, Hermeneutics and the Unity of Luke-Acts." *JSNT* 28 (2005): 131–57.
Rowe, C. Kavin. *Early Narrative Christology: The Lord in the Gospel of Luke*. Grand Rapids: Baker Academic, 2006.
Rowe, C. Kavin. "Literary Unity and Reception History: Reading Luke-Acts as Luke and Acts." *JSNT* 29 (2007): 449–57.
Rowe, C. Kavin. *World Upside Down: Reading Acts in the Greco-Roman Age*. Oxford: Oxford University Press, 2009.
Rubin, Benjamin. "Ruler Cult and Colonial Identity: The Imperial Sanctuary at Pisidian Antioch." In *Building a New Rome: The Imperial Colony of Pisidian Antioch (25 BC–AD 700)*, edited by Elaine K. Gazda, and Diane Y. Ng, 33–60. Ann Arbor: Kelsey Museum Publications, 2011.
Sack, Robert. *Human Territoriality: Its Theory and History*. Cambridge: Cambridge University Press, 1986.
Salmeier, Michael A. *Restoring the Kingdom: The Role of God as the 'Ordainer of Times and Seasons' in the Acts of the Apostles*. PrTMS. Eugene, OR: Pickwick, 2011.
Sanders, E. P. *Judaism: Practice and Belief 63 BCE–66 CE*. London: SCM, 1992.
Sanders, Jack T. *The Jews in Luke-Acts*. Philadelphia: Fortress, 1987.
Sanders, Jack T. "The Jewish People in Luke-Acts." In *Luke-Acts and the Jewish People: Eight Critical Perspectives*, edited by Joseph B. Tyson, 51–75. Minneapolis: Augsburg, 1988.
Sanders, Jack T. "Who Is a Jew and Who Is a Gentile in the Book of Acts." *NTS* 37 (1991): 434–55.
Sanders, James A. "Isaiah in Luke." *Int* 36 (1982): 144–55.
Sanders, James A. "From Isaiah 61 to Luke 4." In *Luke and Scripture: The Function of Sacred Tradition in Luke-Acts*, edited by Craig A. Evans, and James A. Sanders, 46–69. Minneapolis: Fortress, 1993.
Satterthwaite, Philip E. "Acts against the Background of Classical Rhetoric." In *The Book of Acts in Its Literary Setting*, edited by Bruce W. Winter, and Andrew D. Clarke, 337–80. BAFCS 1. Grand Rapids: Eerdmans, 1993.
Schendel, Joshua. "'That Justice Might Not Be Infringed Upon': The Judgment of God in the Passion of Christ in Irenaeus of Lyons." *SJT* 71 (2018): 212–25.
Schmithals, Walter. *Das Evangelium nach Lukas*. ZBK 3.1. Zürich: TVZ, 1980.
Schmithals, Walter. *Die Apostelgeschichte des Lukas*. ZBK 3.2. Zürich: TVZ, 1982.
Schnabel, Eckhard. *Early Christian Mission*. 2 vols. Downers Grove, IL: InterVarsity Press, 2004.
Schnackenburg, Rudolf. *God's Rule and Kingdom*. Freiberg: Herder, 1963.
Schneckenburger, Matthias. *Über den Zweck der Apostelgeschichte: Zugleich eine Ergänzung der neueren Commentare*. Bern: Christian Fischer, 1841.
Schneider, Gerhard. *Die Apostelgeschichte*. 2 vols. HTKNT 5. Freiberg: Herder, 1980.
Schreck, Christopher J. "Luke 4,16–30: The Nazareth Pericope in Modern Exegesis: A History of Interpretation." STD diss., Katholieke Universiteit Leuven, 1990.

Schreiber, Stefan. *Weihnachtspolitik: Lukas 1–2 und das Goldene Zeitalter*. NTOA 82. Göttingen: Vandenhoeck & Ruprecht, 2009.
Schürer, Emil. *The History of the Jewish People in the Age of Jesus Christ (175 B.C.–A.D. 135)*, edited by Geza Vermes, and Fergus Millar, 2nd ed., 5 vols. Edinburgh: T&T Clark, 1973.
Schürmann, Heinz. *Das Lukasevangelium*. 2 vols. HTKNT 3. Freiberg: Herder, 1969.
Schweizer, Eduard. "The Concept of the Davidic 'Son of God' in Acts and Its Old Testament Background." In *Studies in Luke-Acts: Essays Presented in Honor of Paul Schubert*, edited by Leander E. Keck, and J. Louis Martyn, 186–93. Nashville: Abingdon, 1966a.
Schweizer, Eduard. "Concerning the Speeches in Acts." In *Studies in Luke-Acts: Essays Presented in Honor of Paul Schubert*, edited by Leander E. Keck, and J. Louis Martyn, 208–16. Nashville: Abingdon, 1966b.
Schweizer, Eduard. "υἱός, υἱοθεσία." *TDNT* 8 (1972): 363–92.
Schweizer, Eduard. *The Good News according to Luke*. Atlanta: John Knox, 1984.
Scott, James M. "Exile and the Self-Understanding of Diaspora Jews in the Greco-Roman Period." In *Exile: Old Testament, Jewish, and Christian Conceptions*, edited by James M. Scott, 173–218. JSJSup 56. Leiden: Brill, 1997.
Scott, James M. "Acts 2:9–11 as an Anticipation of the Mission to the Nations." In *The Mission of the Early Church to Jews and Gentiles*, edited by Jostein Ådna, and Hans Kvalbein, 87–124. WUNT 127. Tübingen: Mohr Siebeck, 2000.
Scott, James M. *Geography in Early Judaism and Christianity: The Book of Jubilees*. SNTSMS 113. Cambridge: Cambridge University Press, 2002.
Seccombe, David P. "Luke and Isaiah." *NTS* 27 (1982): 252–9.
Seccombe, David P. *Possessions and the Poor in Luke-Acts*. SNTSU B6. Linz: Fuchs, 1983.
Seccombe, David P. "The New People of God." In *Witness to the Gospel: The Theology of Acts*, edited by I. Howard Marshall, and David Peterson, 349–72. Grand Rapids: Eerdmans, 1998.
Seesemann, Heinrich. *Der Begriff ΚΟΙΝΩΝΙΑ im Neuen Testament*. BZNW 74. Giessen: Töpelmann, 1933.
Segal, Alan F. "Heavenly Ascent in Hellenistic Judaism, Early Christianity and Their Environment." *ANRW* 2, no. 23.2 (1980): 1333–94.
Seifrid, Mark A. "Roman Faith and Christian Faith." *NTS* 64 (2018): 247–55.
Sellner, Hans Jörg. *Das Heil Gottes: Studien zur Soteriologie des lukanischen Doppelwerks*. BZNW 152. Berlin: de Gruyter, 2007.
Seo, Pyung Soo. *Luke's Jesus in the Roman Empire and the Emperor in the Gospel of Luke*. Eugene, OR: Pickwick, 2015.
Shepherd, William H., Jr. *The Narrative Function of the Holy Spirit as a Character in Luke-Acts*. SBLDS 147. Atlanta: Scholars Press, 1994.
Shin, W. Gil. "The 'Exodus' in Jerusalem (Luke 9:31): A Lukan Form of Israel's Restoration Hope." PhD diss., Fuller Theological Seminary, 2016.
Sidebottom, E. M. "The So-called Divine Passive in the Gospel Tradition." *ExpTim* 87 (1976): 200–4.
Skinner, Matthew L. "Who Speaks for (or against) Rome?" In *Reading Acts in the Discourses of Masculinity and Politics*, edited by Eric D Barreto, Matthew L. Skinner, and Steve Walton, 107–25. LNTS 559. London: Bloomsbury T&T Clark, 2017.
Sleeman, Matthew. *Geography and the Ascension Narrative in Acts*. SNTSMS 146. Cambridge: Cambridge University Press, 2009.

Sleeman, Matthew. "The Ascension and Spatial Theory." In *Ascent into Heaven in Luke-Acts: New Explorations of Luke's Narrative Hinge*, edited by David K. Bryan, and David W. Pao, 157–74. Minneapolis: Fortress, 2016.

Sloan, David B. "Interpreting Scripture with Satan? The Devil's Use of Scripture in Luke's Temptation Narrative." *TynBul* 66 (2015): 231–50.

Sloan, Robert B. *The Favorable Year of the Lord: A Study of Jubilary Theology in the Gospel of Luke*. Austin: Schola, 1977.

Smart, Ninian. *The World's Religions: Old Traditions and Modern Transformations*. Cambridge: Cambridge University Press, 1989.

Smit, Peter-Ben. "Negotiating a New World View in Acts 1.8? A Note on the Expression ἕως ἐσχάτου τῆς γῆς." *NTS* 63 (2017): 1–22.

Smit, Peter-Ben, and Toon Renssen "The *passivum divinum*: The Rise and Future Fall of an Imaginary Linguistic Phenomenon." *FN* 27 (2014): 3–24.

Smith, Dennis E. "Table Fellowship as a Literary Motif in the Gospel of Luke." *JBL* 106 (1987): 613–38.

Smith, Jonathan Z. *Imagining Religion: From Babylon to Jonestown*. Chicago: University of Chicago Press, 1982.

Smith, Jonathan Z. "Religion, Religions, Religious" In *Critical Terms for Religious Studies*, edited by Mark C. Taylor, 269–84. Chicago: University of Chicago Press, 1998.

Smith, Steve. *The Fate of the Jerusalem Temple in Luke-Acts: An Intertextual Approach to Jesus' Laments over Jerusalem and Stephen's Speech*. LNTS 553. London: Bloomsbury T&T Clark, 2017.

Smith, Wilfred Cantwell. *The Meaning and End of Religion: A New Approach to the Religious Traditions of Mankind*. New York: Macmillan, 1962.

Smyth, Herbert Weir. *A Greek Grammar for Colleges*. New York: American, 1920.

Soards, Marion L. *The Speeches in Acts: Their Content, Context, and Concerns*. Louisville: Westminster John Knox, 1994.

Soja, Edward. *Thirdspace: Journeys to Los Angeles and Other Real-and-Imagined Places*. Malden, MA: Blackwell, 1996.

Sourvinou-Inwood, Christiane. "Further Aspects of *Polis* Religion." In *Oxford Readings in Religion*, edited by Richard Buxton, 38–55. Oxford: Oxford University Press, 2000a.

Sourvinou-Inwood, Christiane. "What Is *Polis* Religion?" In *Oxford Readings in Religion*, edited by Richard Buxton, 13–37. Oxford: Oxford University Press, 2000b.

Spencer, Patrick E. "The Unity of Luke-Acts: A Four-Bolted Hermeneutical Hinge." *CBR* 5 (2007): 341–66.

Stalder, K. "Der Heilige Geist in der lukanischen Ekklesiologie." *US* 30 (1975): 287–93.

Stanton, Graham N. "Jesus of Nazareth: A Magician and a False Prophet Who Deceived God's People?" In *Jesus of Nazareth: Lord and Christ: Essays on the Historical Jesus and New Testament Christology*, edited by Joel B. Green, and Max Turner, 164–80. Grand Rapids: Eerdmans, 1994.

Stenschke, Christoph W. "The Need for Salvation." In *Witness to the Gospel: The Theology of Acts*, edited by I. Howard Marshall, and David Peterson, 125–44. Grand Rapids: Eerdmans, 1998.

Stenschke, Christoph W. *Luke's Portrait of Gentiles Prior to Their Coming to Faith*. WUNT 2/108. Tübingen: Mohr Siebeck, 1999.

Sterling, Greg. "*Mors philosophi*: The Death of Jesus in Luke." *HTR* 94 (2001): 383–402.

Stott, John R. W. *The Spirit, the Church, and the World: The Message of Acts*. Downers Grove, IL: InterVarsity Press, 1990.

Strahan, Joshua Marshall. *The Limits of a Text: Luke 23:34a as a Case Study in Theological Interpretation*. JTISup 5. Winona Lake, IN: Eisenbrauns, 2012.
Strathmann, Hermann. "λατρεύω, λατρεία." *TDNT* 4 (1967): 58–65.
Strauss, Mark L. *The Davidic Messiah in Luke-Acts: The Promise and Its Fulfillment in Lukan Christology*. JSNTSup 110. Sheffield: Sheffield Academic Press, 1995.
Strobel, August. "Die Ausrufung des Jobeljahrs in der Nazarethpredigt Jesu: Zur apokalyptischen Tradition Lc 4,16–30." In *Jesus in Nazareth*, edited by Walther Eltester, 38–50. BZNW 40. Berlin: de Gruyter, 1972.
Stronstad, Roger. *The Charismatic Theology of St. Luke: Trajectories from the Old Testament to Luke-Acts*, 2nd ed. Grand Rapids: Baker Academic, 2012.
Swartley, Willard M. "Politics and Peace (Eirēnē) in Luke's Gospel." In *Political Issues in Luke-Acts*, edited by Richard J. Cassidy, and Philip J. Scharper, 18–37. Maryknoll, NY: Orbis Books, 1983.
Sweetland, Dennis M. *Our Journey with Jesus: Discipleship according to Luke-Acts*. Collegeville, MN: Liturgical Press, 1990.
Sweetland, Dennis M. "The Journey of Discipleship in Luke." *TBT* 41 (2003): 277–82.
Sylva, Dennis D., ed. *Reimaging the Death of the Lukan Jesus*. BBB 73. Frankfurt am Main: Anton Hain, 1990.
Tacitus. *The Histories and The Annals*. Translated by Clifford H. Moore, and John Jackson. 4 vols. LCL. Cambridge, MA: Harvard University Press, 1937.
Taeger, Jens-W. *Der Mensch und sein Heil: Studien zum Bild des Menschen und zur Sicht der Bekehrung bei Lukas*. SNT 14. Gütersloh: Gütersloher Verlagshaus Mohn, 1982.
Taeger, Jens-W. "Paulus und Lukas über den Menschen." *ZNW* 71 (1990): 96–108.
Tajra, Harry W. *The Trial of St. Paul: A Juridical Exegesis of the Second Half of the Acts of the Apostles*. WUNT 2/35. Tübingen: Mohr Siebeck, 1989.
Talbert, Charles H. *Luke and the Gnostics: An Examination of Lucan Purpose*. Nashville: Abingdon, 1966.
Talbert, Charles H. *Literary Patterns, Theological Themes, and the Genre of Luke-Acts*. SBLMS 20. Missoula, MT: Scholars Press, 1974.
Talbert, Charles H. *Reading Acts: A Literary and Theological Commentary on the Acts of the Apostles*. New York: Crossroad, 1997.
Tannehill, Robert C. "Israel in Luke-Acts: A Tragic Story." *JBL* 104 (1984): 69–85.
Tannehill, Robert C. *The Narrative Unity of Luke-Acts: A Literary Interpretation*. 2 vols. Philadelphia: Fortress, 1986.
Tannehill, Robert C. "Rejection by Jews and Turning to Gentiles: The Pattern of Paul's Mission in Acts." In *Luke-Acts and the Jewish People: Eight Critical Perspectives*, edited by Joseph B. Tyson, 83–101. Minneapolis: Augsburg, 1988.
Tanner, Kathryn. *Christ the Key*. Cambridge: Cambridge University Press, 2010.
Taylor, Charles. *Modern Social Imaginaries*. Durham, NC: Duke University Press, 2004.
Taylor, Charles. *A Secular Age*. Cambridge, MA: Belknap, 2007.
Thomas, Derek W. H. *Acts*. REC. Phillipsburg, NJ: P&R, 2011.
Tiede, David L. *Prophecy and History in Luke-Acts*. Philadelphia: Fortress, 1980.
Tiede, David L. "The Exaltation of Jesus and the Restoration of Israel in Acts 1." *HTR* 79 (1986): 278–86.
Tiede, David L. "'Glory to Thy People Israel': Luke-Acts and the Jews." In *Luke-Acts and the Jewish People: Eight Critical Perspectives*, edited by Joseph B. Tyson, 21–34. Minneapolis: Augsburg, 1988a.
Tiede, David L. *Luke*. ACNT. Minneapolis: Augsburg, 1988b.
Tripolitis, Antonía. *Religions of the Hellenistic-Roman Age*. Grand Rapids: Eerdmans, 2002.

Trocmé, André. *Jesus and the Nonviolent Revolution*. Scottdale, PA: Herald, 1998.
Trompf, G. W. *The Idea of Historical Recurrence in Western Thought: From Antiquity to Reformation*. Berkeley: University of California Press, 1979.
Turner, Max. *Power from on High: The Spirit in Israel's Restoration and Witness in Luke-Acts*. JPTSup 9. Sheffield: Sheffield Academic Press, 1996.
Turner, Max. "The Spirit and Salvation in Luke-Acts." In *The Holy Spirit and Christian Origins*, edited by Graham N. Stanton, Bruce W. Longenecker, and Stephen C. Barton, 103–16. Grand Rapids: Eerdmans, 2004.
Tyson, Joseph B. *The Death of Jesus in Luke-Acts*. Columbia: University of South Carolina Press, 1986.
Uehlinger, Christoph. *Weltreich und "eine Rede": Eine neue Deutung der sogenannten Turmbauerzählung (Gen 11,1–9)*. OBO 101. Göttingen: Vandenhoeck & Ruprecht, 1990.
Vaux, Roland de. *Ancient Israel: Its Life and Institutions*. Grand Rapids: Eerdmans, 1961.
Vielhauer, Phillip. "Das Benedictus des Zacharias (Lk 1,68–79)." In *Aufsätze zum Neuen Testament*, 28–46. TBü 31. Munich: Kaiser, 1965.
Vielhauer, Phillip. "On the 'Paulinism' of Acts." In *Studies in Luke-Acts: Essays Presented in Honor of Paul Schubert*, edited by Leander E. Keck, and J. Louis Martyn, 33–50. Nashville: Abingdon, 1966.
Vinson, Richard B. "The Minas Touch: Anti-Kingship Rhetoric in the Gospel of Luke." *PRSt* 35 (2008): 69–86.
Wainwright, Arthur W. "Luke and the Restoration of the Kingdom to Israel." *ExpTim* 89 (1977): 76–9.
Walaskay, Paul. *"And So We Came to Rome": The Political Perspective of St. Luke*. SNTSMS 49. Cambridge: Cambridge University Press, 1983.
Wall, Robert W. "The Acts of the Apostles in Canonical Context." In *The New Testament as Canon: A Reader in Canonical Criticism*, edited by Robert W. Wall, and Eugene M. Lemcio, 110–28. JSNTSup 76. Sheffield: JSOT Press, 1992.
Wall, Robert W. "The Function of LXX Habakkuk 1:5 in the Book of Acts." *BBR* 10 (2000): 247–58.
Wall, Robert W. *"Acts of the Apostles: Introduction, Commentary, and Reflections."* In *Acts, Introduction to Epistolary Literature, Romans, 1 Corinthians*. NIB 10, 1–368. Nashville: Abingdon, 2002.
Wallace, Daniel B. *Greek Grammar beyond the Basics: An Exegetical Syntax of the New Testament*. Grand Rapids: Zondervan, 1996.
Walters, Patricia. *The Assumed Authorial Unity of Luke and Acts: A Reassessment of the Evidence*. SNTSMS 145. Cambridge: Cambridge University Press, 2009.
Walton, Steve. "The State They Were In: Luke's View of the Roman Empire." In *Rome in the Bible and the Early Church*, edited by Peter Oakes, 1–41. Carlisle: Paternoster, 2002.
Walton, Steve. "A Tale of Two Perspectives? The Place of the Temple in Acts." In *Heaven on Earth*, edited by T. Desmond Alexander, and Simon J. Gathercole, 135–50. Carlisle: Paternoster, 2004.
Walton, Steve. "'The Heavens Opened': Cosmological and Theological Transformation in Luke and Acts." In *Cosmology and New Testament Theology*, edited by Jonathan T. Pennington, and Sean M. McDonough, 60–73. LNTS 355. London: T&T Clark, 2008a.
Walton, Steve. "Primitive Communism in Acts? Does Acts Present the Community of Goods (2:44–45; 4:32–35) as Mistaken?" *EvQ* 80 (2008b): 99–111.
Walton, Steve. "Ascension." In *Dictionary of Jesus and the Gospels*, 2nd ed., edited by Joel B. Green, Jeannine K. Brown, and Nicholas Perrin, 59–61. Downers Grove, IL: InterVarsity Press, 2013.

Walton, Steve. "Jesus, Present and/or Absent? The Presence and Presentation of Jesus as a Character in the Book of Acts." In *Characters and Characterization in Luke-Acts*, edited by Frank E. Dicken, and Julia A. Snyder, 123–40. LNTS 548. London: Bloomsbury T&T Clark, 2016a.

Walton, Steve. "Jesus's Ascension through Old Testament Narrative Traditions." In *Ascent into Heaven in Luke-Acts: New Explorations of Luke's Narrative Hinge*, edited by David K. Bryan, and David W. Pao, 29–40. Minneapolis: Fortress, 2016b.

Wanke, Daniel. *Das Kreuz Christi bei Irenäus von Lyon*. BZNW 99. Berlin: de Gruyter, 2000.

Wasserberg, Günter. *Aus Israels Mitte—Heil für die Welt: Eine narrative-exegetische Studie zur Theologie des Lukas*. BZNW 92. Berlin: de Gruyter, 1998.

Watson, Francis. "Roman Faith and Christian Faith." *NTS* 64 (2018): 243–7.

Webb, Robert L. *John the Baptizer: A Socio-Historical Study*. JSNTSup 62. Sheffield: JSOT Press, 1991.

Weinfeld, Moshe. *Social Justice in Ancient Israel and in the Ancient Near East*. Minneapolis: Fortress, 1995.

Weinstock, Stefan. "The Geographical Catalogue in Acts II, 9–11." *JRS* 38 (1948): 43–6.

Weinstock, Stefan. *Divus Julius*. Oxford: Clarendon, 1971.

Weiser, Alfons. *Die Apostelgeschichte*. 2 vols. ÖTK 5. Gütersloh: Gütersloh Verlaghaus, 1985.

Weiser, Alfons. "'Reich Gottes' in der Apostelgeschichte." In *Der Treue Gottes Trauen: Beiträge zum Werk des Lukas: Für Gerhard Schneider*, edited by Claus Bussmann, and Walter Radl, 127–35. Freiberg: Herder, 1991.

Weiss, Johannes. *Über die Absicht und den literarischen Charakter der Apostelgeschichte*. Göttingen: Vandenhoeck & Ruprecht, 1897.

Wendt, Hans Hinrich. *Die Apostelgeschichte*. KEK 5. Göttingen: Vandenhoeck & Ruprecht, 1913.

Wenell, Karen J. "Kingdom, Not Kingly Rule: Assessing the Kingdom of God as Sacred Space." *BibInt* 25 (2017): 206–33.

Wengst, Klaus. *Pax Romana and the Peace of Jesus Christ*. Philadelphia: Fortress, 1987.

Wenham, Gordon J. *The Book of Leviticus*. NICOT. Grand Rapids: Eerdmans, 1979.

Wenk, Matthias. *Community-Forming Power: The Socio-Ethical Role of the Spirit in Luke-Acts*. JPTSup 19. Sheffield: Sheffield Academic Press, 2000.

Wenkel, David H. "Jesus at Age 30: Further Evidence for Luke's Portrait of a Priestly Jesus?" *BTB* 44 (2014): 195–201.

Westermann, Claus. *Isaiah 40–66*. OTL. Philadelphia: Westminster, 1969.

Wilckens, Ulrich. *Die Missionsreden der Apostelgeschichte: Form- und Traditionsgeschichtliche Untersuchungen*. Neukirchen: Neukirchen Verlag, 1961.

Williams, David J. *Acts*. NIBCNT. Peabody, MA: Hendrickson, 1995.

Williams, Delores S. *Sisters in the Wilderness: The Challenge of Womanist God-Talk*. Maryknoll, NY: Orbis Books, 1993.

Wilson, Benjamin R. *The Saving Cross of the Suffering Christ*. BZNW 223. Berlin: de Gruyter, 2016a.

Wilson, Sarah Hinlicky. "Water Baptism and Spirit Baptism in Luke-Acts: Another Reading of the Evidence." *Pneuma* 38 (2016b): 476–501.

Wilson, S. G. "Lukan Eschatology." *NTS* 16 (1970): 330–47.

Winkler, Lorenz. *Salus: Vom Staatskult zur politischen Idee: Eine archäologische Untersuchung*. AG 4. Heidelberg: Archäologie und Geschichte, 1995.

Winter, Paul. "Magnificat and Benedictus—Maccabaean Psalms?" *BJRL* 37 (1954–5): 328–47.
Witherington, Ben., III. *The Acts of the Apostles: A Socio-Rhetorical Commentary*. Grand Rapids: Eerdmans, 1998.
Witherington, Ben., III. *New Testament Rhetoric: An Introductory Guide to the Art of Persuasion in and of the New Testament*. Eugene, OR: Cascade, 2009.
Wolter, Michael. "'Reich Gottes' bei Lukas." *NTS* 41 (1995): 541–63.
Wolter, Michael. *Das Lukasevangelium*. HNT 5. Tübingen: Mohr Siebeck, 2008.
Wolter, Michael. "Jesu Tod und Sündenvergebung bei Lukas und Paulus." In *Reception of Paulinism in Acts: Réception du Paulinisme dans les Actes des Apôtres*, edited by Daniel Marguerat, 15–35. Leuven: Uitgeverij Peeters, 2009.
Wright, N. T. *The New Testament and the People of God*. Vol. 1 of *Christian Origins and the Question of God*. Minneapolis: Fortress, 1992.
Wright, N. T. *Jesus and the Victory of God*. Vol. 2 of *Christian Origins and the Question of God*. Minneapolis: Fortress, 1996.
Wright, N. T. *The Resurrection of the Son of God*. Vol. 3 of *Christian Origins and the Question of God*. Minneapolis: Fortress, 2003.
Yamazaki-Ransom, Kazuhiko. *The Roman Empire in Luke's Narrative*. LNTS 404. New York: T&T Clark, 2010.
Yao, Santos. "Dismantling Social Barriers through Table Fellowship: Acts 2:42–47." In *Mission in Acts: Ancient Narratives in Contemporary Context*, edited by Paul Hertig, and Robert R. Gallagher, 29–36. Maryknoll, NY: Orbis Books, 2004.
Yoder, John H. *The Politics of Jesus: Vicit Agnus Noster*, 2nd ed. Grand Rapids: Eerdmans, 1994.
Yoder, Joshua. *Representatives of Roman Rule: Roman Provincial Governors in Luke-Acts*. BZNW 209. Berlin: de Gruyter, 2014.
Zampaglione, Gerardo. *The Idea of Peace in Antiquity*. Notre Dame: University of Notre Dame Press, 1973.
Zanker, Paul. *The Power of Images in the Age of Augustus*. Ann Arbor: University of Michigan Press, 1988.
Zeller, Eduard. *Die Apostelgeschichte: Nach ihrem Inhalt und Ursprung kritisch untersucht*. Stuttgart: Carl Mäcken, 1854.
Zeller, Eduard. *Staat und Kirche: Vorlesungen an der Universität zu Berlin gehalten*. Leipzig: Fues's, 1873.
Zhang, Wenxi. *Paul among Jews: A Study of the Meaning and Significance of Paul's Inaugural Sermon in the Synagogue of Antioch in Pisidia (Acts 13:16–41) for His Missionary Work among the Jews*. Eugene, OR: Wipf & Stock, 2011.
Ziccardi, Constantonio Antonio. *The Relationship of Jesus and the Kingdom of God according to Luke-Acts*. TGST 165. Rome: Gregorian University Press, 2008.
Zimmerli, Walther. "Das 'Gnadenjahr des Herrn.'" In *Archäologie und Altes Testament*, edited by Arnulf Kuschke, and Ernst Kutsch, 321–32. Tübingen: Mohr Siebeck, 1970.
Zwiep, Arie W. *The Ascension of the Messiah in Lukan Christology*. NovTSup 87. Leiden: Brill, 1977.
Zwiep, Arie W. "Assumptus est in caelum—Rapture and Heavenly Exaltation in Early Judaism and Luke-Acts." In *Christ, the Spirit and the Community of God*, 38–67. WUNT 2/293. Tübingen: Mohr Siebeck, 2010.
Zwiep, Arie W. "Ascension Scholarship." In *Ascent into Heaven in Luke-Acts: New Explorations of Luke's Narrative Hinge*, edited by David K. Bryan, and David W. Pao, 7–26. Minneapolis: Fortress, 2016.

Index of Ancient Sources

HEBREW BIBLE/OLD TESTAMENT

Genesis
9:26	37	12:31	44
10	119	13:3	139
11:1–9	118–19	13:9	139
11:30	137	13:14	139
14:18–20	75	13:16	139
15:13	138	13:19	38
17:14	154	13:21	114
17:15–16	137	14:24	114
18:11	57	14:30	42
22:2	76	15:13	39, 73
22:16–18	142	16:1–3	140
49:10	41	16:4	66
		17:1–7	140
Exodus		17:2	66
2:24	43	17:32	140
3:2–3	114	19:19	114
3:12	44	20:6	43
3:16	38	20:18	114
4:23	44	21:30	39
4:31	38	22:24	84
5:23	42	23:6	84
6:1	139	23:10–11	84
6:5	43	30:12	39
6:6	39, 42, 73, 139	32:11	139
7:3	122	32:34	38
7:9	122	34:7	43
7:16	44		
8:1	44	*Leviticus*	
8:20	44	4:20	87
9:1	44	4:26	87
9:13	44	4:31	87
10:3	44	4:35	87
10:7–8	44	5:10	87
10:11	44	5:13	87
10:24	44	5:16	87
10:26	44	5:18	87
11:9–10	122	5:26	87
12:21	59	10:9	56
12:27	42	19:22	87
		23:26–32	73
		23:42	117
		23:43	117

25–6	73	*Deuteronomy*	
25	70–1	1:31	139
25:1–7	70, 73	4:24	114
25:1	73	4:33	114
25:8–55	70–1	4:34	122, 139
25:8–9	70	4:36	114
25:8	69, 74	4:37	139
25:9	74, 75	5:10	43
25:10	70, 72, 73	5:15	139
25:13	73, 74	5:22–7	114
25:24	39	6:22	122
25:25–6	72	7:8	39
25:26	39	7:9	43
25:30	72	7:12	43
25:33	72	7:19	122
25:35–8	74	8:2	66
25:36	74	9:5	43
25:38	70	9:26	39, 139
25:39–55	74	9:29	139
25:39	74	10:12	44
25:42	70, 122	10:15	139
25:43	74	11:2–7	120
25:46	74	11:3	122
25:48–9	72	13	146
25:51–2	39	13:1–11	107, 147
25:53	74	13:2–3	122
25:54	72	13:5 (13:6 LXX)	39
25:55	70, 122	15:1–18	70
26:2	73	15:4	84
26:15	154	15:15	39
26:17	42	18:16–18	114
26:27–39	73	21:8	39
26:34–5	73	21:22–3	146–7, 153, 156
26:40–5	73		
26:44	154	21:23	147
26:46	73	23:2	116
27:31	39	24:18	39
		26:8	122
Numbers		28:46	122
3:49	39	28:49	112
6:3	56	29:2	122
14:11	140, 143	29:18	150
14:19	43	30:17	42, 43
14:32–4	140	31:16	154
15:25	87	31:20	154
15:28	87	32:41	42, 43
15:31	154	32:43	42
24:17	59	33:2	59
25:6–11	155	34:11	122

Joshua
5:6	140
21:22	42
21:31	42
24:14	44

Judges
2:1	154
8:34	42

1 Samuel
1:5	57
1:7	57
1:9	57
1:11	57
1:15	57
1:19–20	57
1:22	57
1:24	57
1:28	57
2:1–10	137
2:1	40
2:5	57
2:10	40
2:18	57
2:25	57
2:27–36	57
3:1	58
7:17	57
8:7	140, 142, 143
9:16	57, 76
10:1	76
10:8	57
10:19	140, 142, 143
11:14–15	57
13:8–9	57
13:14	141
15:10–35	141
15:10–31	88
16:1–13	57
16:1	141
16:13	76
25:32	37
31:9	78, 148

2 Samuel
2:7	76
4:10	78, 148
5:17	76
7:4–17	141
7:6	141
7:8–16	40
7:11–16	123
7:11	141
7:12–17	41
7:12	141, 148
7:13–16	141
7:16	141, 142
7:23	39
12:7	42, 76
12:13	88–9
14:16	42
18:19	78, 148
18:20	78, 148
18:31	78, 148
19:10	42, 76
19:15	89
22:3	40
22:9–16	114
22:18	42, 43
22:41	42, 43
22:44	42
22:49	42
22:50–1	141
23:1–2	76
23:2	77
23:5	40
24	46

1 Kings
1:34	76
1:42	78, 148
1:48	37
5:1	76
8:15	37
8:16	37
8:21	37
8:23–4	40
14:15–16	54
15:19	154
17–18	52
18:20–40	57
18:38	114
19:15	76
19:16	77

2 Kings
2:1–12	103
2:9–15	51
9:3	76

9:6	76	3:5	60
9:12	76	5:20	42
17:6	120		
17:21–3	54	*Psalms*	
18:11	120	2:1–2	146
18:32	42	2:7	76, 148
21:11–15	54	6:5	42
23:26–7	54	7:2	42
24:2–4	54	16:8–11	123
		16:10 (15:10 lxx)	149
1 Chronicles		17:18	42
10:9	78, 148	17:20	42
16:15–18	37	17:44	42
16:19–22	37	17:49	42
16:23	37	18:2	40
16:36	37	18:8	114
17:21	39	21:8 (20:9 lxx)	42, 43
29:10	37	22:4 (21:5 lxx)	42
		22:8 (21:9 lxx)	42
2 Chronicles		23:4 (22:4 lxx)	60
2:12 (2:11 lxx)	37	25:6 (24:6 lxx)	58
6:4	37	25:7	43
6:5	37	27:1	59
6:14	43	28:8 (27:8 lxx)	44
13:5	40	29:7 (28:7 lxx)	114
16:3	154	30:16	42
21:7	40	33:5	42
		34:17 (33:18 lxx)	42
		34:19 (33:20 lxx)	42
Ezra		36:9	59
3:11	43	37:20	42
8:31	42	37:40 (36:40 lxx)	42
9:6–7	54	40:10 (39:11 lxx)	78
9:8	40	40:11 (39:12 lxx)	58
9:13	54	41:1 (40:2 lxx)	42
9:14	154	41:11–12	37
		41:13 (40:14 lxx)	37
Nehemiah		44:10 (43:11 lxx)	42
1:5	43	44:19 (43:20 lxx)	60
1:10	39	51:1 (50:3 lxx)	58
9:16–31	54	53:9	42
9:28	42	54:13	42
9:32	43	55:14	42
9:36–7	40	59:5 (58:6 lxx)	38
		62:7 (61:8 lxx)	44
Esther		68:1 (67:2 lxx)	42, 43
10:3	122	68:5	42
		68:11 (67:12 lxx)	78, 148
Job		69:16 (68:17 lxx)	58
1:11–12	48	72:12–14	37
2:5–6	48		

72:12 (71:12 LXX)	42	106:47	37
72:18 (71:18 LXX)	37	106:48 (105:48 LXX)	37
74:2 (73:2 LXX)	39	107:10 (106:10 LXX)	60
75:4–5	40	107:14 (106:14 LXX)	60
75:10	40	108:8	36
77:16 (76:16 LXX)	39	109:13–15	54
78:43 (77:43 LXX)	122	110:1	38, 103, 123
79:8–10	54		
80 (79 LXX)	38	110:4	75
80:3	38	111:9 (110:9 LXX)	39
80:4	38	112:9	40
80:8–19	38	118:27	59
80:8	38	118:126 (119:126 LXX)	154
80:15 (79:15 LXX)	38	132:11	123
80:18	38	132:17 (131:17 LXX)	40, 59
80:20	38	134:6–7	112
81:6	36	135:9 (134:9 LXX)	122
81:7 (80:8 LXX)	42	148:14	40
83:2 (82:3 LXX)	42		
85:9	36	*Proverbs*	
86:10 (85:10 LXX)	89	6:6–11	84
88:6 (87:7 LXX)	60	6:35	39
88:24	42	13:8	39
89:3–4	40	21:17	84
89:3	36	23:21	84
89:17	40		
89:20	36, 141	*Isaiah*	
89:24	40	1:14	54
89:32 (88:33 LXX)	38	1:17	42
91:14 (90:14 LXX)	42	1:24	42
95:10	140	2:1–4	111
96:2 (95:2 LXX)	78	2:3–4	62
97:10 (96:10 LXX)	42	2:5–11	60
98:2–3 (97:2–3 LXX)	44	2:5	59
98:2 (97:2 LXX)	54	2:6	54
98:3	43	3:13–15	42
103:4 (102:4 LXX)	58	4:3–5	103
105:27 (104:27 LXX)	122	5:7–10	42
106 (105 LXX)	38	5:14	42
106:4 (105:4 LXX)	37, 38, 44	5:20	59
106:5 (105:5 LXX)	38	6:9–10	44, 159
106:6	54	8:8	122
106:7–12	37	8:9	111, 112
106:8–11	37	9	60
106:10 (105:10 LXX)	38, 39, 42	9:2 (9:1 LXX)	60
106:21	37	9:4 (9:3 LXX)	60
106:30	155	9:5 (9:4 LXX)	60
106:42 (105:42 LXX)	42	9:6–7 (9:5–6 LXX)	37, 41, 60
106:43 (105:43 LXX)	37, 42	9:7	41, 62

Reference	Page(s)
9:11	59
10:1–3	38
10:2	42
11:1–16	111, 142
11:1	59, 141
11:2	41
11:4–5	84
11:4	41
11:6–10	62
11:6–9	41
11:10–16	40
11:10	41
11:11	59, 120
11:14	59
14:4	92
14:12	92
14:21–2	112
16:5	41
20:3	122
23:17	38
24:21–3	38
24:22	38
24:23	111
25:6–10	41
25:6–8	131
26:1	44
27:13	111
29:6	38
32:9–20	111, 142
32:15	111
33:20–2	111
33:20	44
35:1–2	66
35:4	38
40–66	72
40:1–2	44, 143
40:2	38, 54, 72, 73
40:3–5	44, 52, 58, 66, 122
40:3	52
40:4	52
40:5	44, 121
40:9–11	111
40:9	78
41:14	72
42:1–9	111, 142
42:1	60, 76
42:4	60
42:7	60, 90
42:18	90
42:24	73
43:1–2	72
43:1	38, 39, 72
43:8	90
43:14–21	72
43:14	39, 72
43:25	54
44:1–5	111, 142
44:1	76
44:6	42, 72
44:21–2	54, 56
44:22–4	72
44:22–3	39
44:22	54, 73
44:23	38
44:28	141
45:1	141
47:1	60
47:4	42, 72
48:16	111, 142
48:17	42, 72
48:20–2	72
48:20	42, 72, 111, 112
49:1–6	158
49:3	111, 112, 156
49:5–6	111, 156
49:6	4, 60, 61, 110–11, 112, 122, 156–8
49:7	42, 72
49:8–13	94
49:8–9	61
49:8	73, 156
49:9–10	60
49:25	42
49:26	42, 72
50:1	73
51:4–5	60
51:5–6	44
51:5	60
51:8	44
51:9–11	72
51:10	72
52:1–10	111
52:3–6	72
52:3	39, 72
52:7–10	62, 148
52:7	62, 75, 78
52:9	42, 62, 72
52:10	62
52:13–53:12	15
53:7–8	15

53:11–12	15	62:6–7	111
53:12	15, 16	62:11	111, 112
54:5	42, 72	62:12	72
54:8	42, 43, 72	63:1	44
54:10	43	63:4	39
54:11	84	63:7–14	72
55:1–5	28, 41, 150–1	63:9	39, 72
55:3–5	41	63:10	140
55:3	41, 149–50	63:15–19	59
55:5	151	63:15	58
55:7	54	63:16	42, 72
56:1–58:14	68	66:15	114
56:1–8	68	66:20	111
56:1	44, 74		
56:3–5	116	*Jeremiah*	
57:14–58:14	73	1:1	57
58:2	74	2:9	54
58:3	62, 73, 74	2:10–11	120
58:4	74	3:17	111
58:5	68, 73	5:1	87
58:6–14	86	5:9	38
58:6–9	73	5:29	38
58:6	65, 68, 73, 74, 76, 84, 85–6	6:22	112
		9:9 (9:8 LXX)	38
58:7–8	86	10:12	112
58:7	68, 74	11:22	38
58:9	74	13:16	60
58:10	60, 74	14:20	54
58:13–14	62, 68	14:21	154
58:13	74	15:4	54
59:6	56, 62	15:15	38
59:8–9	60	16:10–13	54
59:8	62	16:15	56
59:9–15	60	16:18	72
59:9	60	16:19	112
59:20	42, 72	17:25–6	111
60:1–7	111	22:3–4	41
60:1–3	60	23:3	56
60:6	78	23:5–6	41, 59
60:10	73	23:5	59
60:16	72	23:6	41
60:18	44	24:6	56
61:1–11	111, 142	27:8 (34:8 LXX)	38
61:1–2	65, 68, 74, 75, 76, 86, 103	29:10 (36:10 LXX)	38, 56
		29:32 (36:32 LXX)	38
61:1	68, 69, 72, 78, 85, 90, 148	30:8–9	41
		30:20 (37:20 LXX)	38
61:2	68, 73	31:11	39
61:7	72	31:31–4	114–15

32:27	56	*Daniel*	
32:41 (39:41 LXX)	38	3:34	154
33:14–15	41	5:31	120
33:15–16	41	7:2	104
33:17	41	7:4	104
33:20–1	41	7:6	104
34:8–22	70	7:7	104
34:8	72, 73	7:9	104
34:15	72	7:11	104
34:17	72	7:13	104
36:31 (43:31 LXX)	38	8:16	37
39:20–1	122	9	37–8, 39, 74, 75
44:13 (51:13 LXX)	38	9:3–20	74
44:29 (51:29 LXX)	38	9:4–16	38
48:25	40	9:4	43
50:17–20	111	9:15	38
50:19	56	9:16	54
		9:17–19	38
Lamentations		9:18	54
4:22	38, 52, 54	9:20–7	38, 138
5:7	54	9:20	38
		9:21	37
Ezekiel		9:24–7	38, 54, 74, 76
1:3	57	9:24	38, 74, 90
1:13	114	9:26–7	38
1:27	114	9:26	38, 41
5:5	117	9:27	38
11:17–19	111, 142	11:31	38
13:21	42	12:11	38
13:23	42		
16:7	59	*Hosea*	
17:10	59	2:14–23	66
18:30–2	111, 142	2:21	58
20:33–44	66	3:5	41
29:21	40	4:14	38
34:22–4	41	6:1	56
34:22	40	11:11	56
34:23–5	41		
36:22–32	114–15	*Joel*	
36:24–32	111, 142	2:2–11	121
36:26	114	2:20	121
37:1–14	111, 142	2:28–32 (3:1–5 LXX)	111, 114–15, 121–3, 142
37:23	42	2:28 (3:1 LXX)	111, 121
37:24–5	41	2:29 (3:2 LXX)	121, 122
37:24	40	2:30 (3:3 LXX)	122
38:12	117	2:32	111
39:27	56		
46:17	69, 72		

Amos
5:25	140
9:11–12	41, 158

Jonah
2:9	44

Micah
4:2	111
4:10	39, 42
5:4–5	41
5:6 (5:5 LXX)	42
6:4	39
7:8	60
7:20	43

Nahum
1:15 (2:1 LXX)	78

Habakkuk
1:2–4	154–5
1:4	154
1:5	145–6, 154–5, 158
1:6–11	154

Zephaniah
2:7	38
3:9	118
3:14–20	111

Zechariah
1:16–17	111
3:1	48
3:8	59
6:12	59
7:9	58
8:1–8	111
9:9–13	111
10:8	39
11:10–11	154

Malachi
2:8	57
3:1	37, 52, 57, 143
3:3–4	57
3:4	57
3:5	52
4:5–6	37, 52, 57

DEUTEROCANONICAL WORKS

Tobit
3:11	37
13	39
13:18	37
14:5	39

Wisdom of Solomon
2:18	42
9:3	43

Sirach
2:14	38
5:6	58, 59
17:9	120
18:4	120
25:2	84
35:18	38
36:1–22	120
36:2–5	120
36:7	120
36:13	119
40:28	84
41:1–4	84
42:21	120
45:23	155
45:25	40
46:11–20	141
46:13–15	41
48:1–15	52
48:10	37, 52

Baruch
2:11	122
4:18	43
4:21	43

1 Maccabees
1:54	38
2:24–6	155
2:54	155
3:9	112
4:10	43
4:11	39
6:7	38
10:24	134
12:15	42

2 Maccabees

2:7	39
2:21	11
4:11	12
4:13	11, 12
7:37	89
8:1	11
8:17	12
13:14	12
14:38	11
15:11	134

1 Esdras

8:60	42

OLD TESTAMENT PSEUDEPIGRAPHA

Ascension of Isaiah

2.3–4	48

Assumption of Moses

3	39

1 Enoch

91.12–17	74
93	74

Joseph and Aseneth

8.9	59, 61
15.12	61

Jubilees

1.7–18	39
6.15–18	114
8.12–21	117

Letter of Aristeas

92–5	87
123.4	100
132	89

Liber antiquitatum biblicarum

30.7	43

3 Maccabees

6.10	42
6.39	42
7.22	120

4 Maccabees

3.20	12
4.26	11
8.7	12
17.9	12
18.12	155

Martyrdom of Isaiah

2.4	75

Psalms of Solomon

1.4	112
2.37	37
8.15	112
17–18	41
17.3	41
17.4	41
17.5–10	41
17.21–5	41, 42
17.26	41
17.32	41
18.8	41

Sibylline Oracles

3.760	89

Testament of Judah

23.5	38
24.1	59
25.3	118

Testament of Levi

4.2–4	59
4.3	38
16–17	39
18.2–4	59
19.1	59

Testament of Zebulun

3	58
8.2	58
8.6	58

NEW TESTAMENT

Matthew

2:2	59
2:9	59
3:1–6	52

3:2	57	*Luke*	
3:6	57	1–2	18, 25, 34–5, 36
3:8	57	1	35
3:11	55, 57	1:5–23	117
4:23	78	1:5–7	137
9:1–8	86	1:5	37, 56
9:35	78	1:6	152
11:5	78, 148	1:7	57
11:10	52	1:8–23	56, 57
11:14	52	1:8–20	38
13:24–30	81	1:8–9	37
13:47–50	81	1:13–17	51
13:54–8	67	1:14	51, 130
14:3–5	58	1:15	56, 57
15:31	37	1:16–17	37, 56
16:19	87	1:16	52, 157
17:2	52	1:17	41, 51, 52, 137, 152
18:18	87	1:19	37, 78, 148
20:28	15, 27	1:23	44
22:17	46	1:24–5	57
22:21	46	1:26	37
24:14–15	38	1:27	35, 36, 37, 41, 141
24:14	48, 78	1:30–3	2
24:24	122	1:32–3	36, 37, 56, 141
26:13	78	1:32	35, 41, 48, 76, 92, 103, 144
27:43	42	1:33	41, 79
		1:35	92, 103
Mark		1:41–2	77
1:1–4	52	1:41	113
1:1	78	1:44	130
1:4	55	1:46–55	2, 36, 37, 82, 137
1:5	57	1:50	41, 43
1:14–15	93	1:51–3	85
1:14	78	1:52–3	41, 52, 103
1:15	78, 82	1:53–4	96
2:1–12	86	1:54–5	37, 143
6:1–6	67	1:54	41, 43, 157
6:17–19	58	1:55	142
8:35	78	1:58	41, 43
9:13	52	1:64	36
10:29	78	1:66	36
10:45	15, 27	1:67–79	2, 36, 46
12:14	46	1:67	77, 113
12:16–17	46	1:68–79	31–2, 33–64, 82, 120, 163
13:10	78	1:68–75	34, 36, 37–45, 51, 56, 58, 143
13:14	38		
13:22	122	1:68–70	37–42
14:9	78		
16:15	78		

1:68–9	36	2:30	91
1:68	39, 40, 41, 54, 59, 107, 157	2:31	158
		2:32	4, 41, 59, 61, 111, 156, 157, 158
1:69	28, 35, 36, 40, 41, 48, 56, 59, 60, 76, 141, 149	2:34–5	99, 157
		2:34	157
		2:36–8	148
1:70	42	2:38	40, 53
1:71–5	37, 42–4, 127	2:41–51	57
1:71	2, 28, 38, 41, 42, 54, 72, 131	2:41	114
		2:49	92, 108, 142, 165
1:72	41, 43, 58	3:1–2	57, 66
1:73	42, 43, 142	3:1	46, 135
1:74–5	43, 61, 63, 72	3:2	57, 66
1:74	2, 28, 38, 42, 54, 72, 131	3:3	52, 53, 54, 55, 56, 71, 86, 89, 90, 108, 126–7, 143
1:75	41, 54, 60, 152		
1:76–9	34, 36, 45, 51–63		
1:76–7	151	3:4–6	44, 52, 58, 103, 121, 122
1:76	36, 51–2, 103, 143		
1:77	34, 38, 41, 42, 43, 51, 52–6, 58, 86, 89, 90, 108	3:4	66
		3:5	52, 58
		3:6	41, 91, 157
1:78–9	54, 97	3:7–18	52
1:78	41, 43, 59	3:7–14	71
1:79	41, 54, 59–63, 74, 164	3:7–9	94
1:80	66, 157	3:8–9	56
2:1–20	143	3:9	68
2:1–7	35, 82	3:11	131
2:1–4	36	3:12	52
2:1–2	36, 45, 46, 48, 49, 62	3:14	52
2:1	46, 47, 48, 135	3:15–17	56
2:4	35, 36, 56, 141	3:16	55
2:8–20	82	3:18	78, 148
2:8–14	46	3:19–20	58
2:10–14	36	3:19	43
2:10–12	2	3:21–2	66, 76, 102
2:10 78, 2:11	148	3:22	41, 48, 76, 92, 102, 148
	35, 36, 41, 42, 46, 48, 49, 56, 76, 93, 104, 141, 143	3:31	41
		3:38	92
		4:1–13	28, 43, 50, 63, 66, 76, 93, 107, 134, 153, 164
2:13	36		
2:14	41, 62	4:1	41, 134
2:22–38	57	4:2	66
2:22	153	4:3	67, 92
2:25	36, 44, 102, 134, 148, 152, 156, 157	4:5–8	67, 164
		4:5–7	48, 61, 104, 134
2:26	36, 44, 141	4:5	48
2:29–31	36	4:6	48, 92, 93, 104
2:29	41, 62, 63	4:9–12	57

4:9	67, 92	5:2	86, 88–9
4:10–11	146	5:23–4	90
4:13	132, 164	5:24	86–7, 89
4:14–30	147	5:26	91, 93
4:14–15	67	5:27–39	130
4:14	41	5:27–8	52, 91
4:15	65, 67, 82	5:27	130
4:16–30	65, 96, 134	5:29–32	91
4:16–21	67, 75, 82, 164	5:29	130
4:16	67, 86, 134	5:30	130
4:17	67	5:32	152
4:18–21	122	6:3–5	141
4:18–19	31–2, 54, 65–97, 99, 108, 113, 164	6:6–11	86
		6:6	65
4:18	41, 48, 52, 55, 61, 67, 76, 78, 84, 90, 92, 148, 165	6:15	156
		6:18	92
		6:20–49	91
4:19	68	6:20–38	69
4:20	67	6:20–6	85
4:21	76, 80, 86, 93–6, 112, 121	6:20–3	84
		6:20	41, 79, 84, 164
4:22	67, 134	6:23	102
4:22–30	161	6:29–34	131
4:23–30	134	6:30	129
4:24	68, 77, 134	6:35	103, 114
4:25–7	77, 134, 137	6:36	92
4:25	157	6:37–8	92
4:27	157	6:39–49	91, 167
4:28–30	67, 99	6:39–42	91
4:31–41	86	6:42	86
4:31–5	93	6:46–9	91
4:33–7	65	7:1–17	137
4:33–6	92	7:6–9	22
4:34	93	7:9	91, 157
4:39	86, 130	7:11–17	41
4:41	92	7:11	52
4:42	67	7:13	41
4:43–4	67	7:16	41, 149
4:43	67, 78, 79, 108, 142, 148, 164, 165	7:21	92
		7:22–3	84
4:44	65	7:22	41, 78, 84, 148
5:8	103	7:24–7	66
5:11	86, 91	7:29	152
5:16	67	7:30	57, 142
5:17–26	86–90, 134	7:31	94
5:20–5	54, 55	7:34	14, 130
5:20–1	90	7:35	152
5:20	86, 88–9	7:36–50	86, 90, 130
5:21–4	106, 124	7:37	90

7:39	77, 90	10:9	81–2, 92, 93
7:41–3	90	10:11	81–2, 93
7:47–9	90, 106, 124	10:14–15	68
7:48–9	54, 55	10:14	94
7:48	90	10:17–24	92, 103, 104
7:49	103	10:17–20	92, 104
7:50	41, 62, 63, 90	10:17–19	43
7:55–6	103	10:18	92, 103–4
8:1	67, 78, 148	10:19	92, 105
8:2	92	10:21–4	92, 104
8:9–10	83	10:21–2	104
8:10	81–2, 91	10:21	102
8:12	92	10:22	89, 92, 108
8:26–39	92	10:25–37	131
8:28	92,103	10:25–8	153
8:33	41	10:25–7	131
8:35	103	10:29	152
8:48	41, 62, 63	10:30	86
8:51	86	10:37	43
9:6	78, 148	10:38–42	130
9:7–9	43	10:38	130
9:8	77	10:39	103
9:10–17	67, 91, 130	10:43–4	53
9:11	91	11:1–4	86
9:16	103	11:2–4	69, 85
9:17	53	11:2	79, 80
9:19	77	11:4	85, 90, 164
9:21–6	108	11:13	102
9:22	43, 108, 142, 149	11:14–26	92
9:23–4	91, 92	11:15–17	53
9:23	91	11:15	102
9:26–7	48	11:16	102
9:28–36	91	11:20	79, 81–3, 93
9:35	48, 92	11:21	62
9:37–43	92	11:32	68
9:38	41	11:33–6	61
9:43–5	80, 91	11:37–54	130
9:45	83, 91	11:37–44	126
9:46–8	80, 91	11:41	84, 129
9:49–50	80, 92	11:42	61
9:51–6	80	11:52	54, 57
9:51	67	12:10	86
9:54	102	12:12	77, 113
9:57	91	12:13–34	129
9:59	91	12:13–21	85
9:60	86	12:16–21	131
9:61	91	12:21	84
10:5–6	41, 62	12:23	84, 129
10:5	92	12:28	93

Reference	Pages
12:31	81
12:32	81
12:33	84, 102, 129, 131
12:35–50	94
12:38	130
12:39	86
12:51	41, 62
12:54–7	91
12:56	102
12:57	152
13:1	43, 107, 148
13:4	117
13:6–9	94
13:6–8	94
13:8	86
13:10–17	86
13:10	65
13:12	92
13:16	43, 86, 92, 106, 142
13:18–21	81
13:20–1	163
13:24–30	131
13:28–9	79, 80
13:28	68, 142
13:29–30	130
13:31	43, 108
13:32–3	93
13:33	108, 165
13:34–5	77
13:35	86
14:1–23	130
14:1–6	86
14:7–25	130
14:7–14	131
14:7–11	85
14:7–10	103
14:11	103
14:12–24	131
14:12–14	85
14:13	41, 84–5
14:14	152
14:15–24	84, 85, 131
14:15	91
14:21	41, 84–5
14:27	91, 92, 108
14:32	41, 62
14:33	84, 129
15	131
15:1–2	130
15:1	130
15:3–7	14
15:7	152
15:18	102, 103
15:21	102, 103
16:1–31	129
16:1–14	85
16:1–13	96, 131
16:8–9	61
16:8	61
16:9	96
16:15	152
16:16	67, 78, 79, 148
16:19–31	41, 85, 131
16:20	84
16:22	84
16:24–31	142
16:29–31	131
17:1–4	86
17:1–2	90
17:3–4	71, 90
17:4	56
17:15	103
17:20	79
17:21	81
17:22	81
17:25	94, 108, 142
17:26–33	131
17:29	102
17:34–5	86
18:9	152
18:10	57
18:13	102, 103
18:14	103, 152
18:16–17	84
18:16	86
18:18–22	131
18:22–5	81
18:22–3	85
18:22	41, 84, 91, 102, 129, 131
18:28–9	86
18:28	91
18:29–30	167
18:31–4	80, 91
18:34	83, 91
18:35–43	91
18:35–9	80
18:38–9	41

18:38	141	22:1–6	43
18:39	91	22:1–2	114
18:43	91	22:3	43, 67, 104, 107, 132, 134, 165
19:1–10	52, 85, 130		
19:5–7	130	22:7–38	130
19:5	77, 93, 142	22:9	80
19:8	84, 131	22:14–23	91
19:9	41, 77, 93, 142	22:16	79, 80
19:11–36	132	22:17	118
19:11–27	79–80, 112	22:18	79, 80
19:11	35, 79	22:19–20	15, 108, 168
19:18	41	22:20	38
19:27	124, 165	22:22–3	80
19:38	41, 62, 107	22:22	142
19:42–4	154	22:24–30	15, 80
19:42	41, 62, 63	22:24–7	80, 83, 91
19:43–4	41	22:26–32	107
19:43	2	22:28–30	148
19:44	41, 52, 86	22:29–30	79
19:45–21:6	57	22:30	157
19:45–8	52	22:31	104, 107, 165
19:45–6	38	22:32	56
19:47–8	43	22:34	93
20:1–19	57	22:37	15, 108, 142, 167
20:1	43, 78, 148	22:38	83
20:4–5	103	22:41	103
20:9–19	142	22:45	107
20:13–15	132	22:47	107
20:19–26	43	22:48	107
20:20–6	95–6, 146	22:52–3	43
20:20	152	22:53	43, 67, 104, 107, 132, 134, 165
20:22	46		
20:24–5	46	22:54	43
20:24	95	22:59	148
20:37	37	22:61	93
20:41–4	141	22:64	77
20:42	41	22:66–71	43, 107
20:45–21:4	118	22:69	41, 108
20:46	103	22:70	92
21:1–4	41	23:1–5	43, 146
21:3	84–5	23:2	46, 107, 153, 154
21:6	86, 154	23:4	107, 146, 154
21:9	142	23:5–6	148
21:12–19	26	23:6–12	43
21:20–4	38, 154	23:10	43
21:20	38, 41	23:11	107
21:26	48	23:13–25	43
21:28	40	23:13	43
21:31	79, 80	23:14–15	107, 146, 154

23:14	154	24:51	101
23:18–25	107	24:52	117
23:22–5	107	24:53	57
23:22	154		
23:34	54, 55, 86, 89, 105, 107, 108, 165	*John*	
		1:21	52
23:35–9	107	1:25	52
23:41	152, 154	1:45	145
23:42–3	80	3:28	52
23:43	93, 94	4:8	122
23:44–9	122	4:14	114
23:45	57, 117	5:44	89
23:46–7	107	7:37–9	114
23:47	105, 107, 146, 152, 154, 165	11:51	56
		12:31	48
23:49	148	20:22	114
23:50–3	147	20:23	87
23:50	152		
23:55	148	*Acts*	
24:1–53	83	1–2	32
24:6	148, 149	1:2	113
24:7	108, 142, 149	1:3–8	116
24:13–35	91, 130	1:3	26, 109, 116
24:16	91	1:4–8	110
24:19–21	99	1:4–5	110
24:19	77	1:4	117, 130, 142
24:20	43	1:5	111, 143
24:21	40, 157	1:6–8	26, 35, 158
24:25–7	145	1:6	109, 110, 116, 142, 157
24:26	108, 142		
24:27	91	1:7–8	110–3
24:28–35	130	1:7	132
24:29	142	1:8	4, 61, 77, 109, 111, 117–18, 134, 156, 157
24:30–1	91		
24:31–2	91	1:9–11	100, 101
24:31	91	1:10–11	101, 102, 109
24:34	149	1:11	148
24:35	91	1:13	156
24:36–53	130	1:15	100
24:36–43	130	1:16	77, 113, 142
24:36	41, 62	1:19	117
24:42	71	1:20	117
24:44–7	145	1:21	142
24:44	108, 142, 153	1:22	112, 143
24:45–8	157	2	31, 99–132
24:46	149	2:1–4	100–6, 116, 127
24:47	41, 52, 53, 55, 86, 90, 111, 151	2:2	100
		2:3	118
24:49	111	2:4	77, 113

2:5–13	116–21	2:42	91, 127
2:5	100, 101, 117, 120	2:43–7	127–8
2:7	148	2:43	122, 128
2:8	118	2:44–5	128–9
2:9–11	47, 48, 99, 118–20	2:44	128
2:9–10	120	2:45	118
2:9	117, 120	2:46–7	128
2:10	117	2:46	57, 128, 131
2:11	120	2:47	99, 127, 165
2:14–36	121–4	3:1–10	57, 134
2:14–21	121–3	3:2–3	84, 129
2:14	54, 117	3:10	84, 129
2:17–18	77, 113	3:11–16	26
2:17	112, 121–2, 161	3:12–26	77
2:19	122, 123	3:12	54, 137
2:20	122	3:13–15	108, 147
2:21	127, 158, 159	3:13	37, 100, 142
2:22–36	26, 121, 122–3	3:14–15	107
2:22–8	121, 137	3:14	152, 155
2:22–4	108	3:15	41, 112, 124, 149
2:22	54, 122, 123	3:17-19	146
2:23–4	132	3:17–18	145
2:23	121, 123, 124, 137, 142, 145, 146	3:17	26, 91, 145
		3:18	77
2:24	147, 149	3:19–26	157
2:25–36	41, 54, 135, 141	3:19–21	99–100
2:25–8	149	3:19	15, 16, 53, 56, 71, 90, 115
2:26	124		
2:29–36	121	3:20–1	94
2:29	54	3:20	77
2:30	123	3:21	80, 110, 132, 142, 168
2:32–3	112	3:22–4	54
2:32	149	3:22–3	77
2:33	41, 101, 109, 113, 123, 142	3:22	40, 115, 149
		3:24	57
2:34–5	108, 123	3:25–6	134
2:34	41, 103	3:25	43, 54, 142
2:36	91, 104, 123, 145, 157	3:26	56, 111, 134, 149
2:37–47	121, 124–31, 134	4:1–31	100
2:38–41	115	4:1–3	134
2:38–40	124–7, 159	4:1	57
2:38	15, 16, 52, 53, 55, 71, 86, 89, 90, 115, 123, 124–7, 142, 147, 151	4:4	128
		4:5–6	43
		4:7	127
2:39	54, 134, 142	4:8–11	118
2:40	94, 112, 127	4:8	113
2:41–7	122, 132	4:10	108, 124, 147, 149, 157
2:41	127		
2:42–7	127, 130	4:11	145

4:12	41, 100	5:36	66
4:16–21	118	5:37	46, 148
4:16	117, 122	5:38	86, 154
4:17–18	127	5:40–1	127
4:17	123	5:41	110
4:19	152	5:42	57, 78, 148
4:21	101	6:1–7	130
4:22	122	6:7	26
4:23	43	6:8–15	100, 134
4:24–8	146	6:8	122
4:24	102	6:9	117
4:25–7	131, 153	6:10	113
4:25–6	146	7:1	43
4:25	77, 113, 158	7:2–53	139, 153
4:26	104	7:2–47	120
4:27–8	145	7:4	117
4:27	43, 76, 146, 157, 158	7:6	138
4:28	142	7:7	142
4:29	41	7:8	43
4:30	122	7:9	155
4:31	77, 113, 127	7:17	142
4:32–7	127	7:23	138, 157
4:32–5	165	7:25	41
4:32	128, 129	7:26	62
4:34–5	118	7:32	37
5:3	43	7:35–43	140
5:7	138	7:35–8	77
5:12	122	7:35	40
5:14	128	7:37	77, 157
5:17–42	100	7:38	153
5:17–18	43, 118	7:42	157
5:17	156	7:46	37
5:20–6	57	7:48–50	117–18
5:21–4	43	7:49	102
5:21	157	7:51	140
5:27–32	118, 131	7:52	152, 155
5:27	43	7:53	153
5:28	127	7:54–8:1	100
5:29–32	26, 102	7:55–6	41, 102, 103
5:30–2	112	7:55	101
5:30–1	147	7:56	102, 108
5:30	37, 41, 108, 124, 146, 149, 153	7:60	90
		8:4–17	126
5:31	15, 16, 41, 52, 53, 54, 55, 86, 89, 90, 101, 119, 123, 124, 132, 135, 143, 146, 151, 157, 168	8:4	78, 148
		8:6	122
		8:12	26, 67, 78, 109, 112, 116, 127, 148
		8:13	122
5:35	137	8:16	127

8:22	71, 86	10:40	41
8:25	78, 112, 148	10:41	149
8:26–40	47	10:42	54, 142
8:29	116	10:43	15, 16, 52, 53, 55, 86, 89, 90, 115, 127, 146, 151
8:30	91, 145		
8:32–3	15		
8:35	78, 148	10:44–8	116
8:39	116	10:44–5	113
8:40	78, 148	10:46	120
9:1–3	144	10:48	127
9:1–2	43	10:49	149
9:3	61, 102	11:1–18	126
9:14–15	127	11:2	130
9:14	43	11:3	130
9:15	41, 157	11:5	102
9:16	142	11:9–10	102
9:17	53	11:15–17	53
9:18–19	91	11:16	143
9:20	134	11:18	41, 44
9:21	43	11:20	78, 148
9:22	117	11:21	56, 128
9:23–5	100	11:27–30	118
9:28	100	11:28	48, 77, 116
9:31	41, 62	11:29	116, 117
9:32	117	12:1–4	43
9:35	56, 117	12:1–2	100
9:36	84, 129	12:3–4	114
10:1–48	52, 126, 135	12:7	61
10:2	84, 126, 129	12:20	62
10:4	84, 126, 129	12:21–3	43
10:9–16	130	12:24	26
10:11	102	13:1	134
10:15	126	13:2	116, 154
10:16	102	13:4–12	104
10:19	116	13:4	116
10:22	152	13:5–12	135
10:31	84, 129	13:5	134
10:33–4	53	13:6–12	134–5
10:34–48	126	13:6	134
10:34–5	126	13:9	134
10:35	41, 126, 152	13:10	134, 152
10:36	41, 62, 78, 135, 148, 157	13:13–52	31–2
		13:14	134
10:37	148	13:15	134, 144
10:38–40	147	13:16–52	133–62
10:38	43, 127	13:16–25	136–43
10:39–43	112	13:16–17	54
10:39–40	108, 124	13:16	136
10:39	146, 153	13:17–41	159

13:17–31	136	13:34–5	141
13:17–25	136–8, 157	13:34	28, 139, 149
13:17–23	54	13:35	149
13:17–22	120	13:36	142, 144
13:17–21	138	13:37	144, 145, 149
13:17–20	138	13:38–41	136, 151–5
13:17–19	138, 139–40	13:38–9	114, 136, 150, 151–3, 159
13:17	37, 142, 143, 144, 157	13:38	15, 16, 52, 53, 55, 86, 89, 90, 91, 115, 136, 142, 145, 146, 147, 151
13:18	138, 139–40, 150		
13:20–5	57, 140–2		
13:20–2	138, 140		
13:20	57, 138, 141, 143	13:39	151, 153
13:21	141, 150	13:40–1	136, 139, 140, 151, 154
13:22–3	26, 41, 42, 54, 77		
13:22	141, 149	13:40	155
13:23–4	157	13:41	158
13:23	135, 141, 142, 143, 144, 148	13:42–52	155–60
		13:42–3	134, 155
13:24	53, 141, 143, 144	13:42	136, 155
13:25	56	13:44–52	157
13:26	41, 54, 136, 144	13:44–50	134
13:26–37	136	13:44–8	134
13:26–31	136, 144–8	13:44–6	100
13:27–37	136	13:44–5	155
13:27–31	144	13:44	155
13:27–30	108	13:45	156
13:27–9	118, 139, 142, 145, 148, 150	13:46–8	41
		13:46	111, 134, 154, 157, 159
13:27	26, 91, 117, 141, 142, 144, 145		
		13:47	4, 61, 111, 156, 157
13:28	144, 146, 153	13:50	100, 146
13:29–30	124	14:1	134
13:29	144, 145, 146–7	14:3	122
13:30–7	139	14:5	100
13:30–6	148	14:7	78, 148
13:30	41, 147, 149	14:8–10	134
13:31–7	144	14:9	100
13:31–2	156	14:15	56, 78, 102, 148
13:31	112, 144, 148	14:17	86
13:32–7	136, 144, 148–51	14:21	78, 148
13:32–3	144	14:22	26, 109, 116, 142
13:32	54, 78, 136, 142, 148, 149	14:26	154
		15:1	156
13:33–7	41, 54, 141	15:3	41, 110
13:33–5	144	15:5	153
13:33	76, 149	15:6–21	44
13:34–7	26, 41	15:7–9	126
13:34–6	149	15:7	41, 78, 116, 142

15:8–9	126	18:5–6	157
15:8	126	18:5	112
15:9	116	18:7	130
15:10	153	18:10	158
15:12	122	18:12–17	100
15:13–18	28	18:18	153
15:14–18	161, 166	18:19	134
15:14–17	41, 158	18:25	53
15:14	41, 158	18:26	134
15:15–17	141	19:1–7	126
15:16–17	41, 158	19:1–5	53
15:16	41	19:4	53
15:17	154	19:5	127
15:19	56	19:6	113
15:20	130	19:8	26, 109, 112, 116, 134
15:21	145	19:10	117
15:28	116	19:17	117
15:32	134	19:18	116
15:33	62	19:21	116, 142
15:35	78, 148	19:23–41	100
15:38	154	19:27	48
16:1–3	153	20:6	114
16:6–7	116	20:7	130
16:10	78, 148	20:11	130
16:14–15	130	20:16	114
16:16–24	100	20:21	112
16:17	41	20:22	116
16:29	61	20:24	78, 112
16:34	130	20:25	26, 109, 112, 116
16:36	62	20:27	142
16:37	95, 163	20:28	15, 168
17:1–8	100	21:4	116
17:1–2	134	21:19	41
17:3	142, 145, 146, 149	21:20	156
17:5	156	21:21	153
17:6–7	166	21:23–4	153
17:6	48	21:26–30	57
17:7	120, 146	21:26	153
17:10	134	21:27–8	100
17:13	26	21:28	66, 153
17:16–34	4	21:37	118
17:17	134	22:3	95, 156
17:18	78, 148, 149	22:5	43
17:23	26, 91, 145	22:6	102
17:24	102	22:9	61
17:30	26, 91, 145	22:11	61
17:31	41, 48, 94, 142, 149, 152	22:12	117
17:37	149	22:14	37, 54, 91, 145, 152, 155
18:4	134		

22:15	157	28:14	130
22:16	55, 86, 90, 127	28:18–20	71
22:17–21	118, 119	28:20	157
22:17	57	28:21–2	145
22:25–9	163	28:23–8	35, 157, 159
22:28	95	28:23	26, 109, 112, 116, 153
22:30	43		
23:2–5	43	28:25	77, 113
23:11	142	28:26–8	44
23:14	43	28:26–7	44
23:18	110	28:27	56
23:22	110	28:28	44, 91, 145, 159
23:35	43	28:31	26, 109, 116
24:1	43		
24:2	62	*Romans*	
24:5	48	1:3–4	148
24:6	57	1:16	134
24:12	57	2:9–10	134
24:14	37, 143	2:13–17	142
24:15	152	2:13	152
24:17	84, 129	2:17–19	61
24:18	57	3:20	152
24:21	143	3:21	145
24:25	41, 152	3:24	152
25:2	43	3:26	152
25:8	57, 153	3:28	152
25:10	142	3:30	152
25:15	43	4:2	152
26:6–7	143, 148, 151	4:5	152
26:6	142	4:7	52
26:10	43	5:1	152
26:12	43	5:9	152
26:13	61	6:7	151, 152
26:15–18	26	8:9	114
26:16–18	61, 111, 157	8:13	153
26:17–18	4, 61, 92, 156	8:14	114
26:18	26, 43, 50, 52, 53, 56, 86, 89, 90, 93, 104, 105, 115, 124, 134, 147, 151, 161, 166, 167	8:30	152
		8:33	152
		10:18	48
		11:25	82
		15:25–32	129
26:20	41, 56	15:31	42
26:21	57	16:25	82
26:23	41, 61, 156	16:26	145
27:24	142		
27:35–6	130	*1 Corinthians*	
28:4	152	2:1	82, 83
28:5	110	2:7	82, 83
28:7	130	4:4	152

6:11	152	1:26–7	82
15:51	82	1:27	82
16:1–4	129	2:2–3	82
16:8	114	3:12	58
		4:3	82

2 Corinthians

		1 Thessalonians	
1:10	42	5:4–7	61
2:7	82	5:12	112
2:14	54		
4:4–6	61	*2 Thessalonians*	
4:6	54	2:7	82
8–9	129	3:21	42

2 Thessalonians

		1 Timothy	
3:21	42	3:16	82
		4:13	134

Galatians

		2 Timothy	
1:13	11	3:11	42
1:14	11	4:17	42
2:10	129	4:18	42
2:16–17	152		
2:16	153	*Titus*	
3:2–3	114	3:7	152
3:8	152		
3:11	152	*Hebrews*	
3:13	146	1:5	148
3:24	152	1:6	48
5:4	152	2:5	48
		5:5–10	75
Ephesians		5:5	148
1:7	53	6:20	75
1:9	82	7:1–28	75
1:10	100	9:12	40
3:3–4	82	9:22	53
3:3	82	10:18	53
3:5	82	13:22	134
3:9–10	82		
6:19	82	*James*	
		1:17	59
Philippians		5:15	53
2:1	58		
2:9–11	50	*1 Peter*	
3:8	54	1:10–12	145
4:15–20	129	2:9	59, 61
		2:13	120
Colossians		2:17	120
1:12–14	59	2:24	146
1:12–13	61		
1:14	53		

2 Peter
   2:7   42
   2:9   42
   3:18   54

1 John
   1:9   53
   2:12   53

Revelation
   3:10   48
   7:2   59
   12:9   48
   16:14   48
   22:16   59

DEAD SEA SCROLLS

1QM
   I, 3   39
   I, 10–15   75
   XI, 6–7   59
   XI, 7–8   77
   XIII, 1–15   75
   XIII, 2   37
   XIV, 3   35
   XIV, 4   35, 37

1QpHab
   II, 6–10   146

1QS
   II, 1   58
   III, 13–15   38
   III, 18   38
   IV, 9   38

Damascus Document
   I, 7   38
   II, 12   77
   III, 9   77
   VI, 1   77
   VII, 9   38
   VII, 18–21   59
   VIII, 2–3   38
   XIX, 15   38

1Q22
   III, 6–7   71

4QpNahum   146
   3–4 I, 7–8   147

4QFlorilegium
   (4Q174)   40, 141
   I, 7–13   123

4Q175
   9–13   59

4Q378
   11, 2–3   43

4Q503   37

4Q504
   1–2 V, 9   43
   4, 7–14   39
   6, 7–17   39

11QMelchizedek   74–6, 104
   II, 2   74
   II, 4–5   74
   II, 6–9   75
   II, 6–8   74
   II, 6   75
   II, 7–9   73
   II, 9   74
   II, 12–14   75
   II, 25   74

11QTemple
   LXIV, 6–13   146, 147

TARGUMIC TEXTS AND RABBINIC LITERATURE

Babylonian Talmud
   b. Megillah
      31a   73, 114

   b. Sukkah
      52a   148

Mishnah
   m. Megillah
      3:5   114

Targumic Texts
   Targum of the Prophets
      2 Sam 7:20   141

Targum Isaiah
61:1   77

Other Rabbinic Works
Genesis Rabbah
44:8   148
49:8   142

Midrash on the Psalms
1.2   77
2.9   148

Shemoneh 'Esreh 37
15   40, 59

Sipra on Deuteronomy
26.1.C   77

APOSTOLIC WRITINGS

Barnabas
5.11–13 147
19.8   129

1 Clement
59.2   59

Didache
4.5–8   129
11.11   83

Ignatius
To the Romans
2.2   112

ANCIENT CHRISTIAN WRITINGS

Ambrose
Epistulae
41.7   29

Anselm
Cur Deus Homo?
1.3–7   29

Augustine
Sermons
263.1   29

Basil
Epistulae
261.2   29

Gregory of Nazianzus
Oration
39.13   29
45.22   29

Gregory of Nyssa
Great Catechism
5.21–6   29
5.22   106

Irenaeus
Against Heresies
2.20.3   30
3.5.2   30
3.5.3   106
3.12.7   106
3.16.9   105, 106
3.18.2   105
3.18.5   30, 108
3.18.6   28, 29, 105, 164
3:21.10 105
3.23.7   105
4.5.4   106, 107, 108, 132
4.8.2   106
4.13.4   107
4.20.2   106
4.20.10 29, 30, 105, 106
4.37.1–4 29, 105, 106
5.1.1   29, 30, 105, 106, 108, 132, 169
5.16.3   29, 30, 92, 105, 108, 164
5.17.1   106–7
5.18.3   31, 105
5.21   28
5.21.1–2 105, 164
5.21.2–3 29, 30, 92
5.21.2   67, 105
5.21.3   93, 105

Demonstration of the Apostolic Preaching
17   28
29–31   105

34	29, 30, 31, 92, 105, 164	*Poetics*	
36	105	1450b27	4
37	28	*Politics*	
38	105	1253a3	5
49	105		
56	105	*Rhetoric*	
59	105	3.16	148
62–4	105		
69	105	Aspines	
83	28	*Rhetoric*	
97	105	10	151

Justin
  Dialogue with Trypho
  32   147
  96   147

Origen
  Commentary on the Gospel of Matthew
  16.8   29

  Commentary on Romans
  2.13.29 29

Tertullian
  Against the Jews
  7   119–20
  10.1–5   147

  Apology
  21   21

CLASSICAL WRITINGS AND OTHER ANCIENT SOURCES

Anonymous Seguerianus
  1.1   136
  198–253 151

Appian
  Civil Wars
  2.86   120

Aristotle
  Nicomachean Ethics
  1181b15 5

Augustus
  Res gestae divi Augustus 135
  12   45
  25–33   119

Cicero
  De officiis
  1.121   155
  2.21   155
  2.32   155
  2.38   155

  De oratore
  1.85–6   155
  2.326–30 148
  2.343–4 155

  De invention rhetorica
  1.27–30 148
  1.98–109 151

  Orationes philippicae
  6.19   47

  Pro Balbo
  16   47

  Pro lege manilia
  56   47

  Pro Sestio
  67   47

  Rhetorica ad Herennium
  2.47–50 151

Index of Ancient Sources

Dio Cassius
   53.16.18   50

Dio Chrysostom
   To the People of Alexandria
   18   45

   Defense
   4   62

Diodorus Siculus
   40.4   47

Diogenes Laertius
   Lives of Eminent Philosophers
   1.45   39
   9.10   129

Dionysius Halicarnassus
   Antiquitates romanae
   1.3.3–5   47
   1.3.3   47
   4.9.2   43

Epictetus
   Diatribai
   4.1.12   62

Florus
   2.24.63   48
   2.24.64   49
   2.34.66   50

Geminus
   Astronomy
   18.1–3   100
   18.10   100
   18.18   100

Herodian
   2.4.4   120

Herodotus
   Historiae
   3.25   112

Hippocrates
   Joints
   30.38   100

Homer
   Iliad
   257–62   83

Horace
   Odes
   1.12.49–57   122
   1.24.5–8   155
   3.5.1–4   48, 120
   4.5.5–8   60
   4.14   119
   15.4–16   49
   15.4–7   45

Josephus
   Against Apion
   2.17–8   145
   2.282   119

   Jewish Antiquities
   3.192   56
   6.92   88
   6.142–54   88
   6.166   77
   6.378   141
   11.63   100
   11.112   138
   13.299–300   56
   14.114–18   119
   16.118   62
   18.23–6   46
   18.116–19   58
   20.34   146
   20.38   146
   20.97–9   66
   20.167–72   66

   Jewish War
   1.68–9   56
   1.397   117
   1.437   117
   1.672   117
   2.118   46
   2.261–3   66
   2.379   120
   2.398   119
   2.433   46
   3.351   120
   3.352   56

3.399–408	56
4.618	78, 148
7.158	49

Joy at the Accession of Mer-ne-Ptah 70, 71

Livy
1.16.6–8	47
9.43.25	50
10.1.9	50

Lucan
Civil War
1.18–32	48
1.33–66	49
1.45–66	45
1.60	49
9.20	62

Lucian
Ocypus
78	45

Marcus Aurelius
12.1	43

Martial
Epigrammata
8.2.5–6	62

Ovid
Fasti
1.608	50
2.130	48

Metamorphoses
15.858–61	48, 50
15.868–70	48, 50

Oxyrhynchus Papyri
1130.12	39

Philo
Hypothetica
7.11–12	145

On the Decalogue
33	114
46	114
164	100

On the Embassy to Gaius
149–51	45
281–2	119
283	120

On the Life of Abraham
208	43

On the Sacrifices of Cain and Abel
57	43

On the Special Laws
1.68–70	123
1.69	117
1.304	43
2.64	43

On the Virtues
47	43

Who Is the Heir?
293	100

Philostratus
Vita Apollonii
1.15	95–6

Plato
Laws
679B–C	128
684C–D	128
744B–746C	128
757C	128

Protagoras
333B	43

Republic
420C–422D	128
424A	129
449C	129
449D	128
462B–464A	128
550C	128

Pliny the Elder
Natural History
3.38–9	47
5.94	135
7.98	119

11.26	48		*Epistulae morales*	
36.118	47		90.38	128
37.78	48			

Pliny the Younger
Epistulae
52   49

Plutarch
Aratus
11.2   39

Caesar
23.3   47

Marcius Coriolanus
11.2   45

Moralia
275A   155
857A   43

Polybius
1.1.5   47
1.2.7   47
1.3.1–6   63
3.1.4–5   47
3.4.2–3   47
6.2.3   47

Priene Inscription
(*OGIS* 458)   45, 49, 78,
                         148

Quintilian
Institutio oratoria
3.8.12   148
4.2.1–3   148
6.1–2   151

Quintus Curtius
History of Alexander
6.3.2–3   119

Rhetoric to Alexander
30   148

Seneca
De clementia
2.1.4   45

Stoicorum veterum fragmenta
2.599   100
2.625   100

Strabo
Geography
1.1.6   112
1.2.31   112
1.4.6   112
2.5.8   47
2.5.12   48
3.1.8   112
4.3.2   119
12.557   135
12.569   135
12.577   135
17.1.53   46
17.3.25   47

Suetonius
Divus Augustus
8.2   120
94   49

Divus Julius
44.3   120
88   122

Nero
13.2   49

Tiberius
58   95

Vespasian
9.1   49

Tacitus
Agricola
30   63

Annals
6.41.1   46
11.24   118

Histories
1.2   120
4.74   46

Thucydides
  History of the Peloponnesian War
    1.76.2–3   137
    3.39.5   137
    3.45.7   137
    3.83.2   137
    4.19.4   137

Vergil
  Aeneid
    1.278–9   47
    6.781–2   119
    6.788–807 49
    6.788–94   45
    6.791–5   48
    6.850–3   63
    8.714–28   119

  Eclogues
    1.6–8   49
    1.17–20   49
    4   45
    4.19   36
    4.46–9   122

  Georgics
    1.24–43   45

Index of Modern Authors

Abraham, M. V. 69
Ackroyd, Peter R. 39
Agamben, Giorgio 83, 94–5
Ahn, Yong-Sung 26
Alexander, Loveday C. A. 18, 23, 109, 110, 147
Allison, Dale C. Jr. 22
Anderson, Charles 102
Anderson, Gary A. 72, 73, 90
Anderson, Kevin L. 16, 17, 143, 149
Ando, Clifford 46–50, 70, 95
Armstrong, Karen 2
Arndt, William F. 33
Asad, Talal 2, 6, 8, 9
Ash, Anthony 126
Atkinson, Kenneth 41
Aulén, Gustav 27, 28–30, 107
Avemarie, Friedrich 126

Bacchiocchi, Samuele 69
Bacon, Benjamin Wisner 153
Bakhtin, Mikhail M. 6
Baltzer, Klaus 39
Bandstra, Andrew J. 106
Barclay, William 110
Barrett, C. K. 20, 108, 110, 118–19, 128, 135, 137, 139, 140, 149
Barth, Karl 94
Barton, Stephen C. 22
Bauckham, Richard 36, 37, 40, 56, 115, 117
Beale, Gregory K. 115
Beard, Mary 3, 11
Beasley-Murray, George R. 124, 126
Beck, Brian E. 15, 107
Beck, Norman 46
Beers, Holly 31, 76, 77, 111, 112, 156
Bell, Catherine 126–7
Benoit, Pierre 54
Berger, Klaus 43
Bergsma, John Sietze 39, 70, 72, 73, 74–5

Beyer, Hans F. 99
Billings, Drew W. 21, 23
Bird, Michael F. 1
Black, C. Clifton, II 136, 144, 148, 151
Blomberg, Craig L. 22, 80
Blum, Matthias 159
Blumenthal, Christian 52
Blumhofer, C. M. 120, 122
Bock, Darrell L. 31, 33, 34, 55, 59, 66, 76, 86, 104, 114, 119, 139, 150
Bockmuehl, Markus 82
Boer, Roland 118
Boersma, Hans 30, 105, 106
Bonz, Marianne Palmer 48
Bovon, François 31, 36, 53, 54, 66, 76, 80, 81, 86, 93, 94, 96, 104, 112, 113
Bowker, J. W. 141
Boyarin, Daniel 8
Braun, Adam F. 80
Braun, Willi 130
Brawley, Robert L. 119, 142, 159
Bremmer, Jan N. 146
Brent, Allen 50
Bright, John 148
Brinkman, J. A. 119
Brown, Raymond E. 34, 36, 43, 44, 46, 53, 54, 146
Brown, Schuyler 126
Brownlee, William H. 87
Bruce, F. F. 21, 79, 110, 113, 117, 124, 137, 140, 149, 153
Brückner, Martin 11
Brueggemann, Walter 68, 76
Bryan, Christopher 22–3, 46
Bryan, David K. 101
Bryan, Steven M. 40
Buckwalter, H. Douglas 111
Bultmann, Rudolf 4, 53
Burgess, Andrew 94
Burkert, Walter 11, 45

Buss, Matthäus Franz-Josef 137, 142, 155, 156
Buzzard, Anthony 17, 110

Cadbury, Henry J. 1, 15, 16, 19, 21, 150
Caird, G. B. 33, 34, 36, 53
Calvin, John 110
Camp, Ashby L. 125
Campenhausen, Hans von 22
Capper, Brian 128
Carpinelli, Francis Giordano 108
Carroll, John T. 13, 79, 80, 95, 112
Carter, J. Kameron 9, 12, 31, 34, 105
Carter, Warren 51
Cassidy, Richard J. 24
Cavanaugh, William T. 7, 8, 9
Certeau, Michel de 6–7
Chance, J. Bradley 91
Charlesworth, James H. 123
Childs, Brevard S. 68, 72, 77, 111
Chilton, Bruce 83
Cho, Youngmo 79
Christiansen, Ellen Juhl 126
Chrupcała, L. Daniel 33, 142
Clark, David George 57
Cohen, Shaye J. D. 12
Coleridge, Mark 34, 52
Collins, Adela Yarbro 123
Collins, John J. 59, 68, 72, 74, 75
Constantelos, Demetrios J. 30
Conzelmann, Hans 5, 13–14, 15, 18, 21, 22, 25, 77, 79, 80, 94–5, 101, 110, 112, 118, 138, 145, 149, 157
Corley, Kathleen E. 130
Courtés, Joseph 1
Crawford, Michael 3
Crisp, Oliver D. 30
Culpepper, R. Alan 80
Culy, Martin M. 137, 139
Cumont, Franz 11

Dahl, Nils 158
Dana, H. E. 125
Danker, Frederick W. 39, 44, 45, 68, 94
Darr, John A. 56
Das, A. Andrew 125, 126
Davies, Jason P. 3
Davies, J. G. 118

Davis, J. C. 125
Dean-Otting, Mary 103
DeClaissé-Walford, Nancy 148
Denova, Rebecca 119, 134
DeSilva, David A. 136–9
Destro, Adriana 71
Dibelius, Martin 4, 15, 107
Dillon, Richard J. 34–5, 36, 38, 54
Dionne, Christian 136, 137, 144, 156
Doble, Peter 15
Doeve, J. W. 141
Douglas, Mary 130
Driver, John 28
Du Plessis, Isak J. 22, 91
Dumais, Marcel 139, 141, 144
Dungan, David Laird 9
Dunn, James D. G. 79, 82, 87, 113–15, 117, 124, 126, 159
Dupont, Jacques 114, 134, 150, 151, 156
Dyson, Stephen L. 46

Easton, Burton Scott 21
Eißfeldt, Otto 120
Ellis, E. Earle 36
Epp, Eldon Jay 145
Erdmann, Gottfried 36
Esler, Philip Francis 19, 21, 22–3, 130
Eubank, Nathan 105
Evans, C. F. 35, 36, 43, 55
Evans, Craig A. 39, 66

Falk, Daniel K. 123
Farris, Stephen 36, 43, 44, 53, 59
Farrow, Douglas 30
Fears, J. Rufus 49, 50, 62, 63
Fee, Gordon D. 126
Festugière, André Jean 10
Finger, Reta Haltemann 128, 130
Finger, Thomas 30
Finney, Paul Corby 95
Fitzgerald, John T. 129
Fitzgerald, Timothy 2, 9
Fitzmyer, Joseph A. 13, 34, 36, 39, 42, 44, 53, 74, 76, 77, 104, 110, 114, 123, 136, 137, 138, 139, 140, 142, 144, 149, 150, 152, 153, 154
Flanagan, Neal 1, 17
Flender, Helmut 79

Fletcher-Louis, Crispin H. T. 87
Flichy, Odile 136, 137, 140, 144, 152
Foakes-Jackson, F. J. 21
Foerster, Werner 45, 61
Ford, J. Massyngbaerde 34-5, 55
Forsyth, Neil 29, 106
Foucault, Michel 5, 6
Franklin, Eric 23
Franklin, Lloyd David 126
Fredriksen, Paula 21
Friedrich, Gerhard 78, 87
Fuller, Michael 18, 37
Fusco, Vittorio 37

Galinsky, Karl 48
Gane, Roy E. 71
Garrett, Susan R. 92, 104, 143
Gasque, W. Ward 20
Gathercole, Simon 59, 104
Gaventa, Beverly Roberts 14, 25, 110, 112, 136, 146, 153, 154
Geldenhuys, Norval 53, 104
Genz, Rouven 111
Gerber, Daniel 34, 43
Gerlot, P. 156
Gerstenberger, Erhard 71
Giambrone, Anthony 39, 85, 90
Gilbert, Gary 25, 27, 49, 51, 63, 119-20, 143
Giles, Kevin 112
Glöckner, Richard 17, 111
Gnilka, Joachim 53, 59
Goldingay, John 55-6, 68, 72, 73, 76, 77, 111
Goldsmith, Dave 141
Goodblatt, Martin 157
Goodman, Martin 117
Gräßer, Erich 79
Green, Joel B. 1, 16, 17, 31, 36, 39, 53, 55, 56, 65, 69, 71, 76, 77, 81, 84, 86, 88, 91, 92, 93, 99, 103, 104, 111, 118, 126, 127, 146, 147
Gregory, Andrew F. 1
Gregory, Bradley C. 68, 72, 73
Greimas, Algirdas 1
Grenz, Stanley J. 29
Griffiths, Paul J. 95
Gross, Michael B. 20

Gunkel, Heidrun 126
Gunkel, Hermann 148
Güting, Eberhard 119
Guy, Laurie 80

Haacker, Klaus 143
Haenchen, Ernst 21, 101, 110, 112, 114, 139, 153, 157
Hägerland, Tobias 87, 88
Hahn, Scott W. 41, 79
Hamm, Dennis 91
Hanks, Thomas D. 73, 94
Hansen, G. Walter 144
Harland, Philip A. 21, 117
Harris, Sarah 41
Hart, Trevor A. 30
Hays, Christopher M. 129, 131
Hays, Richard B. 68, 152
Heath, Malcolm 151
Heil, John Paul 130
Heitmüller, Wilhelm 11
Hendrickx, Herman 35
Hengel, Martin 117
Herzog, William R., II 117
Heumann, C. A. 19
Heusler, Erika 21
Heywood, Andrew 5
Hiers, Richard H. 79
Hill, Andrew E. 57
Himmelfarb, Martha 103
Hochban, John I. 29, 108
Hofius, Otfried 87, 88
Holladay, Carl R. 110, 118, 119, 134, 139, 145
Holladay, William L. 72
Horn, Friedrich W. 19
Horsley, Richard A. 46, 82
Houston, Walter J. 69
Huddleston, Jonathan 137
Hull, J. H. E. 113
Hurtado, Larry W. 145
Hutt, Curtis 80

Isasi-Díaz, Ada María 3

Jacobson, Rolf A. 148
Jantsch, Torsten 17, 59, 157
Jennings, Willie James 12, 17, 113

Jeremias, Joachim 88–9
Jervell, Jacob 23, 37, 111, 117, 119, 120, 137, 139, 140, 142, 145, 156–9
Jeska, Joachim 139, 140, 141, 142
Jipp, Joshua W. 130
Johansson, Daniel 87, 88
Johnson, Andy 103
Johnson, Luke Timothy 33, 39, 69, 77, 80, 81, 86, 92, 93, 110, 114, 117, 121, 129, 134, 140, 150
Johnson, Mark 103
Jones, Douglas 35
Jonge, M. de 74, 75
Juel, Donald H. 119
Jung, Franz 49
Just, Arthur A., Jr. 91, 131

Kaiser, Walter C. 43
Karris, Robert J. 15, 130
Käsemann, Ernst 25
Kaut, Thomas 53, 54
Kawashima, Robert S. 71
Keener, Craig S. 113, 114, 117, 134, 136, 139, 140, 143, 145, 150
Kennedy, George A. 136
Kilgallen, John J. 142, 150, 151
Kim, Seyoon 22–3
Kimbell, John 15
Kinman, Brent 21
Kittel, Gerhard 104
Klager, Andrew P. 107
Klauck, Hans-Josef 134
Klawans, Jonathan 57
Klein, Hans 21, 33, 39, 53, 55, 65
Kloppenborg, John S. 137
Koch, Klaus 87
Koester, Helmut 58
Koet, B. J. 69, 77, 86, 110, 111, 155, 156
Kort, Wesley A. 8
Kotsko, Adam 30
Kremer, Jacob 119, 120
Krodel, Gerhard A. 117, 140
Kuhn, Karl Allen 24, 79
Kümmel, Werner Georg 2, 13, 14, 16
Kurz, William S. 140

Lake, Kirsopp 21, 150
Lakoff, George 103

Lang, Friedrich Gustav 33, 34, 43
Lawson, John 30, 107
Laytham, D. Brent 91
Le Cornu, Hilary 110, 114, 119
Lebourlier, Jean 81
Lefebvre, Henri 6–7
Lennartsson, Göran 100
Levick, Barbara 135
Lindemann, Andreas 47
Locke, John 9
Loewe, William P. 29, 30, 107, 108
Lohfink, Gerhard 103
Lohse, Eduard 114
Loisy, Alfred 150
Lövestam, Evald 141, 150
Lundbom, Jack R. 72

MacIntyre, Alasdair 9
MacMullen, Ramsay 11
Maddox, Robert 19, 21, 22, 79, 116
Malina, Bruce J. 137
Mallen, Peter 110, 111, 156
Mantey, Julius R. 125
Marcus, Joel 104
Marcus, Ralph 125
Marguerat, Daniel 22, 108, 117, 136, 137, 138, 139, 140, 159
Marshall, I. Howard 14, 15, 16, 33, 34, 36, 38, 53, 59, 65, 93, 104, 110, 113, 114, 139, 140
Martin, Luther H. 10
Marty, Martin 7
Martyn, J. Louis 25
Mason, Steve 12
Maston, Jason 17, 79, 110
Matera, Frank J. 107
Mattill, A. J., Jr. 20
May, Jordan Daniel 156
McCutcheon, Russell T. 10
McIntyre, Luther B., Jr. 125
McKnight, Scot 146
McRay, John 135
Medina, Gilberto J. 26
Meiser, Martin 22
Méndez-Moratalla, Fernando 4, 56
Menken, Maarten J. J. 58, 77
Menzies, Robert P. 113, 115, 126
Merk, Otto 79

Merrill, Eugene H. 138
Metzger, Bruce M. 59, 119, 120, 140
Meyer, Ben F. 54
Milbank, John 6, 102
Milgrom, Jacob 70, 71
Miller, Amanda C. 26
Miller, Merril P. 74
Minear, Paul S. 18
Minns, Denis 30, 105
Mitchell, Alan C. 129, 130
Mitchell, Stephen 135
Mittelstadt, Martin William 130
Mittmann-Richert, Ulrike 2, 16, 59
Miura, Yuzuru 41, 76, 77, 123, 141
Moehring, Horst R. 46
Moessner, David P. 157, 159
Molthagen, Joachim 21
Montgomery, James A. 74
Moore, George Foot 73
Moralee, Jason 45, 50
Morgan, Teresa 128, 155
Morgan-Wynne, John Eifion 137, 139, 149, 152
Morris, Leon 39
Moule, C. F. D. 101
Moxnes, Halvor 7, 117, 130
Müller, Paul-Gerhard 152
Muñoz-Larrondo, Rubén 26

Nave, Guy D., Jr. 56
Neagoe, Alexandru 19, 20
Neyrey, Jerome H. 130
Nielsen, Anders E. 14
Noack, Bent 114
Noble, Joshua A. 84
Nolland, John T. 14, 65, 76, 77, 79, 86, 112
Nongbri, Brent 3, 5, 8, 11–12
Nordgaard, Stefan 23, 157
North, John 3, 11
Novick, Tvzi 145

O'Banion, John 148
O'Neill, J. C. 157
O'Toole, Robert F. 16, 24, 41, 53, 76, 79, 101, 108, 111, 149
Oakman, Douglas E. 117
Oegema, Gerbern S. 123
Osborn, Eric 105
Osburn, Carroll D. 125

Page, Sydney H. T. 104
Palmer, D. W. 103
Pao, David W. 18, 60, 69, 76, 77, 94, 110, 111, 119, 130, 131
Parsons, Mikael C. 1, 109, 134, 136, 137, 139, 140
Pascut, Beniamin 88
Pattison, Stephen 19
Paul, Shalom M. 68, 72, 77, 90, 111
Peirce, Charles Sanders 83
Perrin, Nicholas 69, 71
Perrin, Norman 83
Pervo, Richard I. 1, 31, 110, 128, 134, 136, 138, 139, 149, 159
Pesce, Mauro 71
Pesch, Rudolf 136, 137, 141
Peterson, David 16
Petterson, Christina 118
Pilch, John J. 137
Pilcher, Josef 139
Pilgrim, Walter E. 15, 69
Pillai, C. A. Joachim 134, 139, 145
Pitre, Brant 54
Plummer, Alfred 39
Poirer, John C. 77
Poon, William K. 130
Powell, Mark Allan 17
Price, Simon R. F. 2–3, 11, 48
Prieur, Alexander 71
Prior, Michael 77

Rad, Gerhard von 61
Radl, Walter 54, 134, 137
Räisänen, Heikki 151, 158
Rajack, Tessa 21
Ramelli, Ilaria L. E. 100
Ramsay, W. M. 11, 135
Ravens, David 37, 158
Reardon, Timothy W. 1, 13, 84, 102, 108, 116, 126, 127, 146, 147, 153, 155
Reeder, Caryn A. 147
Reitzenstein, Richard 11
Renssen, Toon 88
Resseguie, James L. 66
Ricoeur, Paul 4
Rindoš, Jaroslav 57
Ringe, Sharon H. 70, 81
Ringgren, Helmer 70
Rive, James B. 5, 11

Robbins, Vernon K. 22, 56
Robinson, Thomas A. 10
Rodrigues, Hillary 10
Roloff, Jürgen 114, 136, 149
Romm, James S. 112
Rossing, Barbara 47
Rothschild, Claire K. 134, 137
Rowe, C. Kavin 1, 24–6, 27, 76, 79, 82, 89, 118, 120, 127, 154
Rubin, Benjamin 135

Sack, Robert 6
Salmeier, Michael A. 79
Sanders, E. P. 87
Sanders, Jack T. 157, 158
Sanders, James A. 69, 70, 74, 90, 110, 111
Satterthwaite, Philip E. 138
Scharper, Philip 24
Schendel, Joshua 105
Schmithals, Walter 55, 149
Schnabel, Eckhard 129
Schnackenburg, Rudolf 116
Schneckenburger, Matthias 19–20
Schneider, Gerhard 117, 136, 139, 155
Schreck, Christopher J. 69
Schreiber, Stefan 25, 27, 45
Schürer, Emil 40
Schürmann, Heinz 39, 44, 66
Schweizer, Eduard 39, 149, 152
Scott, James M. 40, 109, 112, 114, 117, 118, 119, 120
Seccombe, David P. 84, 156, 159
Seesemann, Heinrich 128
Segal, Alan F. 103
Seifrid, Mark A. 128
Sellner, Hans Jörg 16, 53, 55, 60, 61, 88
Seo, Pyung Soo 26
Shepherd, William H., Jr. 113
Shin, W. Gil 18
Shulam, Joseph 110, 114, 119
Sidebottom, E. M. 88
Skinner, Matthew L. 18–19
Sleeman, Matthew 7, 100, 101, 111, 112
Sloan, David B. 93
Sloan, Robert B. 68, 69, 86, 94
Smart, Ninian 10
Smit, Peter-Ben 88, 109
Smith, Dennis E. 130

Smith, Jonathan Z. 8, 10
Smith, Steve 119
Smith, Wilfred Cantwell 11–12
Smyth, Herbert Weir 39
Soards, Marion L. 136, 140, 144
Soja, Edward 6–7
Sourvinou-Inwood, Christiane 11
Spencer, Patrick E. 1
Stalder, K. 100
Stanton, Graham N. 146
Stenschke, Christoph W. 4, 33, 34, 53
Sterling, Greg 15, 107
Stott, John R. W. 110
Strahan, Joshua Marshall 91, 105
Strathmann, Hermann 44
Strauss, Mark L. 40, 41, 43, 59, 76, 94, 114, 123, 134, 139, 141, 142, 149, 150, 156, 158
Strobel, August 69
Stronstad, Roger 113
Swartley, Willard M. 62
Sweetland, Dennis M. 91
Sylva, Dennis D. 15, 107

Taeger, Jens-W. 4
Tajra, Harry W. 21
Talbert, Charles H. 20, 117, 129, 137
Tannehill, Robert C. 69, 91, 94, 134, 137, 139, 143, 152, 155, 159, 160
Tanner, Beth LaNeel 148
Tanner, Kathryn 30, 105
Taylor, Charles 2, 9
Thomas, Derek W. H. 110
Tiede, David L. 34, 54, 61, 77, 80, 111, 112, 159
Tripolitis, Antonía 10
Trocmé, André 69
Trompf, G. W. 137
Turner, Max 18, 37, 53, 69, 77, 79, 113, 114, 115, 126, 127
Tyson, Joseph B. 134

Uehlinger, Christoph 118

Vaux, Roland de 148
Verheyden, Joseph 137
Vielhauer, Phillip 4, 53, 54, 59, 152
Vinson, Richard B. 80

Index of Modern Authors

Wainwright, Arthur W. 37
Walaskay, Paul 19, 22
Wall, Robert W. 1, 20, 110
Wallace, Daniel B. 88–9
Walters, Patricia 1
Walton, Steve 18, 20, 22, 24, 84, 100, 101, 103, 119, 120, 128, 129
Wanke, Daniel 29, 105
Wasserberg, Günter 137
Watson, Francis 128
Webb, Robert L. 57
Weinfeld, Moshe 70
Weinstock, Stefan 47, 119
Weiser, Alfons 79, 116, 134, 136, 138
Weiss, Johannes 20–1
Wendt, Hans Hinrich 150
Wenell, Karen J. 3
Wengst, Klaus 22, 62
Wenham, Gordon J. 71
Wenk, Matthias 113, 115, 118, 127
Wenkel, David H. 87
Westermann, Claus 68
Wilckens, Ulrich 15
Williams, David J. 110

Williams, Delores S. 67
Wilson, Benjamin R. 15
Wilson, Sarah Hinlicky 126
Wilson, S. G. 112
Winkler, Lorenz 50
Winter, Paul 35, 36
Witherington, Ben, III 134, 136, 139, 144, 145, 153
Wolter, Michael 15, 34, 51, 76, 79, 87, 116
Woude, A. S. van der 74, 75
Wright, N. T. 40, 54, 69, 76, 102

Yamazaki-Ransom, Kazuhiko 25–7, 48, 60
Yao, Santos 130
Yoder, John H. 69
Yoder, Joshua 23

Zampaglione, Gerardo 62–3
Zanker, Paul 47, 49, 50, 62, 95
Zeller, Eduard 20
Zhang, Wenxi 136
Ziccardi, Constantonio Antonio 79, 116
Zimmerli, Walther 68
Zwiep, Arie W. 101, 103

Subject Index

anthropology 4, 14, 28, 30 n. 148
Abraham 37, 42–3, 142–3
   covenant, *see under* covenant
   sacrifice 107 n. 43, 108
acceptable year of the Lord 68, 73–4, 76, 93–6, 115
Acts' ending 159–60
almsgiving 84, 126 n. 140, 129 n. 157
Antioch of Pisidia 134–5
apocalyptic 24–5, 48, 82–3, 104, 122, 132
Aristotle 4–5
atonement, 27–8, 31, 97. *See also Christus Victor*
   baptism 57, 89
   Christus Victor 3, 27–30, 64, 92–3, 96–7, 105–9, 160–1, 166–7
   cleansing 38, 71 n. 29, 106
   corporate 27, 38, 71, 74
   cosmic 27, 32, 65, 70–1, 75, 90, 99, 100, 108, 132, 164, 166, 168–9
   God and 97, 167
   Jubilee and 70–5, 96, 164
   Luke-Acts perceived lack 1–2, 14 n. 62, 16, 27
   moral exemplar 30–1, 64, 105, 167
   propitiation 106–7
   priests and 87
   ransom 27, 29, 30 n. 146, 39 n. 35, 105–6
   "religious" 18
   sacrifice 105–8, 165
   satisfaction, substitution, vicarious expiation 15–16, 27, 29, 97, 105–8, 147, 160, 165, 169
   social ordering 70–1, 75, 90, 164
   spatial 27–8, 32, 65, 71, 75, 78, 90, 132, 164, 168
Atonement, Day of 32, 70–1, 73–5
Aulén, Gustav 28–9, 30 n. 146
Augustus 36, 42, 45–50, 60 n. 146, 63, 78, 119, 135, 143

baptism, water 55–6, 124–7, 165. *See also* John the Baptist
   embodied act 56, 64, 124
   and Spirit 53, 55, 115
Babel 118–19
Belial. *See* Satan
Benedictus 33–64
   composition 34–5 n. 10
   structure 35–6
blasphemy 87–8
blindness. *See* sight

Caesar. *See also* Augustus *and* census
   cosmic legitimation 122 n. 125
   fidelity to 153–4, 165, 167
   imagery of 47, 63, 95–6
   and the Jerusalem leadership 107 n. 44, 146, 165, 167
   Jesus and 62–3, 84 n. 84, 120, 127, 131, 135, 146
   Lord of all 62, 127, 131
   savior 45, 49–50
   taxation 46, 95–6, 146
causal εἰς 125
census 36, 42, 46–7, 62, 82, 143
Certeau, Michel de 6–7
Christology 76–8, 84, 89, 149 n. 73
   absentee 101
Christus Victor. *See under* atonement
chronotope 6
church, community. *See* state
   apocalyptic 24–6, 122, 132
   baptism and 126–7
   being saved 32, 99, 127, 131–2, 165
   and complex space 95, 160, 169
   economic fellowship 118, 121, 128–30
   era of 94, 166
   institutionalization of 13
   and Israel 12
   and kingdom 81, 83, 116
   kinship 92

mission 109, 112, 115–16, 133, 156, 165–6
mystery 83 n. 82
liberal conception of 8–9, 13, 19–21
participation in 30, 32, 81, 132, 162
signs and wonders 122
spatially productive 32, 81, 83, 95–6, 126–7
Spirit and 32, 109, 112–13, 115–16, 118, 131, 161
table-fellowship 130–1
(theo)political body 3, 7, 12, 121, 126, 132, 165
civilized world (οἰκουμένη) 47–8, 62, 82, 104, 120, 164
cleanliness, cleansing 38, 71 n. 29, 106, 116, 126
coins 95–6
Conzelmann, Hans 13–14, 25, 112
cosmic drama 32, 65, 92–3, 97, 103–9, 131–2, 134, 161, 164
cosmology 84 n. 84, 101–2
Covenant 37, 42–4
 Abrahamic 37, 43, 142 n. 45
 Davidic 40–1, 43, 114–15, 141–2, 148, 150
 Levitical 57
 Mosaic 43
 Noahic 114
 Pentecost 114
 people 31, 44
covenant fidelity
 and the cross 108–9, 132, 164
 of David 150
 God to Israel 3, 30, 42–4, 58, 64, 132–3, 143, 151, 157–61, 164–5, 167
 Habakkuk and 154–5, 158
 and Jesus's resurrection/ascension 124, 132
 and national restoration 45, 57
 in Paul's rhetoric 136, 139, 142–4, 147–8, 151, 159–60
cross, crucifixion, death of Jesus 15–16, 27, 30–1, 86, 92, 94, 103–9, 165
 and forgiveness 105, 108, 166
 hanging on a tree 146–7
 revelatory 106–8, 123–4, 132, 147, 153–4, 165–6, 168
 rhetoric of 107–8, 123–4, 132, 153–4

David, Davidic 57, 137
 anointing 76
 blessing formula 37
 branch 59, 61
 city of 36, 46, 49
 covenant, *see under* covenant
 enthronement 76, 123, 148
 God's selection of 140–1
 holy things, blessings of 28, 149–50, 155, 160
 horn 34, 38, 40–1, 63–4
 and Jubilee/Atonement 70, 74–5
 and justice 84
 line, messiah 38, 40–2, 54, 60, 62, 75–6, 84, 123, 141–2. *See also* Jesus
 and Moses 77
 and national restoration 41–2, 54, 62, 131, 143, 150, 153
 prophet 77, 123
 suffering (righteous) servant 76–7, 141, 146
 tent, booth 28, 41, 158, 161, 166
decentralization 110, 117–18, 121
delay of the Parousia 13, 19, 21, 25, 94–5, 112
demonic authority/captivity 4, 26, 28, 61, 67, 74–5, 92–3, 97, 104–6, 134, 153, 161, 164–8. *See also* Satan *and* idolatry
the devil, *see* Satan
diaspora 39, 117 n. 96, 119–20
disciples
 ascension questioning 110–13, 116, 130
 ignorance, *see* ignorance
 ministry 90, 104, 111–13, 123, 156, 158
 as servant 112, 123, 156
 testing 106
 witnesses 112, 148
discipleship. *See also* imitation *under* Jesus 63–4, 82, 84, 91–3, 97, 164–8
divine passive 87–9
dualism 9–10, 31, 33 n. 5, 92

economy of God's kingdom/Jubilee 32, 56, 73, 85–6, 90–2, 97, 124, 126, 128–9, 132, 151, 153, 160, 164

election 137, 139, 142, 144, 157–61
   and supersession 12 n. 56
Emmaus 99
end of the earth 61, 109–12, 132, 163–4
epilogue 141
exile 38–40, 44, 52, 54, 72, 85
exodus 70, 122, 137–40
exodus paradigm 37–9, 42–4, 64, 66, 72–3, 122, 139
   New Exodus 18, 115 n. 86

faith, faithfulness, fidelity 128, 128 n. 149, 155
   and discipleship, *see* discipleship
   the faithful, faithfulness 90, 128–9, 132–3, 151, 155–6, 160
   of God, *see under* covenant fidelity
   inner experience 10–13, 126 n. 40
   of Jesus, *see under* Jesus
   justification and 153–5, 159
   obedience/fidelity 30, 63–4, 97, 105–6, 108, 164, 166–7
   unfaithfulness/disobedience 93, 97, 108 n. 47, 153
forgiveness of sins. *See also* atonement
   baptism and 55, 124–7
   corporate/communal 38, 45, 54, 61, 71, 74, 85
   cosmic order and 71, 75, 90, 92, 161
   debt language 39 n. 35, 52, 56, 70–2, 72 n. 37, 85–6, 90
   gentiles 92
   God's initiative 27, 54–6, 58–9, 64, 90, 94, 99, 107–8, 132, 164–7
   Jesus and 53, 55–6, 86–90, 94, 105–8, 123–4, 132, 151, 165, 167
   John the Baptist, *see* John the Baptist
   Jubilee and 71–5, 85, 89, 94, 151, 165
   justice in 123, 166–7
   knowledge and 52–6, 58, 151
   national restoration 38, 42, 45, 52–4, 58, 61, 64, 115, 142, 146, 151, 153
   political 33, 38, 51, 86, 92
   priestly 86–7, 89
   prophets and 86, 88
   release 85–90, 92, 151, 164–5
   and resurrection/ascension 15–16
   and salvation 53–6, 64, 85, 127, 163

   socially/spatially productive 27–8, 56, 71, 86, 90, 94, 126, 151, 164, 166–7
   subjective, "religious" 2, 17, 34, 51, 53, 64, 86, 126–7, 133, 164
   unmerited 43, 90
friendship 129–30

Gabriel 37–8, 51–2, 56, 74
gentiles 41, 44, 92, 111, 113, 121–2, 130, 133, 137, 142, 150, 155–61, 166
God. *See* covenant fidelity
   as Father 89 n. 110, 104, 132, 165
   great things of 120
   and heaven 102–3
   of Israel 37
   judgment 4, 27, 38, 52, 68, 94, 121–2, 158–9
   justice/justness 27, 30, 60, 68, 85, 97, 107, 123, 143, 160–1, 166–8
   king 140
   mercy 43, 58–9, 124
   redeemer 73
   uniqueness 89
   visitation 38–9, 43, 52, 58–9, 108, 164
   wrath 4, 106–7
good news, gospel 49, 62, 67–8, 76, 78, 83–4, 93, 148, 156, 165

heaven, heavenly 8, 65, 94, 99–103, 116
   and authority 102–3, 116
   cosmology 101–2
   and earth 102, 122, 131–2, 164
   invading 132
   orientation 102, 109, 112, 131
   and Satan 104
   and Spirit 113
Heilsgeschichte 13–14
Herod, Herodian line 43, 66, 146
historical recurrence 133, 136–42, 145, 153, 160
holiness 43, 54, 61, 63–4, 72, 102, 127
hospitality 91, 130–1

idolatry 4, 28, 96–7, 146–7, 153–4, 160–1, 164–7
ignorance 26, 30, 41, 147. *See also* blindness

of the disciples 80, 83, 91, 110–13
Jerusalem leadership 145–6
Irenaeus 28–31, 92–3, 105–8, 169
Israel. *See* covenant fidelity
　asking for a king 140–2
　consolation 44
　forgiveness of sins 38, 54, 71
　history of 137–43
　ingathering 118–19
　priority of 4, 18, 28, 137, 143 150
　restoration/deliverance 3, 18, 28, 34–5, 37–8, 40–4, 53–60, 62–3, 66, 72–4, 84–6, 110–11, 113, 115, 121–2, 131, 133, 143, 151–3, 155–6
　supersession 12, 157–60
　unfaithfulness 138–42, 147–8
　vocation 110–12, 156–8, 161
Isaianic servant 15–16, 76–7, 111–13, 123, 156–8

Jerusalem, Jerusalemites
　atonement for 38, 52
　centrality 99, 109, 111, 117–18, 144–5, 165
　Jesus in 41, 107, 132, 142, 165
　missional trajectory 109–10
　opposed to Jesus 123, 136, 139, 145–8, 154–5
　power center 57, 66–7
　restoration 62
Jerusalem leadership 42–3, 57, 127, 141, 145
　collusion with foreign leaders 146, 150–1, 153, 165, 167
　opposition to Jesus 57, 67, 104, 144–6, 165
Jesus. *See* cross, crucifixion
　ascension/exaltation 15–18, 55, 76, 84 n. 84, 94, 100–104, 108–9, 133, 144, 149
　authority 86–7, 89–90, 92, 100, 103–4, 120, 123
　baptism of 76, 104, 149
　birth 35–6, 82, 149
　blood of 15, 106
　burial 147
　curse 147
　Davidic Messiah/Savior 2, 26, 34–8, 40–2, 49, 56–7, 64–5, 76–8, 84,
　　96, 103–4, 116, 123, 131, 135, 137, 141–4, 146, 148–50, 155, 160, 164
　Davidic servant 141, 146
　enthroned 120, 144, 149, 161, 165
　false prophet 146–8
　God's son 76, 164, 167–8
　and heaven 101–3
　imitation of 30, 63, 91–2, 164
　incarnation 31, 105, 107
　justice and 30, 105–8, 123–4, 132, 165, 167
　life and ministry 102, 107
　Lord 121–4, 127, 135
　martyrdom 15
　Mosaic prophet 114
　mystagogue 91, 97
　name 55, 89, 123–4, 127, 159
　obedience/fidelity 29–31, 67, 105–7, 123, 164–5, 167
　prophet 77
　servant 112
　Savior 44, 46, 49, 104, 138, 143–4, 163
　temptation of 30, 48, 63, 66–7, 75, 93, 105, 107, 164
　trial 146
Jews. *See* Israel
John Locke 9
John the Baptist 51–8, 66, 143, 164
　baptism 53–8, 64, 66 n. 2, 103, 126–7
　and Elijah 51–2, 57
　forgiveness and 51–8, 89
　preparing the way 44, 52, 143
　priest 56–8, 89
　and Samuel 57, 141
Jubilee 65, 68–78, 81, 84–5, 89, 93–4, 96, 122, 151, 164–5
Judaism(s), Jewishness
　anti-Judaism 12, 17, 34, 110, 125, 159
　as "religion" 11–12
Judas 104, 107, 165
Jupiter 47–8, 50
justice, justness 28–9, 43 n. 67, 44, 60–3, 154–5, 160
　church and 24, 28
　cosmic order 70–1
　cross and 30, 104–8, 123–4, 156, 161, 165, 167
　God's servant and 60
　Jubilee and 74

prophets and 52, 86
Roman 24, 154, 165
salvation and 61–2, 160
social-political 84–5, 97, 167
justification 114, 147, 150–5, 159
Justin Martyr 147

kerygma 13–14, 15
kingdom of God 3, 63, 65, 67, 78–85, 113
   in Acts 115–16
   cosmic drama and 92
   economy of 97
   and Israel 110
   moral vision 101
   mystery 81–4, 164
   other kingdom 164
   practices of 99
   spatial 3 n. 12, 7, 67, 78–82, 93–6, 100, 102, 163–5, 167
   knowledge 30–1, 51–6, 61, 64, 91–2, 97, 99, 109, 116, 121, 123–4, 132, 145–6, 151, 165–7
koinonia 118, 128–9. *See also* church

law of Moses 147, 151, 153–5, 160
Lefebvre, Henri 6
light imagery 59–61, 72, 90, 92, 110, 156

Marshall, I. Howard 14
Melchizedek 74–5
mission 109–13, 156–7
Moses 40, 43, 54, 77, 114
mystery 81–4, 90–3, 97, 164
mystery religions 10–11

narrative 4, 8, 27. *See under* salvation, soteriology

obedience/fidelity 29–31, 63, 92–3, 97, 106–7, 153–5, 160, 164, 167. *See also* Jesus
οἰκουμένη. *See* civilized world

Parthia, Parthians 48, 120
Paul, Pauline
   citizenship 95, 163
   missionary preaching 134
   rhetoric 136–9, 153, 160

and the temple 119
theology 2, 16, 152–3
peace 34, 41, 45–7, 49–51, 60–3, 75, 92, 97, 163–4
Pentecost 100, 113–14, 117–18, 127, 133
persuasion 29–31, 64, 97, 105–8, 113, 123–4, 132, 153, 161, 165
Phineas 155
pilgrims, pilgrimage 117–18
Pilate 43, 66, 146
politics 2–3, 5–13
   apologia pro ecclesia 13–14, 18, 19, 20–1
   apologia pro imperio 18, 22
   apologia pro Paulus 19–20
   history of research 18–27
   legitimation 22–3
   non-political 23
   politically subversive 23–6
   politics *simpliciter* 24
poor, poverty 41, 68, 76, 84–6, 102, 129–30, 165, 167
Priene inscription 49, 78
promise 142–3, 148
   to Abraham 142–3
   to David 142
   of the Father 100, 110, 142
   to Israel's ancestors 2, 32, 142–3

reconciliation 28, 32, 85–6, 90, 106, 108, 131–2, 164, 166–7
redeemer 72–3
release, redemption from captivity 28–31, 39, 44, 68–70, 72–6, 85–6, 89–90, 96–7, 164, 166–7
religio licita 21
religion 2–3, 5–6, 8–13
   antiquity 9–12
   compartmentalization 8–13, 20, 22, 33–4
   embedding 3
remnant 40, 111, 159
repentance 56, 71, 132, 146
   apostles' baptism 124–7
   forgiveness and 27, 71, 89–90, 97, 123–4, 132, 151, 161, 164, 167
   Israel's 44, 54, 62
   John's baptism of 53, 56, 64, 143
   wilderness and 66

resurrection. *See* covenant fidelity
  Israel's hope in 143, 150
  of Jesus 16–18, 26, 76, 94, 102, 104, 112, 122–3, 149, 151, 168
  as revelation 147, 149, 153
reversal 14, 17, 26, 164–5
the rich 66, 85, 167
Rome, Roman 3, 7 n. 28, 13, 66. *See also* Augustus *and* Caesar
  and Antioch of Pisidia 135, 143
  authority, *auctoritas* (CHECK) 96, 120
  conquest lists 119–20
  cosmic legitimation 49–50, 84, 131
  ideology 25, 45–51, 62–3
  justice 154, 165
  and language 118
  Luke-Acts and 3, 18–27, 31, 35
  Pax Romana 46–7, 49, 62–3, 64
  Salus, salvation 49–50, 143
  and Satan 25, 50
rule of concord 125

Sabbath 62, 68–9, 73–4, 86 n. 92, 145
salvation, soteriology 1–2, 4–5, 32, 42–4
  deliverance/liberation 2, 28–30, 39–40, 74
  comprehensive 131
  cosmic 27–8, 69–71
  embodied 17–18, 27–8, 30–1, 34, 60, 166
  era of 75
  Greco-Roman 45–51
  history of research 18–27
  and Israel 133, 136, 143
  knowledge of salvation 51–6
  message of 144
  narrative 3–5, 28, 31, 64, 99–100, 164–6
  "political" 1–3, 8, 13, 31, 33–4, 37, 150–1, 163, 169
  "religious" 2–3, 13, 33
  spatial 27–8, 65, 77–8, 99, 109, 113, 115–16, 127–32, 160, 163, 166
  theopolitical 75, 163
  universal 3, 18
Samuel 57, 88, 141
Satan 25–6, 28–31, 43, 48, 50, 63, 65, 67, 75, 93, 97, 134, 153–4, 164, 166

authority 26, 48, 50, 61, 92–3, 104, 108, 124, 161, 167
Belial 74–6
conflict with 51, 76, 93
falling from heaven 92, 103–4
in Jerusalem 104, 107, 164
ransom to 29
release from/captivity to 28–30, 65, 97, 106, 132, 167
victory over 29–32, 94, 105–6, 109, 154, 164–7
violence of 29–30
and world powers 48, 65
Saul 140–2
Savior 36, 45, 78
Scripture 146–7, 153–4
sight 28, 72, 90–3, 97, 99, 102, 154, 164–7
signs and wonders 122–3
sin, sinfulness 4, 14, 90 n. 114
  corporate 52, 72–3
Sinai 114
Smith, Wilfred Cantwell 11–12
Soja, Edward 7
space 5–8, 12, 65
  chronotope 6
  compartmentalization of 2–3, 5–6, 8–13, 20, 22, 31, 96, 101–2
  complex 6–8, 63, 81, 84, 94–6, 161, 163
  cosmic-comprehensive 8, 45, 70, 83, 92, 96, 100–3, 109, 112, 116, 163
  directional metaphor 104, 109
  mapping 118–21
  modern, Enlightenment 6, 8–9, 12
  mundane 81–3, 89, 94, 99, 102–3, 109–10, 131–3, 160–1, 164, 166
  orientation 100–3, 109–10, 112, 144
  place 5–7
  production of 8
  restoration geography 111–12
  salvific 113–16, 127–31
  simple 6, 13, 83, 94, 101–2
  social-political 8, 28, 37, 52, 58, 63, 65, 75, 81, 85, 101–2, 131, 163, 165, 167
  thirdspace 7, 100
  trajectory 109–13, 117–18, 131, 161
Spirit 44, 76–7, 100, 113–16, 123
  and baptism 53, 55, 110, 115, 124, 126
  donum superadditum 113, 115
  dispersal 118

empowering mission 131–2, 161, 165
eschatological 114
ethical impact 115
inward transformation 114
Jesus and 41, 44, 76, 115, 164
legitimizing readings 35, 82
missional 116–17, 165
presence of Jesus 101
prophetic speech 77, 113, 115
restoration of Israel 111, 115
social ordering 122, 131–2, 161
as soteriological 113–15, 132
spatial movement 109
"spiritual," spiritualization 2, 12–14, 33–4, 53
state
   church and 6–7, 7 n. 28, 9, 19–21, 26
   nation-state 6
   and politics 12
synagogue 134

table-fellowship 91, 128, 130–1
table of nations 119
taxation 95
temple 71, 87, 117
time 79–80, 83, 93–7, 102, 112–13. *See* today

Enlightenment 6
last days 112, 121
soteriological 4–5
tension 161
that remains 94, 104, 112, 21, 132, 159–60, 164, 166
times and seasons 112–13, 132
today 76, 80–1, 83, 86, 93–4, 96, 112, 121, 164, 169
tongues of fire 100, 118, 121

unity of Luke and Acts 1 n. 4
universal restoration 99–100, 110, 116, 161, 168
universalism 12, 28, 34

Vespasian 78
violence 28–30, 34, 63, 68, 80, 96–7, 105–8, 123–4
and time 112–13

wilderness 57–8, 66–7, 100
Wisdom 152
witness 26, 83, 112–13
Word of God 26, 58, 66
Zeal 155–6
Zeller, Eduard 20

www.ingramcontent.com/pod-product-compliance
Lightning Source LLC
Chambersburg PA
CBHW072139290426
44111CB00012B/1922